CRITICAL COLLABORATIONS

TransCanada Series

The study of Canadian literature can no longer take place in isolation from larger external forces. Pressures of multiculturalism put emphasis upon discourses of citizenship
and security, while market-driven factors increasingly shape the publication, dissemi-
nation, and reception of Canadian writing. The persistent questioning of the Humanities has invited a rethinking of the disciplinary and curricular structures within which
the literature is taught, while the development of area and diaspora studies has raised
important questions about the tradition. The goal of the TransCanada series is to publish
forward-thinking critical interventions that investigate these paradigm shifts in interdisciplinary ways.

Series editor:
Smaro Kamboureli, Avie Bennett Chair in Canadian Literature, Department of English,
University of Toronto

For more information, please contact:

Smaro Kamboureli
Professor, Avie Bennett Chair in Canadian Literature
Department of English
University of Toronto
170 St. George Street
Toronto, ON M5R 2M8
Canada
Phone: 416-978-0156
Email: smaro.kamboureli@utoronto.ca

Lisa Quinn
Acquisitions Editor
Wilfrid Laurier University Press
75 University Avenue West
Waterloo, ON N2L 3C5
Canada
Phone: 519-884-0710 ext. 2843
Fax: 519-725-1399
Email: quinn@press.wlu.ca

CRITICAL COLLABORATIONS

INDIGENEITY, DIASPORA, AND ECOLOGY IN CANADIAN LITERARY STUDIES

Smaro Kamboureli *and* Christl Verduyn, *editors*

WILFRID LAURIER
UNIVERSITY PRESS

Wilfrid Laurier University Press acknowledges the support of the Canada Council for the Arts for our publishing program. We acknowledge the financial support of the Government of Canada through the Canada Book Fund for our publishing activities. Smaro Kamboureli would also like to acknowledge her Canada Research Chair Tier 1 in Critical Studies in Canadian Literature, held at the University of Guelph, 2005–2013, for the support it provided toward the publication of this book.

Library and Archives Canada Cataloguing in Publication

    Critical collaborations : indigeneity, diaspora, and ecology in
Canadian literary studies / Smaro Kamboureli and Christl Verduyn, editors.

(TransCanada series)
Includes bibliographical references and index.
Issued in print and electronic formats.
ISBN 978-1-55458-911-1 (pbk.).—ISBN 978-1-55458-912-8 (pdf).—
ISBN 978-1-55458-913-5 (epub)

    1. Canadian literature—History and criticism—Theory, etc.—Congresses.
2. Criticism—Canada—Congresses. 3. Literature and society—Canada—Congresses.
I. Kamboureli, Smaro, writer of introduction, editor of compilation II. Verduyn, Christl, [date], author, editor of compilation III. TransCanada: Literature, Institutions, Citizenship Conference (3rd : 2009 : Sackville, N.B.) IV. Series: TransCanada series

PS8041.C75 2014   801'.950971   C2014-901342-6
                                                                       C2014-901343-4

Cover design by Martyn Schmoll. Front-cover image by Erín Moure, from research for O Cadoiro, 2005. Text design by Angela Booth Malleau.

This book is printed on FSC recycled paper and is certified Ecologo. It is made from 100% post-consumer fibre, processed chlorine free, and manufactured using biogas energy.

Printed in Canada

CONTENTS

ACKNOWLEDGEMENTS

This edited volume arises out of TransCanada 3: Literature, Institutions, Citizenship, the third conference in a series designed to address the formation of Canadian literature as an institution and the shifts it has been undergoing in the late twentieth and early twenty-first century. Organized jointly via the University of Guelph and Mount Allison University, it took place in July 2009. We would like to thank all the delegates who participated in that event, and to acknowledge the valuable contributions of the members of the organizing committee (http://www.transcanadas.ca/2d_transcanada3.html).

Beyond the conference, the opportunity to work with the contributors to this volume has been one of tremendous intellectual stimulation, collaboration, and collegiality. We thank them for their insights and commitment to continuing the critical development of Canadian literary studies. Their work has made this volume possible.

For assistance with the manuscript's preparation, and related research, we would like to thank the graduate and undergraduate research assistants at TransCanada Institute, in alphabetical order, Marcelle Kosman, Cameron Kroetsch, Hannah McGreggor, Mishi Prokop, Andrew Whitfield, and Robert Zacharias, and Prathna Lor at the University of Toronto. We are especially thankful to our respective institutions, University of Guelph and Mount Allison University, for their generous financial and in-kind support toward the conference. We also wish to express our gratitude to the Social Sciences and Humanities Council of Canada and the Canada Research Chair program in Critical Studies in Canadian Literature (2005–13) that helped make the publication of this volume possible. Finally, our sincere thanks to our editor at Wilfrid Laurier University Press, Lisa Quinn, for her editorial ingenuity, and to Rob Kohlmeier for his impeccable attentiveness to the entire production process.

Smaro Kamboureli
University of Toronto

Christl Verduyn
Mount Allison University

INTRODUCTION

Smaro Kamboureli

The world needs an epistemological change that will arrange desires.
Gayatri Chakravorty Spivak,
—*An Aesthetic Education*
in the Era of Globalization (2012)

I From CanLit to Canlits: White Diaspora, Filiation, and Complicity

Literary fields develop by means of a double trajectory: while they remain in a state of constant flux, they acquire their disciplinary status by posing as stable categories, feigning the kind of constancy that allows readers to take a lingering and critical look at them. The field of Canadian literature is not an exception to this normative state. As a literature with a colonial descent, it has always been inscribed by the anxiety and insecurity typifying the ambivalent desire of settler cultures: to differentiate themselves from their imperial origins by establishing a literary idiom representative of the local even while craving recognition from the metropole under the rubric of its presumed universal literary values. Far from being linear, this route is palindromic, for in the process of coming into their own, literatures of settler cultures strive to come to terms with the double ethos of filiation and complicity. At the same time that they are driven by an emancipatory impulse as they strive to attain the status of national literatures, the residual memory of their elsewhereness compels them to keep looking back; they thus remain eager to disassociate themselves from their colonial heritage but also to emulate its time-honoured paradigms. They behave like prodigal kin; theirs is a "schizoid consciousness" (Huggan 30),[1] hence their ambivalence. This ambivalence takes different configurations, but the recitability of white settler cultures' acute desire to exceed their colonial origins that is attended by compulsory nation building endures; moreover, white settler cultures rarely fail to reproduce the colonial vestiges of their history. Colonialism, even when it is not directly evoked or is presumed to have been eradicated in this so-called postcolonial era, survives in how "white diasporas" (Ashcroft et al. 19) behave. "This pattern," as Graham Huggan writes, "reconfirms the dis-ease—the epistemological, even metaphysical uncertainty—which accompanied historical processes of white settlement" (29).

This filiative and complicitous conduct is aptly summed up by Lee Maracle, who calls white settlement "Diaspora" and equates this "Diaspora" with "the mother countries" (55).[2] For Maracle there is no distinction between the imperial centre and its colonies that have evolved into nation-states; the sliding of one signifier into the other exposes their filiative structural relationship and speaks to the displacement that marks such metonymic relations, a displacement that works in this context in more ways than one. Diaspora is displaced from and attempts to displace the mother country, a recognition (in part) of its complicity with it, while it itself displaces the others it encounters. While Diaspora writ large in Maracle's essay refers to the hegemonic role of white settler culture and its pervasive impact on Indigenous peoples, I also take it to refer to the subsequent diasporas it has accommodated and instrumentalized in its process of becoming a nation-state. Maracle is not being reductive when she collapses the differences between white settler cultures and diasporic communities within such cultures; rather, Diaspora as a condensed signifier evokes the archives of Western violence, archives here to be understood not only "as repositories of state power but as unquiet movements in a field of force, as restless realignments and readjustments of people and the beliefs to which they were tethered, as spaces in which the senses and the affective course through the seeming abstractions of political rationalities" (Stoler 32–33). As such an archive, one whose violence is not just a thing of the past but has a durability that continues to warp the present, Diaspora as Maracle's choice term also works to produce "a condensed historicity" that "exceeds itself in past and future directions" (Butler, *Excitable Speech* 3). Diaspora has played a "usurp[ing]" role, Maracle writes, by "claim[ing] discovery, and then proceed[ing] to define, delineate, and demarcate the cultural, intellectual, economic, spiritual, and physical being" of those it has "established exclusive dominion over" (55–56). Nevertheless, by rendering it as a site located at the same level as that of the other diasporic communities it contains and manages, Maracle curbs its power. She thus undoes the epistemic habit[3] that applies the designation diaspora to people other than white settlers, and in the process affirms the unceded nature of Indigenous sovereignty. Beyond this, she further complicates the question of whether or not Canada is truly postcolonial.[4]

Maracle's particular inscription of Diaspora opens "Seeing Ourselves Through Story vs Western Models," the first part of her essay "Oratory on Oratory," which was presented as a plenary talk at the first TransCanada conference and was subsequently revised and published in *Trans.Can.Lit: Resituating the Study of Canadian Literature*, the first volume of the TransCanada project.[5] Maracle's critical gesture unsettles the disciplinary matrix of Canadian literary studies. In doing so, it exemplifies the ways in which critics and writers have responded to the TransCanada project's double incentive: to consider the epistemic breaks that are necessary to engage with the displacements and conjunctions that characterize the study of the literary at a time when we cannot afford to ignore what Gayatri Spivak calls "the uneven diachrony of global contemporaneity" (11). *Trans.Can.Lit* draws attention to what I call in its preface the elsewhereness[6] of Canadian literature as an institution, namely, that Canadian literature "intimates that Canada is ... constituted in excess of the knowledge of itself" (x); the second volume of the TransCanada project, *Shifting the Ground of Canadian Literary Studies*, elaborates this condition as an opening out of the field beyond its conventional confines. Responsive and proactive, and thus symptomatic of the times, this outward movement suggests that the field is under stress from internal as well as external forces at the present moment—a long moment. As Diana Brydon and Marta Dvořák put it in their introduction to *Crosstalk: Canadian and Global Imaginaries in Dialogue*, "the shifting forms of collective imaginaries ... challenge cultural commentators within various theoretical and political movements" and produce "exchanges between texts and readers" that result in Canadian literature being situated "within different geopolitical and theoretical locations" (1). It is "this unraveling of Canadian literature as an object of study across different thresholds," what I identified in my introduction to the second volume as the undisciplining of the discipline ("Shifting the Ground" 8), that the TransCanada project has invited scholars to examine. The present volume, the third in the series, further realizes this goal by bringing to view what happens when, as Christl Verduyn states in its concluding chapter, the study of Canadian literature "shift[s] ... from its familiar foundations into what may at first seem to be strange new fields" (231).

Critical Collaborations: Indigeneity, Diaspora, and Ecology in Canadian Literary Studies thus speaks directly to the epistemic breaks that have occurred in the field, as my discussion of Roy K. Kiyooka at the end of this Introduction demonstrates, and points to those that still need to take place. These epistemic breaks derive from multiple and imbricated fronts: the critical turns the study of Canadian literature has taken in recent times, especially regarding the intensified attention to Indigenous, diasporic, and ecological concerns; the kinds of Canadian literature published today and the cultural, social, and political conditions that inflect their publication and study; this literature's ongoing charged relationship with the Canadian state and its registering, as well as challenging, of globalization; and the recognition that the study of literature has a role to play in shaping and articulating our engagement with Canada and the world. The critical perspectives this volume offers are not necessarily filtered through a corrective lens, one that seeks to dismiss entirely or simply critique existing models of reading; rather, acknowledging that both CanLit and its study continue to grow more robust while at the same time facing considerable challenges,[7] they operate in transdisciplinary[8] contexts that help expand the range as well as the methods of our inquiry.

By putting to the test existent, but also proposing novel, ways, of responding critically to Canadian literature and its different contexts, this volume continues the collaborative interrogation of the field launched by the Trans-Canada project. It thus contributes to the ongoing dialogue that examines the formation of Canadian literature as a field, a dialogue that has been taking place within and across different constituencies. With its focus on Indigeneity, diaspora, and ecology, *Critical Collaborations* draws attention to three distinct yet at certain levels coincident points of entry into Canadian literature as a body of diverse works *and* as a discipline. Featured as what Cheryl Lousley calls in this volume "matters of concern" (147), Indigeneity, diaspora, and ecology, addressed separately but also in criss-crossing ways—ways that bring into the open these areas' relationalities and even, as I argue below, kinship—invite a refiguration of the perceptual and material fields within which we have been studying and teaching CanLit. Indeed, at a time when "mainstream" literature can include texts that range from chick lit to nature writing, from Indigenous literature to diasporic voices, we can no longer speak of CanLit as a singular construct; operating more as a historical sign of Canadian literature's formation, CanLit has now become Canlits.

II Where Is CanLit? Situatedness and Force Fields

My use of spatial rhetoric above—field, site, locus, origin, and the underlying emphasis on Canada as a geopolitical space—is not intended to suggest that *Critical Collaborations* privileges the spatial dimensions of Canadian literary studies. Instead, it is meant to draw attention to the importance of reflecting on and renegotiating the situatedness of Canadian literature and its criticism, a situatedness inflected by the elsewhereness of CanLit. Where and how the field is situated is obviously not a simple matter. Indeed, Northrop Frye's question

"Where is here?" (220) declares situatedness to be a formative element in the development of literary production in Canada and of that literature's Canadian character. Not to be understood, then, in static or stable terms, situatedness as it is inscribed in this collection functions as a compelling yet fluid trope in Canadian literary studies. As David Simpson argues in his book of the same title, situatedness "is at once something given and something created or inter-pellated" (7). The prominence it has gained since the last part of the twentieth century in discussions of subject positionality—"the self-other vocabularies of modernity" (8)—exposes the "embeddedness" (12) of our discourses, as well as of our self-location or assigned positions as subjects and/or others. Nevertheless, while the persistence of situatedness partly reflects the militancy of culturalist habits, it also announces the need to realign "elective and invol-untary affiliations" (7).[9] It may be a necessity or have become, depending on one's point of view, a banal trope in its own right, but situatedness allows us to exercise "our powers of modification" (6). It is the simultaneous mutability and embeddedness of situatedness that unmoors any stability that may be inscribed in spatiality. Modified by geopolitical and cultural conditions, by de- and re-territorializations, spatiality is rendered as a spatial-temporal and thus dynamic structure, construing the local, to quote from Roy Miki's essay in this collection, as "a site of immediacy" (48) that is constantly modulated by the differences and mobilities it embodies. Or, as Laurie Ricou puts it in this volume, when the mobility we track includes that "of plants and ani-mals," a movement that is "always already transnational and diasporic," "the long-standing primacy of landscape-place in Canadian literary criticism" is "disturbed" because we begin to understand the bioregion we inhabit with a critical difference. "Where the earth is disturbed," he writes, "the other moves in; it transforms.... This is disturbing. It is intended to disturb" (162).

The spatial tropes I employ here, then, are better understood in terms of Theodor Adorno's "force field" (*Kraftfeld*), a concept that describes "a rela-tional interplay of attractions and aversions that constitute[] the dynamic, transmutational structure of a complex phenomenon" (Jay, *Adorno* 14).[10] As Martin Jay has shown, in his reading of Adorno and also in his work on intel-lectual history, a force field is constituted of "conflictual energies" that do not resolve the tensions between the past and the present; it is "a nontotalized juxtaposition of changing elements" that lack a single originary point or gen-erative principle (*Force Fields* 2) but maintain a dialectical relationship. As such, a force field doesn't invite a fusion of contrasting elements, nor does it annihilate the very conflicts that give rise to it. Instead, it exposes points of contact,[11] constellations of discordant elements that activate zones of engage-ment.[12] These zones constitute the spatial-temporal structures that derive from

various coercive or otherwise ambivalent encounters, as well as from the flux
of history and of the present moment. *Critical Collaborations* is such a force
field. It operates as a zone of engagement composed of critical discourses that
emerge from the fluctuating intersections of different terrains, disciplinary
fields, critical approaches, and communities. It consists of essays that are as
much about Canadian literature and Canadian critical discourses as about the
body politic in Canada and the role and responsibilities of critical readers—be
they literary, legal, or educational scholars and cultural practitioners.

The tone of the volume is set by the seminal question Miki raises in this
volume, how "to do justice to CanLit?" (40) Not an aporetic gesture, this question frames the determination of the contributors to examine what Jacques
Rancière calls "the politics of literature." For Rancière, however, literature does
not refer exclusively to linguistic aesthetic products; it also comprises the condition of "literality" (*The Politics of Literature* 13–14),[13] that modality of the literary that threatens to undo the regime of writing (40) and the ways in which
it upholds the rules of the sensible. If the sensible for Rancière stands for what
is proper—the governing laws of what a state considers to be a sensible order,
the hierarchies supported by "the police logic" (*Disagreement* 32) that are both
"visible and invisible," "speech and noise" (*The Politics of Aesthetics* 13)—then
literariness is precisely what allows the circulation of "democratic disorder"
(*Dissensus* 158). It actualizes the collapse of representational paradigms (159),
thus making it possible for the politics of literature to have an effect. This effect
does not manifest itself in the sense that literature has a mission, for such a
mission, in Derrida's words, would "assign it a meaning, a program and a regu-
lating ideal" (Attridge 38), which would be counterproductive. The "politics of
literature" for Rancière is not to be confused with "the politics of writers," nor
does it refer to the writers' "personal engagements … in the social or political
struggles of their times"; rather, the political efficacy of the literary entails its
capacity to "'do[]' politics simply by being literature" (*The Politics of Literature*
3), thus uncoupling the link "between saying and doing," a phrase that occurs
frequently in his work.[14] What this politics *does*, then, is assert itself as an institution in its own right, in Derrida's words, an "institution of fiction," which "is
linked to an authorization to say everything, and doubtless too to the coming
about of the modern idea of democracy" (Attridge 37).

III *Critical Collaborations'* Zones of Engagement

In light of the above, "Where is here?" echoes in this collection as a historical
referent that is deliberately and continuously unsettled, at once a topos con-
figured in multiple ways and a trope that reveals the aporetic nature of Frye's
question. A question that generates further questioning rather than inviting a

definitive answer—Frye did call it a "riddle" (220), after all—it figures prominently in Miki's essay, which opens this volume. Acknowledging the "illustrious[ness]" and "provocative" nature of this question, Miki reads it via Freud's
Civilization and Its Discontents to show that "the alignment in their work *of
the imagination with the un-real*, the latter being illusion in Freud and myth
in Frye," produces a "consciousness" that is "situated in an aesthetic sphere,"
a sphere "separated from the ... dynamic and conflicted world of social and
cultural concerns" (34). Frye's question also serves as the impetus for Laurie
Ricou's essay later in this book, though Ricou's troping toward it follows a
different equally important trajectory: "I seek to answer the cherished and
well-worn Canadian question 'Where is here?' by teaching habitat," he writes
in his opening sentence. Whereas Ricou practises "Habitat Studies" by adopt-
ing a microcosmic model—tracking, for example, the behaviour of a local
species like kinnikinnick—his attention on habitats of "soil conditions and
microclimates" is designed to "disrupt[], even disturb[] ... familiar approaches
to Canadian literature," a disturbance that is "necessary to thinking bioregionally" (161).

Catriona Sandilands and Cheryl Lousley's ecocriticism advances a more
discursive approach to habitat. Seeing literature, "literally, as an 'act' of nature,"
Sandilands attests its importance to "the ecopolitical realm" (136). Concerned
primarily with methodological issues, she posits her essay as a response to her
question, "How is it that the act of doing literary criticism can be an expression
of ... environmental concern[s]?" (128), and demonstrates that "literature"
and "criticism" are "points of environmental activity" in the realm of "public
culture" (128). Lousley's essay engages with the same question, setting out "to
look for connections, to follow flows, and to read in context (subject-in-envi-
ronment, animal-in-habitat, worker-in-workplace)" (149–150); so the critical
act, for Lousley, is not just a "matter" of "reading for nature or for culture," as
her reading of Larissa Lai's *Salt Fish Girl* exemplifies, but a matter of reading
"for narratives of new or re-assembly," "for attachments," or "against a text ...
to politicize boundaries that have been unjustly stabilized" (159). Cast differently but equally concerned with movement across diversely constructed
spaces, Julie Rak's essay asks, "what is it about the literary that seems to make it
travel so well between states, regions, institutions, and economies?" (177–78).
Her answer lies in her notion of the translocal, a concept that allows her to
"track," through her reading of the figures of Vernon-Wood and Long Lance,
"their rather bumpy course across spaces and identities in order to interpret
what cannot be fully 'placed' within a state, a body of writing, or an identity" (178–79). Space, place, and mobility are similarly important in Winfried
Siemerling's and François Paré's essays that focus on diaspora. Their diverse

approaches, and the different locations within which they situate the diasporic imaginary—the former dealing with Montreal's black diaspora, the latter
with the Acadian diaspora—suggest that the diasporic imaginary, as Maracle
shows, does not behave as a singular or homogeneous construct; rather, it
must be considered in relation to the particular sites that produce it. Whereas
Siemerling demonstrates that Montreal's black diaspora places emphasis on
"both black culture *and* its intercultural or transcultural options" (213), Paré
shows that "the concept of pluralism [can] be used to describe effectively contemporary Acadia," which "form[s] a national community within Canada"
(216) in all "its national and diasporic manifestations" (216).

The correspondence between critical method and situatedness in these
essays is equally prominent in the other contributions to this volume. Writing
from "the place of a personal ethics-under-construction, one that acknowledges [her] condition as a participant in settler culture," Larissa Lai sets out to
restructure the dominant paradigm of anti-racist work that "constantly puts
both First Nations people and people of colour in conversation with European
settler cultures, but not with each other" (99). Thus at the same time that Lai
acknowledges "the problems of immigrant complicity in the colonization of
the land" (99), she develops "a poetics and a politics of relation between Asians
like [herself] and the Indigenous peoples of the land we call Canada" (100).
Using as her point of departure two texts that directly address the politics and
literary history of Asian/Indigenous relations, Maracle's "Yin Chin" and SKY
Lee's *Disappearing Moon Cafe,* Lai advances what she calls an epistemology
of respect that echoes Miki's call for an approach that does "justice to CanLit"
studies, an act that demands critical attentiveness to the past but that is also
"future-directed" (Lai 114). This call to establish political and cultural affiliations between Diaspora and Indigenous peoples through a practice of respect
that remains mindful of the past—a central concern in this volume—is also
exemplified in Julia Emberley's essay. Emberley examines how "testimonial
practices unsettle national and transnational histories," but she also identifies
"the need for an epistemic shift in the field of postcolonial testimonial studies
influenced by ... Indigenous storytelling knowledges and practices" (70). Her
reading of Eden Robinson's novel *Monkey Beach* demonstrates that its "narrative design ... belongs to a kinship web of affiliations" (73). She invites us
to understand kinship not only in its "traditionally overdetermined" meaning
as "a filiative set of human relations," but also, and more productively so, as
"affiliative contingencies: a set of personal and political relations that critically
generate interwoven ways of knowing and being" (71).

The emphasis on relationality and epistemic shifts that underlies the contributions to which I have referred so far is most evident in the essays by the
Indigenous scholars in this collection, Marie Battiste and Sa'ke'j Henderson.

Battiste employs the concept of Indigenous renaissance not only as a signal of Indigenous people's "resilience" against knowledge invented elsewhere and imported, knowledge experienced as "a sword of cognitive imperialism" (86), but also as a "strategic" deployment "for communicating with Eurocentric thinkers." Referring specifically to the trajectory of her own family as well as that of her kin group, the Mi'kmaq nation, away from the "assimilationist and disempowering agenda in [their] education," she demonstrates the "multiple forms of struggle, resistance, and conscientization" that Indigenous renaissance entails (88). Recognizing "the limits of the knowledge" produced in "colonial society," Indigenous renaissance calls for "allied work" with "white feminists and anti-racist and social activists, as well as ecologists"; both a philosophy of life but also a "practical and pragmatic" approach, it contests the "contradictions and paradoxes in discourses, histories, assumptions, beliefs, and values between Indigenous and non-Indigenous peoples" (91). Indigenous renaissance, then, involves both revival and cooperation; what is more, as Len Findlay puts it, this renaissance "is being wrested from Eurocentric contexts to help redress historical and perceptual imbalance" ("Redress Rehearsals" 229); as "an organic consciousness unfolding to meet urgent crises" (Battiste 90), it concerns as much Aboriginal as non-Aboriginal people. Significantly, as Battiste points out, it "has shifted the agenda from recrimination to rebirth, from conflict to collaboration, from perceived deficiency to capacity" (98). This process has had an immense impact on many fronts, from literary and performance production in Canada[15] to the UN's 2007 Declaration of the Rights of Indigenous Peoples, in the formation of which Battiste was directly involved. The "ambidextrous consciousness" that Battiste identifies as her "core tool" (86) in this process allows for the "regeneration of new relationships among and between knowledge systems" and results from the deployment of "trans-systemic analyses and methods" (97).

The trans-systemic method that Battiste's ambidextrous consciousness is aligned with and performs is more fully and historically addressed by Sa'ke'j Henderson.[16] Henderson's work is not new to the TransCanada project. Findlay paints an evocative picture of this legal scholar as a "public" and "'indigenous intellectual'" in Shifting the Ground (236), "urg[ing] readers to place trans-systematics alongside trans-Canadas on all occasions in a preparatory act of sui generis solidarity" (246). Henderson introduces "trans-systemia" as a "transformative method" that can safeguard Aboriginal peoples' sovereignty, lands, and rights, but also as "a model for other Eurocentric disciplines and scholars" (49). The product of "trans-generational alliance[s]" among First Nations Elders and legal scholars, it relies on "Aboriginal world views and legal traditions, as well as Eurocentric strategies and persuasion, to accomplish the art of the impossible," namely, the affirmation of "Aboriginal and treaty rights over the objections of the provinces" (50). As his condensed narrative of what is a long and complex history demonstrates, the constitutional reality that has emerged from this process builds on "convergence and reconciliation" (51). This method, unique to Canadian constitutional jurisprudence because it affirms "constitutional supremacy over parliamentary supremacy" (52), is the result of a *sui generis* approach that does away with the positivism of common law. Directly engaging with the causal effects of Eurocentric logic, the *sui generis* method—Eurocentric in its origins, as Henderson reminds us—affirms the inalienable sovereignty and rights of First Nations peoples. The Canadian legal system's "use of *sui generis* illustrates," then, as Henderson writes, "a distinct constitutional method for Aboriginal and treaty rights," practising in effect "an Aboriginal method of synthesis" (60). A "collaborative enterprise" (50), it advances "a more profound and coherent understanding of fundamental epistemologies" that are of immediate concern to Canadian law and legal scholars but also to literary and, more generally, humanist scholars. Engaging as it does with "the deep structure of humanity, ecology, and civilizations" (67), it encourages a particular kind of transdisciplinarity that leads to "*sui generis* solidarity" (Findlay, "The Long March" 274).

IV From Hauntologies to Heterologies: Beyond the Canadian Oedipus

As the essays gathered here suggest, *Critical Collaborations* points to the productive allegiances that can emerge when epistemic shifts recast the technologies of knowing that beget uneven relations; expose the universalisms produced by Eurocentric thinking to be just that, Eurocentric; dismantle binaries like nature and culture; demolish hegemonic practices that construct dominant and subjugated subjects; and eliminate the distance between legitimized and disqualified knowledge. If literature as an institution has been an instrument often put in the service of the state, this collection invites us to read the CanLit archive by entering the space of what Michel de Certeau calls "displaced history." De Certeau develops this notion of history via Alexandre Dumas, who, "a regular at court, knew too much about the 'ceremonial gowns' history drapes over the shoulders of its actors in order to give itself an air of majesty," and so took "a look behind the scenes ... [to] show[] the back-hall 'dramas' and 'comedies'" (150).[17] De Certeau calls the historical legal dramas Dumas unearthed displaced because they comprise a "history recounting both the proximity of the past and the foreignness of your private life, or the present as a metaphor for a somewhere else." This kind of history brings into relief the phantoms of the "*ancien régime*" but also sheds light on the "shadow[s] of what history assassinated" so that they "become the lexicon of the living" (151).

Such displaced histories—like the Indigenous legal and spiritual traditions that Henderson and Battiste invite us to consider, the contiguous relations between Asian Canadians and First Nations people that Lai addresses, the non-binary understanding of nature and culture that Sandilands, Lousley, and Ricou discuss, and the displaced Acadians that Paré writes about—do not haunt only those who embody them. They also haunt the political unconscious of Canada. But this "haunt[ing] from within from other nations," as Marlene Goldman and Joanne Saul put it (648), is not exactly what is evoked in Earle Birney's poem "Can. Lit," especially its lines "It's only by our lack of ghosts / we're haunted." As frequently cited as Frye's question, these lines stress absence and lament the dearth of a Canadian literary tradition equivalent to that shaped by Emily Dickinson and Walt Whitman. The richness of black culture in Montreal that Siemerling reveals, for example, wouldn't have helped fix the cultural deficit conjured up in Birney's poem. Though satirical in spirit, albeit with an admonishing undertone, Birney's is a trope that derives not from something that has been and is now lost but, instead, from something that has never been—cannot be—because it is extraneous to the circumstances. Birney suggests that with the eagles gone, "leaving no shadow bigger than a wren's," nature—nature not as Sandilands, Lousley, and Ricou read it in their essays—has gone awry; thus, despite Canada's construction of a national myth of unity ("hacked railway ties"), a myth that ushers it into modernity by reifying the binary of nature/culture, CanLit is imaged as a cultural wilderness, "a bloody civil bore." Yet the poem's meta-figural structure reiterates a desire for affiliation, a craving for a new (autochthonous) literary tradition that would nevertheless mimic in its formation the Eurocentric patterns of cultural maturation. Latent in this desire for what CanLit is seen as missing is the unarticulated admission—fear, desire, and longing—that Canadian culture may no longer be a/kin to the Empire.

As a trope that continues to engage critics over half a century after the publication of Birney's poem, being haunted by a lack of ghosts[18] registers the impact of colonialism exclusively from the perspective of the settlers. If the Canadian *genius loci* is "elusive," as Jonathan Kertzer writes, it is because it "is given no place to *settle*" (58, my emphasis). That he attributes to this ghost the Latin "common name" of "*genius loci*" (40) both affirms the desire for CanLit to release itself from its colonial vestiges by assuming an identity that "serv[es] as the voice of local history and national destiny" (61) and belies this spirit of independence by reinstalling its settler identity. "Settle" does not challenge either what the local entails (more precisely, how it has been claimed as such) or how its history is constructed. Though Kertzer uses this verb without a sense of irony, it ironically discloses that what validates the constitutive role of the ghostly in the formation of CanLit are the direct consequences of settlement. His notion of elusiveness, then, which is at the core of his study, far from referring to an intangible ghost, becomes synonymous with the nation's "monstrosity," as Justin Edwards states, and the "mangled, mutilated and marginalized" people/s it has produced, those "who have stood in [the nation's] path" (111), what I have called elsewhere scandalous bodies. These displaced subjects and their histories are not spectral, nor do they belong to the past alone; they have a materiality that is unambiguously inscribed in the national, cultural, and socio-political lexicons of today.

Thus, as I read it, Birney's trope provides a highly economical way of registering that the desire to be haunted by non-existent ghosts effects a tropological transformation that animates the spectral figures of those whom history has assassinated. If, like Frye's question, Birney's lines too have become one of the foundational tropes in the formation of CanLit, then the ghosts in question signal the return of the repressed, a figure that inserts psychoanalysis into the fray of things. At the same time that CanLit is assigned the aspirational and performative function of raising settler culture above its double colonial condition of filiation and complicity, believing to be haunted by a lack of ghosts discloses a psychological disturbance bordering on paranoia, the very same that afflicts the central figure in Margaret Atwood's poem "Progressive Insanities of a Pioneer."[19] It is only when read synchronically and diachronically that Birney's poem begins to air Canada's dirty colonial laundry. Revealing the kind of inadvertent knowledge[20] that is released in a psychoanalytic session, the trope reflects the ambivalence of what Robert Young calls colonial desire, a desire for the other that is always already convoluted because it has shown itself to be invariably accompanied by fear for that same other.[21]

Hence CanLit as (or caught in) a cul-de-sac, when viewed in terms of its formation history and against the ecologies of knowledge that its history has ignored or distorted. To put it in terms of Kertzer's reading of this same trope, "we actually are haunted, but only by a palpable absence that marks our peculiar identity crisis" (38). However, Kertzer's notion of "crisis" turns this haunting into a positivist construct. Referring to W.H. New, he attributes to crisis a "positive virtue[]" (38), and thus grants it a meta-spin, seeing it as a "ghost-of-a-ghost" (38) that is shown to have the uncanny, indeed fortuitous, ability to generate writing, both literature and criticism. This is why Kertzer, and other critics along with him, cannot afford to exorcise the ghost that such a notion of crisis produces. Instead, by domesticating crisis—"Canadian culture generally," he writes, "exists in a state of permanent crisis, always on the verge of being overwhelmed by outside forces" (171)—he contains any unsettling effect the ghostly may have.[22] He may be intent on defining this ghost in local terms—he affectionately claims it as "*our* ghost" (40, my emphasis)—but he ascribes to it an identity by borrowing heavily from the Enlightenment and later Western philosophical and aesthetic traditions. In Kertzer's argument, then, the elusiveness of the ghost and the habitual role of crisis form a symmetrical structure that contains the unruliness of Canada's *genius loci* and releases its energy in predictable directions. It doesn't then come as a surprise when we find out that what is supposed to be the distinguishing mark of CanLit and CanCrit is comparable to the history of American letters and entails (Birney's "Can. Lit" again), significantly so, "assimilation" and "adapt[ation]" of the legacy of romantic historicism (444). In other words, as an institutional formation, CanLit has unfolded by indigenizing[23] its anxiety about its state of belatedness by way of shifting its gaze from what is local to what lies outside it. This turning away from a (distorted) familiar locus in search of critical paradigms executes (in both senses of the word, putting to death and performing an action) an apostrophe[24] that resurrects the spectres of race that in this scenario of hauntology are rendered, yet again, invisible.[25]

The lack that CanLit sets out to overcome reflects a denial of its congenital (mal)formation. Moreover, in a fashion that shows this malaise to be decidedly Eurocentric, it enacts a certain kind of script wherein it performs double Freudian duty: not quite liking where it stands, it indulges in a family romance that, nevertheless, returns it to the very Oedipal site it strives to move beyond. This overdetermined familialism exposes a number of things simultaneously: the Oedipal infrastructure of colonialism,[26] which explains, in part, why Freud suppressed the implications of the Oedipal complex by rendering it a normative aspect of subject formation in capitalist society; romancing Eurocentrism; perceiving the intimate local as a space that deterritorializes the settlers who have already deterritorialized the indigenous population and, subsequently, others; and, of course, the principal reason why hauntology recurs in examinations of the formation of CanLit, namely, the preoccupation with yet repulsion from the racialized others that reduce them to heavily coded figures, ghosts of a kind, that the white gaze fails to see for what and who they are.

While conventional understandings of Birney's trope privilege the white settlers' "haunted minds" (Sugars and Turcotte ix), the true spectre peeking through his lines is that of the repressed. And it is crucial that we read this figure in a manner that disrupts the Freudian trope of the return of the repressed, a trope that, when read in colonial contexts, operates virtually outside of time because it normalizes repression. The thing is, the Indigenous people have never left in order to return—never mind all the colonial scripts, chief among them that of the "vanishing Indian"[27]—nor have they capitulated to their colonial condition. Kertzer may end his book by contending to be developing a vision of justice, but he does so in a rather tepid fashion. Though he acknowledges the "fractious[ness of the] Canadian family" (171), his is a vision that relies on "tolerant people [who] can tolerate each other's differences" (193), that aspires to go only as far as "*some kind* of accommodation, *some* vision of adequacy and redress" (193, my emphasis). Beyond anticipating the politics and limits of reasonable accommodation in Quebec,[28] this rhetoric of tolerance and moderation advances not a new vision but rather a liberal metrics that reflects a reluctance to do away with colonial mastery, the direct result of the fact that he only "chide[s] colonialism as an 'incivility' because [he] want[s] to keep the civil forum in view" (178).[29]

This hauntology, as it emerges in Birney's poem but also in Kertzer's study over thirty years later, shows Canada to be a dysfunctional family that has been practising a politics of twisted intimacy. If intimacy is not just a matter of "private … [relations] constructed within the lines of private consent, intention, and will" (Berlant 79), but a matter of critical relationality, then the ways in which Canada has been trying to bring these others into the family fold—hailing them as its own yet curtailing their differences, and thus infantilizing them in the process—employ a politics of intimacy that belongs to the governmentality exercised by both political and non-political institutions. The policy of multiculturalism that excludes First Nations people, the various official apologies to First Nations and diasporic communities, and the reconciliation processes with regard to the traumatic legacies of residential schools are instantiations of an intimacy that involves both familiarity and defamiliarization, management and containment. The Canadian state has advanced these policies in the name of the nation's unity and its imaginary of benevolence, as gestures towards redress and restitution, but they often depend on tactics that defer true and just reconciliation, hence the persistence of hauntology. Indeed, reconciliation may not even be the right word; as David Garneau writes, "*[r]e-conciliation* refers to the repair of a previously existing harmonious relationship. This word choice imposes the fiction that equanimity is the status quo between Aboriginal people and Canada … the imaginary the word describes is limited to post-contact narratives," the result being that it "anaesthetizes knowledge of the existence of pre-contaiginal sovereignty" (35). A consequence of such tactics of incorporating others into the Canadian family, it runs the risk, as Scott Macfarlane puts it, of "stag[ing] the haunting of race—its very 'otherness' as encrypted within the institutional, cultural and political bodies that ostensibly represent people of colour and First Nations people" (26). Reading this settler tradition via a politics of intimacy that includes First Nations and other minoritized subjects only by means of special dispensation invariably encompasses collaboration with the epistemic violence of Western forms of thought. From Birney's Dickinson and Whitman to Kertzer's Enlightenment and the Romantic tradition, to the ever-present spirit of Empire that manifests itself in different guises, this continuous turning to various *hors-textes* in a way that validates the civilizational roots of colonialism does not necessarily deliver justice but instead justifies (however unwittingly) its *ancien régime.*

Still, we can cross this methodological and ideological threshold by turning this hauntology around, by engaging with *hors-textes* that come from a different repertory, that of displaced histories, and doing so in trans-systemic ways. Barbara Godard, for example, shows that the repressed do not necessarily *return* as repressed; what she calls "a deterritorialized literature" comes from "the *rise* of the repressed" that "dislocat[es] and undermin[es] the logic of the literary systems of the Anglo-American world" (79, my emphasis). Godard's shift from "return" to "rise" introduces a wedge in the familiar tropes of hauntology that implodes the Oedipal structure of the Canadian family. More specifically, her notion of deterritorialization echoes Deleuze and Guattari's trenchant critique of the Oedipal sign and its tight connections to colonialism: "Oedipus is always colonization pursued by other means, it is the interior colony, and ... even here at home, where we Europeans are concerned, it is our intimate colonial education" (170). So, if the Canadian family, like other families, "does not engender its own ruptures" (Deleuze and Guattari 97), it is through a series of anti-Oedipal gestures that we can begin removing its masks of civility that allow its politics of intimacy and incorporation to be perpetuated. The complicity of the Canadian "unrepentant familialism" (Deleuze and Guattari vii)[30] can be exposed for what it is when we no longer consider the repressed as belonging to an Oedipal genealogy whereby the other is forcibly adopted by the colonial logic and assimilated into the family as both a desirable and feared figure, or as a figure belonging exclusively to a traumatized culture or a culture of complaint. Such an incorporation would invariably constitute the other as a site of lack, an unruly and uncivilizable figure that has to be rescued from itself. Rather, if we recognize the repressed as an anti-Oedipal subject, that is, a subject "grant[ed] full credit to the *otherness* of [its] alterity" (Terdiman 7), its colonial familialism can be turned upside down. Instead of looking for missing ghosts, we can expand the repertoire that delimits the horizon of inherited histories by engaging in a particular configuration of de Certeau's historical practice of heterologies: in shorthand, the infusion of alterity into familiar/familial territory in ways that do not subsume or understand the other solely in terms of dominant categories.

V Of Politics and Ethics: Towards a Practice of Kinship

I hope it has become apparent by now that if this book is marked by the persistent need to address the lingering impact of hegemonic structures—from colonialism to entrenched critical paradigms—the essays in it respond to the gravitational pull exercised by the concern with politics and ethics as they are embodied in literature and in criticism. If the political stems from and is responsive to the public sphere, and if the ethical entails a subject's movement towards others premised on their irreducible differences, then politics and ethics are invariably entangled with each other. The ethical, as Simon Critchley states, "always take[s] place within a political context, within a public realm where the question of justice for others and for humanity as a whole can be raised" (273). *Critical Collaborations* posits this complex and often fraught connection between politics and ethics, especially with regard to how it is inscribed both in Canadian literature and its study and in the various contexts that inform it. More specifically, it materializes through these essays' critical narratives about relationality, which attempt to establish bridges and thereby create routes and crossings even when the terrain seems to be impassable—an instance of cultural portage—but also through the relations that emerge when we read them through and against one another.

Findlay employs the trope of cultural portage to refer to the "effortful move of ideas and experiences from one navigable site to another," a mode of mobility embodying a trans-systemic approach. Historically associated with the tradition of the voyageurs and the fur trade, and employed by the First Nations "long before contact with newcomers," portaging is an "activity redolent of development yet profoundly dependent on Aboriginal knowledge and the reliable technologies of prior occupation." Described by Findlay as "a moment of going beyond where we currently are and transforming some things we take with us while preserving others unchanged" ("Lori Blondeau" 24),[31] cultural portage aptly accounts for the critical practices advocated and practised in this collection. Hence the title *Critical Collaborations:* critical in the triple sense of the word—diagnostic, analytical, and consequential—with the emphasis on the plural, intended to thwart an overarching approach, a programmatic or single-minded way, as the answer to the many questions the contributors raise, but also suggesting the collaborative labour that any such project that involves cultural portaging relies on.

Criticism as a collaborative activity may invoke T.S. Eliot's notion of criticism as "a place for quiet co-operative labour," but his sense of the critical act demands that the critic "endeavour to discipline his personal prejudices and cranks … in the common pursuit of true judgment" (69) in an effort to achieve a depersonalized position. In contrast, critical collaboration as it emerges in this book doesn't bracket but instead problematizes the subject's position/s as critic, teacher, citizen, or member of a particular community. It does so by decanting the privileging of disinterested objectivity, the kind that would result in Eliot's "true judgment," which, to quote Spivak, is "in fact, an unacknowledged partisanship to a sort of universalist humanism" ("Responsibility" 20). If there is any partisan element in this collection—at least in my reading of it—it is that emphasis is placed equally on relationality and responsibility, the latter in the sense of "let[ting] oneself be approached by the resistance which the thinking of responsibility may offer thought" (Derrida, "From *Shibboleth*" 373).[32] In the context of a scholarly project like this one, responsibility signals a recasting of the ways in which we are expected to relate to the university as "a community of thought," a community whose "responsibilities cannot be purely academic" (Derrida, "The Principle of Reason" 16). If the role of the university today, as Derrida argues, involves "political, ethical, and jurid-ical consequences" (16), then responsibility entails disturbing the university's economies and ecologies of knowledge that "regulate[] university life accord-ing to the supply and demand of the marketplace" (17), on the one hand, and questioning the normative paradigms that determine disciplinary structures and research, on the other. As these essays suggest, such disturbances cannot be solely "intra-institutional" (19); they must occur as much inside as outside the university but also, and equally importantly, in the interstices between the university and the communities outside it, a case of portaging across and through institutional structures and community sites. In this light, respon-sibility and collaboration operate as conditions that shape not only the sites within which critics work but also the methodological avenues their work pursues. At once a form of accountability towards the sites critics are affiliated with and a sign of social, political, and cultural engagement, responsibility provides "the stimulus of a persistent critique" (Spivak, "Responsibility" 45).

It is this kind of stimulus that compels this volume's contributors, at least in my estimation, to continue addressing the enduring impact of hegemonic structures, especially as they pertain to the production and institutionalization of Canadian literature. What stands out as perhaps the single most import-ant aspect of these essays—most important in that it keeps resurfacing in different guises and ways—is the consistent weight placed on kinship and its related equivalents: kinship (Emberley), affiliation (Emberley, Miki, Rak), affinity (Siemerling), allegiance (Verduyn), alliance (Lousley), collaboration and relations (Battiste), contingency (Sandilands), convergence (Hender-son), engagement and contact (Ricou, Paré). Not necessarily synonyms of one another, these terms nevertheless emerge as variations on the theme of kinship. Coming from different terrains and practices, they must be read in the particular contexts in which they are employed. In a volume that focuses on Indigeneity, diaspora, and ecology, kinship cannot possibly figure as a transparent concept, a set of relations conceived in the traditional sense of the term or a set of cultural notions of filiation socially acknowledged and in many cases legally validated.

There is no doubt kinship is a loaded term. The fact that its meanings and functions, as well as its study, have continued to be the object of intense discussions for a long time now in the field of anthropology, the discipline that has systematized its importance, speaks to its inherent complexity but also to the fraught and complicitous history that characterizes its development. James Clifford wrote in 1997 that "kinship, once a disciplinary core [in anthropology], is now actively forgotten in some departments" (59). Yet questions about kinship continue to unfold and to be debated in contexts that problematize subject relations, communities, nation-states, and the (re-)production of bodies.[33] They demonstrate, as Thomas Strong puts it, that "'kinship' is definitely back on the anthropological agenda, but did it ever leave?" (401). Three important issues that have emerged from these among other arguments are that kinship should no longer be exclusively understood biogenetically; that as a unified construct kinship does not necessarily exist in non-Western societies; and that the tendency today is not to delimit and thus bound kinship but, rather, to employ it as a trope reflective of how it is produced by, is responsive to, and unsettles inherited technologies of knowledge. Hence ~~kinship~~, kinship under erasure, what Strong after Butler proposes to call the persistent questioning and engagement with it (404).

If genetics is at the core of how kinship has long been commonly defined, blood emerges as a literal and metaphorical figure that both affirms and disturbs the reciprocity attached to kinship. Blood "links the living to each other and also to the dead and conjoins place and identity," but when it is "shed in fighting" it also speaks of "the struggle of the 'civilized' against the 'savage,'" of sacrifice and violence. It is, then, a double sign, a sign of inheritance and of brutality, that is "etched in the land" (Alonso 188) and in memory. When its flow crosses borders and bodies that it is not supposed to, then it also becomes a sign of contamination and impurity that can be welcomed or feared, or both. Today kinship does not function exclusively in terms of filiation and closely knit groups but in terms of diversity as well. As Marilyn Strathern writes, "*diversity … [is] a … fact of modern kinship*" (22). This shift in conventional notions of kinship is evidenced, for example, in *Cultivating Canada: Reconciliation through the Lens of Cultural Diversity*, the third volume produced by the Truth and Reconciliation Commission (TRC), which includes, as Georges Erasmus says in his "Introduction," "the perspectives of new Canadians and those outside the traditional settler communities of British and French." Comprising writing and visual art, these contributions are by writers, artists, academics, and cultural activists representing communities ranging from Afro-Canadian to Chinese Canadian, from the Roma to Arab Canadian. In this instance, kinship emerges from their shared experience of "wrongdoings and redress" but also from their shared desire for "healing[] and reconciliation." As Erasmus goes on to say:

Because Canada is a nation of diverse cultures, its people drawn from every region of the world, any discussion of reconciliation must include the perspectives of those who have arrived in more recent days and those who trace their family histories beyond western European colonial states. The reason for this is simple. Aboriginal people have a unique historical relationship with the Crown, and the Crown represents all Canadians. From this it follows that all Canadians are treaty people, bearing the responsibilities of Crown commitments and enjoying the rights and benefits of being Canadian. (vii)

The experience of systemic injustices experienced both personally and collectively as a community, accompanied by the desire to heal traumas and achieve reconciliation and restitution, is what grants "all Canadians" in this instance their "necessary place in the circle" for reconciliation. Here kinship functions not biogenetically but as a web of relations across multiple fronts that brings together Indigeneity and diaspora and does so in relation to the land, land understood at once as the geopolitical space of Canada and as the larger ecological system whose sustenance is intimately linked with humanness.

By "crossing both the material and notional boundaries that assign Aboriginal people to the margins" (Erasmus viii), the TRC practises a performative gesture, thus effecting an epistemic shift that shakes up the epistemological construction of the "'Indian problem'" (Erasmus viii), while at the same time nullifying the exclusionary clause in the Canadian Multiculturalism Act that leaves Aboriginal peoples out of its mandate to "preserve" and "enhance" the "cultural heritage" of "ethno-cultural minority communities." If traditionally the study of kinship was "based on the assumption that it creates divisions in society by conceptually separating those who are genealogically related to each other from those who are not so related" (Ladislav 143), kinship as a methodological and socio-political trope has the potential to suspend the Western privileging of blood as the single most important element of kin relations. If it is their mutual relationship to the Crown that the contributors to *Cultivating Canada* share, then kinship is a problematized *and* desirable condition that pivots around inherited paradigms of knowledge production and the need to challenge their obstinate hold on how we understand our presence in this land and our relations with it and with others.

Aaron James Mills's "An open letter to all my relations: On Idle No More, Chief Spence and non-violence" signals these shifts powerfully:

All my relations,
My Anishinaabe name is White Wolf and the name my mother gave me is Aaron James Mills. I'm a Bear Clan Anishinaabe, a Canadian and the son of a single mother. I say "Anishinaabe" not "aboriginal" intentionally, for this is

who I am and how you should understand me. Regarding our relationship, I'm from Treaty #3 Territory. I'm also from Couchiching First Nation, North Bay, Ottawa, Vancouver, Toronto, and now Victoria. I'm a lawyer. I have a graduate degree from Yale Law School where last year I was a Fulbright scholar. I'm 31 years old and I have a partner I love very much.

Mills' apostrophe addresses "all [his] relations Indigenous and other," while the ways in which he self-identifies evoke different degrees of kinship between himself and those whom he apostrophizes. By situating himself as a subject in a chain of relations, he views kinship to be as much a matter of biogenetics as of contingency. Moreover, and equally important, not only is the nation, long assumed to be analogous to a family, pluralized—he is both Anishinaabe and Canadian, and more specifically from Couchiching First Nation—but it also figures as an unsettled construct in more ways than one, its putative unity as a legal and affective entity shaken up. Defining "our relationship" in reference to the Anishinaabe Nation's 1873 Treaty #3 with the Crown, Mills shows that the realignment of kin relations is actualized "in the idiom of the land" (Ladislav 150), an idiom that in this instance further expands and complicates relationality. By identifying himself via his Anishinaabe Nation's Treaty, Mills recalibrates non-Indigenous Canadians' relationship with the Canadian state and Indigenous people/s. Thus his open letter evokes Henderson's notion of "'sui generis and treaty citizenship,'" a reminder that "Canadian citizenship is not a gift or even a reparative gesture to be bestowed upon Aboriginal peoples by the state; instead, Canadian citizenship is the product of Aboriginal peoples' conditional permission, though historical treaty processes" (Henderson, "Incomprehensible Canada" 115–16). In this context, the inclusiveness that "all my relations" registers speaks of a kinship that does not annul long-term legal and ethical responsibilities; rather, it entails intricate and multifarious relationships that demand a re-evaluation of the politics of intimacy, but also of the social, affective, and political bonds among people/s. As Krista E. Van Vleet writes, "kinship is *lived* among people with diverse experiences of identity and inequality, within and between households and communities that can no longer be viewed as isolated from global processes and transnational discourses" (10). This multi-layered process manifests that, while kinship is lived in the present, it remains concerned with the past and is historically contextualized.

Seen in these terms, kinship operates as a trans-systemic method that brings to the fore the materiality of histories that conjoin different subjects and their respective communities with one another, as well as with Canada as a nation-state and the land it inhabits. Promising to recompose the Canadian national imaginary, it also functions as a route that challenges the limits of boundaries, boundaries of sites and of bodies, of literary texts and cultural paradigms; it thus points to reconfigurations of communities and their representations in ways that realign how they have been constructed—without, however, abrogating their inherited traditions or inhibiting the circulation of various kinds of asymmetries that are crucial to understanding the production of literary and critical discourses. The accent on "re-" here does not simply signify the return or circulation of the same; it also indicates the demands that kinship places on constant engagement with the conditions that produce and uphold it.

Coda: Two Artists, a Bedraggled Moose, and a Quill

The potential inscribed in a critical mode that engages with and questions existing paradigms to produce epistemic shifts is amply evident in Roy Kiyooka's posthumously published *The Artist and the Moose: A Fable of Forget* (2009). As Miki's reading of the same text in this volume (44–47) also demonstrates, in this highly intertextual, parodic, comical, and historically situated narrative, at once historiographic meta-fiction and allegory, the chief player is the Canadian paradigms that have established Canadian nationalism and CanLit. The text's nameless narrator, perhaps a poet since he "had the misfortune of attending" a League of Canadian Poets conference (23), is invited to compose a White Paper for "the Royal Commission on 'The Status of a Genuine Multi-Cultural Aesthetic for Canadians in the 21st Century.'" It doesn't take him long to realize that such a project cannot just be forward-looking; it must involve "the copious Texts"[34] in the National Archives. So off he goes to Ottawa: "Page after page of Anglo-Canadian History, with all its linguistic peculiarities, proposed parenthetical alignment with Indo-European man and his clandestine appropriation of all of the Aboriginal Land that had virtually remained unsullied til 1492. Despite himself he had unwittingly blundered on a Textual Paradigm that threatened his alacritous quest" (18). Never mind that he hails from Forget, Saskatchewan, a tiny, economically forsaken hamlet that, though named after Saskatchewan's first Lieutenant Governor, Amédée E. Forget, was left "out of the National Dream" (15); the narrator knows better than to "succumb[]" to these Texts "without" questioning "their authorial Colonial Tropes" (19). Indeed, he constantly stumbles on nationalist paradigms such as the "unmitigated Garrison Mentality" (85), often to the detriment of his safety—"(Inadvertently, he stubbed his big toe on a paradigm that threatened to undermine his Mandate)" (78)—a relentless reminder that such constructs have material and lasting consequences.

What helps steer the direction of his quest—Kiyooka calls it by one of his favourite words, a "probe" (11)—is his self-appointed mentor, Ol' Moose. Ol'

Moose is both plagued by the memory of and inspired by "his illustrious forebears [that] once roamed the length and breadth of North America and the
only fleet two-legged critters they ever encountered never called themselves
'Indian'" (84). He may suffer from his own share of "baleful guffaws" (57), but
this doesn't undermine the wisdom he imparts to the narrator. Quite the contrary, the palimpsestic history Ol' Moose embodies makes him as important
an asset in the narrator's research as the National Archives. Hence his ability
to probe the narrator's conscience, his ubiquitous presence and embodied
history providing both poignant cues as to what Canada's "awful rhetoric of
progress" (69) entails and a host of intimations about the future. "Since 1492,"
the narrator finds out, "Ol' Moose had contracted, without his consent, syphi-
lis, trench mouth, gangrene, small pox, AIDS and cancer plus a whole array of
noxious pimples. All these plus endless codicils, institutions, and surveillance
systems" (68). As Miki writes in his Afterword to *The Artist and the Moose*,
which he edited, Ol' Moose "is both a victim of colonialism and an embodiment of the lands appropriated through invasion ... [but also] a source of
contact with a spirit of place that is still accessible to the active imagination
of artists" (155). The kinship that ensues between the narrator and Ol' Moose
is highly instructive and largely determines the former's insight that he must
first come to terms with "the iconography of Canadian Nature" and "all the
fugitive tropes before he begins to elucidate a truly benign Multi-Cultural
Aesthetic" (29). His relations with Ol' Moose and with a cast of other non-
human characters, ranging from the text's Plot and the nation-state's Text to
a Pipe and a tiny bird, no matter how parodic and allegoric, allow kinship in
Kiyooka's Plot to deconstruct the anthropocentrism of the Western tradition
but also to illustrate that kinship, depending on the paradigms that constitute
it, can create highly productive alliances while at the same time operating as
a discriminatory tool with dire consequences.

Despite, or because of, the vestiges of "the unredeemed paradigms clogging
[the] conduits" of his White Paper (65), there is precious little in Ottawa—
what with "our heroes made to order, and in our own image" (35)—that makes
the narrator feel at home. Not one to "kick[] the old tropes around" (94), he
soon discerns that "Ottawa and its legions of Civil Savants ... had no intention of introducing, let alone endorsing anything as fraught as a New Multi-
Cultural Aesthetic for the 21st Century" (90). If he has discovered anything
about the mandate of his probe, it is that the "word *Aesthetic* had to be among
the meanest words in a Canuck's lexicon. Bring it up in a pub if you want some
lout to tell you where to get off" (85–86). Indeed, precisely because he realizes
that the White Paper he has been commissioned to write is intended to pay
only lip service to differences, he concludes that "Aesthetics proposes to take
measure of all the unsung Beauty beneath our cultural politics. Otherwise, it's

just a pile of deer shit beside the tumbleweed tracks. Nothing to scream off the top. Nothing much to shout 'HURRAY!' about" (86).

This recognition comes to him via his exploration of how the figure of Tom Aplomb / Tom Thomson was granted a place "in the Legendary Hall-of-Fame" (30), a process initiated by a package mailed to him in Forget that contains a precious cultural artifact, Tom Aplomb's Pipe. "*Who is Tom Aplomb?*" the narrator wonders. "*And is he truly the 'Blameless Hero' at the Heart of the Eastern Historian's mytho-poetic enterprise? And does his untold demise comprise one of the forsaken paradigms for a renewed aesthetics?*" (28). The turning point in his quest, the entrance of Tom Aplomb/Thomson into the narrator's life signals Kiyooka's fascination with this national icon while also exposing, in an unmitigated fashion, the canonization process of artists and their appropriation by the Canadian national imaginary. Yet the narrator's response to the unexpected gift he receives—"*Who is Tom Aplomb?*—is not just a rhetorical question; echoing as it does the question of "Canadian Identity" that literary critics and writers alike have long been obsessed with, especially in the 1960s and '70s, it becomes the central trope in the narrator's quest. Turned sleuth, he sets out to answer it by trying to figure out both how and why Aplomb/Thomson emerged as a cultural hero and the circumstances of his death.

In *The Artist and the Moose*, as Miki observes, Kiyooka does not hold Thomson responsible

> for what was made of him by cultural nationalists. [Kiyooka's] critical stance accounts for the distinction that needs to be maintained between the legend of Tom Thomson invented by centralist cultural nationalists, who needed an icon to validate the state's cultural control of the so-called wilderness, and Tom Aplomb the artist in Kiyooka's narrative, who was possessed by the desire to enact in the materiality of this art, his affective relationship to natural phenomena. (Afterword 143–44)

Read in the context of Kiyooka's own personal and artistic trajectory, the hegemonic, colonial, and racializing paradigms at the core of the Canadian nationalist mythos that has elevated Thomson to the status of national cultural hero are put under the microscope in Kiyooka's text. Kiyooka's sensibility as an artist and writer had been shaped by the same nationalist ethos that has identified Thomson as a quintessential Canadian artist, only in his case this formation followed a parallel yet diametrically opposite route to Thomson's. With his education and life interrupted by the internment of Japanese Canadians, Kiyooka was identified as an "enemy alien," akin to the Canadian nation-state's Yellow Peril narrative that haunted the nation at the time of the Second World War. Forced to reside outside the Canadian family, Kiyooka, born in Moose Jaw, Saskatchewan, turned his racialization and deterritorial-ization around.[35] Feeling "athwarted" (Miki, "Interface" 71), he neither stayed in the periphery of the Canadian family nor fully adopted it. In a manner that resonates with Mills's self-identification above, Kiyooka posited himself in relation to Canada as an anti-Oedipal subject *and* as a Canadian. As he wrote in a conference paper included in his *Pacific Rim Letters,* "We Asian North Americanos," he saw himself as "a white anglo-saxon protestant with a cleft tongue" (117). Speaking in the first-person plural with a cleft tongue allows Kiyooka to embody in his discourse his history as a Japanese Canadian subject and artist while disclosing the uncanny relations that have shaped the mythos of the Canadian family. He thus asserts a kinship with Canada that, nevertheless, deconstructs the Canadian Oedipal apparatus. As Miki puts it, the "in-between critical space[,] between the inclusionary and exclusionary boundaries of the cultural nationalism he had to negotiate," allowed Kiyooka "to empathize with Tom Thomson, the consummate artist, whose death was commodified to serve the WASP nation, but whose work exceeded, and con-tinued to exceed, the assumptions of the narrow nationalism in which it was valorized" (Afterword 145–46).

It is this tension between inclusion and exclusion, between being adopted and being appropriated, that propels the narrator in *The Artist and the Moose* to delve more deeply into the mystery of Aplomb/Thomson's death. This inves-tigation takes the narrator into Algonquin Park, where Aplomb/Thomson lived after 1912, "canoeing, fishing, and sketching in the forests and lakes" (O'Brian and White 131) until he met his death there. Miki reminds us that Algonquin Park is "a state-owned construct ... established in 1893 through regulatory boundaries that specifically displaced the members of the Algon-quin tribe who inhabited its spaces" (141). Expropriated from the Algonquins as their natural and hereditary habitat, Algonquin Park exemplifies what John O'Brian and Peter White call "the nationalization of nature in Canada, par-ticularly ... the development of foundational ideas about northernness and wilderness" (4). More an attempt to forge a kinship with this "New Found Land" (35) than an ecologically minded endeavour, this national/ist project needed artistic legitimation. Enter Aplomb/Thomson, "who had everything a Greek or a Canuck could possibly want and then some. Take a strapping six-footer with an eye for the changing seasons in both trees and women. Add to this his fly-tying skills, his swiftness in water, his down-to-earth paintings, his re-doubtable hunting and culinary skills, and presto! you've got a fulsome Socratic Hero: one tailor-made to take his place in the Legendary Hall-of-Fame" (30).

Aplomb/Thomson's mysterious death in the park was a catalyst in his mythologization. Thomson's "dead body," Sherrill Grace notes, "has come to represent a complex web of meanings and associations that rivals, if not over-shadows, the body of his work" (qtd. in Miki, Afterword 139), a process that the narrator intuits on his own and through the interviews he conducts. The ongoing preoccupation of critics, historians, biographers and judges with how Thomson died and where his body is buried is reproduced in Kiyooka's text in virtually all its complexity,[36] and then some,[37] thus reinforcing my earlier point about the dominant desire in Canadian culture to be haunted by non-existent ghosts, a desire that inadvertently unearths those history has assassinated. The elusiveness of Aplomb/Thomson's dead body mimics that of Kertzer's *genius loci*. Yet the fact that it is replaced—or displaced in turn—by the Algonquin man's skeletal remains shows elusiveness to be a master trope managing the cohesiveness of the Canadian family. Moreover, the mystery surrounding the circumstances of Aplomb/Thomson's death—or wandering body, as it were—is not just about this Canadian cultural icon; it also broaches the question of murder. While some of Aplomb/Thomson's associates and official figures are intent on exploring who might have killed him, none of them except the narrator is concerned with what might have happened to or who killed the "Nameless Indian" (56).

One of the "*Remembrances*" the narrator collects about Aplomb/Thomson sums up concisely why Canada attempted to fabricate a cultural cord linking it with Turtle Island that it colonized.

> For Canada to find a true racial expression of herself through art, a com-plete break with European traditions was necessary; a new type of artist was required—a type with sufficient creative equipment to initiate a technique of his own through handling new materials by new methods—and what was required more than technique was deep-rooted love of the country's natural environment. (36)

This testimonial Kiyooka devises takes my argument in this introduction back to its beginning: the double ethos of filiation and complicity that char-acterizes the making of literary traditions of settler origins, and the ensuing tension between (de-)oedipalization and family romance that arises from the desire to invent a Canadian Oedipus. But, as Deleuze and Guattari write, "only in appearance is Oedipus a beginning, either as a historical or prehistorical origin, or as a structural foundation. In reality it is a completely ideological beginning.... Oedipus is always and solely an aggregate of destination fab-ricated to meet the requirements of an aggregate departure constituted by a social formation" (101). The ideological apparatus behind these paradoxes and tensions emerges in all its "multilateral sublime" (Findlay, "TransCanada Col-lectives" 174) in what I take to be the pivotal moment in this text, a moment that turns the Canadian Plot to find a true Canadian Aesthetic upside down: the skull discovered in what is supposed to be Aplomb/Thomson's burial spot is that of an Algonquin man with "an exemplary hole in his temple" (57). The return of the dislocated, deterritorialized figure in Kiyooka's text not only "displace[s]" or "misplace[s]," as Miki suggests, Aplomb/Thomson but also reveals "the body of indigeneity." "No longer in the closet of colonial cover-up" (Miki, Afterword, 160), the Algonquin skull brings to light yet another plot repressed in the Colonial Texts the narrator has been poring over. The affiliation suggested here between Aplomb/Thomson and the unknown Algonquin man is of the kind that speaks of complicity, as well as of misbegotten and denied af/ filiations, a kind of kinship that "appears to be invented and re-invented out of the abrogation of its constitution taboos" (Strong 402).

As a consequence of this Algonquin skull, the narrator's probe goes astray. He realizes that "Aesthetics got bored and turned its back on the humble sod roof shack with its Old World relics" (86). This Native's remains, the narrator surmises, should justly haunt the Canadian nation-state, so he gives up on his project and flies back to Forget. But he doesn't give up entirely on what he has unearthed in the course of his probe; he keeps a record of his discoveries and thoughts in a "thick Notebook, labeled 'Historical Paradigms, Incorporated.' Tom Aplomb's death, and the White Paper's bite of breath, had been laminated onto his dumbfound skull so long he couldn't forego either of them without forfeiting himself" (96).

And so, at the end of this short narrative, leaving behind "a hastily penned circle with a question mark in the middle" (107), the narrator performs his own vanishing act. Perhaps a sign of his capitulation to his "exemplary failure" (107) to script a 21st-century Canadian Aesthetic, his disappearance results in part from his inability to any longer see his own reflection in his small round pond back in Forget. The absence of his reflection in the pond renders his gaze empty, symptomatic of his oath "to tell the Truth, the Whole Truth, by unconditionally forgetting 'everything'" he has "perused" and come upon on his "improvidential Quest." This resident of Forget keeps his word, but he does so in a gesture that totally unscripts the Plot to re-oedipalize Canada: he signs his declaration by placing "his name (in Cree) on the bottom of the line of the official Document that gave him back his freedom" (102).

The Cree signature inserts into the cultural, historical, and political archive of Canada what has been rendered as an *hors-texte*, an *hors-texte*, however, that incurs a profound epistemic shift as it comes from sources other than those of the "Eastern Establishment" (37). Not just a sleuth but also a saboteur, Kiyooka's narrator reveals his true "colors" in his personal meditations: "If his faithful Notebooks knew anything, it had to do with [his quill's] own native alliances" (106). The quill, the same one with which he signed in Cree and penned the question mark in his departing note, is the implement that recasts the national Texts, creates the scripts that remain of him, and enables him to "join[] Ol' Moose in the Tundra" (107).

Is the narrator's anonymity, along with the fact his tale unfolds through a third-person voice, a kind of conspiratorial wink to those who have been silenced by the Old Paradigms? Is he a Cree poet or does he sign in Cree out of solidarity with and as a sign of respect towards the Algonquin man whose dead body was found in the park? Becoming as he does an elusive ghost himself, is his vanishing act one of mimicry or resistance, or both? Does he kill himself or is he spirited away by Ol' Moose? Whatever the answers might be, the Plot—Kiyooka's but also that of Canadian history and of our ongoing engagement with critical paradigms and their colonial vestiges—continues.

BELIEF AS/IN METHODOLOGY AS/IN FORM
Doing Justice to CanLit Studies
Roy Miki

To be in any form, what is that?
—Walt Whitman, "Song of Myself" (1959)

A Grace Note

In one of many talks on poetics that bpNichol gave during the 1970s and 1980s, he returned to a preoccupation—perhaps more tellingly an obsession—with the question of form, not limiting himself to the practice of creative writing, but also taking into consideration the somatic conditions of the human organism in its production of the spatial and temporal boundaries of its enactments. When asked to explain a phrase he had once used, "syntax equals the body structure," he referred to the emotional and psychological processes by which we "armour the body, the easiest illustration of which is: if I live in a house with a low doorway, I'm probably going to end up walking like this a lot" (hunching). In thinking about this deformation of body structure in relation to the restricted spaces of syntax in his writing, he says that he discovered that "the order in which I wrote my poems allows certain contents in and keeps other content out, i.e. the syntax I choose, the way I tend to structure a piece, form per se, permits some contents and excludes others." For a creative writer to maintain a vital and generative relationship to form, then, the trick is to "keep moving the structure of the poem around," so that "hopefully I can encompass different realities and different ways of looking at things." What is revealing in Nichol's notion of form are the intimate connections he draws

between the body of the writer and the "body of the poem" (276), both constantly engaged in a somatic process where form is crucial to the workings of
our consciousness. If the body of the poem, and by implication other forms
of writing, can undergo "hunching" by restrictive forms, then readers who
inhabit these forms will be subject to the same limits. Even if their bodies
will not be physically hunched, their consciousness may be by the formal
restrictions of the texts.

Taking Nichol as a cue, then, we can assume that writing—and specifically
our writing as intellectuals and researchers—has worldly effects and consequences that necessitate ongoing self-reflection as well as reflexivity of form.
These will vary according to, on the one hand, the contexts of its unpredictable
circulation in networks of often conflicting and asymmetrical discourses, and,
on the other hand, the assumptions we bring to the moment of composition.
This interplay of networks and assumptions constitutes a basic operation of
our work in literary studies, an operation that to a large extent establishes
the agenda of our institutional affiliations as custodians and interpreters of
creative texts. With this thought before us, I want to return to one of the key
moments in the history of CanLit studies.

Northrop Frye and the Pastoral

In thinking though the implications of form, it is revealing to turn, once
again, to Frye's essay, a constituting document of CanLit as an institution and
one that has received ongoing attention since its first publication.[1] In Imre
Szeman's recent engagement with Frye's "Conclusion to *A Literary History
of Canada*"—which was published in 1965, a year in the Cold War era when
a powerful cultural nationalism was ascendant—Frye's essay is described as
"an unavoidable text, the Urtext for the critical analysis of Canadian literary
criticism" (176). Szeman resituates Frye's reading of the Canadian literary
scene in relation to "nation" as a formation in Canadian literature and criticism. Criticism receives more attention because, according to Szeman, it is
primarily through its development that "the nation has become the concept
around which every other consideration revolves" (176). By literature, Szeman
means primarily fiction, and here he notes an absence of national cultural
preoccupations, which leads him to argue that the valorization of the nation
by critics goes contrary to the decline of the nation as a vital force for the two
most prominent intellectuals whose work has been generative for criticism:
George Grant and Northrop Frye.[2]

In his essay, Frye says (famously) that the "forms of literature are autono-
mous" (232), but since Canadian writers, as part of a colonial society, are so
distant from these forms, they necessarily encounter a disconnection between

reference and these forms, which have become foreign, or exist back there in a pre-colonial space and time. Consequently, writers of British or European origin in Canada have no choice but to represent their experiences of place through foreign forms. Supposedly, we would get the kind of hunching that bpNichol says is the result of forms being imposed rather than created out of the actual conditions of existence. Having established a cultural and historical context for his imagined Canadian writers, Frye concludes with a Cartesian flourish but with little sense of doubt: "The separation of subject and object is the primary fact of consciousness, for anyone so situated and so educated" (233). We have moved from a particular instance of an alienated condition, the result of colonial displacement, to a general state of consciousness.

Frye qualifies his assertion somewhat in acknowledging that some writers have overcome the shortcomings of their colonial situation to access "the real headwaters of inspiration" (234), but the general rule is that Canadian literature begins as a tradition that is already estranged from its literary roots, which accounts for the "separation of subject and object." If left untended, such a fraught, even traumatic, state could become unbearable. What is needed is the invention of tradition, and this brings us to his central notion of the "pastoral myth" (238) that functions as the origin of Canadian literature. Leaving aside for now his use of the pastoral myth, what remains exceptional is the way Frye strategically frames the inaugural power of this literature's dislocated state. Applying the metaphor of organic growth in cultural formations, he proposes that, unlike American literature, Canadian literature did not undergo a historical phase during which a "social imagination can take root and establish a tradition" (219). English Canada went from being "part of the wilderness, [to] a part of North America and the British Empire, [to] a part of the world" (219). His account, which does not recognize the state's efforts to produce a national culture in the postwar era—a period that was formative for Frye's own work—implies that English Canada bypassed a national formation phase. Consequently, "Canadian writers are, even now [circa 1965], still trying to assimilate a Canadian environment at a time when new techniques of communication, many of which, like television, constitute a verbal market, are annihilating the boundaries of that environment" (219). Frye does not explain the term "environment," but presumably he would include, aside from natural phenomena, the social, economic, political, and technological factors that were drawing Canada into a global network of relationships, in other words, away from the bounded elements of nationalist forms. For Frye this truncated development helps account for Canadian culture's "fixation on its own past, its penchant for old-fashioned literary techniques, its preoccupation with strangled articulateness" (220).

It is at this point in his argument that Frye enunciates his now illustrious question, the one that has generated so much speculation about the nature of English Canadian consciousness: "It seems to me," he writes, "that Canadian sensibility has been profoundly disturbed, not so much by our famous problem of identity, important as that is, as by a series of paradoxes in what confronts that identity. It is less perplexed by the question 'Who am I?' than by some such riddle as 'Where is here?'" (220). When we, as current readers steeped in the proliferating discourses around globalizing processes, step out of the frame of Frye's endlessly provocative question, we may wonder who can, or would have the state of consciousness to, formulate such a question, and out of what conditions of apprehensiveness. Where is here, when posed as a question, presumes a subject who is not here but elsewhere, at least in consciousness, and further that an estrangement causes an anxiety, an anxiety that can perhaps be healed through the question. Further speculation might suggest that the question not only enables the positing of an answer, but also is designed to function as a rhetorical move that pre-empts the void threatening to dissolve the very possibility of the question—the real anxiety being the hunch that no here is here to be a where. The process of deferral, in any case, seems to motivate the writer to offer as a model for Canadian literature an aesthetic and national formation that compensates for the potentially debilitating split between subject and object in Canadian life, and thus for the threat of the inarticulate—an absence of meaning that, if left untended, will turn into a rational humanist nightmare.

On the surface, Frye's argument makes good and even pragmatic sense. The creation of a working relationship between subject and object—and by implication between literature and place—has been a generative preoccupation of nation-based CanLit studies in providing a thematic and methodological purpose for its cultural and institutional development. What has not been adequately noted, in my view, is that its formation functions as compensation for the otherwise anxious state of estrangement with its sense of "strangled articulateness." In displacing the anxiety through an aesthetic form, Frye's model of CanLit bears striking resemblances to Freud's model of "civilization" in *Civilization and Its Discontents*, which functions as a form of compensation for the natural conditions of human suffering. For Freud, each individual organism with its ego drives and libidinal energies seeks to maximize its pleasure and minimize the pain it inevitably suffers because it is alive and mortal. As a humanist and rational formation, civilization works to manage individual egos, which left on their own would be in endless battles with other egos. It does so by cordoning off a space in the ego for the superego, a force that is internalized as conscience. Conscience, in turn, ensures that individuals will become socialized in working together to produce a civilization. While

speaking about the regulatory power of conscience, Freud invokes the metaphor of the garrison in a way that prefigures Frye's use of "garrison mentality"
to identify colonial settler consciousness in Canada: "Civilization ... obtains
mastery over the individual's dangerous desire for aggression by weakening
and disarming and by setting up an agency within him to watch over it, like
a garrison in a conquered city" (70–71). Significantly, for Freud civilization
progresses through a process akin to colonization: its power derives from its
ability to appropriate and transform the materiality of the earth into objects
that serve its own human-centred interests, acting in this sense as a rapa-
cious force of technological empowerment. As he comments, "countries have
attained a high level of civilization if we find that in them everything which
can assist in the exploitation of the earth by man and in his protection against
the forces of nature—everything, in short, which is of use to him—is attended
to and effectively carried out" (39).

Within the terms of Freud's civilization, art and other creative forms manu-
facture "illusions" or fantasy sites to make suffering palatable. In such aesthetic
forms, we show the "intention of making oneself independent of the external
world by seeking satisfaction in internal, psychical processes" (27). Through
the "displacement of libido" in art forms, "the connection with reality," so
Freud would have us believe,

> is loosened; satisfaction is obtained from illusions, which are recognized
> as such without the discrepancy between them and reality being allowed
> to interfere with enjoyment. The region from which these illusions arise is
> the life of the imagination; at the time when the development of the sense
> of reality took place, this region was expressly exempted from the demands
> of reality-testing and was set apart for the purpose of fulfilling wishes which
> were difficult to carry out. (27)

For Frye, serious literary work begins when writers individuate themselves,
detaching themselves from the social world of the "garrison mentality" (analogous to Freud's "reality") to enter the world of literature (analogous to Freud's
"illusion"). The "pastoral myth, the vision of a social ideal," which is derived
from the forms of literature, embodies the innocence of "childhood," both as
a state of pure consciousness and a stage of innocence in the history of civilization. The pastoral myth functions to invent an idealized origin in which
the split between subject and object has not occurred. At this pure site, the
Canadian writer's wish to assume the condition of indigeneity is fulfilled, and
this, Frye says, enables a "kind of rapport with nature which the Indian sym-
bolizes" (239). The pastoral myth, which substitutes for the lack of tradition in
a colonial space, also enables a nativization process through which indigenous

presence is supplanted, or otherwise appropriated in the interests of Canadian national identity.

Reading Frye's question—"Where is here?"—alongside Freud's *Civilization and Its Discontents* is instructive to understand the turn in his model of CanLit away from actual contemporary conditions. Frye believed that his country had already moved beyond the strict boundaries of nationalist forms, yet he himself desired an aesthetic space for CanLit where the fantasy of the pastoral myth could play itself out. In other words, the turn away from his own contemporary conditions necessitated the invention of literary origins in the pastoral as an aesthetic formation, one that could compensate for the void of colonial displacement and the imagined threats of a brutal and amoral nature that is antithetical to settler consciousness. For Freud, "civilization" as a form of order constitutes itself through a violent appropriation of what lies outside its domain, and this begins with the appropriation of nature, including Indigenous presence, to serve its human-centred social ends.

What is striking in reading Frye and Freud together is the alignment in their work *of the imagination with the un-real*, the latter being illusion in Freud and myth in Frye. In both instances, this capacity of consciousness is separated from the more dynamic and conflicted world of social and cultural concerns and situated in an aesthetic sphere that compensates for the dualism of the self and the other. Szeman notes that Canadian literature, primarily fiction, exhibits few signs of the nationalist concerns evident in the criticism, but this may signal the effects of the separation of aesthetics from the political sphere, the result of which is the overall devaluation of the imagination as a creative critical force in our lives as citizen consumers. He hints as much at this situation when he asserts that "literature is itself constituted within the circuits of ideological operations of which the belief in the ahistorical autonomy of the literary is itself one of the chief and most powerful examples" (195). In their conceptions of the imagination, both Frye and Freud remain staunch humanists for whom reason is hierarchically valued over imagination, just as culture-as-civilization is valued over nature, and mind is valued over body.

Although, as Szeman says, Frye does not himself advocate a nation-based literature, his model of an origin in the pastoral myth could be incorporated into a nation-based literary criticism that needed a conceptual framework. The belated condition of the nation in Frye's model could, with little difficulty, ground the call for a national culture to bolster a drive for Canadian exceptionalism in the face of liberal US mass media to the south and the conservative pull of European and British antecedents. Here the pastoral as analogous to contact with nature could function temporally as a "pre-colonial" (and thus "pre-modern") ground for the contemporary, a strategy that could enable a nativization process that would displace or otherwise cover over the violence of colonial civilization. What then lies beneath the pastoral is not an ancient wellspring of collective spirits, but the void of spaces—where is here?—that dark "nature" that Frye says scared the heck out of the settlers who built their garrisons to keep this "wilderness" imagined in their Protestant assumptions at bay.

This reading of Frye's essay as a constituting moment in the history of Can-Lit studies raises at least three points of importance for thinking through the connectives that bring form, belief, and methodology into a dynamic alignment. First, as simple as this point may be, the strategic use of the pastoral myth shows that CanLit has no necessary existence, as some nationalists would have us believe, but was invented as a form through the methodological split between subject and object. It was this split, posited as a condition of existence, that allowed the products of CanLit to be understood as the creations of the individuation process and not as embedded in the cultural and political trajectories of colonialism. Second, in the production of an identity formation, the analogy between a return to childhood and the turn to becoming native— the basis of the indigenization process—rendered invisible the displacement of Native cultures and collectives. And third, the teleological imperative of "identity" as an end product established a model of literary formation—and this would include minority formations, such as Asian Canadian—that would focus more on reference and interpretation than on the politics of differential relations that has always underwritten acts of the imagination. It is, in this sense, quite ironic that the current shift in technology towards the personal as the site of mobile bodies has opened up, even necessitated, a rethinking of the ethical implications of creative critical reading and writing practices, practices that sometimes get lost in the rationalist-dominated forms of research and thought that are promulgated and sanctioned in literary studies.

Meanwhile in the University

In their introduction to *Retooling the Humanities: The Culture of Research in Canadian Universities*, Daniel Coleman and Smaro Kamboureli draw attention to the policies of the Social Sciences and Humanities Research Council (SSHRC) as the "barometer" of the "culture of research" governing Canadian universities, and rightly so in light of the central role played by SSHRC in vetting and funding the work of academics and graduate students. They conclude that "research capitalism" has become the dominant model of knowledge production in universities, and that in this model, as if to mirror a neoliberal code of conduct, research is valued and validated according to capitalist standards of profit from investment, commercialization, and benefits for consumers. Thus, the public imagined in research capitalism is the "consumer" rather than the "citizen," as the case would be with humanities scholarship that functioned to question and critique such normative economic values. The genealogy informing "research capitalism," which Coleman and Kamboureli trace from the early postwar Massey Commission through the 1980s to the present, exposes the marginalization of critically conscious and progressive humanities research and the complementary formation of institutional policies and attitudes that give priority to projects that service the economic interests of profit, commodity production, and consumerism. So, they conclude that

> the university has transfigured the resilience it has always displayed into a widespread accommodation of the ideologies and practices of capitalist logic. In so doing it has surrendered its responsibility to generate knowledge that produces critically aware and informed national and global citizens by submitting to the pressure to generate knowledge that meets the needs of the marketplace—a marketplace shaped as much by the demands of the present economic climate as by the desire to meet the challenges of the twenty-first century. (31–32)

What we are left to contend with is the corporatization of university spaces, along with a fiercely competitive struggle for research grants, intellectual property rights, and the branding of research. Reinforcing the "buyer/seller paradigm," researchers come to be seen more and more as "entrepreneurs" rather than "scholars."

Research capitalism advocates the powerful assumption, in line with a neoliberal agenda, that knowledge is a commodity that is produced, exchanged, and sold in the form of patents and intellectual property rights. This instrumental view of knowledge is, of course, not new, but it has intensified in light of the alliances being forged between university researchers and corporations whose goal is the maximization of profits for shareholders, not a critical awareness of the perils of commodification. Within this conjunction of knowledge and commodification, humanities scholars—and perhaps, even more specifically, literary scholars—find themselves having to address the belief that researchers, including their students in the classroom, are nothing more than talking heads constituted through rationality as the only method of determining what is valued as knowledge and what is not. The ever-present creativity of the living body and the unpredictable resources of the imagination, as well as the plethora of non-rational tensions and uncertainties that operate in everyday intellection, have to be stabilized and rendered coherent to produce a performatively successful discourse for knowledge production. Knowledge and rationality are so consonant in academic culture that other modes, such as intuition, spiritual vision, and non-local communication (e.g.,

ESP or telepathy), including poetic texts that do not conform to norms of rationality, are discounted and often ridiculed. This is not to deny the power of rationality, but assuming that it is the only form of legitimate knowledge production establishes a boundary that abnormalizes the creative and displaces its central importance in the invention of new forms and the necessary critiques of existing ones.

One of the greatest disservices that has been promulgated in literary studies as a discipline—and this has permeated the modes of assessing performance for graduate studies, publication, promotion, and grants—is the distance assumed between the creative act and the critical contexts brought to visibility in the methodologies we adopt in our teaching and writing practices. Even when we pay lip service to the creative as an embodied mode of consciousness, it is the rational that is sanctified as the sign of legitimate knowledge acquisition. Creative texts are assumed to be outside of legitimate knowledge formations. Can we conceive of an institutional future in which a poem or novel that performs the boundaries of representation and an academic essay that talks about the boundaries of representations can be read as equivalent forms of knowledge production in the university? Probably not, at least not in the near future. Are we to conceive of creative texts then as the innocent victims of the appropriating claws of institutional mechanisms? Of course not. Texts can never be free from contextualization because their creators are themselves social and somatic beings whose desires are mediated by the same assumptions as are held by their critics. But the unquestioned rational interpretations of textual processes enabled by the various methodological approaches we have devised and continue to devise—whether progressively postcolonial or reactionary postcolonial, hip postmodernism or status quo postmodernism, whether critical multiculturalism or management multiculturalism, and so on—often exert their discursive power at the expense of the rich field of indeterminacies that the creative process thrives on, a field that produces the somatic fluidities and disequilibriums we associate with the life energy of the imagination.

Say what? Is it fair to question the honest and hard work of literary scholars who have honed their ratiocinative skills to produce critical essays that present powerfully cogent arguments? Well, perhaps, given that success in the disciplinary space of the university depends on these skills. But my concern is that the largely normalized ascendancy of rationality as the measure of knowledge production in our institutional practices has resulted in the fall of the (excuse my language here) stock value of the imagination, despite the often begrudging acknowledgment that art production constitutes a form of knowingness. Even then, such acknowledgment arises usually after some form of institutionally sanctioned interpretation has validated its worth. Overall, universities function under the constituting assumption of rationalism: that its methodology—self-consistency, thesis and proof, and logic—is superior to the affective and sensorial flows of the imagination, affiliated as the latter is with a somatic consciousness tied to the becomingness of life processes. We see this in the starkly simplistic contestation between subject and object—comparable to the split in Frye's essay—that still underlies much academic work, even in the face of theoretical work that has demonstrated that this divide serves to structure the value-constructing systems of institutions and their state benefactors. This divide, which resembles a colonial model of knower and known, becomes a big lie without which the fruits of knowledge production could not be picked so easily, and helps explain the undermining of autonomy (and therefore personal agency) in current research methodologies. Instead of empowering the personal to assume responsibility for the effects of knowledge production, it hands power over to the regulatory mechanisms of what can broadly be called disciplinarity, the belief that rational forms of knowledge form the sole objective of its institutions, and hence the exclusion of other forms of knowing such as spirituality, myth, belief, ESP, and other translocal phenomena, and even poetry. Much of this non-rational material reveals the workings of consciousness as a manifestation of living organisms that are also social beings, ourselves included in our research methods and the thought processes we undergo to arrive at the writing forms we use to represent our work.

Just as the mind is never simply a receptacle but a producer of what comes to appearance in its forms, so too, as Cornelius Castoriadis reminds us, the living organism is never just a passive receptor of external phenomena but is always creating "its sensations," so that "there is a *corporeal imagination*" that is always in play in consciousness. Since the "body is always, in a sense, psychical and the psyche always, in certain regards, somatical" (180), critical thinking, as it unfolds on any given occasion, is bound up with non-visible somatic affects (e.g., of desire, love, hate, disgust, pleasure, fear, anxiety, and so on) that texture the outcome of its more overt intellectual negotiations. Such a range of affects, often at odds with one another, can play a large role in the interpretation or discursive representation of creative texts, perhaps more visibly so in those texts—my own interest in CanLit and Asian Canadian Studies—that embody either prescribed or inscribed signs of difference, or so-called deviance from normative regulatory formations. We have referred to these texts variously in social terms as minority texts, racialized texts, multicultural texts, other texts, and in cultural terms as (fill in the blank identity) Canadian texts. Post-Frye, and in the wake of the identity politics that marked the decades prior to the more powerful ascendancy of neoliberal tenets in the 1990s, such marked texts generated a considerable amount of oppositional and resistant critical work, as well as a considerable amount of defensive critical work. In the process the model of nation-based CanLit became highly unstable, as the shifting desires of its readers gave way to a range of reading practices. If, in the dominant language of commodity culture, we have gone *post*, from IP as identity politics to IP as Internet provider, the latter our current source of consumer empowerment, then I believe the time has come to reassess the potency of the reading processes that form both the creative and the critical parameters of our work in CanLit studies, and by implication literary studies in general.

Creative Critical Reading Practices

Of all the intellectual activities that are prominent in literary studies, the reading of texts is both the most taken for granted and the most creative of critical acts. For students conditioned to see themselves as receptacles rather than as producers of knowledge, reading becomes largely an unconscious act that gets them through courses. The only time it becomes visible is when a text is no longer decipherable and therefore no longer consumable or otherwise commodified. Literary studies, I think, is very fortunate to have for its sphere of inquiry a methodology that enables an approach to broader dimensions of interpretive processes that involve, if we allow for it, both creative and critical concerns. For what I call creative critical reading I have in mind the kind of reflexive reading practices that complement the multi-faceted contexts that make up the shifting spaces of consciousness in readers who are themselves mobile subjects and, in potential at least, capable of initiating ethical acts that have justice and social equity as modes of desire.

Here, at the risk of faltering in my own terminological deficits, I want to suspend focus on the outcomes of interpretations—those discursive entities we call critical papers or essays that advance an argument—and draw attention to the methodological possibility offered in the reading process itself. Notwithstanding the rigorous training of literary specialists to produce cogent arguments based on a demonstration of contents and sources mastered, the imaginatively saturated immersion in the reading of texts is where, I would predict, we encounter our desires, fears, anxieties, and so on, mirrored in the materiality of the texts, although unfortunately in the instrumental process of constructing a rationally sound argument, much of the non-rational, affective whirlpool of phenomena experienced gets reduced to the plane of logic, commodity, intellectual ownership, and institutional stature.

In active forms of reading, we are allowed to undergo the throes of unknowingness, doubt, excitement, repulsion, attraction, frustration, discovery, revelation, and all comparable states of a consciousness that awaken to the virtual images, narratives, and language that constitute the forms of creative texts. In direct contrast to the more appropriative strategies of reading in disciplines that emphasize the mastering of theme and concept, literary studies begins with the seemingly unproblematic but, as we know, highly unpredictable, contingent, and open-ended act of encountering and negotiating the complicated material and referential elements of texts. While nothing in the arsenal of reading literary signs can prevent appropriative readings based on predetermined assumptions and frameworks, the performance of what I call creative critical reading practices calls for a willingness, not only to be open to images, narratives, language forms, and the experience of alterity, but also to reflect on the overlapping contingencies that govern the assumptions, both personal and social, that are brought into play. The activity of reading then holds the potential of releasing creative (and somatic) energies as well as opening a site for critical (self-)reflection, and therefore a site wherein ethical questions can be posed and explored. As a pedagogical methodology, as well as a primer for writing critical interpretations, creative critical reading practices have the potential to encounter the imagination, both in oneself and in texts, as a projective force that operates in often wily, non-rational, somatic ways in our reading of texts.

In his discussion of ethics, Michel Foucault talks about the self as "not a substance. It is a form, and this form is not primarily or always identical to itself" (*Ethics* 290). This loss of the self's armouring, which bpNichol recognized as part of the creative process, opens up the formal dimensions of its precarious embeddedness in somatic and social transferences, with far-reaching implications for our relations with others and with the contingencies that compose our imagination of otherness. Daniel Coleman's *In Bed with the Word* draws attention to the "outward-reaching energy" that is inherent in the simple desire to read. "What is important about it is that … it flies in the face of solipsism, the myth of autonomy and self-completeness. The desire to read emphasizes a basic generosity toward the Other that is the condition of all language" (14). Without turning a blind eye towards the potential for reading to be used as a means of indoctrination and social engineering, along with Coleman, we need to recognize (even celebrate) reading as a form in which consciousness can enact a more malleable and inclusive range of questions and reflections—about references, for instance, and intent, meaning, framing, positioning, voice, and other literary and extra-literary elements. In such a mode of attention, the reading subject becomes more attuned to fields of differential and asymmetrical relations that constitute the complex of representations that produce the limits of language, thought, and knowledge. How, for instance, might this mode of attention connect with our desire to do justice to CanLit?

In the not too distant past, at a time when so-called minority texts were finding their way onto course lists, their mere inclusion was read as an ethical and therefore just act. After all, by including minority texts, we were supposedly making space for what had been excluded, and we were thereby enabling minority voices to have a place in the institution, even though, as I recall, we tended to shy away from asking how and why they came to be marked or minoritized in the first place. Now that we have, again supposedly, gone beyond this dimension of identity politics, we can see that the institutional incorporation of minority texts as ethical, even when such incorporation made certain minority writers and communities more accessible to readers, remains problematic. I agree with Vikki Bell in *Culture and Performance* that ethical practices are not dependent solely on taking a position for the inclusion of formerly excluded work, or against perceived injustices, or even promoting a cause that might lead to the amelioration of hardships. These can be noble acts that should be encouraged, but whether they constitute ethical acts depends on our modes of questioning the extent of our critical understanding of the contingencies out of which such acts have taken formation. Bell sees ethics "figured neither as a source of politics nor as a political weapon, but as a check on freedom, an inspiration that prompts a continual questioning of one's own positionality, including ... the conditions of possibility of one's ethical sensibilities" (51). Or to cite from Foucault's *Ethics:* "Freedom is the ontological condition of ethics. But ethics is the considered form that freedom takes when it is informed by reflection" (284). Smaro Kamboureli takes this line of thinking further in her provocative critical essay on Yann Martel's *Self,* "The Limits of the Ethical Turn," where she distinguishes between the recent turn to ethics in literary and cultural theory and the necessity, in an "ethical turn," to "remain mindful of the transactions it involves lest they incur violence in lieu of the violence we try to remedy" (945). Much of the difficulty in assessing what constitutes an ethical act has do with recognizing the conditions and contingencies that produce differential relations from which we benefit or not according to our differing access to dominant representational schemata. In the forms of literature—in their very textuality—we encounter the imagination's potential either to open up or to foreclose a reflexive approach to the somatic and social production of cultural values—values that I believe call for constant critique.

The critical reflexivity associated with the ethics of reading practices, as effective as it can be as a methodology for literary studies, is also vulnerable to the discursive forms that translate their fluidity into the regulatory systems of academic norms—norms in which, as I have already noted, the rules of rationality (thesis, argument, evidence, coherence) become the only measure of legitimacy and authority. There are, however, strong grounds for maintaining the experience of reflexivity, even or especially when that experience finds itself drawn into forces of non-rational incommensurability, incoherence, and the absence of proper syntax and grammar. In his account of reading, drawing on the work of Ronald Rolheiser, Coleman goes so far as to compare the reading act to the form of prayer, not prayer as a "series of requests," but prayer as "a specific form of pondering, a patient bearing of tension" (109). He develops this point by referring to theologian Rolheiser's notion of prayer as a form in which "one is willing to live in unresolved tension" (110). Creative critical reading, then, might be considered a kind of pondering that slows down the interpretive process to the point where readers can imagine the differential relations that are mobile in their consciousness. Such a temporality, in stark contrast to the speeding up of time in the technoscape of commodity culture, allows for a process of reflection in which questions of justice and equity rise to the surface. In this respect, a recent study conducted by specialists of somatic affects is telling. In experiments measuring subjects' responses to the pain and suffering of others, the researchers concluded that the speed of information flow in the latest technological outlets, such as cellphones and Internet, may actually impede the development of affects such as empathy and compassion. "The rapidity and parallel processing of attention-requiring information, which hallmark the digital age, might reduce the frequency of full experience of such emotions, with potentially negative consequences" (Immordino-Yang et al. 8024).

Against the rapid flow of information in current neoliberal commodity culture, creative critical reading practices, which are the hallmark of literary studies, may be one of the most profound aspects of our work. If, through some technological invention, we could make visible the vast network of energies set in motion when one reader, whose subjectivity has been shaped by an immeasurable complex of somatic and discursive variables, undergoes the language of a text and interacts with other readers who bring to the texts their own complex of variables, we might begin to respect the power of the creative critical imagination, even in instances of misidentification of references, semantic slippages, and all the so-called failures to decode the text through conventional or discipline-specific rules and assumptions. Few disciplines practise reading processes in which the boundaries between self and other become so porous that we necessarily begin to engage in immediate relations with one another. Here pedagogical interventions become a crucial means of preventing collective engagements with texts from falling into solecisms, at which point the "unresolved tension" between self and other would default to dominant power formations. When the tension is maintained, reading practices enter into negotiation with the limits of representations as formations that constitute what comes to be both visible and legible and therefore what becomes invisible and illegible according to normative measures of truth-value.

A Take on Asian Canadian

Genealogically, the abstraction Asian Canadian, which strangely enough never referenced anyone in particular, other than those who were abstractly identified or who self-identified under the racialized term Asian, embodies the long history of racialization by the Canadian state. Many who would happily identify themselves as Chinese Canadian or Japanese Canadian or South Asian Canadian would resist referring to themselves as Asian Canadian. As a formation, Asian Canadian came to appearance in the wake of CanLit, during the Cold War era that also shaped Northrop Frye's model of the "garrison mentality." Through the production of cultural nationalism, the state sought to shape a more standardized citizenry around coherent beliefs and symbols, but the nation imagined in its policies suffered instability under pressure from external (transnational) and internal (intranational) forces. At the risk of over-simplification, we can trace the shifting parameters of cultural politics through a legacy of concerns that conditioned the arrival and continuing transformation of Asian Canadian:

- from the cultural homogeneity proposed by the Massey Commission and enacted through agencies such as the Canada Council and the National Film Board and its notion of the nation as coherent;
- to the emergence and problematics of multiculturalism with its heated debates over the inclusionary and exclusionary boundaries of cultural representations, racialization, and social justice;
- to the ascendancy of the discourse of globalization, which heralded the politics of neoliberalism and the commodification of culture;
- to a highly indeterminate and volatile globalization in which transnational flows are uncertain and unpredictable, new nationalisms are invented, and old-style or fundamentalist identity politics can have dire consequences.

One advantage of studying formations like Asian Canadian as simultaneously minoritized and emergent is that the contradictory effects of differential relations among subjects can be more visible than in dominant and therefore normalized formations. Similar to CanLit, with which it has been aligned, Asian Canadian functions in a kind of virtual mode with always-provisional references to socially constituted groups, and as such, it has no necessary existence. Despite what some supporters and skeptics might argue, it has no essential reason to be. It could sever its connection to Canadian to become Asian, which it might do in time, and its existence would become no more

substantial. And, again in time, it might come to signify Canadian alone without the Asian qualifier, and even then, it would remain the floating signifier it
has always been. Does this tentative status as a mirage-like form mean that it
loses its cultural and aesthetic value as a body of literature and a subject worthy of specialization in literary studies? To the contrary, its very malleability
and vulnerability may make it the ideal type for literary studies at a time—
such as the present—when we are called to a radical rethinking of critical
methodologies that can result in progressive social transformation. Asian and
Asian Canadian as terms are both continually produced and created, shaped as
effects within vast and overlapping social and cultural histories, and created as
affects in multiple ways by subjects who choose to situate themselves in their
field of references.

For me, a limit frame for this discussion is a recently published posthumous
text by Roy K. Kiyooka, one that I was fortunate to edit. Kiyooka's *The Artist
and the Moose: A Fable of Forget* is striking for the ways in which it enters
into negotiation with a nation-based cultural centrism that has honed the
unidentified narrator's subjectivity even while placing him on its almost invisible margins. In good Canadian fashion, perhaps to accommodate "regional
disparities" (17), he is appointed by Prime Minister Jason Decentbaker to head
a Royal Commission whose task it is to develop a twenty-first-century multicultural aesthetic. To achieve his mission, the narrator undertakes research
on the most iconic Canadian artist of his time, the landscape artist Tom
Thomson—in Kiyooka's text, Thomas Aplomb. Aplomb's mysterious death in
Algonquin Park in July 1917 had provided the fodder for cultural nationalists to erect a now-creaking national identity. Is it possible that the clues to a
twenty-first-century aesthetic lie in solving the mystery of the artist's death?
If Aplomb was murdered—and some evidence points that way—who killed a
nascent Canadian icon?

Off the narrator goes to the National Archives, acting very much like a
diligent academic in pursuit of a hot research project, and there he immerses
himself in the archival traces of Aplomb's untimely death while at the same
time experiencing the political culture of his nation's capital. The fabulous tale
that unfolds, with an exiled-from-his-natural-home Ol' Moose as the intrepid
narrator's mentor, performs a creative critical reading of the construction of
Canadian cultural nationalism, a formation constituted through the displacement of its colonial violence. The displacement, and subsequent invention of
a national identity, enabled the erasure of the Aboriginal communities whose
lands had been appropriated. Soon after his death, indeed *because of* his death,
the aesthetic spaces of Aplomb's art in Algonquin Park—a provincially managed site—became the material through which cultural nationalists invented a
so-called Native tradition that validated the sovereignty of the Canadian state.

In perhaps the most prescient moment in the text, Kiyooka's narrator zeroes in on the work of one Judge William Little. In the 1950s, when Thomson's reputation as national icon was still developing, Judge Little decided to clear up at least one of the mysteries surrounding the case. Contrary to the official story that the artist's body was moved to his childhood home, did it remain where it was first interred in Algonquin Park?

While drawing on William Little's narrative in his book *The Tom Thomson Mystery*, the narrator twists his own narrative to reveal the darker underbelly of colonial history. From the mounds of colonial documents in the archives, he has come to recognize the violence of representation in the nation's official history, noting that the documents "had been pitilessly mined from the slag heaps of the Laurentian Shield since the advent of Christianity in the New World. Otherwise, his own ruminations kept turning into palimpsests with each new entreaty, whereas the Official Documents kept reiterating (in bold italics) the litany of a hostile Tundra, with every footnote diminishing both 'Moose' and 'Native'" (24). There are shades of the representation of nature as an amoral threatening force in Northrop Frye, who makes a cameo appearance in Kiyooka's text as Friar Northtrope when the narrator informs his readers: "Ol' Moose balefully agreed with his adversary … that the Angles and the Saxons had an unmitigated Garrison Mentality, one that harkened back to the Black Plague and other scourges of the Middle Ages" (85). In any case, back with Judge Little, the narrator recounts that Little and a small band formed an expedition to dig up the gravesite. They came upon a skeleton that they quickly decided had to be the body of the iconic artist. After professional forensic testing, however, they were dismayed to learn that the skeleton was too short and, surprise surprise, also Aboriginal. For the narrator, fact in a sense has transmogrified into a fabulous turn in his narrative, one that raises a contradiction that has exposed the limits of representation. Has the white settler/artist, Thomas Aplomb, in death, replaced the Native, as the advocates of cultural nationalism would have it? Or has Aplomb *become* Native, so that his whiteness has been subsumed on entering the condition of death in its dislocated condition? Or does the act of digging up the past expose the visibility of a Native presence that has been suppressed? The interpretive possibilities multiply along with the shifting positions of readers.

In *The Artist and the Moose*, Kiyooka performs a creative critical reading of a national cultural formation that does not account for the limits of its representation. What is interesting for my discussion is that Kiyooka began his Tom Thomson writing project in the mid- to late 1960s, a period of heightened nationalism and also the period in which Northrop Frye wrote the final words to the *Literary History of Canada* (1965), a nationalist literary project edited by Carl F. Klinck. The synchronicity of events, I would suggest, is no accident.

But the kind of creative critical intent that is evident in Kiyooka's narrative would have been contrary to the object of desire for cultural nationalists of the time. For literary studies, the model of the pastoral myth was much more conducive to institutionalization and allowed for the development of a referential mode of criticism that could stabilize itself around notions of identity and place, the hallmarks of nation-based CanLit studies. Strangely—or not, depending on our critical lens—the aesthetic and cultural spaces of Kiyooka's *Transcanada Letters*, a companion text to *The Artist and the Moose*, are extensions of those contemporary Canadian conditions identified by Frye, which Frye bypasses in his turn to the pastoral, revealing perhaps his own desire for a more homogenous and conservative literature in Canada. In *Transcanada Letters*, Kiyooka recognizes the limits of a nationalist culture that identifies and excludes minorities as well as the generative possibilities of transnational cultural work. Tellingly, the first text in *Transcanada Letters* is not a letter but a report to the Canada Council written from the perspective of Japan, and it ends with an affirmation of aesthetic forms produced in the conditions of the contemporary, a principle that Frye may very well have approved:

> *possibilities*
> HERE
> > (or, Anywhere
> > no larger than Everyman's Vision —
> > > has it ever been more
> > > than this ?
> > ALL THINGS SWIRL
> > making for whats possible
> > > HERE / NOW (3)

While Frye reflects on the cultural history of Canadian settler culture and methodically constructs a model of literary formations in which the European humanist binary so necessary to colonization—civilization over nature—remains intact, Kiyooka goes trans-Canada, traversing the geographical and cultural extent of the nation as he assembles a multiplicity of voices and subjects who form metonymically the matrix of the body politic in which writers and artists are embedded; significantly, his nation already includes signs of the transnational and global forces that Frye says pose a threat to the autonomy of Canadian literature. In the interplay of methodology and belief, Kiyooka's artist negotiates fragments and contingencies, contradiction and revelation, as he moves in and out of the multiple variables that inform the boundaries of his subjectivity to construct a kind of living encyclopedia of Gertrude Stein's "continuous present," which he refers to in the epigraph of *Transcanada Letters*. As weird as it may sound initially, I think it is instructive to imagine the subsequent history of Canadian literary studies had this work achieved the canonic status of Frye, so that "our" beginnings had been more preoccupied with forms of difference in our actually existing conditions rather than with the demarcation of identity boundaries.

The narrator's skepticism in Kiyooka's narrative extends to his research in the National Archives, where he discovers that the representations of the present and the past are highly determined by the discourses of dominant institutions. The eventual failure of his own quest to unravel the mystery of Thomas Aplomb's death takes on symbolic importance to suggest a productive crisis of knowledge production. Knowledge has limits, and these limits become visible in the experience of finitude. Any pinning down of meaning leads to the appropriation of the creative for predetermined ends. Representations, as such, are precarious forms that can never be taken at face value.

Unfortunately, literary studies do not have access to a crystal ball to see what might have been or what might yet come to appearance. It remains, nevertheless, for these eyes a speculative possibility to imagine *Transcanada Letters* to be the body found when an intrepid group of scholars went in search of Frye's "Conclusion to a *Literary History of Canada*." Is this kind of transformation, or exchange of critical spirits, possible in our world of belief in the rational method? If Kamboureli is right, and I believe she is, "the constancy of the ethical is infinitely postponed" ("The Limits" 947); because ethics is conditioned by acts in the here and now, it is always possible to invent new possibilities that can alter our understanding of the past. Asian Canadian texts such as *Transcanada Letters* and *The Artist and the Moose*, as well as Fred Wah's *Diamond Grill*, Hiromi Goto's *The Kappa Child*, Larissa Lai's *Salt Fish Girl*, Ashok Mathur's *The Short, Happy Life of Arthur Kumar*, and, most recently, Rita Wong's *Forage* and her collaborative text with Lai, *Sybil Unrest*, and there are many others, inhabit always-provisional frameworks that take on shifting contours according to the reading practices brought to them. The more effective they are as creative critical forms that make us more conscious of differential relations of power and representation, the more they can make us aware of our responsibilities in generating the desire, not for commodities, but for justice.

A Tentative Conclusion

If, in a post-Frye context, we understand the invention of CanLit to be a strategic move on the part of cultural nationalists in a belated nation, then CanLit has no necessary existence and, similar to other identity formations, such as Asian Canadian, needs to be approached as a provisional and contingent formation and therefore a limit frame that is always open to collective reinvention. As Jacques Derrida reminds us in *Specters of Marx*, "an inheritance is never gathered together, it is never one with itself. Its presumed unity, if there is one, can consist only in the *injunction* to *reaffirm by choosing*" (16). The future of this "inheritance" is governed by the agency of its advocates and the forms they produce—and whether actions generate ethical acts or not needs to be judged according to the methodologies and beliefs those advocates adopt and practise. It can no longer be measured simply on the authenticity (or not) of any given identity formation, since any identity formation as such is constituted on exclusionary/inclusionary boundaries. When CanLit is approached as a provisional and contingent formation, the representational frames of its ties to the geographical, legal, cultural, and symbolic elements of Canada manifest a multiplicity of unresolved desires, discourses, and publics. What then comes to be called "the local" is a site of immediacy for differing and deferring subjects whose mobility is always inflected by networks of determinants and indeterminacies, both close to the skin and globally distant in the overlapping conjunctions of moment-to-moment existence. Research at these limits needs to draw on the resources of the imagination to invent writing forms consonant with those limits. Belief in such a methodological potential is crucial to its enactment in creative critical practices wherein the desire for justice is never far away.

TRANS-SYSTEMIC CONSTITUTIONALISM IN INDIGENOUS LAW AND KNOWLEDGE

Sa'ke'j Henderson

> Treaties serve to reconcile pre-existing Aboriginal sovereignty with assumed Crown sovereignty, and to define Aboriginal rights guaranteed by s. 35 of the Constitution Act, 1982.
> —Chief Justice McLachlin, *Haida Nation* (2004)

My essay will explore the trans-systemic synthesis of the Supreme Court of Canada's (hereafter Court) constitutional framework of Canada that is in the process of being advanced as a transformative method to protect Aboriginal peoples and generate constitutional reconciliations. The subject is crucial, and its importance is daunting not only for the development of a legal system that can bring justice to Aboriginal rights and treaty rights but also for any scholarly project that seeks to understand Indigenous knowledge and cultures in the context of Canada. In its cautious, case-by-case approach, the Court has generated innovative methods and principles to displace colonialism and racism in the law according to its constitutional mandate. These principles inform institutional change, peoplehood, and citizenship in Canada, and embody both conceptual and practical arrangements. These principles can be a model for other Eurocentric disciplines and scholars. Before I provide some necessary context for my argument here, I should disclose that, as one of the Aboriginal drafters and negotiators of Aboriginal and treaty rights, and as someone who has been involved in the various litigation designs in relation to Aboriginal rights, I have more than a non-aligned interest in how the courts should interpret this constitutional framework.

Context

After a long and difficult struggle to implement treaty rights and recognize Aboriginal rights in both the political forum and the courts, the United Kingdom's Parliament repatriated Aboriginal and treaty rights. Through the Canada Act 1982, the imperial Crown in Parliament transferred these rights from imperial law to the constitutional law of Canada, vesting them in the Aboriginal peoples of Canada. Section 35 of the Constitution Act 1982, which is part of the Canada Act 1982, elegantly summarizes the catalytic transformation of an old truth: "The existing Aboriginal and treaty rights of the Aboriginal peoples of Canada are hereby recognized and affirmed." Section 25 of the Canadian Charter of Rights and Freedoms affirms that existing Aboriginal and treaty rights, as well as other rights and freedoms that pertain to them, cannot be as construed as being abrogated or derogated by the Charter's rights and freedoms. These sections reflect the imperative to constitutionally accommodate, recognize, and implement Aboriginal and treaty rights. They also require reconciliation with other constitutional powers.

These constitutional clauses were not a new statement of rights; they merely affirmed pre-existing Aboriginal sovereignty through the asserted British sovereign rights and the more than three hundred imperial treaties that established the original constitutional order, and now the postcolonial constitutional order, of Canada. The affirmation of these rights reflects the constitutional commitment to shape a new order guaranteeing Aboriginal peoples' effective enjoyment of constitutional rights, both collectively and individually. Thus the patriated Constitution that directs Canadian life locates the shared or overlapping sovereignty of Canada in the First Nations and the imperial Crown.

The leaders of the constitutional movement were the First Nations Elders and the first generation of First Nations peoples educated in the Eurocentric systems in Canada (Cardinal; Barsh and Henderson; Mercredi and Turpel). This trans-generational alliance used Aboriginal world views and legal traditions, as well as Eurocentric strategies and persuasion, to accomplish the art of the impossible by affirming Aboriginal and treaty rights over the objections of the provinces.

The various peoples of Canada did not merely craft the constitutional vision as a collaborative enterprise; this enterprise generated new and needed institutional forms of the patriated society and life. The Court in *Sparrow* held that as part of the supreme law of Canada, which is embodied in fragmented imperial treaties and acts, s. 35 specifically directs and mandates recognition and affirmation of existing Aboriginal and treaty rights at every level of Canadian society. This has created new contexts for the honourable interpretation of governmental responsibility and treaty rights in Canada.

Canadian politicians and Canadians in general were (are) taken aback by these constitutional reforms and the transformations they made necessary. Superimposing a vision of constitutionalism on people's consciousness is a difficult and complicated task, especially if some of them have never shared that vision. The anxious public and resisting politicians were lost in the implausible reform. They faced myriad challenges in the new, rights-based regime that had displaced a colonial system based on a theory of race and its supposed characteristics. Perhaps the greatest challenge governments and the public faced in the constitutional regime was transforming their knowledge and consciousness to conform to the emerging postcolonial order. This bewilderment was, and continues to be, reflected in Canadian literature, institutions, and citizenship.

Faced with the federal and provincial governments' resistance to implementing Aboriginal peoples' rights, as well as government attempts to litigate against the exercise of those rights, the Canadian courts became an asymmetrical centre of the transformation in consciousness, knowledge, politics, and law. When the Court began to explore ways of ensuring the practical conditions for the effective enjoyment of constitutional rights, it discovered that these rights had changed the existing institutional structure of Canada. Beginning in *Delgamuukw*, the Court understood the need to reinvent Canadian institutions and procedures through constitutional reconciliation as it confronted constitutional reforms that stressed liberation from oppression, and justice rather than injustice. It found that it was no longer able to be the rational apologist of colonial federalism and legislation confined to its "proper function," for it had no legal authority to invalidate statutes on the ground that they are contrary to fundamental moral or legal principles. Thus it also found that the judiciary was inadequate to the task of directing the constitutional transformation. Most lower courts and courts of appeal failed in their initial attempts, leaving the Court to articulate the correct principles and insights. At first, it chose conceptions and strategies that left present institutional arrangements intact, while controlling their consequences through judicial review of legislation. Its later conceptions and strategies, however, flipped the concept of sovereignty; in order to realize the sources of these constitutional rights, and to implement them more effectively, the Court introduced new structural arrangements with Aboriginal peoples that asserted institutional changes through constitutional convergence and reconciliation. It is this process that my essay tracks, along with its implications.

In over forty cases since 1982, in its attempt to create fair processes for just and trans-systemic convergences and reconciliations, the Court has generated a truly Canadian legal system based on symbiotic constitutionalism and legal and epistemic plurality. That is, it has had to develop innovative principles of

adjudication that seek a convergence of Aboriginal and Eurocentric legal traditions. This trans-systemic approach reflects the unique nature of Canadian
constitutional jurisprudence. Nevertheless, both politicians and the public
have been flabbergasted (Rotman) by the Court's unfamiliar trans-systemic
constitutional synthesis, for they still operate on an unreflective colonial paradigm and remain an intolerant and perplexed society.

In recognizing the phrase "recognized and affirmed" in s. 35(1) of the
Constitution Act 1982, the Court in *Van der Peet* and *Marshall* has not only
established constitutional supremacy over parliamentary supremacy, thus
affirming the ultimate principle of Aboriginal sovereignty, but also has opened
the way for a trans-systemic constitutional approach that acknowledges, and
brings within the protection of Canadian constitutional law, the fact that First
Nations lived on the land in distinctive societies with their own sovereignty,
legal orders, practices, traditions, and cultures. This recognition has constitutionalized their knowledge and legal traditions. This recognition in turn has
generated a *sui generis* approach to Aboriginal and treaty rights designed to
displace positivism and the common and civil law. This recognition has also
established honourable government over the colonial-era concept of good government. The Court has articulated, then, that constitutionalizing Aboriginal
and treaty rights displaces and transforms the colonial and racial understanding of Aboriginal peoples' rights in relation to other constitutional powers
and rights. Section 35 affords constitutional protection to existing Aboriginal
peoples' rights against provincial and federal legislative power as a "restraint
on the exercise of sovereign power" and requires that a strict justification
test be met (*Sparrow*, ibid.). Thus, while it does not constitutionalize existing
federal or provincial regulatory laws, it has forced federal and provincial law
to be consistent with Aboriginal peoples' rights (ibid.).

Moreover, in aiming to help Aboriginal peoples improve their situation and
achieve self-sufficiency, the Court in *Kapp* held that Charter rights of individuals cannot override Aboriginal and treaty rights, ameliorative or remedial
law, or policy and programs of the Crown designed to proactively combat discrimination. It has thus determined that legislation that distinguishes between
Aboriginal and non-Aboriginal people in order to protect interests associated
with Aboriginal sovereignty, territory, culture, way of life, or the treaty process
and its implementation must be shielded from Charter scrutiny in order to
promote substantive equality.

In their efforts to comprehend Aboriginal knowledge and legal traditions, the Canadian courts have been burdened by the lack of a method for
comprehending the constitutional rights of Aboriginal peoples. The ways in
which common and civil law jurists have approached issues of method and
evidence in these cases have been largely determined by the severely limited

fund of basic schemes of explanation available in Eurocentrism, that is, by an entrenched prejudice in knowledge (Blaut; Lambropoulos; Battiste and Henderson). In fact, one might say that all of these methods are variations on two types: logical analysis and causal explanation. The logical and the causal methods serve as the starting points for two ways of dealing with the problem of rational method, explanation, and justification. Each method attempts to provide an interpretation of what it means to account for something both in the sense of telling what it is like (description) and in the strict sense of establishing why it had to follow from something else (explanation).

The problem of establishing a transformative method for approaching Aboriginal and treaty rights cases encompasses four main issues, all of them unresolved: the possibility of an Indigenous alternative to Eurocentric logic and causation, capable of overcoming the inadequacies of both logic (rationalism) and causality (historicism) in procedural and evidence codes; the link between *sui generis* analysis and natural rights and positivism analysis; the connection between the meaning of an act for Aboriginal peoples and its meaning for Eurocentric consciousness; and the relationship of holistic world views to Eurocentric understanding.

Constitutional Supremacy Displaces Parliamentary Supremacy

Section 52(1) of the Constitution Act 1982 expresses the innovative concept of constitutional supremacy: "The Constitution of Canada is the supreme law of Canada, and any law that is inconsistent with the provisions of the Constitution is, to the extent of the inconsistency, of no force or effect." The same section creates a different, if not distinct, theory of the written Constitution of Canada as compared to the unwritten Constitution of the United Kingdom, which has no supremacy clause. Furthermore, in the *Quebec Secession Reference*, a unanimous Court established an analytical framework and the principles necessary for constitutional supremacy, implicitly including unwritten imperial common law principles, norms, and rules that created the framework for Aboriginal rights and imperial treaties with First Nations (par. 72).

The convergence doctrine that characterizes these developments entails a complicated nexus of constitutional supremacy. Under the principle of constitutional supremacy and the rule of law, the Court has established not only that individual elements of the Constitution are linked to one another, but also that they must be interpreted by reference to the structure of the Constitution as a whole (par. 49). Thus, the defining principles function in constitutional "symbiosis." Although this term is not a familiar legal expression, "symbiosis" articulates the fundamental premise that no single principle or text trumps or excludes the operation of any other (*Paul* par. 24), which is the basic rule of constitutional supremacy. This convergent or symbiotic doctrine of the constitutional supremacy principle ushers in an innovative and enduring interpretative process that, as the Court suggests, breathes new life into the Constitution of Canada.

Manitoba Language Rights and *Sparrow* affirm that the constitutional law prevails over the laws of Canada and each of the provinces. In the *Manitoba Language Rights* decision, the Court stated that the words in s. 52 "of no force or effect" mean that a law that is inconsistent with the Constitution has "no force or effect" because it is invalid:

> The Constitution of a country is a statement of the will of the people to be governed in accordance with certain principles held as fundamental and certain prescriptions restrictive of the powers of the legislature and government. It is, as s. 52 of the *Constitution Act, 1982* declares, the "supreme law" of the nation, unalterable by the normal legislative process, and unsuffering of laws inconsistent with it. The duty of the judiciary is to interpret and apply the laws of Canada and each of the provinces, and it is thus our duty to ensure that the constitutional law prevails. (745)

Thus the courts cannot allow either federal or provincial legislation to exceed the limits of the established constitutional mandate; the consequence of such non-compliance continues to be invalidity of the legislation. In effect, this introduces a constitutional veto of legislation, regulation, and policy.

In *Sparrow*, the Court applied the constitutional supremacy principle to protect Aboriginal and treaty rights under s. 35(1). It has acknowledged that the constitutional rights of First Nations are part of the supreme law of the nation, unalterable by the normal legislative process and unsuffering of laws inconsistent with it (1107). Thus, the Court has held that the judiciary has a vital duty "to ensure that the constitutional law [must] prevail[]" (1107), if the constitutional rights of the Aboriginal peoples of Canada are to be protected. In other words, legislation and regulations must be consistent with Aboriginal peoples' rights. Furthermore, these rights cannot be extinguished by governmental power (*Delgamuukw* par. 173). The Court in *Marshall* rejected the argument that Aboriginal and treaty rights are subject *ab initio* to governmental power; it established that express governmental standards in legislation or regulations respecting Aboriginal and treaty rights are required (par. 54). Thus, governmental legislation and regulations must give explicit direction to a minister that is consistent with Aboriginal peoples' rights. These governmental regulations must explain how public servants should exercise their discretionary authority in a manner that respects these constitutionalized rights (par. 64).

The centrepiece of constitutional convergence and reconciliation of constitutional supremacy is the Court's articulation of a new version of Canadian "sovereignty": "[t]he Constitution is the expression of the sovereignty of the people of Canada" (*Quebec Secession Reference* par. 85). If different peoples can generate different institutional forms of life and society, then constitutionalism, too, can function in ways that reflect and are responsive to the diversity of a people. The will of the peoples creates constitutionalism, which informs and broadens the conversation about the institutional present and the institutional futures of society:

> Constitutionalism facilitates—indeed, makes possible—a democratic political system by creating an orderly framework within which people may make political decisions. Viewed correctly, constitutionalism and the rule of law are not in conflict with democracy; rather, they are essential to it. (par. 78)

The Court has also stated that "the law … creates the framework within which the 'sovereign will' is to be ascertained and implemented" (par. 67). This is a simple conclusion of a postcolonial sovereignty and constitutional legitimacy, a principle that is consistent with the language and insights of sovereignty as understood by Aboriginal peoples. Constitutionalism seeks not only to humanize Canadian institutions but also to change them based on notions of peoplehood, not citizenship. Thus, the colonial legal regime's understanding of constitutional law and its practice of legal synthesis has to change from the bottom up and from the inside out. The public, politicians, and scholars have to comprehend that they can no longer assume that constitutional law, institutions, and legal theories are inherited, ready-made European systems.

This conceptualization of the relationship of political sovereignty to constitutional supremacy displaces the imperial Crown and United Kingdom's concept of an unwritten constitutional law that posits parliamentary sovereignty over the peoples of Canada. It replaces the colonial framework and sociocultural narratives developed during the era of parliamentary supremacy (Austin; Dicey). The distinctive principle of parliamentary sovereignty or supremacy was entirely the construction of Oxford men like Coke and Blackstone and was widely popularized in the imperial age by Albert Venn Dicey. According to Dicey:

> The principle of parliamentary sovereignty means neither more nor less than this, namely, that Parliament [defined as the Queen, the House of Lords, and the House of Commons, acting together] … has, under the English Constitution, the right to make or unmake any law whatever; and, further, that no person or body is recognised by the law as having a right to override or set aside the legislation of Parliament. (38)

A.W.B. Simpson notes that Dicey cites neither a clear judicial decision of bind-
ing authority for his absolutist view of parliamentary power, nor any reference
to it in any statute or constitutional instrument. J. Goldsworthy argues that
Dicey's analysis of the sovereignty of Parliament was a restatement or a declaration of a central theme in English legal history.

    Although this principle is not laid down in any parliamentary legislation,
it was adopted by the North American colonialists in their local government
(Wade, "The Basis" 188). They based their governments on British parliamentary traditions as affirmed in imperial acts, rather than the antecedent
imperial treaty delegations from Aboriginal nations. Thus they founded their
assumptions and beliefs on an unwritten British constitutional tradition (Winterton), which they viewed as close to perfect (Cruikshank 321–22). In their
path from imperial rule to self-rule, the colonialists never critically inquired
about the validity of these principles. Thus the validity and authority of their
use of power and law could ultimately and comfortably be traced back to the
Sovereign's prerogative, to the decisions of the Sovereign's judges, and to the
Sovereign in Parliament at "home."

    The colonialists' beguiling and enduring identification of the fundamen-
tal source of law with parliamentary sovereignty concealed the constitutional
lineage of Aboriginal sovereignty and of the imperial treaties that delegated
authority to the imperial Crown. In the colonial narrative of Canada, as created
by legislation and judicial decisions, Aboriginal sovereignty and treaty orders
were masked by parliamentary supremacy and the delegation of that supremacy to responsible and good government for the British and French colonialists (Mercredi and Turpel 168–85). According to these colonial assumptions,
the sovereignty of Parliament was "received" or carried over into the Canadian constitutional order by the imperial Parliament through the Constitution
(British North America) Act, 1867. However, this construction was marred
by legal anomalies that were the product of colonialist ideologies—for example, the new Canadian Parliament and its distinct provincial federation was
still legally subordinate to the imperial Parliament, and Canadian courts were
subject to review, on appeal, by an imperial tribunal, the Judicial Committee
of the Privy Council, sitting in London. In the late nineteenth century, the
Judicial Committee of the Privy Council in *Burah* held that when the imperial
Parliament granted power to colonial legislatures to make laws for the "peace,
welfare, and good government" of their colonies, this granted them power of
the same nature, as plenary and absolute, as its own power.

    None of these colonial assumptions and judicial interpretations had been
challenged in Canadian ideology, legislation, and precedents prior to the Canada Act 1982. The colonialists—be they academics or legal professionals—
never suggested that their assertion of Crown sovereignty was an "ugly fiction"

(Ryder), a "huge, ugly, Victorian monument that has dominated the legal and constitutional landscape and exerted a hypnotic effect on the legal perception" (Walker 161; Conaglen 666). No British-trained lawyers were ever told that they had been "brain-washed ... in [their] professional infancy by the dogma of legislative sovereignty" (Wade, *Constitutional* 68). Yet this is part of the truth of colonized legal consciousness. As Justice Michael Kirby of the High Court of Australia (1998) said, colonial legal consciousness is characterized by the times of "fairytales"; it belongs to the time of Aladdin's cave of common law; it is a "Victorian monument[]" of legal positivism. The sovereignty of the Crown—that is, parliamentary supremacy, as the colonial legal *grundnorm* (Kelsen)—may still prevail in the courts (Borrows), but the Court is displacing many of its principles. Aboriginal and treaty rights, and the interpretative doctrine of constitutional convergence and reconciliation discussed above, have modified the inherited principle of parliamentary supremacy with constitutional supremacy.

The Court has recognized that Aboriginal and treaty rights in the Constitution require a new, complex, and comprehensive theory of constitutional supremacy. Interstitially and incrementally, it has developed innovative doctrines out of many constitutional principles, while paying due regard to constitutional stability and practicality. In trying to work out answers to these questions today, it has faced fictions and inconsistent claims regarding the basis of sovereignty and rights in postcolonial Canada. Based on these innovative case-by-case interpretations of constitutional law, the Court has found that Aboriginal knowledge and philosophy affirm and protect Aboriginal sovereignty in the constitutional framework of Canada. This evolving and living constitutional law is challenging governments and Aboriginal peoples to develop more effective approaches for addressing Aboriginal and treaty rights and to create trans-systemic convergence and reconciliation.

Recognizing the Constitutional *Grundnorm* of Aboriginal Sovereignty

The Court has recognized that Aboriginal and treaty rights presuppose Aboriginal sovereignty, which is the *grundnorm* that serves as the foundation not only for the constitutional rights of Aboriginal peoples but also for other constitutional powers and rights. Although the Court has not worked out the conclusion or implications of this insight in existing cases—a task that has been left up to future litigation and scholarship—it has established this *grundnorm* as the new foundation for constitutional law and legislation in Canada, and it has acknowledged that it must play a converging role in shared governance in the "eternal future."

In *Van der Peet*, the Court began to explain why the diverse Aboriginal confederacies, nations, tribes, peoples, societies, cultures, communities, and

families exist in imperial constitutional law, and why they have been recognized and affirmed as holding Aboriginal rights as specified in s. 35(1) of the
Constitution Act 1982:

> [B]ecause of one simple fact: when Europeans arrived in North America,
> Aboriginal peoples *were already here*, living in communities on the land, and
> participating in distinctive cultures, as they had done for centuries. It is this
> fact, and this fact above all others, which separates Aboriginal peoples from
> all other minority groups in Canadian society and which mandates their
> special legal, and now constitutional, status. (par. 30)

More than a historical description, this is the premise that establishes the
grundnorm as the ultimate constitutional principle of the patriated constitutional law of Canada. Thus it affirms not only that the pre-existing sovereignty
of the First Nations was manifest in imperial treaties and affirmed constitutionalizing Aboriginal peoples' rights, but also that this deeper and invisible,
impalpable yet powerful, constitutional *grundnorm* in North America has
always been an integral element of Aboriginal sovereignty.

While the *grundnorm* was the foundation of the imperial treaties and
prerogative acts, it was not disclosed as such in the ensuing imperial parliamentary acts that established delegated responsible government among the
non-Aboriginal settlers in British North America. When the arrival of Europeans and the assertion of European sovereignty over Aboriginal territories
generated questions about sovereignty, jurisdiction, and ownership of land
and resources, the British Crown's response was to enter into imperial treaties
with the Aboriginal sovereigns. This situation reflected the division of prerogative jurisdiction of the Crown and its treaties from Parliament's competen-
cies. As Chief Justice McLachlin noted in *Haida Nation* at par. 20: "Treaties
serve to reconcile pre-existing Aboriginal sovereignty with assumed Crown
sovereignty, and to define Aboriginal rights guaranteed by section 35 of the
Constitution Act, 1982." These sovereign treaties permitted the Crown certain
delegated responsibilities and rights in Aboriginal territory, including British
settlement, and provided for British law to control the conduct of the settlers.
These treaty delegations created the source for the king's delegation of self-rule
to the colonialists and led to the establishment of provinces and the federal
government. It was the patriation of the Canadian Constitution from residual
imperial authority, and its ensuing recognition and affirmation of Aboriginal rights and existing treaty rights, that brought about the re-emergence
of Aboriginal sovereignty. Aboriginal sovereignty provides a trans-systemic
constitutional norm (Little Bear) and rule of recognition (Hart) that together
protect Aboriginal legal traditions, heritage, and imperial treaties, and this

is the beginning of a chain of normative validity of *sui generis* analysis. This foundational norm revises Crown sovereignty of the colonial era. Thus the *grundnorm* of Aboriginal sovereignty mandates a reorientation of the constitutional framework of Canada. This *grundnorm* derives from pre-existing Aboriginal knowledge and legal traditions and is recognized and affirmed by the British sovereign in the imperial treaties. Aboriginal sovereignty, then, derives from Aboriginal knowledge and legal traditions about what makes them a certain kind of people (Canada, Royal Commission on Aboriginal Peoples vol. 1 616–97).

In Aboriginal thought, sovereignty is not about absolute power; rather, it is about the subtle art of generating and sustaining relationships (Henderson and Battiste). It is a distinct vision about the way humans live together and behave in a kinship and an ecosystem, a distinct tradition of philosophies and humanities. It is a distinct philosophy of justice and legal traditions based on spiritual and ecological understandings, as well as linguistic conventions that are interconnected with these. It operates as an implicit, inherent, epistemic, unwritten, and living concept.

In constitutional law and its relationship to federal and provincial legislation and policy, Aboriginal sovereignty separates Aboriginal peoples from all other peoples in Canada who migrated to Canada. It generates a distinct theory of equality of law in constitutional supremacy. These constitutional obligations contain many principles and manifestations—some implicit, others explicit—such as pre-existing systems of Aboriginal knowledge and law (*Delgamuukw* par. 126; *Van der Peet* pars. 38–40) and their distinctive sovereignties, nations, societies or legal orders, and Aboriginal title or land tenures (*Delgamuukw* par. 111; *Van der Peet* par. 74). These judicial interpretative principles rely upon and animate Aboriginal peoples' latent knowledge and traditions, which provide the content for Aboriginal sovereignty, title, and rights as well as the substantive, evidentiary, and procedural processes of Aboriginal and treaty rights (*Van der Peet* pars. 29, 31, 40). They clarify the underlying jurisprudential framework of Aboriginal peoples' rights. Thus the *grundnorm* of Aboriginal sovereignty can animate a resourceful constitutional approach that can provide the Canadian scholarly and legal profession with a foundation for developing a *sui generis* constitutional method, one that could perhaps even be based on Aboriginal languages, a method that can reconcile imported jurisprudences with Aboriginal jurisprudence.

Properly understood, Aboriginal sovereignty is the source of all law in Canada. It flips over the colonial concept that all power derives from the imperial Crown or imperial Parliament, and it creates a distinct way of looking at the patriated constitution of Canada and the division of powers. However, most courts, politicians, academics, and Canadians have a poor understanding, if any at all, of the principle of the *grundnorm*. Much dialogue and discussion are required, although at present avoided, to actualize this new *grundnorm*.

The *Sui Generis* and Positivist Approaches

In searching for a way to characterize the constitutional framework of Aboriginal peoples' rights, in *Sparrow* the Court has chosen to characterize these rights as *sui generis*. It has rejected using the existing categories of legal theory and judicial reasoning embedded in the common or civil law or legal positivism for these extraordinary constitutional rights. Thus the judiciary struggles to generate a trans-systemic method to displace the Eurocentric monopoly and baggage of colonial attitudes and sympathies embedded in familiar judicial methods, reasoning, and rules of evidence. The Court borrowed its concept of *sui generis* from the language of empire to discuss distinct legal traditions and rights. The expression was originally coined by European scholastic philosophy to indicate an idea, an entity, or a reality that cannot be included in a wider concept, and that is structurally outside legally defined categories—a species that heads its own genus. Derived from Latin—*sui* (of its own) connected with *generis*, genitive of *genus* (kind)—it means self-generating; of a kind of one's own; without equal; absolutely unique. In other words, a knowledge system distinct from Eurocentrism.

The legal concept of *sui generis*, then, has been used to signify an independent legal tradition that the Court cannot acknowledge as its own. In *Sparrow*, the Court defined the *sui generis* nature of Aboriginal rights by awkwardly focusing on specific activities, rather than methods, that were "an element of a practice, custom or tradition integral to the distinctive culture of the Aboriginal group claiming the right" (1101–2). While uncomfortable with and incapable of articulating the *sui generis* interpretative paradigm outside the existing legal traditions and knowledges of the Canadian legal system, it realized that imperial and Canadian jurisprudence was neither a legitimate nor an adequate framework for explaining or redressing Aboriginal or treaty rights. This realization has generated the need to protect and enhance the distinct Aboriginal knowledge system and distinctive cultures. Thus the Court's use of *sui generis* illustrates a distinct constitutional method for Aboriginal and treaty rights. It attempts to describe and explain an Aboriginal method of synthesis—one that is not derived from British, French, or other kinds of European jurisprudence and that is distinct from these.

In *Van der Peet*, the Court rejected the application of the European Enlightenment or colonial ideology as informing Aboriginal rights and articulated the distinct nature of Aboriginal knowledge

Aboriginal rights cannot, however, be defined on the basis of the philosophical precepts of the liberal enlightenment. Although equal in importance and significance to the rights enshrined in the *Charter*, Aboriginal rights must be viewed differently from *Charter* rights because they are rights held only by Aboriginal members of Canadian society. They arise from the fact that Aboriginal people are *Aboriginal*. (par. 19)

This constitutional exclusion makes most, if not all, Eurocentric Enlightenment philosophies of very limited utility in recognizing and describing Aboriginal legal traditions, sovereignty, and rights. Legal science's rationalism, a direct product of the European Enlightenment, aspires to become a system of propositions whose interdependencies are governed by precise logical notions of entailment, consistency, and contradiction. Often called reasoned elaboration, this common law tradition gives a central role to a context-bound analogical method of comparison and distinction; it clings to usage and precedent as judicial and legal reasoning and thus fails to grasp abstraction, generalization, and holistic relationships in rationalizing legal analysis. The purpose of the *grundnorm* in civil law and of the Crown in the common law has been precisely to generate such general premises.

Eurocentric logic and causality as methods of legal analysis fail to address Aboriginal and treaty rights because they are distinct from Aboriginal consciousness, languages, and traditions. Logic addresses the Eurocentric order of ideas; causality, the Eurocentric order of events. But neither logical nor causal analysis can read and interpret that which has never been written. The Court can apply Eurocentric logic or causality, but the results may well be biased by the imposition of Eurocentric methods on Aboriginal knowledge. Moreover, no justification exists for granting primacy to Eurocentric methods over Aboriginal methods in Aboriginal and treaty rights. Neither the continued reliance on logical entailment nor causal explanation has been reconciled with Aboriginal verb-centred languages and consciousness that represent a holistic approach to life. It is precisely this holistic consciousness that grants Aboriginal conduct its distinct legal, social, and human meaning. To disregard this Aboriginal meaning is to neglect an integral part of the experience for which an account is to be given, and thus also to ignore perspectives that are intrinsic to Aboriginal and treaty rights.

Recognizing this paradox, the Court has declared in *Van der Peet* that rights associated with Aboriginal sovereignty and jurisprudences are equal to (but distinct from) the rights contained in the Charter (par. 19). Thus the task of the judiciary is to recognize and define these distinct Aboriginal rights by employing Aboriginal thinking which recognizes that Aboriginal rights are *rights* but which does so without losing sight of the fact that they are rights held by Aboriginal people because they are Aboriginal. The Court must neither lose sight of the generalized constitutional status of what s. 35(1) protects, nor can it ignore the necessary specificity which comes from granting special constitutional protection to one part of Canadian society. The Court must define the scope of s. 35(1) in a way which captures *both* the Aboriginal and the rights in Aboriginal rights. (par. 20)

The Dickson Court in *Sparrow* emphasized the importance of this internal vision of Aboriginal rights by stating that, under s. 35(1), "[i]t is ... crucial to be sensitive to the Aboriginal perspective itself on the meaning of the rights at stake" (1112). Similarly, in *Delgamuukw*, the Court has acknowledged that these perspectives can be "gleaned, in part, but not exclusively, from their traditional laws, because those laws were elements of the practices, customs and traditions of Aboriginal peoples" (par. 148).

While the negative side of the Court's characterization of Aboriginal rights is fully developed, the positive side is in a rudimentary state. This is inevitable, since the Court is engaged in a revisionary analysis of great difficulty and profundity. But it is imperative that rationalist legal analysis reject some of its received legal understandings as invalid, in keeping with how the Court refines and implements constitutionalism. The Court has been struggling to define Aboriginal rights in a context that has been shaped by the Eurocentric tradition, but it has not attempted to articulate the Indigenous methods or procedures that are embedded in the distinct Aboriginal legal traditions. It has yet to clarify the relations between purpose and being in performance-based Aboriginal legal traditions, the link between traditions that describe and those that ordain, its own approach to factual irregularities and customs, or the nature of Aboriginal reasoning about necessity, sequence, time, causation, and objectivity as expressed in Aboriginal languages.

Still, because of the *sui generis* nature of Aboriginal and treaty rights, the Court in *Delgamuukw* has already demanded that a unique approach to the existing procedural and evidentiary law of the various courts be devised, an approach that can accord due weight to the perspective of Aboriginal peoples (pars. 82, 84–87). Thus the Court found in *Delgamuukw* that the "traditional values of evidence law," values that constitute the consciousness of the Court, were not necessarily conducive or appropriate to a culturally sensitive consideration of Aboriginal knowledge, legal traditions, or histories. The Court has held that in adjudicating Aboriginal and treaty cases, trial courts must adapt the law of evidence to accommodate Aboriginal law and oral histories, approach the rules of evidence in light of the evidentiary difficulties inherent in these claims, and interpret that evidence presented in the same spirit (pars. 82, 87). Until the law of evidence is made consistent with Aboriginal peoples' rights, judges should apply the existing rules in a broad and flexible manner commensurate with Aboriginal knowledge and legal traditions until Aboriginal traditions and methods are placed on an equal footing with other types of historical evidence (pars. 84, 87). This *sui generis* concept needs developing in social sciences and humanities scholarship.

The initial way the Court has sought to accomplish this substantive task in *Sparrow* is through a constitutionally purposive approach that identifies the activities or interests that Aboriginal and treaty rights were intended to protect (1106). This purposive approach in *Van der Peet*, based on a principle-based and policy-oriented style of legal reasoning, ensures that the recognition and affirmation of Aboriginal and treaty rights are constitutional rights (par. 21). These rights should not be viewed as static or relevant only to current circumstances; they are dynamic and transforming in new contexts (par. 21).

Distinct Legal Traditions

The Court has noted in *Van der Peet* and *Delgamuukw* that Aboriginal legal traditions are based on oral traditions and histories that illuminate Aboriginal law. These are primary evidence of both Aboriginal and treaty rights, but they are distinct from Eurocentric disciplinary approaches to these traditions and histories. According to the Court in *Delgamuukw*, Aboriginal legal traditions include things passed down, and arising, from the pre-existing legal teaching, heritages, and customs of Aboriginal peoples (pars. 84–88). But to Aboriginal peoples and their system of knowledge, understanding traditions involves a process that is distinct from the Eurocentric thin and static meanings of pastness, the replication of past practices of a social order, and the contrast between traditional and modern (or postmodern, for that matter) ways of thinking. Aboriginal concepts of tradition rely on a distinct method of learning and contemplation that involves oral processes or ceremonies that integrate new insights, attitudes, and practices through dynamic ways of life and learning that adapt to changing environments and situations. This also involves a way of thinking about time that is different from the Eurocentric linear extension of the past to the present and a discernible future. Aboriginal traditions are not comprehensive; open and ongoing, they are always in the process of becoming. They have never been static forms of social order, as the disruptive concept of "the trickster" reveals in Aboriginal traditions and literature.

Thus Aboriginal legal traditions contain many perspectives concerning Aboriginal knowledge and sovereignty. They do not present a singular vision of a good mind or a balanced relationship, but many. For example, Aboriginal knowledge and sovereignty have always been based on the subtle art of sustaining peaceful relationships. As such, when determining Aboriginal sovereignty, jurisprudences, and perspectives, trans-systemic and *sui generis* analyses are critical, since one culture cannot be judged by the norms of another and each must be seen in its own terms. Governments, bureaucracies, academics, scholars, and the legal profession, who have refused to step outside Eurocentric traditions to comprehend Aboriginal traditions, fail to understand that Aboriginal traditions are distinct from Eurocentric ones.

Aboriginal legal perspectives are transmitted through Aboriginal knowledge, languages, visions, and ceremonies. In that alone they comprise a method that is distinct from those of Eurocentrism. In Eurocentric legal thought, a legal tradition is usually conceptualized as "a set of deeply rooted, historically conditioned attitudes about the nature of law, about the role of law in the society and the polity, about the proper organization and operation of a legal system, and about the way law is or should be made, applied, studied, perfected, and taught" (Merryman 2). As law professor Robert Cover writes:

> A legal tradition ... includes not only a *corpus juris*, but also a language and a mythos—narratives in which the *corpus juris* is located by those whose wills act upon it. These myths establish the paradigms for behavior. They build relations between the normative and the material universe, between the constraints of reality and the demands of an ethic. These myths establish a repertoire of moves—a lexicon of normative action—that may be combined into meaningful patterns culled from meaningful patterns of the past. (9)

These legal traditions are shaped by the structure of European languages. For example, Eurocentric civil law of the *Justinian Institutes* is structured by the trichotomy of the linguistic approach reflected in the sacred and secular trinity of person–thing–action, while the common law is shaped by the trichotomy reflected in the subject–verb–object structure of the English language, which translates into person–action–thing (1.2.12). Language is a fundamental aspect of systems of knowing, a process of communication of knowledge, doctrine, or technique.

European languages, *mythos*, knowledge systems, and legal traditions derive from a separation within the classic traditions of Eurocentrism through the intellectual lens of the eighteenth-century Enlightenment, the development of physical and social science, the rise of exclusivist nation-states, and the development of informational system theories in the twentieth century. The social theorists of the imperial age—Tocqueville, Marx, Durkheim, and Weber—rejected the established intellectual traditions in Eurocentrism, especially the Platonic and Aristotelian philosophies, and generated a new, identifiable "modern" movement in Eurocentrism. Eurocentric law was reconstructed based on the legacy of concepts, methods, theories, and tacit assumptions handed down by the leading social theorists of the late nineteenth and the early twentieth centuries. In many ways, the Canadian legal system is characterized by its ongoing denial of its historical roots and its belief that it is modern rather than traditional. As Patrick Glenn argues, a legal system may reject tradition, but cannot escape from it.

Since Aboriginal legal traditions are distinct from Eurocentric traditions, Aboriginal knowledge, sovereignty, and legal traditions are best studied in the structure and context of Aboriginal languages and consciousness. Most of these languages are being- or action-centred, that is, they are verb-centred (Battiste and Henderson 50; Inglis; Lomosits). Aboriginal vocabularies, stories, methods of communication, and styles of performance and discourse all encode values and frame understanding. The Court in *Delgamuukw* had noted that Elders and designated persons who speak Aboriginal languages are primary sources for and authorities on *sui generis* Aboriginal jurisdictions (pars. 12–13). Such integrated methods of knowing cover all aspects of stored heritage as revealed through Aboriginal languages, memories, stories, and ceremonies, and as learned and expressed through the oral and symbolic traditions and teachings of Aboriginal peoples.

Aboriginal legal traditions generate a constitutional order that is simultaneously heard, seen, felt, and savoured through holistic ceremonies and communal performances (Henderson, *First Nations* ch. 4). This order is comparable to the "synesthetic" tradition of early Greek and Hebrew societies (Hibbits). Through dynamic synthesis, Aboriginal traditions exist not as a thing or noun or rule but rather as overlapping and interpenetrating processes or activities that represent teachings, customs, and agreements. Aboriginal peoples understand law as a force that lives through personal conduct, rather than as something that has to be written or produced by specialized thought and reasoning. It is more a matter of processes than a matter of Eurocentric logic, causality, or structural theory.

Trans-systemic Reconciliation

Understandably, the Court is uneducated about Aboriginal knowledge and its languages, traditions, and performance methods. While the Court has firmly acknowledged that Aboriginal peoples have generated a distinct structure, medium, and content of Aboriginal sovereignty, out of necessity in each case it has had to develop its methods and understanding of Aboriginal knowledge and legal traditions from analogy to the Eurocentric legal traditions. This has been a challenging, complex, and incomplete process. Significantly, the Court has also affirmed in *Côté* that each substantive Aboriginal right would normally include the constitutional right of the Aboriginal peoples to teach such customs and traditions to ensure their continuity (pars. 27, 31 and par. 56). This is an important principle of trans-systemic synthesis and reconciliation.

As the Court has affirmed, Aboriginal legal traditions represent a distinct legal system with its *sui generis* method of analysis. It is based on narrative and categories integral to Aboriginal languages that give normative force to interpretation and analysis of its performances. It presents a unique set of interpretive and consensual methods of problem solving. It has a unique set of rhetoric operations and decisional conventions, engrained through performance and dialogue. It has affirmed the divide of different legal traditions and the generations of "intersocietal" (or métis) legal systems, and it has constructed diverse ways of reconciling, sustaining, and synthesizing these traditions.

The Court has yet to reveal an established constitutional reform in a manner that acknowledges its transformative possibilities, giving Canadians the power to decolonize the past and make the future, freeing us from fictions about the present. This necessitates the creation of new tools and methods to aid in the transformation and structural change of law, institutional arrangements, and associated beliefs that shape the practical and conversational routines of people. While the Court has not been able to identify a way to move beyond the Eurocentric method of rationalizing analysis in explaining Aboriginal peoples' rights, it understands the value of articulating a holistic method that would account for all the elements of a situation and that would bring out their reciprocal, non-linear interrelatedness. But the Court's case-by-case approach has not yet fashioned a coherent *sui generis* method based on Aboriginal knowledge, language, and traditions that displaces what the logical and the causal modes of explanation have in common (despite their important divergence): the concern with sequence and the search for relationships of necessity. It is still searching for a persuasive model (or models) of constitutional analysis and *synthesis* based on Aboriginal traditions rather than Eurocentric traditions, one that is dynamic, coherent, and legitimate. It cannot construct this model as long as Aboriginal peoples are not in a position to transmit their knowledges or traditions. Hence the need to adopt a trans-systemic approach to constitutional reconciliation.

The simplest way to define trans-systemic legal synthesis is to say that it represents a way to think clearly and connectedly about the many legal traditions that inform Canadian law. It is based on the ability to recognize and affirm that extraordinary thought. Trans-systemic analysis is designed to promote a more profound and coherent understanding of fundamental epistemologies that mould the jurisprudential consciousness and legal principles of Canadian law rather than simply teaching the logic of a single system of law. It is an attempt to understand the deep structure of humanity, ecology, and civilizations, an attempt to appreciate knowledge over information. This approach is a valuable model for social and human sciences to adopt.

Through its convergence of knowledge, humanity, and sovereignty, trans-systemic legal synthesis acknowledges and affirms Aboriginal sovereignty and knowledge. Trans-systemic legal synthesis is an indispensable antidote to the ethnocentric bias in Canadian legal reasoning, court decisions, and scholarship. It enables Aboriginal peoples to become secure in their constitutional entitlements and densely shared traditions and culture while restraining popular majorities and their legislative and policy power under law. It relieves distinct ways of living and cultural diversity of some of its terrors, both past and present. Trans-systemic legal synthesis establishes the premises to understand, respect, and substantially converge and reconcile the Eurocentric legal traditions of common law and civil law with the distinct, constitutionalized legal traditions of the Aboriginal peoples. Trans-systemic synthesis must reveal not only the uneasy distinctions between these legal traditions and their methods but also the latent shared consciousness (if any) about the terms of life. Many distinct challenges exist in both searches towards a justified order.

Trans-systemic constitutional synthesis is a way to sustain the commitment to patriated constitutionalism, the rule of law, legal traditions, and a regime of rights. It is a way of animating the constitutional commitment to remedy the past legal and political abuses of Aboriginal legal traditions by the extraordinary problems created by colonialism. This *pianissimo* remedy of affirming their Aboriginal and treaty rights and their *sui generis* legal traditions makes the powerless peoples in Canada the beneficiaries of constitutional reform. These constitutional reforms and the doctrine of the honour of the Crown establish the legal authority to tame the power of the majority with its rights-defeating advantages and to protect the impoverished from obvious disadvantages.

Trans-systemic synthesis creates a method both for the courts and for legal scholars, as well as for other scholars. It offers a way of being cognitively alive, conscious of the decolonization of legal inheritances and the transformation of past intellectual traditions in order to create a just Canada. It seeks to honourably converge and reconcile Aboriginal knowledge with Eurocentric knowledge (Battiste 2013). It allows for an imaginative and noble intellectual effort to construct and reconstruct power, both politically and intellectually, into honourable action, policy, and practices. It operates in specific ways to generate decent and just action to improve governance and scholarship. It addresses what is the distinct nature of legal knowledge and what it means to think like a patriated Canadian lawyer and scholar. It brings together the theoretical, the constitutional, and the practical. It has a potential for sharpening, deepening, and expanding the lenses through which every person can perceive and generate justice.

THE ACCIDENTAL WITNESS
Indigenous Epistemologies and Spirituality as Resistance in Eden Robinson's *Monkey Beach*
Julia Emberley

The accident is known, in other words, both to the extent that it *"pursues"* the witness and that *the witness is, in turn, in pursuit of it* ...
But if, in a still less expected manner, it is the witness who *pursues the accident*, it is perhaps because the witness, on the contrary, has understood that from the accident a *liberation* can proceed and that *the accidenting*, unexpectedly, is also in some ways *a freeing*.
—Shoshana Felman, "Education and Crisis, or the Vicissitudes of Teaching" (1992)

By their very nature, testimonies are unsettling. Produced in order to verify, supplement, or provide a subjective account of what are often traumatic and violent events, they disrupt any sense of normalcy in the continuum of life experience. The unsettling effects of testimonies, however, are often manufactured by the circumstances of their delivery. In our media-saturated manipulation of emotional intensities, the unsettling effects of testimonies are becoming less and less powerful. In addition, the pretense that testimony is a direct account of an event and as such more truthful or valuable to historical accountabilities belies the seemingly singular importance registered to the oral over the written, as if orality itself were not an unmediated practice, as if the narratives of oral delivery fell outside the realms of rhetoric, composition, and editorial decisions—even if they are self-imposed. Testimonies, today, are also in need of being unsettled, as in critically analyzed. They are

69

discursive formations that include texts, narratives, physical sites, spaces, and even objects. In all their likely and unlikely forms, testimonial discourses unsettle our capacities to connect or relate to another person's experience, and in the exchange between any given testimony and its audience trigger our analytical capacities to understand trauma and its trail of affect. In these multiple ways, I seek to comprehend how testimonial practices unsettle national and transnational histories, while also insisting that such practices be subject to critical examination themselves. Of significance to the latter is, I would argue, the need for an epistemic shift in the field of postcolonial testimonial studies influenced by the production, reception, and analysis of Indigenous storytelling knowledges and practices. This shift situates the need to recognize oneself as an "accidental witness," a position that Felman affirms, in the passage cited above, emerges often in testimonial practices as the listener or reader pursues the truth of a traumatic event and then finds her or himself pursued by something else, a type of haunting, that urges the reader on yet is oftentimes something that the reader does not want to know, because the knowledge itself is painful and overwhelming. And yet, the story must be told and the truth must be known. As I discuss below, Eden Robinson's novel *Monkey Beach* depicts a central character, Lisamarie, as one who is in pursuit of the knowledge of the death of her brother, and the structural organization of the novel, based on the Haisla Spirit Canoe journey, takes the reader on a journey into the history of residential school violence and its intergenerational consequences for Indigenous families and communities.

With the rise of *testimonio* in Latin and South America during the 1970s and 1980s, testimonial discourses, concerned with narrating the historical realities of colonial and postcolonial political oppression, determined a set of practices that linked individual eyewitness accounts to collective struggles and, without conflating the distinction between the private and the public, substantiated their interwoven complexities and complicities. This literary or "anti-literary" movement, as John Beverley would have it, does bear, historically, on the epistemic shift I wish to talk about here, although the geopolitical context differs, given that I focus on a Canadian state initiative as well as on kinship relations between epistemic frameworks, the imaginary figure of the witness, and the interconnections of private and public spaces. Testimonial discourses have undergone significant theoretical challenges especially in the wake of several controversies, including, of course, that of the testimony of the Nobel Peace Prize winner Rigoberta Menchú. The uses—perhaps especially because of the "abuses" to which these cultural technologies of the self have been put—open up many interesting questions not only about the limits of the text and its rhetorical undecidabilities, but also about the limits of epistemologies of truth and their investments in balancing the critical ledgers of state-imposed practices of "reconciliation."

In pursuit of the questions raised by state- and non-state-initiated testimonial practices, this discussion of testimony and Indigenous storytelling epistemologies is situated in the context of the Canadian Indian Residential Schools Truth and Reconciliation Commission (TRC), established in June 2008 on the recommendation of the *Report of the Royal Commission on Aboriginal Peoples* (1996). The RCAP's brief was to gather testimonial evidence—largely by way of public hearings with Indigenous people—on how government policy has affected Indigenous people in Canada. These hearings, held from 1991 to 1996, led to recommendations such as the establishment of the TRC with a view to creating healthier and happier Indigenous communities (Canada, Royal Commission vol. 1: xxiii). Residential schools were viewed by the commissioners as one of the most significant government policy initiatives to have had detrimental effects on Indigenous people. In making its case for a public inquiry into residential schools, the authors of the report emphasized that such an inquiry would represent "an appropriate social and institutional forum to enable Aboriginal people to do what we and others before us have suggested is necessary: to stand in dignity, voice their sorrow and anger, and be listened to with respect" (vol. 1: 383–84).

This essay on testimonial practices and Indigenous storytelling epistemologies is guided by the conceptual metaphor of kinship. The meaning of kinship is traditionally overdetermined by a filiative set of human relations that are more productively understood, I would suggest, as affiliative contingencies: a set of personal and political relations that critically generate interwoven ways of knowing and being. Epistemic kinship involves recognizing the dialogue that exists between Indigenous and Western Enlightenment discourses by demonstrating the ways in which the latter have always been, and continue to be, implicated in and indebted to Indigenous knowledges (Emberley). Reading Indigenous knowledges within the Western episteme entails in Western critical theory a *dialogic* practice. Even in its critical formation, however, the knowledges that have emerged from the European or Western Enlightenment tradition represent a particular perspective, one that must also be subject to epistemic decolonization.

I want now to turn to Robinson's *Monkey Beach* and read it in the context of Indigenous spiritual epistemologies.

The Haisla Spirit Canoe Journey in *Monkey Beach*

Robinson's collection of short stories, *Traplines*, and her novels *Monkey Beach* and *Blood Sports* are each, in their own narrative ways, concerned with the violence of historical discontinuities brought about by Canadian government policies to establish control over the citizenry and class constitution of the nation, particularly as those policies affect Aboriginal people, the Métis, and the Inuit. But if discussions of her work are limited only to the study of violence as an object of analysis, instead of understanding it as an integral part of the writing and representational process with which she is engaged, then an important dimension of her work will be missed. Representation and violence are inseparable in her writing. Furthermore, I would argue, embedded in her textual practice is a critique of the limits of the materiality of the text and its potential to rehearse *representational violence*. In Robinson's works, notions of identity, spectatorship, sexuality, and childhood are held up to scrutiny as material forms of social life whose representational power can, indeed, make or break a life.

Consider the following example from Robinson's short story "Queen of the North," a text that her novel *Monkey Beach* further extends and develops:

> I use a recent picture of Uncle Josh that I raided from Mom's album. I paste his face onto the body of Father Archibald and my face onto the boy. The montage looks real enough. Uncle Josh is smiling down at a younger version of me.
>
> My period is vicious this month. I've got clots the size and texture of liver. I put one of them in a Ziploc bag. I put the picture and the bag in a hatbox. I tie it up with a bright red ribbon. I place it on the kitchen table and go upstairs to get a jacket. I think nothing of leaving it there because there's no one else at home. The note inside the box reads, "It was yours so I killed it." (213)

This passage represents the narrative voice of a young Indigenous woman named Karaoke, who, as her name suggests, becomes yet another victim of the original violence of residential schooling that Robinson's texts are representative of. As the excerpt above shows, Karaoke transplants her face onto that of Josh as a young boy, and overlaps the face of the Priest with a photo of Josh as an adult man. It is precisely by addressing and acknowledging the representational powers of reproduction (both physical and aesthetic) that she is able to turn them to other purposes, that is, to writing the postcolonial genders of violence that are Aboriginal, female and male.

In the case of Indian residential schools, there is the need to wrench individual pain and victimization from the world of repeated substitutability, where child after child, within and across generations, was subjected to the repeated abuses of civil, religious, and familial authorities, day after day, night after night. Also at stake is the need to be wrenched from the logic of substitution itself, where government policies and bureaucracies assumed that they could substitute an Indigenous way of life for one manufactured and managed by the colonial bourgeois order, a colonial bourgeois order that held the substitutability of bodies as the final resolve of its labouring and desiring needs and wants.

The narrative design of *Monkey Beach* belongs to a kinship web of affiliations. The Indigenous emphasis on the interrelationship of story, people, and land lends itself to an understanding of what I call *kinship narrative*, which is formed on the basis of relations that intertwine and interconnect characters in a cosmic web of "the specific geographic, genealogical, and spiritual histories of peoples" (Justice 151).

The name "Monkey Beach" is one of the key sites of these geo-genealogical and spiritual histories. Place is significant to the novel's framing, for Robinson, at the beginning of the novel, traces the knowledge of Haisla territory on an imaginary "cognitive map." The narrator gives instructions such as "find a map of British Columbia" (4), and proceeds to outline the Hailsa land, including its overlap with the adjacent Tsimshian nation and its territory just north of the Douglas Channel. The cartography of Indigenous territories is interspersed with other inscriptions, such as those made by the Tsimshian and by Alcan Aluminum (which respells Kitamaat as Kitimat). Regardless of these variant spellings, Lisamarie, the narrator of *Monkey Beach*, insists Kitamaat be recognized as Haisla territory. Although the map provided divulges its colonial cartography, it also gives way to a different cartographic scale, one that is tied to the sea, especially the ebbs and flows of its permeable boundaries. In addition to the land, Robinson maps out the central relationships of the characters she is about to unfold in the novel. Lisamarie is twenty years old and is named after the wife of Elvis Presley. The story begins with her waking in the morning, thirty-six hours after Jimmy, her younger brother by a year and half, has been reported missing at sea on the boat *Queen of the North*, with his girlfriend's, Karaoke's, uncle Josh. Her mother and father are also waiting for news of his whereabouts.

In addition to the kinship of lands and people, Robinson maps a cartography of spiritual relations based on the Indigenous episteme of the medicine wheel. Just as there are four parts to the medicine wheel, there are four parts to the novel, with each part relating to the key principles depicted on the medicine wheel (see below). I have taken my representation of the medicine wheel from a Haisla author. There are many representations of it, but given that Robinson is herself Haisla, it seemed appropriate to use a Haisla source.

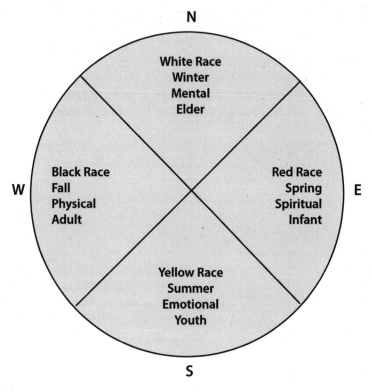

Figure 2.1   The Medicine Wheel (Dumbrill and Green 496)

While each part of the novel emphasizes one section of the wheel, all four parts are interwoven into each section; thus, the separation between the parts is neither formally nor rigidly maintained; rather, all four are interconnected. The "mental" zone of the wheel emerges in the form of Lisamarie's childhood memories. Memory itself is a site of spatial and temporal displacement throughout the text and a primary resource in her spiritual journey to the land of the dead. In Haisla knowledge, the journey to the land of the dead is called the "Spirit Canoe Journey." Traditionally, it was taken by a Shaman, but as with much Indigenous knowledge today, Robinson emphasizes its modern significance, in this case, through a speedboat journey in Part Two. This is the physical aspect of her journey. The emotional section appears in Part Three, when Lisamarie mourns the loss of two important people in her life, her Uncle Mick and her grandmother Ma-ma-oo. The fourth and final section is about her spiritual journey to the land of the dead, where she is able to connect to her brother Jimmy and to learn the truth about how and why he died.

Lisamarie is a young woman with spiritual powers of which she is unaware; when she does draw attention to them, her mother jokes that she needs Prozac (3). Whether she hears birds talking to her or finds in her dreams a suspended reality that helps her see things differently, it is only Ma-ma-oo, her grandmother—her father's mother—who sees her dream world as offering insight into the turmoil of the events that surround her. It is her dreams that trigger the memories of her childhood and point to the place called Monkey Beach. Those memories will come to represent her "spirit canoe journey."

Her first memory of Monkey Beach involves Jimmy's desire to take a picture of the B'gwus, the wild men of the woods, or sasquatches. He is only a young seven-year-old boy at this point, and he believes in the story of B'gwus "as if it were from the Bible" (9). But it is Lisamarie who encounters the B'gwus while searching for Jimmy in the woods: "Just for a moment, just a glimpse of a tall man, covered in brown fur. He gave me a wide, friendly smile, but he had too many teeth and they were all pointed. He backed into the shadows, then stepped behind a cedar tree and vanished" (16). Later, Lisamarie cringes at the thought of telling anyone what she saw: "They'd snicker about it the way they did when Ma-ma-oo insisted they were real" (17). Instead, she returns to the present moment and wonders what her dream of Jimmy standing on Monkey Beach means. She tries to interpret it but concedes: "I used to think that if I could talk to the spirit world, I'd get some answers. Ha bloody ha. I wish the dead would just come out and say what they mean instead of being so passive-aggressive about the whole thing" (17).

Lisamarie does, however, take a journey to the land of the dead, and she does so in the context of her modern life, thus demonstrating that sacred time and modern time can merge on the same plane of existence. The intertwining of the modern and the sacred occurs in the text in a variety of signifying forms, in references to popular commodity culture and naming, such as Lisamarie's attachment to Elvis Presley, Jimmy's girlfriend's name, Karaoke, and Tab, named after the popular soft drink. Popular culture and the sacred intertwine when Lisamarie performs a ceremony with Ma-ma-oo in honour of her dead husband's memory. Lisamarie throws Twinkies onto a fire, because it was one of her grandfather's favourite foods, although she would rather eat them herself (79).

The narrative conjunction of childhood and memories has a significant structural component as it allows for the unfolding of knowledge during a time of intense learning and development. In this way, the pedagogical aspects of Indigenous knowledges are incorporated into the novel's structure as Lisamarie learns the sacred traditions from Ma-ma-oo, such as the importance of oolichan grease to the Haisla (85–86).

Although *Monkey Beach* is narrated largely in first person, unassimilated second-person monologues are interspersed throughout the text. Their narrative voice is instructional, imposing, and directive. In Part Two, "The Song of Your Breath," in which Lisamarie remembers her youth and transition to adolescence, several such passages disrupt the narrative with a graphic description of the anatomical construction of the heart:

> Make your hand into a fist. This is roughly the size of your heart. If you could open up your own chest, you would find your heart behind your breastbone, nestled between your lungs.... Your heart is shrouded at the moment by a sac of tissue, a membrane called the pericardium, which acts like bubble wrap by both protecting your heart and holding it in place. Peel away this sac. Inside is a watery lubricant that minimizes friction when your heart beats. Shooting down from the aorta—the large tube arching on top of your heart—are two large arteries that branch out like lightning forks over the heart muscle. Behold, your heart. Touch it. Run your fingers across this strong, pulsating organ. Your brain does not completely control your heart. (163–64)

The emotional aspect of the medicine wheel is interwoven into these disruptive passages about the heart and its physical properties. Just who is being interpellated by these passages is, however, an open question. Several of these passages, which read like a series of instructional lessons, focus on "how to contact the dead" (82–83, 139, 179–80, 191, 212, 366). The second lesson in contacting the dead, for instance, involves a set of instructions that place the reader in a large mall on Christmas Eve calling for a lost toddler. The experience of hearing the child call back is likened to the magic of conjuring spirits by calling their names: "Names have power. This is the fundamental principle of magic everywhere" (180). The third lesson on contacting the dead involves seeing ghosts (212). Another set of passages imparts traditional knowledge of Haisla territory and language: "The name Haisla first appeared in print in 1848 as Hyshallain" (194). The history of the Haisla people and their settlement as a Christian mission brings new contestations to the surface, as Lisamarie's mother tells her not to listen to Ma-ma-oo's stories about the past and why her own grandmother refused to move to the missionary village, choosing instead to spend her whole life in the different summer and winter camps (194). Although the reader is left to question the intentionality behind the voice of these "instructional" passages, I would suggest that this voice is that of the *accidental witness*. The accidental witness is driven by a certain will to knowledge: to seek, to trail, to track down the truth of an unexpected or accidental event that dramatically and traumatically encapsulates historical significance. Like B'gwus, the hairy monster lurking on the periphery, however, the pursuant witness appears with fleeting irregularity to detect with epistemic precision the violent effects of colonization. Such a monstrous figure, a stalker if you will, could be said to occupy the position of the colonial or postcolonial spectator, a position that implicates, I would suggest, any non-Indigenous reader of *Monkey Beach*. Although the tone of the directional "you" is not necessarily accusatory, its uneasy pedagogical tone appears to mimic the paternalistic voice of the religious instructors of the residential schools, whose seemingly benevolent desire to protect and save Indigenous children masked an insidious violence of sexual abuse and rape. This ambiguous voice also recalls the middle voice, the repositioning of the past in the present tense, and positions the reader, however uneasily, as part of the narrative as it draws her or him into a liminal space between the present and the past, the material and the sacred. In these passages, the temporalities of the sacred and the present intertwine and become indistinguishable. In his definition of the middle voice, Roland Barthes relates it to the "problem of the relation between the present and the past, notably in terms of one's relation as speaker to one's discourse in the present, in contradistinction to one's account of a past discourse or phenomenon" (Barthes 144). In discussing Barthes's notion of the middle voice, Dominick LaCapra argues that the undecidability that results from the ambivalence of a clear-cut subject position threatens to

> disarticulate relations, confuse self and other, and collapse all distinctions, including that between present and past, [and is] related to transference and prevail[s] in trauma and in post-traumatic acting out in which one is haunted or possessed by the past and performatively caught up in the compulsive repetition of traumatic scenes—scenes in which the past returns and the future is blocked or fatalistically caught up in a melancholic feedback loop. In acting out, tenses implode, and it is as if one were back there in the past reliving the traumatic scene. (21)

In other words, for LaCapra, the middle voice represents the experience of trauma. What LaCapra does not grasp, however, is that the representation of traumatic experience is also a mode of discursive delivery that in Robinson's employment of the "you" creates another effect, that of a provisional and momentary reconciliation between writer and reader. Although the pursuant witness wants to learn the truth in no uncertain terms, Robinson's text suggests that this cannot happen unless a balance is maintained among all dimensions of existence, including the emotional, the mental, the physical, and the sacred. Lisamarie's journey is about learning the truth of what happened to her brother, Jimmy, and seeing that truth unfold in the context of the trans-generational effects of residential schooling on Indigenous youth.

What LaCapra views as the transference of a traumatic haunting becomes, in Robinson's web of sacred knowledge, a way to go into the past and come back from it released from its traumatic hold. In these sections, the readerly subject is interpellated by the second-person "you" and allowed—encouraged in fact—to momentarily join forces with the "I" of the text.[1]

As the novel progresses, residential schooling becomes the site that links people together, as well as the foundation of the many things that are left unsaid and silenced. The three characters whose lives were directly affected by residential schools include Uncle Mick, Aunt Trudy, and Josh. Alcohol and drug abuse plays a significant role in their lives. Josh is Uncle Mick and Aunt Trudy's schoolhood friend, but he is the one who eventually rapes Jimmy's girlfriend, Karaoke, and gets her pregnant. Jimmy's discovery of the rape and Karaoke's abortion is what sends him on his perilous journey of revenge. Like Lisamarie, who must struggle to comprehend what is at stake in the sometimes difficult and strained relations that permeate her family, the reader must piece together the story and construct the web, as it were, of trans-generational relations and colonial violence and their present-day effects. From a sociological perspective, Kai Erikson argues that trauma "is normally understood as a somewhat lonely and isolated business because the persons who experience it so often drift away from the everyday moods and understandings that govern social life ... paradoxically, the drifting away is accompanied by revised views of the world that, in their turn, become the basis for communality" (198). Although Erikson is primarily concerned with clinical work on trauma and how acknowledging trauma as a communal experience can affect and possibly change such forms of work, he asks a relevant question: "does it make sense to conclude that the traumatized view of the world conveys a wisdom that ought to be heard in its own terms?" (198). Robinson's novel not only marks out the terrain of how the trauma of residential schooling shaped Indigenous communities, but also offers a non-clinical approach, grounded in Indigenous epistemologies of the sacred, to how such communal trauma can be acknowledged. Jimmy's death not only becomes an act of revenge, but also has a sacrificial dimension to it, for his death shifts Lisamarie's knowledge of her family's history. She becomes aware of how the traumatic effects of colonial and national violence reshaped Indigenous communities by destroying a political economy of affiliative kinship relations and supplanting them with ones determined and overdetermined by the reality of violence in daily life.

Sexual violence represents a key site of trauma in the novel. In one incident, Lisamarie stands up to a carload of four young white men in order to defend her school enemy, Erica (250–51). Everyone in her family tells her never to do this again. Aunt Trudy tries to explain how First Nations children were treated in residential schools—girls and young woman in particular: "Fact of life, girly. There were tons of priests in the residential schools, tons of fucking matrons and helpers that 'helped' themselves to little kids just like you. You look at me and tell me how many of them got away scot-free" (255). Again, Lisamarie is left on her own to figure out why she is the one getting blamed "for some assholes acting like assholes" (255). Soon after this incident, Lisamarie is drugged at a party and raped by her supposed friend Cheese, who wanted to be her boyfriend and to whom she said no (258). In this upsidedown world of violence and confusion, Lisamarie experiences the trickery of the land of the dead.

In Part Three, "In Search of the Elusive Sasquatch," Lisamarie physically arrives at Monkey Beach on her journey to find out about her brother, Jimmy. The section begins with reference to the trickster, the Raven, and how he "mellowed in his old age" (296). Apparently he's now a respectable fellow who "sips his low-fat mocha and reads yet another sanitized version of his earlier exploits" (296); but whether he appears respectable now or not, he is still the trickster, ready to pull the wool over everyone's eyes (296). The trickster figure's appearance represents the moment in the novel when the protagonist, Lisamarie, is caught in a cycle of self-destruction. She, too, is now part of a community of despair, one that appears inevitable, a permanent site of incarceration from which there is no escape. Like the accidental witness as described by Felman, the trickster, however, turns incarcerated spaces into unexpected sites of liberation and freedom.

At Monkey Beach, Lisamarie is transported into the near past, which includes Pooch's funeral after committing suicide and the turmoil of Karaoke and Jimmy's relationship (319). She remembers that while searching for the promise ring that Jimmy bought for Karaoke, she came across the picture Karaoke created to give to Josh to get back at him for raping her:

> In the pocket of Jimmy's brown leather jacket, I found an old photograph and a folded-up card. The picture was black-and-white. Josh's head was pasted over a priest's head and Karaoke's was pasted over a little boy's. I turned it over: *Dear Joshua*, it read. *I remember every day we spent together. How are you? I miss you terribly. Please write. Your friend in Christ, Archibald.*
>
> I asked Karaoke about it later, and she uncomfortably said it was meant as a joke, Jimmy was never supposed to find it. But she wouldn't look at me, and she left a few minutes later. Jimmy'd picked it up the same way I had. The folded-up note card was a birth announcement. On the front, a stork carried a baby across a blue sky with fluffy white clouds. *It's a boy!* was on the bottom of the card. Inside, in neat, careful handwriting it said, "Dear, dear Joshua. It was yours so I killed it." (365)

After recalling this event, Lisamarie returns to the present time at Monkey Beach. This section ends with her cutting into the palm of her hand and letting the blood run down her forearm as she makes her offering to the trees. In Part Four, "The Land of the Dead," we are still at Monkey Beach, but the section begins in dreamtime in which Lisamarie is with Mick and Ba-ba-oo picking out a Christmas tree. Lisamarie then returns to the present and bargains with the tree spirits, who want more blood, but Lisamarie insists, "You tell me where Jimmy is first" (369). In exchange, the tree spirits give her the account of how Jimmy killed Josh (369–70): "For what he did to Karaoke, he knew that Josh deserved to die" (369). Jimmy is last seen swimming to shore. Lisamarie tries to scramble back to the boat at Monkey Beach, but as she is in the water trying to push the boat to shore against the rising tide, she knocks her head and slips underwater (370). In her semi-conscious state, submerged in the water, she sees Ma-ma-oo greeting her and taking her to the land of the dead. Ma-ma-oo reminds her: "You have a dangerous gift," she says. "It's like oxasuli. Unless you know how to use it, it will kill you" (371). Ma-ma-oo then tells her she has to go back, that she has come too far into "this world" (372). She rises to the surface but submerges again because she wants to see Jimmy. Finally, she sees him under the water, and he takes her and shoves her towards the surface (373). In this mixed state of the sacred and the present, Lisamarie gets to the beach, where she sees the ghosts of Mick and Ma-ma-oo and other "dark figures against the firelight." They sing a farewell song in Haisla, and Jimmy's ghost reminds her to "tell her"—Karaoke, that is—goodbye (374).

While European testimonial discourses reimagine traumatic residues in terms of the haunting of the past by ghostly figures such as those created by its Gothic traditions, and insist that the only authentic account of a traumatic history is one marked by the impossibility of its representational authenticity, Indigenous storytelling epistemologies shift the terrain of comprehension by introducing the sacred as a site of resistance to the enforced silencing that occurred with residential school violence. Memory and memorialization are similarly disarticulated from the pathologizing intent of the analytical frameworks of psychoanalysis and the historical nationalization of a sense of belonging. Robinson's narrative use of memory situates it as part of the cognitive web of Indigenous knowledges that move the question of "historical truth" beyond the need to supply evidentiary veracity. Rather, memory provides traces of knowledge that can and must be sorted out into narrative modes of learning, comprehending, and, finally, accepting in the sense of coming to terms with the realities of what did happen at the residential schools to Indigenous children and their families. The Haisla Spirit Canoe Journey to the land of the dead is the vehicle to such comprehension, for entry into an epistemic site that also extends towards the making of a healing knowledge.[2] Sacred knowledge resists the surrogate logic of state power and its domestication of technologies of authority in relation to Indigenous youth and children.

Lisamarie learns about the silent traumas of sexual abuse in residential schools through her ability to comprehend what has happened to her family relations. The sacred enables her to transform how she views those relations, which seemed to be constituted only by a history of abuse and violence, into a different mode of connection and interrelationality. *Monkey Beach* offers up a renewed insight into Canada's postcolonial nation-building enterprise, its legacy of violence, and how Indigenous scholars, artists, and writers are providing knowledge to comprehend and heal from it.

As a non-Indigenous reader of the text, I occupy the position of the accidental witness, occasionally getting a glimpse at the truth of that history. I come away knowing that entry into the middle passage is by no means an easy journey to take. Persistence is key, as Lisamarie's character demonstrates, but it is a gentle form of persistence that is required, one that makes use of the knowledges at our disposal to pursue a range of necessary truths in the many forms in which they appear. While an enlightened critical consciousness may begin with the recognition that residential schools were sites of violence and incarceration, it is not enough to remain within such a narrow scope of vision. Indigenous writers such as Robinson open the way to a trickster mode of resignification whereby the past and the present maintain a kinship that pursues the reader and helps her or him find the way to a possible freedom from pain, trauma, and violence.

AMBIDEXTROUS EPISTEMOLOGIES
Indigenous Knowledge within the
Indigenous Renaissance

Marie Battiste

Nꞌ

wejiwskwijinuꞌlisen
from whom You
got your humanity

Indigenous Protocols of Place

As is customary in Indigenous protocols, I take this opportunity to acknowledge where the TransCanada Three conference took place, within the homelands of the Mi'kmaw people on the territories within Sackville and beyond,
whose protocols of place the conference delegates acknowledged. It is these
lands and their ecological sovereignty that have nurtured my Mi'kmaw family
and ancestors for uncountable generations.

Around the earth, Indigenous peoples continue to feel the cognitive conflict created by Eurocentric educational systems that subjected them to forced
assimilation and cognitive dissonance. Eurocentrism has damaged and eroded
the Indigenous consciousness and their knowledges at multiple levels, fostering injustices for Indigenous peoples worldwide. Yet, despite the centuries of
wariness, mistrust, and barely controlled rage towards Eurocentrism, Indigenous peoples are undergoing a transformation evidenced in their re-engage-
ment with their Indigenous knowledge and traditions (IK) and their helping
others rethink how we can interact with the earth and with one another. As

well, the inability of Eurocentric technological knowledge to sustain ecologies has increasingly brought the world's attention to the latent possibilities and potential of IK, to the cognitive loss of Indigenous languages, and to the desperate need to restore our ecologies with earth-friendly energies, knowledge, and care. These tensions create many quandaries that touch on developing issues of trans-systemic knowledges, diversity, inclusivity, and respect, themes that are emerging with increasing frequency and volume and that point to the relevance and importance of the themes raised here.

The theme of this conference, "Literature, Institutions, Citizenship," points to sites for decolonizing, transforming, and relearning. It speaks to the strengths and limitations of our embodied perceptions and our formal education, which have proved to be a foundation of strength for many but a formidable weapon of mass destruction for Indigenous consciousness and the lives of Indigenous peoples. These textual and imaginative themes continue to be artificial dream sites of promise, fascination, and hope, as expressed not only by Indigenous peoples around the world, but also by peoples disenfranchised by Eurocentrism generally and racism and poverty more specifically. The *Report of the Royal Commission on Aboriginal Peoples* (1996) aptly noted that despite the tragic effects of education as a result of misinformed educators and policies, Aboriginal peoples view education as the transforming agenda for undoing and superseding colonial myths and practices, and as creating transforming practices that recognize the value and validity of Aboriginal knowledges, cultures, and communities as foundational to the future capacity-building of their peoples.

For me, there is no greater promise and hope than that coming from the increasing awareness and work of Indigenous peoples that has been emerging for a generation or two, and that has been so evident since the early 1970s. This theme of trans-systemic knowledge, which operates across two or more distinct knowledge systems, displacing Eurocentrism, suggests sites of emerging change and innovation that come from Indigenous peoples animating IK, as well as from Eurocentric scholars and students actualizing social justice and the human rights of Indigenous people in the academy and in schools. I would like to acknowledge and honour the renaissance of Indigenous peoples by recognizing the resilience of my own peoples' journey.

From Resilience to Renaissance

I am a Mi'kmaw woman, a status Indian from Potlotek First Nations in Nova Scotia, Canada, and a member of the Aroostook* Band of Micmac in the United States of America. Within my life journey, my learning spirit became attracted originally to the teaching profession, and later to correcting the failed educational system that had inflicted trauma upon my people and family and from which we are trying to decolonize ourselves, to heal and stabilize. When I first entered the teaching profession, my formal education gave me no idea of the depth of the shared trauma and its impacts not just on Mi'kmaq and other First Nations peoples on the eastern seaboard of Canada and the United States, but also on the world's Indigenous peoples. My formal education only accentuated notions of Indigenous inferiority and of the need for education founded on Eurocentric principles. Nor was my formal education concerned with global humanity that included my people.

During my early years living in Maine, Mi'kmaq and First Nations peoples were evolving from a generation at best characterized by resilience. My own family's choices characterized that resilience. They were uneducated in the formal systems of Eurocentrism, and unemployed or underemployed most of the time, but also hard working and thoroughly learned in Mi'kmaw language, knowledge, and skills, which extended from Cape Breton Island to Newfoundland to Boston.

When the federal government, under its notorious centralization policy,[1] forced my family to relocate from their self-sustaining homelands of Potlotek to the central location of Eskasoni, my parents reluctantly joined others. However, they left that reserve soon after, in 1948, convinced that off-reserve employment and education would be better than being forced into centralized reserves where employment was sparse at best, and where their own experiences with day and residential schools were oppressive. With nothing remotely resembling hope in the residential school system, education became a tool for eliminating Mi'kmaw consciousness and language. While my family worked in migrant farm camps, my eldest sister was sent for several years to a residential school. As was the case with others who were forced to enter it, the residential school system was traumatic to her, creating disruptions and dissonance well into her later years. It was also destructive to our family. It became apparent to us that this was a failed system, one that would generate an endless search for ways to heal the collective soul wound it has caused.

For most of my years at a school in rural Maine, in the border town of Houlton, my family survived on Mi'kmaw knowledge and skills. I recall my dad—big, strong, and brown—working in the potato or blueberry fields as a migrant labourer; he also worked in the woods, either taking out logs for loggers or searching for logs for our family's business, which was making axe handles, ash baskets of all kinds, and other hardwood crafts, to enrich our living when he could not find local employment. My mother worked mostly as a domestic, and in her spare time she carried on the ancestral traditions of making Mi'kmaw arts and crafts. All the members of my family, depending on our age and capabilities, took on parts of that family work, learning how to make products from ash and maple, and harvesting and living within our beloved woodlands to make Mi'kmaw baskets.

We lived in the cognitive spaces of our parents' stories, which were told in either Mi'kmaq or English. Their rich experiences and knowledge of place helped us learn both languages separately and differently, depending on context and place. This allowed us to generate an ambidextrous consciousness that has proven to be immensely helpful. This consciousness became my core tool as I continued through school in Houlton.

No less important was my learning to understand and cope with overt and systemic racism, which I encountered among students, teachers, and townspeople, who held deeply engrained prejudices against Indians and who held our poverty in disdain. But I survived this thanks to my parents' encouragement, and to their own coping strategies, which we modelled, as they had been modelled to them by their parents. These were lessons in character, honesty, creativity, perseverance, and resilience. Their insights into racism formed a Mi'kmaw theory of anti-racism long before academic literature did so. This knowledge, first derived from experience and discussion, eventually provided cognitive tools for me as I continued through school.

At that time, it puzzled me to witness my cousins and relatives leaving school early, having to work hard at harvesting, and moving with the seasons to survive with their families, lest the children be forced back into residential schools. Few of my relatives achieved schooling beyond the elementary grades. It was assumed they were unable to meet the demands of formal education. This form of inferiority consciousness stuck on us, but it also stuck on the educational institutions themselves, which at the time had no tools for dealing with our languages, achievement levels, or entrenched poverty.

Mi'kmaw students in Canada were educated under colonial systems of education in federal residential schools and day schools, and later in the provincial public schools. These institutions emphasized a knowledge and skills base that was Eurocentric to the core, reinforcing foreign ways of knowing and being that built deficits and failures rather than Indigenous capabilities and enriched knowledges (McConaghy). These "civilizing" missions (Gandhi 16) quietly condemned Mi'kmaw students to a derivative and subjugated epistemic existence. Knowledge invented elsewhere and imported to educational settings is often, and rightly so, understood to be a sword of cognitive imperialism (Battiste, "Mi'kmaq Literacy"; Moore and Deloria). That sword is wielded by educators against those who suffer the conquest or occupation of their minds (Nandy), and this further colonizes the life worlds of First Nations peoples (Duran and Duran) by marginalizing IK and voices (Battiste, *Reclaiming*). Currently, 61 to 69 percent of First Nations students are failing to graduate from high school. It will take approximately twenty-seven years to reach parity with the overall Canadian rate for high school completion (Canada, Auditor General, para. 4.44).

As one of the first Indigenous educators, I was often called upon to address special education issues that non-Indigenous educators thought were beyond their capacity. Despite my Eurocentric education and lack of formal cultural education, I was thought to hold the tools that were necessary for dealing with Aboriginal students' issues. Yet these issues were not immediately understood, for many Indigenous families and students were still dealing with intergenerational trauma as a result of residential schooling, cognitive assimilation, the loss of Indigenous consciousness and languages, negative images embedded in Eurocentric discursive practices of hegemony and superiority, and dissonance between school and home. So the need to identify and generate therapeutic methodologies for educators—and not just for Indigenous peoples—was at the forefront of my mind as I continued with graduate studies. With a focus on therapeutic understandings, sensitivities, and knowledge(s), an Indigenous education has had to address the resignation and lack of hope among Indigenous youth who drop out of school or who find a lack of inspiration, engagement, and identity formation within (and beyond) current humanities classes and Eurocentric disciplines (Hill). Contemporary trans-systemic approaches in Indigenous education seek to displace assimilation strategies and find new ways of engaging Indigenous students' understandings of their heritages, humanities, and identities. This transformative initiative seeks to provide Indigenous Elders, educators, and youth with political tools that can work at both an international and a national level, as well as with an Indigenous pedagogy of hope and agency.

Indigenous Renaissance

The story of the resilience of my parents and ancestors has been transformed into one of renaissance, built by that generation of Indigenous people (my own) who were the first to achieve "higher" education. By the time I got my first university degree, only a small handful of other Indigenous people had already done so. They included my older brother, Tom Battiste, who received a bachelor's degree in business and a master's degree in education. In 1984, I was one of the first Indigenous people to gain a doctorate (in education, in my case), and the first woman from a First Nation in Canada to do so. During those years of education at stellar institutions like Harvard and Stanford, I was not taught anything about IK. That part of my learning came from discussions with the Elders in my family and with the handful of Indigenous students in graduate studies, who also had begun re-engaging with Elders, family, and community to renew and restore their own languages, cultures, and knowledges generated from their own particular places. With our Elders' and communities' guidance, support, and encouragement, Aboriginal students' accomplishments have grown.

Today the number of Aboriginal graduates has risen in Canada. Approximately 300 Aboriginal people now hold a doctorate; more than 1,000 are lawyers; nearly 400 are physicians; and hundreds more are social workers or educators. This emergent renaissance may be small, but it is growing, and it represents a critical mass of Indigenous learners who have survived an assimilationist and disempowering agenda in education with determination, a critical edge, and a desire to move the imposed boundaries of Eurocentric education so that they can begin to walk their own path towards empowering and liberating not just themselves but their communities and nations. For some, their accomplishments have come at a high price in terms of cultural, linguistic, and spiritual erosions and losses; for others, their language, culture, and spiritual communities have been the source of their strength and their success.

The word "renaissance" has French origins, meaning rebirth, but I employ it here by way of acknowledging a rebirthing of consciousness among Aboriginal peoples and what I have witnessed among Indigenous peoples at the international level. The term is deployed strategically for communicating with Eurocentric thinkers. The Indigenous renaissance arose from multiple forms of struggle, resistance, and conscientization—for which I thank Paulo Freire, Graham Smith, Linda Tuhiwai Smith, Leroy Littlebear, and J. Y. (Sa'ke'j) Henderson (2008), as well as Willie Littlechild, Murdena and Albert Marshall, Alex Denny, and diverse other community activists, theorists, and writers. Struggling to make sense of Eurocentric systems in our lives, we realized the limits of the knowledge available for making a difference in our living conditions; thus, many of us have pushed the boundaries of conventional colonial education in the process of helping Eurocentric society find its new story. As Thomas Berry, author of *The Dream of the Earth*, asserts: "It's all a question of story. We are in trouble just now because we do not have a good story. We are in between stories. The old story, the account of how we fit into it, is no longer effective. Yet we have not learned the new story" (qtd. in Suzuki 4). The emergence of this new story is one that involves a conscientization about the limits of colonial society, its foundations and assumptive values, and about the integral role Indigenous peoples have played in an interdependent world. Modern global societies are beginning to connect to our stories within the social sciences, the humanities, and the sciences and in ecological sustainability contexts. In fact, as Paul Hawken reveals in *Blessed Unrest*, Indigenous peoples and ecological and social justice have together helped create one of the largest movements in the world.

In my generation, the story arose from social justice, equity, and cultural pursuits, which became sites of regeneration for the first generation of Indigenous scholars and professionals. Oddly, the forums for the Indigenous renaissance were UN bodies such as the International Labour Organization, UNESCO, the General Assembly, the Working Group on Indigenous Populations, and the Permanent Forum on Indigenous Issues. The settler states continued to suppress and deny IKs in favour of assimilation. This first generation, aided by Indigenous lawyers, politicians, and educators, succeeded in using international law to expose the prejudices and policies of Eurocentric education against Indigenous peoples—something that the settler states refused to acknowledge. Since the professions of law, education, and social work were the first ones that Indigenous peoples sought out in order to address their problems, it was Indigenous lawyers, educators, and social workers who became the front-line workers for developing anti-racist approaches to education, for rebuilding culturally inclusive discourses and programs in schools, for representing Aboriginal peoples in the courts, and for helping heal the intergenerational soul wounds of colonization, racism, and poverty. Their critical historical perspectives on the colonial model of Eurocentrism were foundational to the changes that have since emerged. They have developed the skills to translate Eurocentrism (its discourses, beliefs, and attitudes) into Indigenous languages, and vice versa, thus creating ambidextrous epistemologies that have helped unpack how Eurocentric dominance and superiority have functioned in the context of their professions. They have used their own Indigenous teachings, values, and knowledges to contest Eurocentric dominance and superiority in all areas of contemporary knowledge. Throughout, they have struggled to eliminate racial discrimination and to generate official apologies from church and state, as well as to achieve ratification of the UN Declaration of the Rights of Indigenous Peoples (2007), which all states have now signed (including Canada, in 2010).

It was through the creation of the Working Group on Indigenous Populations by the UN Human Rights Council that the first generation of international Indigenous activists began talking to one another about their local situations and the remedies required. These dialogues then worked their way through various UN institutions (Henderson, *Indigenous Diplomacy*), where they encountered extreme obstinacy when it came to asserting human rights and Indigenous knowledge within nation-states. But Indigenous leaders and scholars were relentless in asserting their ideas about ecological sovereignty in discussions on the Convention on Biological Diversity (1992); about Indigenous knowledge in UNESCO's Declaration on Science and the Use of Scientific Knowledge (1999); and about the Indigenous view of humanity in the Principles and Guidelines for the Protection of the Heritage of Indigenous

People (1995), which became the subject of *Protecting Indigenous Knowledge and Heritage* (Battiste and Henderson). While co-authoring this book, I had the great but nerve-racking honour of chairing the UN session on the Principles and Guidelines for the Protection of Indigenous Knowledge in 2000, becoming the first Indigenous woman to hold that responsibility and to have the experience of managing Eurocentric resistance to the principles.

My colleagues brought the discussions home in 1996 with the SSHRC Summer Institute held at the University of Saskatchewan. The theme of that gathering, Cultural Restoration of Oppressed Indigenous Peoples, would become the foundation of *Reclaiming Indigenous Voice and Vision* (Battiste). The contribution of that volume, as many young Indigenous scholars have relayed to me, lay in the fact that the essays it gathered together addressed issues they already knew were important: the need for analytic tools that would help them unpack issues for themselves; the hostile Eurocentric environment within which our laws, policies, and education systems were situated; the Eurocentric literature and knowledge that had long been embedded in higher education; the background of the theoretical and practical strategies that had enabled Eurocentric dominance; and, finally, need for us to reclaim our own Indigenous voice, vision, and knowledge if we were to empower ourselves. That volume reflects—and continues to do so—a powerful story for those who lack the words or the examples of transformation. It raises awareness of discrimination and racism, of what Elizabeth Minnich called "hierarchical invidious monoism" (110), and, ultimately, of the need to sensitize everyone to the Eurocentric consciousness whose colonial and neo-colonial practices continue to marginalize, racialize, and diminish Indigenous students. This process has required a critical engagement with the imposed Eurocentric categories of race, culture, poverty, gender, and identity—all of which have diverted our attention from our own knowing, living, and being.

All educated people today have been marinated in Eurocentrism. Few of us have escaped its pursuit of domination. Eurocentrism is not a prejudice or attitude that can be erased by a course, a lecture, or a weekend retreat. Rather, it is in every fibre of contemporary Western societies, in their laws, their courts, their books, and their global corporations. It projects, employs, and diffuses the superiority of certain ideologies, laws, structures, schools, and knowledges while diminishing others. Eurocentric attitudes and discourses inflicted a soul wound on our people so deep that, by the middle of the nineteenth century, we had two options: submit utterly (as was hoped), or fight submission in new ways. These were the conditions that generated the first wave of the Indigenous renaissance.

The Indigenous renaissance is not an elitist group; it is an organic consciousness unfolding to meet urgent crises. It generates the missing stories of

Indigenous peoples and brings them to global consciousness, and in the process it has helped overcome the status quo, enrich the future of other peoples with Indigenous rights, and articulate the need for us to be connected with our ecology, our ancestors, and our guiding spirits. It has allowed us to see the strength of the double helix of an anti-racist educational strategy that is entwined with IK—a strategy that encompasses Creation stories, spirituality, teachings, traditions, and holistic lifelong learning. These have become the building blocks for reviving the best of our civilizations and constructing a just, enlightened, and shared future. In the past, we had not benefited from that shared knowledge. Only recently have we acquired the potential and the opportunity to share our knowledges with humanity and construct a sustainable life.

The agenda of the Indigenous renaissance has been immensely practical and pragmatic: to transform the status quo of educational curricula to more effectively include IK. The goal is to transform the persistent poverty of Aboriginal peoples into a civilization marked by education and prosperity for the next hundred years, and to reform attitudes and beliefs not only about the capacity of Indigenous peoples but also about our inherent capacity to foster a participatory consciousness with our environment, ecology, and the inner spirits. Not yet resolved, though, is how to address non-Indigenous peoples' feelings of denial, guilt, or anger over the disruption of their settler attitudes. With the allied work of white feminists and anti-racist and social activists, as well as ecologists and friends of the earth, this work continues to contest the layers of contradictions and paradoxes in discourses, histories, assumptions, beliefs, and values between Indigenous and non-Indigenous peoples. The challenges are great.

There is much for us still to learn, and much more for Indigenous peoples to unlearn. For example, we must somehow come to recognize that what that we have learned in public schools about our own capacities, our strengths, our knowledge, and our relations with one another has only diminished us as part of a strategy to maintain Eurocentrism's status quo. Meanwhile, Indigenous peoples have been studied, pathologized, and projected in ways that falsely render them deficient, dependent, and distrustful.

What the Indigenous renaissance has lacked in funding and focus, it has made up for in imagination and nuance. Over the past two decades, it has developed across a variety of disciplines and studies (law, education, history, anthropology, sociology, women and gender studies, languages, fine arts, cultural studies, Native Studies, interdisciplinary and cooperative studies). Since the initial debates about Indigenous human rights, the Indigenous renaissance has begun to achieve a critical mass, as is now reflected in the works of the many Indigenous scholars who are fighting Eurocentrism.

The principles of this critical mass are found in the 2007 UN Declaration on the Rights of Indigenous Peoples. This declaration established the minimum standard of Indigenous rights within nation-states and with regard to the UN's own behaviour; it is also the constitutional framework of the UN's current global consensus. Thus, laws and policies are required to be consistent with it if they are to have mainstream legitimacy.

The UN General Assembly has affirmed through the declaration that Indigenous peoples have the same human rights as other peoples, including the right of self-determination. Article 1 affirms that "Indigenous peoples have the right to the full enjoyment, as a collective or as individuals, of all human rights and fundamental freedoms as recognized in the Charter of the UN, the *Universal Declaration of Human Rights* and international human rights law." Article 2 affirms that "Indigenous peoples and individuals are free and equal to all other peoples and individuals and have the right to be free from any kind of discrimination, in the exercise of their rights, in particular that based on their indigenous origin or identity." Article 3 affirms: "Indigenous peoples have the right to self-determination. By virtue of that right they freely determine their political status and freely pursue their economic, social and cultural development."

The declaration also affirms Indigenous peoples' complementary rights— that is, access to education and participation in either Indigenous or state institutions—thereby ensuring their nationality and citizenship in current society. Article 5 provides that "Indigenous peoples have the right to maintain and strengthen their distinct political, legal, economic, social and cultural institutions, while retaining their right to participate fully, if they so choose, in the political, economic, social and cultural life of the State." The declaration also emphasizes, in Article 9, that "Indigenous peoples and individuals have the right to belong to an indigenous community or nation, in accordance with the traditions and customs of the community or nation concerned. No discrimination of any kind may arise from the exercise of such a right." Similarly, Article 33 affirms that

> Indigenous peoples have the right to determine their own identity or membership in accordance with their customs and traditions. This does not impair the right of indigenous individuals to obtain citizenship of the States in which they live. Indigenous peoples have the right to determine the structures and to select the membership of their institutions in accordance with their own procedures.

The General Assembly further recognizes that Indigenous peoples are organizing themselves for political, economic, social, and cultural enhancement in order to bring to an end all forms of discrimination and oppression wherever they occur. Furthermore, control by Indigenous peoples over developments affecting them and their lands, territories, and resources will enable them to maintain and strengthen their institutions, cultures, and traditions and to promote their development in accordance with their aspirations and needs.

In Article 34 of the declaration, the nation-states stress that "Indigenous peoples have the right to promote, develop, and maintain their institutional structures and their distinctive customs, spirituality, traditions, procedures, practices and, in the cases where they exist, juridical systems or customs in accordance with international human rights standards." Similarly, Article 35 recognizes that "Indigenous peoples have the right to determine the responsibilities of individuals to their communities," while Article 18 affirms that "Indigenous peoples have the right to participate in decision-making in matters, which would affect their rights, through representatives chosen by themselves in accordance with their own procedures, as well as to maintain and develop their own indigenous decision-making institutions."

In addition to these foundational human rights, the Indigenous renaissance has developed a terrain that empowers IK. The declaration answers the question about whose knowledge will count, and in what ways, in the construction of our future—science, health, justice, law, education, and humanities—by translating and merging Eurocentric and IKs.

Yet as important as anti-racism and human rights efforts have been, most Indigenous educators understand that the second wave of the Indigenous renaissance was mobilized by threats to IK. This second phase has involved convincing governments and institutions, as well as our own peoples, to acknowledge the unique knowledge and relationships that Indigenous peoples derive from place and from homeland. Both are central to our notions of humanity and science, and both are passed on in our languages and ceremonies. Indigenous peoples who have lost their own languages as a result of assimilation policies find themselves severely challenged. Losing one's own language for another's is traumatic in itself, but it involves much more than this, for it profoundly affects a community's socialization, ways of knowing, and non-verbal and verbal communications. In many communities, language is fundamental to IK and to the regeneration of Indigenous cultures.

The foundational tools of the Indigenous renaissance have been Indigenous science, humanity, education, and law. That renaissance has drawn its energy and authority from two appeals, one calculating, the other visionary. The calculating appeal is for the fostering of modest prosperity and independence, often identified with traditional forms of commercial and professional independence and with mastery of conceptual capabilities and practical skills that will strengthen cooperation and innovation. The visionary (or prophetic) appeal is for the realization of human potential, which Indigenous educators must somehow awaken. No one has to invent this potential, for the voices that speak to higher hopes already exist. This second appeal engages not only ecological and scientific sensibilities, but also the Indigenous humanities.

This educational reform is on the horizon, as is evident in the promising and successful programs and schools around the Indigenous world and also in the spirit of the TransCanada project itself. Indigenous intellectuals and professionals are animating Indigenous science, humanities, and legal traditions and exploring Indigenous pedagogy in order to produce new ways of developing sustainable education and lifelong learning. Such initiatives constitute the core tools of knowledge translation and needed capacity for revitalizing Indigenous civilizations and languages.

The emergence of Indigenous humanities as a result of educational reforms is especially evident in the growth of Indigenous arts—including the performing arts, literature, historiography, philosophy, and spirituality. This growth has compelled humanities scholars to rethink humanity—that is, how we are to relate to one another, and how we should learn to think together in order to generate a new global consciousness. The UN *Declaration* translated this transformation project in Article 11:

> Indigenous peoples have the right to practice and revitalize their cultural traditions and customs. This includes the right to maintain, protect and develop the past, present and future manifestations of their cultures, such as archaeological and historical sites, artefacts, designs, ceremonies, technologies and visual and performing arts and literature.

Similarly, Article 12(1) affirms that the "Indigenous peoples have the right to manifest, practice, develop and teach their spiritual and religious traditions, customs and ceremonies"; Article 13(1) affirms that "Indigenous peoples have the right to revitalize, use, develop and transmit to future generations their philosophies, their histories, their oral traditions, their writing system, and their literatures"; and Article 31(1) affirms the legitimacy of the Indigenous humanities by recognizing that "Indigenous peoples have the right to maintain, control, protect and develop their cultural heritage, traditional knowledge and traditional cultural expressions … and oral traditions, literatures, designs, sports and traditional games and visual and performing arts."

The UN declaration and its provisions on Indigenous humanities require that we move beyond the Eurocentric static, mythical, and romantic notions of Indigenous peoples as exotic cultures and recognize that Indigenous humanities are contemporary and global knowledge systems with relevance to and deep value for all. Humanity has the right to adopt new methods and techniques in order to displace the Eurocentric monopoly on knowledge production and to craft Indigenous theories and perspectives in law and health to enrich their senses and their cultural expressions.

The unfolding of the Indigenous renaissance enabled by the declaration document establishes the need to understand both how Indigenous peoples learn—their holistic theories of lifelong learning, their methods for nourishing the learning spirit, and the epistemologies that provide a stronger foundation for learning—and how IK and an Indigenous notion of humanities can be transmitted in restructured learning systems (whether in K–12 schools, post-secondary institutions, alternative schools, health and wellness programs, or the workplace) and in reformative and restorative justice. The declaration recognizes these principles in the realm of the arts. Thus Article 14 establishes the following:

1. Indigenous peoples have the right to establish and control their educational systems and institutions providing education in their own languages, in a manner appropriate to their cultural methods of teaching and learning.
2. Indigenous individuals, particularly children, have the right to all levels and forms of education of the State without discrimination.
3. States shall, in conjunction with indigenous peoples, take effective measures, in order for indigenous individuals, particularly children, including those living outside their communities, to have access, when possible, to an education in their own culture and provided in their own language.

And Articles 15 and 16(1) provide that

Indigenous peoples have the right to establish and control their educational systems and institutions providing education in their own languages, in a manner appropriate to their cultural methods of teaching and learning.

Indigenous peoples have the right to the dignity and diversity of their cultures, traditions, histories and aspirations, which shall be appropriately reflected in education and public information.

These rights affirm the many UNESCO conventions that preceded the declaration (Battiste, Bell, et al.). In an attempt to correct the past wrongs of government and education policies, the declaration declares in Article 7 that

1. Indigenous individuals have the rights to life, physical and mental integrity, liberty and security of person.
2. Indigenous peoples have the collective right to live in freedom, peace and security as distinct peoples and shall not be subjected to any act of genocide or any other act of violence, including forcibly removing children of the group to another group.

Article 8(1) specifically acknowledges that "Indigenous peoples and individuals have the right not to be subjected to forced assimilation or destruction of their culture," while Article 8(2) declares that states will provide effective mechanisms that prevent, and redress for

> (a) Any action which has the aim or effect of depriving them of their integrity as distinct peoples, or of their cultural values or ethnic identities; (b) Any action which has the aim or effect of dispossessing them of their lands, territories or resources; (c) Any form of forced population transfer which has the aim or effect of violating or undermining any of their rights; (d) Any form of forced assimilation or integration; (e) Any form of propaganda designed to promote or incite racial or ethnic discrimination directed against them.

Throughout the world, Indigenous scholars and learners are searching for the best current knowledge, for the most promising innovations that, together with the contemporary knowledge of Aboriginal learning, will inform more widely teachers, institutions, training programs, and policy makers in ways that will make a difference at all levels of achievement. As we have found in the work of the Aboriginal Learning Knowledge Centre, under the co-leadership of the Aboriginal Education Research Centre at the University of Saskatchewan and First Nations Adult and Higher Education in Calgary, Aboriginal lifelong learning is about acknowledging that learning is holistic, lifelong, experiential, rooted in Aboriginal languages and cultures, spiritually oriented, communal in nature, and integrative of Aboriginal and Western knowledges (Canada Council on Learning 2008).

Today around the world, Indigenous peoples continue to feel the tensions created by Eurocentric educational systems that teach us not to trust our own IK, and by an increasingly fragile environmental base that requires us to rethink how we interact with the earth and with one another. We are also becoming increasingly aware of the limitations of technological knowledge, of the possibilities and potential of IK, of the nature of our losses, and of the desperate need to repair our own systems. These tensions generate many quandaries that touch on issues of diversity, inclusivity, and respect. In order to protect IK, Indigenous educators must implement principles and rights against the Eurocentric biases and cultural appropriations that have endangered, and continue to endanger, Indigenous peoples' knowledge and languages. In schools, we must engage in a critique of curriculum and examine the connections between, and the framework of meanings behind, what is being taught, who is being excluded, and who is benefiting from public education.

Many Indigenous peoples, whose lands, languages, or relations were stolen, have been left with feelings of inadequacy and inauthenticity that add to their already diminished sense of worth. As a regeneration of community, culture, and ecology emerges, many feel inadequate to participate effectively on their own and thus turn to others. In schools, it is assumed that Indigenous educators are experts in all aspects of anti-racism and IK. This assumption generates further feelings of inadequacy. Such educators must do relational work with Elders in their communities and, above all, with their *place;* they must return to their land to find in its memory the holistic healing and inspiration necessary for the work ahead. Indigenous educators need to help colleagues and teachers become informed and effective participants by offering them protocols and processes for community relations.

It is crucial to protect IK, and not only for the sake of Indigenous peoples in their own environments. It is equally crucial to raise general awareness of the vitality of IK and its dynamic capacity to help solve contemporary problems. Indigenous science, with its sensibilities about the holistic interconnectedness of all things, can provide core foundations even for quantum physicists to rethink how humanity interacts with other life forms on this planet. For Indigenous peoples, that interaction is more direct. It is Indigenous peoples who are cultivating 80 percent of the world's natural biodiversity, a process that is taking place within the cultivation and daily use of our IK for food, health, and livelihood (CDS Indigenous Peoples' Caucus 14). Through Indigenous diplomacy in international forums, scientists and environmental activists have begun to recognize the potential of traditional ecological knowledge with regard to sustainability, although there is still much work to be done. Indigenous science must be made a priority or mission in education, not just for Indigenous students but for *all* students.

Within universities, over the past thirty years, Indigenous students and faculty, from education and law to the humanities, have generated a holistic area of study based on the animation and activation of IK; from this, new categories of knowledge formation and production and research have begun to emerge. Actively pursued as an academic and social agenda to remedy the structural poverty among Aboriginal peoples, the Aboriginal renaissance has created a "brand" for Indigenous educators and scholars to develop their scholarship and has gained a growing national and global reputation—witness, for example, how Indigenous diplomacy has influenced UNESCO and the ILO through the Permanent Forum on Indigenous Issues and the establishment of the Declaration on the Rights of Indigenous Peoples.

In those few exceptional universities that acknowledge IK, the struggle entails developing trans-systemic analyses and methods—that is, reaching beyond the distinct systems of Eurocentric knowledge to create fair and just educational systems and experiences. In engaging with this process, these institutions are involved in restoring not only fundamental educational rights but also human rights. This is part of the ultimate educational struggle, the future horizon of education: a regeneration of new relationships among and between knowledge systems as scholars competent in different knowledge systems seek to converge and reconcile them. Only once these analyses and methods in thought and behaviour materialize will we be able to create truly "higher" educational systems, places of connectedness and caring, places that honour the heritage, knowledge, and spirit of every Indigenous student, places that contribute to the building of trans-systemic knowledge for all students.

The Indigenous renaissance has shifted the agenda from recrimination to rebirth, from conflict to collaboration, from perceived deficiency to capacity. It has also been a major participant in the early shifts in university thinking from a defensive/assimilative story to a receptive/transformative story, one that accepts that the benefits to Aboriginal peoples are benefits to the entire academic community and the multiple publics. This process bears witness to the fact that innovation coming from diverse sources can lead to beneficial change for all. It is hoped that Eurocentric scholars and institutions will recognize the urgent need to respect and promote the inherent rights of Indigenous peoples as affirmed in the 2007 declaration. Those of us involved in the Indigenous renaissance hope that the Eurocentric university, its disciplines as well as its scholars and students, will honour the international law that affirms IK so that we can create a better environment for trans-systemic literatures, institutions, and citizenship.

The Indigenous renaissance is a reflection of the present, a light that is reaching all parts of the globe as the horizon unfolds. It generates a vision of a future that is important and transformative, a voice for the horizon and beyond, rather than preserving artifacts of the past. It does more than set the conditions for a fuller realization and indispensable expression of Indigenous potentiality, whose powers of experience, initiative, and creativity are never exhausted by the social and cultural worlds into which Indigenous people happen to have been born. Becoming active in the Indigenous renaissance allows Indigenous people to generate the good path to the future. But such a future cannot be constructed without creating the requisite space where Indigenous people can be heard and have their values recognized.

EPISTEMOLOGIES OF RESPECT
A Poetics of Asian/Indigenous Relation
Larissa Lai

I would like to begin this essay by acknowledging the Coast Salish people, on whose unceded territory I live and work. I make this acknowledgment for two reasons. First of all, I understand it as a protocol and a gesture of respect within the living practice of Coast Salish tradition. As an outsider to that tradition, however, I also make the gesture from the place of a personal ethics-under-construction, one that acknowledges my condition as a participant in settler culture, who benefits from that culture by virtue of having entered Canada with papers that the Canadian government considers legitimate. That personal ethics also includes a sense of responsibility to participate in the remaking of contemporary culture and an imagining of the nation to address the injustices of the past and present, in order to produce the future differently.

Anti-racist work of the past few decades constantly puts both First Nations people and people of colour in conversation with European settler cultures, but not with each other. This has been the case even though, as Henry Yu has noted, Asian and Aboriginal peoples were living, trading, and interacting with each other on the West Coast of the geographic space we now call Canada for a long time before the concept of "White Canada Forever" took hold on the West Coast, with ongoing repurcussions. But because that history is sparsely documented in text, those of us who were educated in the Western system tend to forget it.

In an essay titled "Decolonizasian," Rita Wong writes that the relationship between those marked as Asian Canadian and those marked as Indigenous is tainted with the problems of immigrant complicity in the colonization of the land, but remains nonetheless rich with possibilities for anti-colonial alliances.

Furthermore, as Sunera Thobani has recently remarked, when those designated as "people of colour" gain business advantage under official multiculturalism they reinforce the marginality of Aboriginal peoples (162). This is not to deny that immigrants of colour have suffered injustice in racialized terms at the hands of the Canadian state. I acknowledge here such historical facts as black slavery in Canada, the *Komagata Maru* incident, the internment of Japanese Canadians, and the Chinese Head Tax. However, even as people of colour struggle for rights, freedoms, and voice in the Canadian context, that very struggle supports the Western colonial project by reinforcing the legitimacy of the Canadian state while perpetuating the disenfranchisement of Indigenous peoples. I note these things not to pass judgment, but rather to acknowledge the historical and political conditions under which I write. Possibilities for alliance thus do exist at the level of anti-racist work, but are fraught at the level of relation to and identification with the state. It is in this tension that the possibility for what the Caribbean critic Édouard Glissant calls a "poetics of relation" arises, but such a poetics requires commitment, imagination, a willingness—in the face of unbreachable historically constituted difference—to not-know, and an acceptance of the fact that the route to alliances between Indigenous peoples and people of colour may be neither direct nor easy.

If land, language, and interdependence are what is at stake, then my initial desire is to backtrack so that the relationship can begin on the right footing, instead of after the fact of European colonization and Asian Canadians' acceptance of—and, indeed, struggles to enter into—the existing structures in the name of belonging to the nation. Yu's work, which recognizes Asian/Indigenous relations prior to the Canadian state, offers possibilities for such a footing, already historically grounded. However, I fear that even as we do recuperative work to insist on our own presence here, we do not always recognize how our actions reinforce the (relatively recent) state and capital in ways that deepen their colonial and neo-colonial relationship with Indigenous peoples. What's worse, it appears that backtracking is not possible. The colonial moment is still with us in the present. There is no romantic return. As the bearer of both US and Canadian citizenship, educated in an English valued through three generations of British colonial presence in Hong Kong, I am complicit even as I am colonized. What I want to ask, then, is how a poetics and a politics of relation between Asians like myself and the Indigenous peoples of the land we call Canada can be enacted, at this late hour, under these imperfect conditions. I recognize both categories—Asian and Indigenous—as Western constructs that are nevertheless materialized through repeated iterations in language, law, and lived experience.

The Mi'kmaq educator Marie Battiste writes about respect in the Mi'kmaw Concordat in a section called "Nikanikinútmaqn" (which she translates as "used to teach first"). With regard to the issue of respect, she writes:

> Since all things have a common origin in the sparks of life, every life-form and every object has to be respected. Just as a person has a life-force, so does a plant, rock or animal. Therefore, they are taught that everything one sees, touches or is aware of must be given respect. This respect requires people to develop a special consciousness that discourages the careless treatment of things ...
>
> The Mi'kmaq believe all people must be balanced: strong and weak, happy and angry, physical and spiritual. Balanced consciousness creates the best possible human beings. It is through the alliances forced by the life soul that such balance is achieved. (15)

Respect, then, involves a deep recognition of life forces as well as active movement towards the balance of life forces, which Battiste describes as spiritual, bodily, and soulful. It requires active knowledge of and engagement with Indigenous epistemologies and ways of being with the human, animal, vegetable, and elemental worlds.

In an essay titled "Go Away, Water! Kinship Criticism and the Decolonization Imperative," Daniel Heath Justice articulates an Indigenous ontology that is relational in its first instance. A practice of relation is necessary for historical continuity, in other words, for Indigenous contemporaneity. Justice emphasizes kinship as a practice that must be engaged and renewed. Kinship does not exist statically regardless of how we act (148). Without relationality, without continuity, Indigenous people and history are relegated to the status of artifacts of the past, in Western primitivist terms. Arguing against a letter by Delphine Red Shirt castigating certain Connecticut Native people for not being "Indian" because of the way they look, Justice attempts to push other Indigenous thinkers into recognizing the validity of Eastern US Indigenous people—including the Pequots, Mohegans, Paugausetts, Paucatucks, and Schaghticoke—noting that the fact that some Connecticut Native people don't look "phenotypically" Native has everything to do with histories of contact. The Pequots, Mohegans, Paugausetts, Paucatucks, and Schaghticoke have acted, Justice writes, as a "buffer" for Western nations such as the Oglala Sioux, shielding them from the worst of European genocidal activity (158). So there are relations among nations, whether this is acknowledged or not. And there is historical continuity within Indigenous nations, but a continuity that bears the marks of history, including changes in gene pools, which tend to happen with contact.

The purpose of Justice's essay, then, is to work through the complicated relations among Indigenous nations with differing orientations towards European
settlers and towards colonial history. For him, respect and acknowledgment
are necessary, from one nation to the next, because there are historical debts.
Respect includes acknowledgment of differences in appearance and genetic
makeup that have emerged from histories of contact, as well as acknowledgment of the heterogenous variety of experiences of "being Indian" and "looking Indian" within a broad community of Indigenous North Americans. While
the issues he discusses arise in the context of Indigenous nationalism, what
is productive in relation to my discussion here is the recognition of kinship
in difference. Sameness and likeness are not necessary in order to recognize
relation. In fact, the challenges of relation arise precisely through difference
and disagreement, as well as, for Indigenous peoples in the Americas, the
painful differential treatment that Indigenous nations received at the hands of
colonizers. Insofar as I am "Asian," I am not Indigenous to this land; yet insofar
as I am affected by the same colonial and neo-colonial forces that also affect
Indigenous peoples, certain aspects of Justice's discussion might be applicable
to the relations between First Nations peoples and Asian Canadians, and the
respect these relations must rely on.

What I want to think through here is twofold, then. First, what could a
politics and practice of respect look like for Asian Canadians engaged and
implicated in a settler culture? And second, for Asian Canadians who occupy
the contradictory site of both settler and colonial subject, what can we contribute towards turning the world to respectful balance? Because such a turn
cannot be a return, what constitutes balance in our contemporary moment
requires that we not romanticize or idealize the past.

I would like to draw attention to two important texts in the written literary
history of Asian/Indigenous relations in Canada: Lee Maracle's "Yin Chin"
and SKY Lee's *Disappearing Moon Cafe*, both of which Wong has discussed
at some length and with great clarity. These texts acknowledge past injustice
and attempt to take responsibility for that injustice in ways that make sense
in relation to their authors' specifically racialized locations. The root tragedy
of *Disappearing Moon Cafe* is the Chinese patriarch Wong Gwei Chan's aban-
donment of his mixed-race Indigenous wife of the Shi'atko clan, Kelora, who
rescued him when he was lost and starving in the mountains (Rita Wong
161). Although he loves her, he leaves her to do his filial duty by marrying
a "real Chinese" woman from China, whom he does not love (Lee 234–35).
Rita Wong notes:

> Gwei Chan's abandonment and betrayal of Kelora takes on both personal
> and social significance when we consider the role of cheap Chinese labour

in facilitating the appropriation of indigenous land by the Canadian government. The labour of Chinese railway workers supported not only their families but also a Canadian nation-building project based on the exclusion and exploitation of both First Nations and people of colour. (162)

For Wong, then, Gwei Chan's debt is specific to him as a character in Lee's novel, but it is also allegorical for the condition of Chinese Canadians within the Canadian state. In other words, we Chinese Canadians are indebted to the Indigenous peoples of the country some people call Canada. The early Chinese in Canada were exploited by the Canadian state and Canadian companies, yet they also participated in the colonial nation-building project that disenfranchised Indigenous peoples.

Wong writes that Gwei Chan's betrayal has "karmic" consequences that spread out to plague three generations of his own family. His grief is the grief of ingratitude. But Wong suggests that that grief and that ingratitude belong also to the likes of her, me, and the author SKY Lee. At the extra-diegetic level, Lee's gesture of respect is her recognition of the wrongs committed by Chinese immigrants against the Indigenous people who helped them. It is also, as Wong notes, a gesture of solidarity in that it recognizes an Asian/Indigenous relationship that includes desire and emotional connection, as well as (differential) subjugation to the same colonial and economic forces and (differential) connection to the land. Wong recognizes also that colonial record keepers repressed Asian/Indigenous relations in order to foreground white claims on the land (162). SKY Lee's gesture of respect is subtly gendered. She portrays Gwei Chan as a fool for betraying Kelora. In so doing, she offers a critique of Chinese/Confucian patriarchy. There is an implicit suggestion in her novel, then, that were this West Coast world left to women, such tragedy and such betrayal would not have occurred.

"Yin Chin," a short story in Sojourner's Truth that Lee Maracle dedicates to SKY Lee and Jim Wong-Chu, is likewise generously self-reflexive. In this story, the narrator recalls a moment when she helped an old Chinese woman being harassed by a Native man on the street. The memory of that moment opens onto another memory from the narrator's childhood, in which she watched old Chinese men for weeks to make sure they didn't snatch and eat young children, as she learned from "the words of the world" (293) that they did. The crucial and telling moment in "Yin Chin" occurs in the aftermath of the narrator's childhood memory, given in a long flashback, about an old Chinese man she observed from inside a Chinese grocery store that belonged to "Mad Sam" (294). As a child, the narrator watched the old Chinese man shuffling down the street and fantasized seeing the old man's face suddenly up against her own. She screamed, which caused Mad Sam and her mother to come running. When Mad Sam and the child's mother wanted to know why she screamed, the child said, "the chinaman was looking at me" (294). Her mother felt ashamed, and Mad Sam felt hurt (294). What is brave and respectful in the narrative voice of "Yin Chin" is the personal and particular ways in which the Indigenous narrator assumes responsibility for what is, at a deeper level, a social and systemic denigration of Asian people that hardly comes from an Indigenous source, although Indigenous people as members of the wider society are not exempt from participating in it. This systemic debasement includes the racist laws of the late nineteenth and early twentieth centuries—the Head Tax and the Chinese Exclusion Act—which functioned, among other things, to keep Chinese men away from their families. The myth about Chinese men eating children might perhaps be read as a racist interpretation of the longing for children that many sojourners experienced.

Both Lee's novel and Maracle's short story are instances of respect in action, a self-reflexive respect that acknowledges the other, that gestures towards taking responsibility for oneself—both personally and historically—in the face of larger social forces. This respect recognizes both that history is not over and that inequities remain, as do possibilities for a turn to balance, as Marie Battiste describes it. Indeed, both of these works are actions towards a renewal of balance, as well as a clarity of vision—the beginnings of seeing one another. They are precisely what the 2006 Harper apology for the Chinese Head Tax and the 2008 Residential School apology, in their drive towards closure, are not. (This, of course, does not mean that the apologies were not necessary or that they haven't had some healing effects. However, both apologies remain controversial, though for different reasons.)[1] The work of both Lee Maracle and SKY Lee does not brush people aside so that Canadian society can get on with the business-as-usual of global capital. Rather, they pose challenges and enter into new kinds of relations between Asian and Indigenous people that do not attempt to deny the ongoing nature of historical inequity that invariably rears its head in new forms.

Having recognized these important early texts, I would like to discuss three recent creative interventions into the possibilities and problems of Asian/Indigenous relations. The first is a 2008 performance called *How We Forgot Here* by The Movement Project, a Toronto-based group of First Nations women and women of colour that includes Marika Schwandt, Gein Wong, Eva Tabobondung, and Malinda Francis. The Movement Project uses a wide range of media—visual projection, film, theatre, live electronic music, spoken word poetry, and audience participation. Set on board a fictional airline called Ojibway Air, the performance begins in the ticket line. The questions "How did you get here?" and "What are your intentions?", when asked by the Aboriginal Customs Officer played by Eva Tabobondung of the Anishinaabe Nation, mean something quite different than when they are asked by a representative of the Canadian state. These questions propel two passengers, Malinda and Jun, as well as the flight attendant, Fatima, into reveries about their own families' histories of displacement, movement, and settlement.

The questions instigated at the outset—who has the right to control movement, and who gives whom the right to stay or go?—remain present throughout and point to a larger set of questions around the legalities and ethics of ownership, particularly in parts of the country that remain unceded territory. What if passport control and airlines were run by Indigenous people instead of the Canadian state and settler corporations sanctioned through Canadian law? The norms, laws, and social practices regarding movement and the settlement of land would be completely different—different in ways that are hard, though not impossible, to imagine.

How We Forgot Here is not a play that strives for resolution. Its drive seems, rather, to be directed towards an articulation that makes (air)space to acknowledge a kind of relationality in movement between Indigenous people and people of colour. Self-consciously interactive, it begins at the site of an airport

How We Forgot Here. Photo: Tanya Lai

lounge, which is, in fact, the lounge of the makeshift theatre space where the play is being put on. Attendees are interpellated as both audience members and airline passengers on a flight run by the fictional Ojibway Air. A number of the actors, in their roles as customs officials, headed by the main Customs Officer played by Eva Tabobondung, draw the attendees in. As passengers and audience, attendees are implicated from the outset, and this implication is deepened when audience members/passengers are separated into "First Class" and "Economy Class," mostly on the basis of racial appearance. Most of the visibly "white" audience members are sent below into Economy Class, and most of the people of colour and Indigenous people are sent upstairs to First Class." A straight, white, male character—John Smith (played by actor Ryan Symington)—is held for questioning and interrogated about his origins and intentions for so long that he misses the "flight."

The engagement and implication of all those attending the performance draw the audience into a sense of responsibility for the events that occur. And, of course, the framework of the play's "discrimination" largely employs the same categories and tactics that the Canadian state has historically employed (without quotations marks) to control its variously racialized citizenry and to ensure the privilege of some over others. But this is precisely the play's point. Many of the settler participants in the performance—both cast and audience members—are heavily grilled about their intentions and origins by the customs officers before they are allowed to settle into the "flight." We witness the Customs Officer played by Tabobondung questioning a passenger called Malinda, who is on her way to attend her mother's funeral. Because the Customs Officer is Aboriginal, the questions she asks, although they sound standard, work in unexpected ways, particularly when she asks Malinda: "Where are you from?" (8). For Malinda, a racialized woman, the question is loaded. She is discomfited and exasperated. "My family is scattered," she says (8). This customs officer, however, is more interested than the ones this attendee usually encounters at borders. She asks, "Did you scatter yourselves, or did you get scattered?" (8). In spite of her uniform and her imposing manner, her engagement is neither comfortably distant nor safely legalistic. She asks hard questions: "Whose land is your house on?" (8). But then she also says strangely intimate things, such as "We've needed help for a long time" (8). The Customs Officer holds Malinda accountable for her presence, but it is not across a great divide, in spite of Malinda's surly impatience. Their conversation is tense with suspicion and resentment but also strangely intimate. We learn how each has come to acquire English, and there is a measure of sympathy between them because each has lost her mother. In the end, the Customs Officer allows Malinda to go to her mother's funeral.

The airline, Ojibway Airlines, is itself humorously aware of the conditions that face immigrants to Canada. The Stewardess's safety demo closes with a list of flight hazards:

> Please note that Ojibway Airlines is not responsible for any unforeseen events occurring after de-planing: if your education isn't recognized; if you are incarcerated; if people yell at you to speak English; if you find the system to be undemocratic; or if your children's children are still serving tables and cleaning floors. For a list of potential side effects of migration, please see your in-flight magazine. (10)

Once the plane rises into the air, it becomes a space of dreams and reminiscences about the suffering of racialized immigrants and the circumstances that have brought them to Native land. Their dreams, hopes, and memories offer a counterpoint to the gestures of policing and judgment that marked the opening of the show.

The second immigrant tale we hear is Jun's, and we hear it high in the air, in mid-flight. The tale of Jun's grandmother's escape from "the new" (i.e., Communist) government of China—she swims across a stretch of the South China Sea to freedom in Hong Kong, with only a basketball to keep her afloat—is relayed to us as an actual audio interview by Jun of her grandmother, which we hear while a dancer mimes the story behind a screen, so that we only see shadows of a human figure.

What makes this performance powerful, then, is its engagement with the world of the actor-participants themselves. While certain of its aspects are necessarily staged and aestheticized, it remains committed to lives lived in the City of Toronto and their connections with other parts of the world, as well as to Indigenous histories in southern Ontario. The play draws no conclusions about the tales of suffering and disillusionment it offers. It does not call for recognition, apology, return, or balance. But in a telling scene towards the end, Fatima the Stewardess talks about the fact that her home exists in movement: "This airspace is where I'm from. This is my neighbourhood, my village. I've always lived here" (17). After Fatima the Stewardess speaks, the Customs Officer tells a story about the storms on her reservation in Wakausing, about playing games of Word Search with her Nookmis, about her move to Toronto, about how Wakausing has changed since her departure, and also about her own sense of displacement even as she feels a connection to the land (18–20).

How We Forgot Here is largely a memory work; its stories are the "true" stories of Indigenous women and women of colour struggling to survive and live in a system built not for them, but around them—existing in order to use them. Like the stories of Lee Maracle and SKY Lee, these characters' stories are relayed both to recognize suffering and to place racialized settlers in conversation with Indigenous peoples. The play does not strive to resolve the shortcomings of Canadian history, except perhaps insofar as the Customs Officer and the Stewardess exercise a kind of power over the passengers that manifests itself in terms that are more favourable to racialized passengers and less favourable to whites than the currently existing system. The Stewardess Fatima's recognition of her own life as one of movement and the Customs Officer's recognition of her grandmother and her place on the land draw them into the cycle of storytelling that engages the plane's passengers. For indeed, although these two positions are embodied, and in a sense "en-historied," in ways that destabilize the Canadian government and airline norms, they retain the power to police, repress, and contain. In giving the Customs Officer and the Stewardess the space to tell their personal stories, the play also recognizes that these characters are more than simply officials. In a sense, it returns their individual humanity, with all the fraughtness attached to such a notion, including individuality's valuation as a colonial ideal that historically marked Europeans as "superior" for holding it; as a national democratic ideal that values universal franchise and other citizenship rights; and as, increasingly, an international humanitarian ideal, one that holds the individual up as human in order that her or his human rights not be violated.

Interestingly, the last personal story to be told is one that was recorded from a random "diasporic person" (1) drawn from the audience as its coalescing members waited in the lobby of the theatre for the play to start. Such a closing gesture, I argue, works—along with audience participation in the checking of passports and the seating of audience members according to the play's internal rules—to produce audience and players as "singular plural" in the sense that Jean-Luc Nancy[2] describes in *Being Singular Plural*:

> The "meaning of Being": not only as the "meaning of with," but also, and above all, as the "with" of meaning. Because none of these three terms precedes or grounds the other, each designates the coessence of the others. The coessence puts essence itself in the hyphenation—"being singular plural"— which is a mark of union and also a mark of division, a mark of sharing that effaces itself, leaving each term to its isolation *and* [emphasis in original] its being-with-the-others. (37)

Hailed this way, audience and cast break the bounds of Cartesian subjectivity without entirely losing the specificity of their historical and personal experience. The question of what to do with grief and the gifts of dubious power remains hanging in mid-air—or Indigenous airspace—as the place of memory and possibility, before touching down on the contested land.

How We Forgot Here is community theatre with an experimental edge. By contrast, David Khang's *How to Feed a Piano* belongs to a Western avant-garde performance tradition, but one infused with concern for embodied histories and a politics of the local. It also offers the possibility of "being singular plural," or a rebalancing of power, although its strategies and contexts are quite different from those of the Movement Project. *How to Feed a Piano* was mounted in 2008 at Vancouver's Centre A, on the corner of Hastings and Carrall Streets, in the heart of Vancouver's Downtown Eastside, on the edge of Chinatown. In other words, Centre A is right at the intersection where the traditional "loh wah kiu" Chinese Canadian community encounters the most downtrodden of the city's poor, many of whom are urban Indigenous people. Centre A is a contemporary art centre with a mandate to "provide a platform for contemporary Asian art that engages, educates, stimulates a reflective experience and provokes critical thought" ("Centre A"). Highly aware of where he is working, David Khang addresses questions of authorship, or the power of inscription. *How to Feed a Piano* is a piece, then, that deals with both agency and "asiancy" in the sense that Roy Miki means it, as the problem of speaking and writing from a racialized location that does not easily reproduce the master's voice. Miki writes:

> At one extreme, in the tension between inside and outside, the inside can be so subordinated to the outside that it cannot recognize its specificity at all. Such a hierarchic determinacy almost inevitably results in an identity formation in which the dominant values outside come to censor, repress, or otherwise propagandize the inside. Once the foundation of this "self" is undermined, however, as it is when a subject begins to mistrust its conditioned reactiveness, a process of reversals can come into play. There is, initially, a recognition that both poles in the interchange, inside and outside, are constructs dependent on each other for their existence, and bounded by social, psychological, cultural, political, and historical constraints characteristic of a body politics in which minority subjects are denied or otherwise contained. ("Asiancy" 113)

Quoting Gail Scott, Miki asks, "'What if the surfacing unconscious stream finds void instead of code?'" (114). If this propagandized, oscillating subject is the one who also occupies the positions "settler" and "author," then surely, from this wounded location, he can offer a kind of movement we have not seen before. For indeed, Khang's work is highly aware of the problems of history, race, embodiment, and geography. However, he also addresses more hegemonic forms of agency—the author as it is conceived by thinkers like Roland Barthes, as the seat of a master discourse but also a potent illusion.

In *How to Feed a Piano*, Khang applies his "asiancy" most directly to the composer La Monte Young's highly formalist work, titled *Piano Piece for David Tudor #1*, which prescribes the following:

> Bring a bale of hay and a bucket of water onto the stage for the piano to eat and drink. The performer may then feed the piano or leave it to eat by itself. If the former, the piece is over after the piano has been fed. If the latter, it is over after the piano eats or decides not to. (2)

Khang ambitiously materializes Young's prescription and simultaneously circulates the agency of writing, painting, and music making through a range of locations. In so doing, he explores whether he can divest himself of authorial/painterly agency, rather than whether he can keep it.

The second major reference for *How to Feed a Piano* is the *Anthropometry* projects of the French avant-garde artist Yves Klein. At the most obvious level, Khang takes up the problem of agency in Klein. Klein himself is interestingly complicated on the problem:

> We must individually practice pure imagination. The imagination of which I am speaking is neither a perception, nor the memory of a perception, nor a familiar memory, nor a habitual sense of colors and form. It has nothing to do with the five senses, with the domain of feeling or even with the purely and fundamentally emotional. That would be the imagination of artists who will never be able to participate, for in their desire to preserve individuality at all cost, they kill their fundamental spiritual selves and lose their lives.... For those artists prepared to cooperate, imagining means withdrawing, leaping forward to a new life. In their combined élan, going out into all directions and dimensions, they are paradoxically at once unified and apart. ("Evolution" 76)

Klein, then, does not value the kind of individual authorship that ignores its connectivity to others. But by the same token, he wields a kind of artistic control that seems egocentric to the extreme (especially in our historical moment, I admit). Speaking of his *Anthropometry* projects, in which he attempted to close the gap between the medium of representation (i.e., canvas) and the object of representation (i.e., the model), he used live models as instruments with which to directly apply paint to the canvas.

These models, all beautiful young (white) women, he designated as "living brushes," directing them from a carefully measured authorial distance.

> Due to the fact that I have painted with living brushes—in other words, the nude body of live models covered with paint: these living brushes were under

the constant direction of my commands, such as "a little to the right; over to the left now; to the right again, etc...." By maintaining myself at a specific and obligatory distance from the surface to be painted, I am able to resolve the problem of detachment. ("Chelsea Hotel" 85)

Of course, the sexist objectification of women's bodies at work here is, at this belated and beleaguered feminist moment, obvious to the point of hilarity, which doesn't stop it from offensively erupting again in the present.[3] While this aspect of Klein's much-respected work seems dated, his concept of the void still has vitality to it and remains productively in play in David Khang's work. For Klein, the notion of the void, or the immaterial, was a key innovation. In a sense, Klein took forms that the public thought it understood and replaced their content with carefully thought through non-content—what Klein called "the immaterial"—in such a way that his viewers could perceive the void being shown them and experience it in a profound way. I would like to suggest here that, just as Klein emptied form of content to produce new artistic experience, so Khang empties the author/artist of agency, in a Barthesian sense, only to have that agency erupt at a range of (raced) human and animal locations, in such a way as to transform both the human and the animal and at the same time reintroduce to his scenario a balance of (inscribing) power.

The performance begins with two piano players seated on a high platform, playing an improvised duet—for David Tudor, as it were—on a baby grand

How to Feed a Piano. Photo courtesy David Khang

How to Feed a Piano. Photo courtesy David Khang

piano. The agency of artmaking appears to reside with them, as performers and improvisers. Khang appears on the platform and begins to feed hay to the piano by forking it under the piano's lid. Through sleight of hand and foot, Khang is "eaten" by the piano. He falls into its centre, only to reappear, once a curtain is pulled, on the ground level, harnessed to a horse. The horse's handler, played by Secwepemc poet and rancher Garry Gottfriedson, covers him in blue paint, while the rider, played by the Tlingit curator Candice Hopkins, puts on boots and chaps and mounts the horse. Horse and rider then pull the naked, paint-covered Khang in a wide circle on the paper-covered floor, in effect "painting" it with Khang's body as the instrument of inscription.

Where agency is located in this scenario depends on what gesture one understands as the gesture of authorship. If it is the gesture of making marks on a page—the gesture that in the Judeo-Christian tradition lies at the root of law-making and knowledge making—then agency moves from Gottfriedson the horse handler to the horse itself to the rider who guides the horse. If one understands agency more broadly, then it moves from the piano players improvising on La Monte Young's piece, to the piano as it "eats" Khang, to Gottfriedson, to the horse, and finally to Hopkins, the rider. One might argue that at a meta-level, Khang's authorial position still permeates this scene, but it can hardly be said to dominate it. If anything, the notion of authorship itself is utterly abjected as Khang's paint-covered naked body is pulled across the floor. It would be possible to argue that there is a kind of abject authorial *jouissance* still in play here, although this is not a reading that the performance seems to foreground. What it does foreground is the movement of the signifying gesture through a range of variously embodied agents, thus intentionally confusing the significance of the sign made by the "living paintbrush." There is a bit of Derridean humour at work here: a chain of signifiers (or what Henry Louis Gates calls "signifying monkeys," i.e., the signifiers are active and embodied) points to a void at the site of the signified. Or, the signifying monkeys produce a sign of their own—a sign that signifies nothing. At the end of the performance, the trace on the floor is one of a giant "O"—a big zero, a sign of Miki's void, Klein's immaterial, or the abject's *jouissance*—a blue depth of profound nothing.

Given the objectification of the naked body pulled behind the horse, with all of its race and gendered significations, if there is a single authority in the mastermind position, its boundaries are rapidly dissolved. It cycles fluidly through the wide range of the performance's participants. As it does so, the bounded subjectivity of the "author"—which is so connected to the Cartesian subject and to the production of master discourses—becomes less bounded and thus enters into a fluid relation with the loosened subjectivities of the other players in the scenario. Subjectivity is not lost here; instead, it retains a kind of nodal quality, but one that is de-emphasized in favour of a kind of flow of agencies through racialized and animal locations.

In querying, shifting, and ultimately obliterating the site of authorship, Khang offers possibilities for relations in difference that do not rely on authorship as a privileged site. Authorship and agency have long been valued terms in Western Enlightenment discourses, and indeed, they remain so, at least to a certain extent, for those of us who belong to non-Western cultures but whose lives are deeply entwined with the West. But through this multiracial and multi-species confounding of the authorial position, Khang reconfigures the subject itself. Subjectivity becomes productively entangled in a poetics of relation that re-produces it as singular plural. Khang, the piano, the piano players, Garry Gottfriedson, Candice Hopkins, and the horse—and by corollary, the audience itself—all enter into the singular plurality produced in this performance and thus become open vessels through which the power to inscribe flows.

One might argue, as the performance's Indian/Cowboy horse rider and catalogue essayist Candice Hopkins does, that there is a kind of Deleuzian becoming at work here (Khang 69).[4] Khang offers us an instance of ontology of the future that does not erase the subjectivities of the colonial past/ present but offers us another form of being-in-addition that frees us from the boundedness of Cartesian subjectivity. Or, perhaps better, he offers us a range of ontologies attached to extra-historical temporalities, not necessarily of the future, but of the past, and indeed of alternative presents. Describing Khang's "becoming animal" as it pertains to the strangely agented horse in *How to Feed a Piano*, and also in relation to another performance of Khang's, *Phallogocentrix*, in which he holds a giant beef tongue dipped in ink in his mouth and uses it to incribe text on the floor in a number of languages, Hopkins notes that to become (an) animal is not to become subhuman but rather to elevate oneself spiritually, since in West Coast Indigenous tradition, animals are superior to humans in both intellect and strength (69). Such a becoming leaps into an Indigenous traditional past, but also across cultures, using intercultural desires and critical methods of the present. It is thus also future-directed, since there is still a kind of utopianism at work here, one that hopes for a future in which we transnational human-animals might all belong, a future in which Indigenous knowledges are respected and the world is re-turned to balance.

Marie Clements's extraordinary *Burning Vision*, the last work I would like to consider in this essay, is a play that might help us think through these multiple becomings and further articulate a knowledge system that foregrounds respect specifically in the context of Asian/Indigenous relations, although not necessarily exclusive to them. Like Khang's performance work, Clements's play emphasizes the relationship between humans and the living world in which we are embedded, as much as she emphasizes relations among humans.

Burning Vision addresses the historical fact of uranium mining on Sathu Dene territory at Great Bear Lake in the 1930s and 1940s. Both Sathu Dene and white men were employed by the mines to extract uranium, without being told of the dangers of radioactivity. As a result, many developed cancer, and many died of it. The power relations at work were such that more often than not, white men were foremen while the Dene men were hired as workers. However, all of the miners were kept equally in the dark regarding the dangers of radioactivity. The mining companies were callous in their treatment of the miners and ore carriers, and their families. Warnings about radioactivity were so absent, that the men brought empty carrying bags home with them and the women used those bags to make tents. Children played in piles of uranium tailings as though they were sandboxes. Between shifts, men would sometimes lie down and rest on the bags of uranium ore. In her research on uranium mining, Clements was shocked to learn that uranium from the mines at Great Bear Lake was the same uranium that found its way into the atomic bombs that were dropped on Hiroshima and Nagasaki in 1945, killing 220,000 Japanese people and leaving a legacy of trauma and illness that haunts us to this day.

Dene elders recognized the connection between Great Bear Lake uranium and those two atomic bombs. In the 1990s a group of them flew to Japan to meet with Japanese survivors (Wong, "Decolonizasian" 168). The expansiveness in this gesture takes us beyond questions of individual accountability in

Burning Vision. Photo courtesy Tim Matheson

the eyes of Western individualist law. It is marked, I would like to argue, by a logic of respect, a logic Clements takes up in her play.

Temporally, Clements structures the play in four movements. Although each has its own opening framing, the first movement implies a co-temporality among all four and among the scenes within each movement. Clements offers us the sound of a radio dial as it picks up different stations, which she calls *"scenes in different cultural tones as if stories are sitting on radio waves"* (19, italics in original). (Clements's stage directions are characteristically difficult here, privileging the evocative over the concretely specific.) The stories of a range of characters unfold in the play, juxtaposed beside one another so that they seem to be happening on different "stations" at the same time. These characters include Little Boy, who is both a young Native boy and the personification of uranium; Fat Man, who is both an American bomb test dummy and the bomb itself; Tokyo Rose, the (in)famous radio announcer who broadcast to American troops during the Second World War and was accused of treason;

Round Rose, a character based on the Japanese American woman Iva Toguri, who after the war was prosecuted, possibly unfairly, by the US government for being "Tokyo Rose"; a Dene widow; her husband, an ore carrier; a Japanese fisherman named Koji who was fishing off the coast of Japan just prior to the atomic blast; Koji's grandmother; Rose, a Métis baker; a white miner at Port Radium; the LaBine Brothers, prospectors who were credited with the "discovery" of the uranium deposit; and many others.

Implicit in Clements's unconventional use of radio stations as a device is, I think, the pun on the word "radioactive." In the atomic age, "radioactivity" produces active radio waves. As a "radio activist," Clements uses the structure of radio time to show us our relations with one another as much more deeply co-present than we are used to imagining them. That co-presence is not utopic; it is fraught will all the violence of colonial and neo-colonial relations blasted into atomic synchronicity.

Let me explain. The first events we witness in Clements's radioactive temporality are the dropping of the atomic bomb on Hiroshima, the discovery of pitchblende by the LaBine Brothers, the Widow of a Dene Ore Carrier speaking to the boots of her dead husband, and the making of bread by a young Métis woman named Rose. These moments are all instances in the history of the movement of uranium from its place beneath the surface of the earth at Great Bear Lake to its detonation at Hiroshima and Nagasaki near the end of the Second World War. Clements uses the sound of a radio dial being turned to offer us these different historical events as though they were playing on different stations. They are co-temporal with one another on her radio, although taking place on different frequencies. In the linear time of colonization and settlement, the events portrayed are disparate from one another. But in the time of Clements's active radio, they are drawn close through the metaphor of the radio dial. By making them co-temporal on her radio dial, Clements makes the players intimates in a way they would not be in the Western linear imagination. In setting them up this way, she produces a kind of "radioactive" kinship among the players in the story of the movement of uranium from its source at Great Bear Lake to its detonation at Hiroshima and Nagasaki.

It is useful to note that the kinship-producing, "radioactive" time of the play is auditory time, time that privileges hearing as a sense. If we are good listeners, we can hear how closely related these events are to one another. While sound holds together a range of scenarios and offers a range of truths, the best listening takes place in the dark, and the deepest truths are offered then. Tokyo Rose lets us in on the connections among sound, the dark, and the truth when she asks her listeners: "Now what memory holds your regret in the dark? Does it come when the lights are out and those you love have gone before you like a silent witness [*sic*]? Does it reach up when the dark gets loud and whispers the truth in your ear like a good mother after death?" Although Tokyo Rose is very clear in these lines, which occur later in the play, we are in fact given the connections among dark, sound, and truth in the very first scene, when we hear Little Boy, as the spirit of "the darkest uranium," speaking about the foolishness of the Western concept of discovery as he waits beneath the earth to be discovered by the LaBine Brothers, and their "radio footsteps" draw closer:

> Every child is scared of the dark, not because it is dark but because they know sooner, or later, they will be discovered. It is only a matter of time ...
>
> *The radio footsteps and laboured breath get closer.*
>
> ... before someone discovers you and claims you for themselves. Claims you are you because they found you. Claims you are theirs because they were the first to find you and lay claims on you ...
>
> *The radio footsteps and laboured breath get closer and closer. The two beams of light circle towards him.*
>
> ... Not knowing that you've known yourself for thousands of years. (20–21)

If, in Clements's metaphysical order, sound and dark offer a kind of ethical truthfulness, then light belongs to the realm of the stupid, brutal, and deceptive. In this early speech by Little Boy, negatively valenced discovery is associated with light, as the flashlights waved by the Brothers LaBine, who are coming to discover him, show us.

But the brothers' flashlights also show us another temporality that simultaneously structures the play—a temporality that relies on our sense of sight. Sight, vision, and light in Clements's metaphysical order are associated with the European Enlightenment and missionary Christianity. These are not positive values for her, since they are tied directly to colonialism, the displacement of Indigenous knowledge systems by Eurocentric ones, and thus to both cultural and physical genocide. For example, Little Boy insists that he (as the "personification of the darkest uranium" [13]) is not bad in and of himself but rather that "the real monster is the light of these discoveries" (41). The LaBine Brothers carry flashlights as they descend into the earth to "discover" uranium. The light of discovery becomes connected to the light of Christian salvation when the second LaBine Brother's flashlight breaks and a scratchy LP rendition of Hank Williams's "I Saw the Light" begins to play over the theatre's sound system. Williams sings:

> I wander so aimless, life filled with sin
> I wouldn't let my dear Savior in.

> Then Jesus came like a stranger in the Night.
> Praise the Lord I saw the light. (qtd. in Clements 25)

The Christian faith that lights the LaBine Brothers' way, after the flashlight of discovery breaks, is connected, in the next scene, to the European proselytization of Indigenous people and to the capitalist colonialism that accompanied it. On the same stage, at the same time—on a different radio frequency, as it were—the Métis baker Rose puts on her mother's Sunday dress, not to go to church but to go to work in her father's Hudson's Bay store—or, as the widow calls it, the "Here Before Christ store" (55). It is important to note here that Rose's father is Irish and her mother Indigenous. (Speaking of her father's gentle pressuring of her to get married, Rose says: "He gave me the old blue eye and said, 'Things are different in the Old country [sic].' My mother would say, 'We are the old country [sic]'" [26].) So, then, it is an Indigenous woman's churchgoing dress that Rose puts on to do the work of commerce. In this moment, the dress is emphasized. Rose says: "Her Sunday dress is carrying this sack of flour" (26). In other words, the churchgoing Indigenous woman does the heavy lifting for colonial capitalism. Or more precisely, the costume she wears makes her body do the labour of colonial capitalism.

But the light of discovery, which becomes the light of Christian faith, is, for racialized people, the last light one sees before dying. Rose casts a fishing line that whizzes across the stage to another frequency on the radio dial, and we meet Koji, a Japanese man fishing off the coast of Japan just prior to the atomic blast. His grandmother walks past him, carrying the body of a man, which we learn is Koji's own body, down a tunnel of light, as though to death. The connection of the tunnel of light to death is emphasized by what we hear played over the speakers—Hank Williams singing:

> I saw the light I saw the light.
> No more darkness no more night.
> Now I'm so happy no sorrow in sight.
> Praise the Lord I saw the light. (qtd. in Clements 31)

Koji is a interesting character because, within the logic of Clements's active radio—that is, within the logic of sound—he lives, and goes on to love Rose and having a child with her. But within the logic of light—that is, the logic of the atomic blast—he is dead at the start of the play. His grandmother is a liminal figure who carries him through deadly light to darkness, sound, and life. Or more literally, she carries him through the tunnel of light and leaves him at a cherry tree. She asks him to always return there and wait for her, should he lose her for any reason.[5] As she leaves him, the Japanese grandmother tells Koji, "You will be safe as long as you talk to the cherry tree's back" (33). Invoking speech and hiddenness—in other words, invoking sound and darkness—she leaves him, and the tunnel of light disappears.

As it does, we see Fat Man turn on his light. This is important because it is the first instance in the play in which Clements uses the turning off of a light in one area of the stage, and the turning on of another light at a separate spot on the stage, as a device to link scenes. All prior scenes are connected through shared sound or, occasionally, the beaming of light from one area of the stage to another. This particular use of light sets Fat Man apart from all the other characters linked through the active radio. Fat Man can hear the radio on his super-high-tech hi-fi set, but he doesn't hear well, and the other characters don't seem to hear him.[6]

Fat Man is an isolated figure and a figure of pure technology. Literally, he is a bomb test dummy, but his name is obviously taken from the name of the bomb dropped on Nagasaki on 9 August 1945. At 4600 kilograms, the atomic bomb code-named "Fat Man" was the bigger of the two bombs and killed between 40,000 and 75,000 people. If Clements's Little Boy is figured as raw uranium and the starting point in nature of the bomb's construction, then her Fat Man is figured as the encultured, technologized, and violent end point.

Although Fat Man has a hi-fi set and is associated with technology in general, he is figured as constantly sitting in his La-Z-Boy chair in front of his television drinking beer (and, on a good night, flipping through *Playboy* magazines and having sexual fantasies about the end of the world). In other words, he owns and uses sound technology as well as technologies of vision, but he is associated more closely with the latter. Short-sighted, stupid, propagandized and propagandizing, but oddly charming in spite of all that, Clements's Fat Man is a figure of that form of Western subjectivity—or, perhaps more accurately, American subjectivity—that can know itself only by radically othering all forms of difference. He is a caricature, and Clements, by making him a bomb test dummy, figures him as such. Fat Man is a dummy in both senses of the word. And he is all about appearances. He tells us about it himself:

> I look good. I mean I'm dressed for the part and frankly between you and me that's half the battle.
>
> *He sits back down and gets comfy in his lazy-boy chair.*
>
> If you look the part people are just as happy to accept that. We want the unreal real thing. We don't want studies. We want tests. We don't want thinking, we want reaction. Highly skilled unthinking reaction. (29)

Here he is essentially offering a critique of himself. Or he is offering the public a critique of itself figured as Fat Man. In spite of his sometimes quite charming self-reflexivity, Fat Man will not and cannot see or know the world except in the ways it comes to him through his technologies, which always provide the "unreal real"—similacra and stereotypes. His technologies are all technologies of radical othering. So, through the television set, he gets Little Boy, who literally steps through the screen into Fat Man's living room, as a son. But he can only understand Little Boy in terms of Indigenous stereotypes; he cannot see Little Boy's complexities; he certainly cannot see that Little Boy is the personification of the darkest uranium. (When Little Boy watches television from Fat Man's living room, he sees the stereotyped head of an "Indian Chief.") And through his hi-fi set, Fat Man gets Tokyo Rose, the radio personality, as a wife. (He does recognize her, occasionally, as Round Rose, a.k.a. Iva Toguri, in other words as a "real" woman, but this recognition is always fleeting.) There is a hilarious but also devastating scene in which Fat Man drives Tokyo Rose and Little Boy from his house because they are aliens and he has to protect his family from them: "I want you two aliens to get the hell out of my living room. You hear me? I want you two aliens to leave" (98). He is stumped and dismayed by the recognition that his family members *are* aliens: "Where is my family? What did I say? I didn't mean you. I didn't mean it. I said it.... I did it ... but I didn't mean it!" (98). But as a piece of othering technology perceiving the world through more othering technology, he cannot see them except as aliens. He is truly a "dummy." After all the devastation he has wreaked, Fat Man apologizes, but cluelessly so: "I'm sorry. What did I do wrong?" (99). Through the figure of Fat Man, Clements offers us a brilliant critique of state violence and its feeble attempts to be accountable.[7] Moreover, she attaches this critique to the rise of technology, particularly technologies of vision that show us the world as separate from ourselves. And of course the ultimate other-producing technology, and the ultimate flash of light, is the atomic bomb itself. The play's title, *Burning Vision*, now makes brutal and horrifying sense. The technologies of vision burn everything in sight.

To summarize, then, in Clements's metaphysics, sound and darkness belong to the radio as a technology, to the drawing close of kinships, to the associative, simultaneous co-temporality of the "active radio," and to life, while vision and light belong to television as a technology, to European Enlightenment knowledge systems and the practice of "discovery," to missionary Christianity, to radical othering, to linear, capital "H" History, to atomic explosion, and to death.

But there is a deeper structure in the play that binds sounds and vision, dark and light, life and death together in a historically specific way, one that places all of these binaries in "radioactive" kinship with one another. These relationships are painful and death-dealing but they are also loving and life-giving.

That "radioactive" structure, I argue, is primarily associative—it is juxtapositional and parallel, as opposed to linear and hierarchical, and the production of this radioactive, juxtapositional structure, I suggest, is Clements's gesture of re-turning the world to balance. It is a gesture of hope. Of course, by holding the juxtapositional over the linear, Clements makes a hierarchy—so there is a paradox here. Or rather, there is a constant movement between the juxtapositional/associative and the linear/hierarchical, the radioactive and the explosive—a kind of reverberation, which I read here as the reverberation of the atomic blast itself, rippling out in all directions.

Glissant has a name for this reverberation. He calls it *echos-monde:*

> The only discernable stabilities in Relation have to do with the interdependence of the cycles operative there, how their corresponding patterns of movement are in tune. In Relation, analytic thought is led to construct unities whose interdependent variances jointly piece together the interactive totality. These unities are not models but revealing *echos-monde.* Thought makes music. (*Poetics of Relation* 92)

I like the notion of an "echoing world" because it folds us all, in our relationality and our complicity, into the reverberation.

It is possible to think about the peaks and troughs of reverberation through the characters of Fat Man and Little Boy because they are, in a sense, the polar ends of atomic history—raw uranium and the bomb. However, there is another character in the play who works as a figure of the reverberation itself—the Métis baker Rose. Towards the end of the play, before the atomic blast (although also, uncannily, after it, because the play is not linear), Rose gets a premonition of the upcoming explosion. In the sound logic of radioactive time, I would argue, it ripples both backwards and forwards in time to vibrate through her. Rose says:

> In the dark I can hear it trying to come inside me like I am the radio. Like, I am the radio and everything is coming through me and everything is getting bigger and louder until …
> The sound of it is getting right inside me, it's coming through the air like waves. I'm breathing it in. Oh God … make it stop. (97–98)

As I have previously discussed, Rose is Métis. Her father is the Irish-born owner of a Hudson's Bay store and her mother is Indigenous. Like Little Boy, Rose and her mother are objects of discovery. As she bakes bread at her home in Fort Nelson, Rose talks about being mixed, being discovered, making bread, and the oscillation through states of being in a single speech:

Mixing, kneading, rising, punching down, shaping loaves. She saved my father, the Irishman, softening him from a journey of Irish potatoes, Indian curries and Chinese noodles. He was a stowaway at fourteen on a clipper that traveled the Orient and by accident discovered my Indian mother. Letting loaves rise. By accident, she discovered me. Letting loaves cool. (58)

But Rose is also identified with the bread she makes, while the bread is identified with the bomb. The stage directions tell us: "*Rose touches herself like a loaf of bread*" (58, italics in original). Of herself, Rose says, "This perfect loaf of bread is plump with a rounded body and straight sides" (58). The bomb-likeness of her own body and her loaves of bread is also hinted at in her cryptic speech about ingredients: "Flour, yeast, sugar, salt, lard, liquid. Bread. Don't let the long list of ingredients frighten you." The odd thing is that this is a relatively short list of ingredients—there are only six of them. That Rose calls it "long," and says it might somehow frighten her interlocutor suggests she is not talking about bread at all; rather, her list of familiar ingredients is a stand-in for a longer list of unfamiliar ingredients that are indeed frightening, both because of what they are and because they are unnamed. Rose's bread is uncanny bread, in that all of its homely ingredients point to something most sinister and *unheimlich*. When she has finished listing her ingredients, Rose moulds the bread into a loaf and tosses it up into the darkness (59). And still later above Koji and his Japanese grandmother, and their cherry tree, like a bomb: "*From the dark sky a loaf of dough falls*" (59, italics in original).

Peter Blow's documentary *Village of Widows* illustrates the fact that the uranium that was extracted from the mines at Great Bear Lake came out as a fine, powdery substance, not so different from flour. It was stored in sacks not unlike flour sacks. These sacks often leaked, and the uranium tailings blew around the town of Port Radium and got into everything. Knowing this history, it is easy to imagine a woman baking uranium tailings into her bread and to imagine people eating it. Knowing about the increased cancer rates at Port Radium, we might read the eaters of uranium tailings bread as, in a sense, "time bombs" themselves.

As a figure of mixing, a figure of the *echos-monde* itself, Rose is both bomb maker and bomb, nurturer and destroyer, colonizer and colonized, white and Indigenous. As her bread bomb lands on Koji, he loses hold of his cherry tree, and through a kind of radioactive magic the bomb maker and the bomb victim are brought together. Koji tries to explain how it happened:

There was this light in the sky when I was talking to this trout and then I was flying and I landed on a branch and then I tried to grab a loaf of bread then I was swimming and … I fell from a branch (89).

Koji's explanation makes no sense in terms of any kind of linear logic; yet in the juxtaposing logic of the *echos-monde*, it makes all the sense in the world. In the logic of the active radio, the originator of the bomb and the bomb victim are intimately connected. Surely there is no more profound or more violent a connection. But Rose, as a Métis woman, and as a figure of mixing, cannot embrace the logic of radical othering that makes Fat Man who he is.

The love between Rose and Koji emerges through the "sound" logic of producing if not sameness, exactly, then likeness from difference. While Fat Man the bomb test dummy mans his post and stoically defends his country and family "no matter who the Indian is.... Even if my family are Indians" (95), Rose and Koji love each other and in that love see the possibility for the end of othering. Rose says to Koji: "If you make me yours do we make a world with no enemies?" (95).

While Clements works through the logic of binary opposition in this scene, she is highly attuned to the fact that Rose and Koji have something in common—both are the unwilling and unwitting objects of a military-industrial complex that has racialized and othered them and placed them on opposite ends of a logic that is using them to benefit Western imperialism and the war machine.

Rose and Koji, a Métis woman and a Japanese man, are brought together in the most unlikely ways, as rare earth from the mine at Great Bear Lake is dropped on Japan with devastating consequences. Just as earth touches earth through the violence of mineral extraction, industrial processing, and colonialist/expansionist logic, people touch people in ways that would not have been possible without the human transfer of Great Bear earth to Japanese earth. The relationship they develop through this terrible history does not occur as a result of the intention to hurt each other. Rather, this Métis woman and this Japanese man have been placed at two ends of the racist logic that cares for neither of them but that is bent on preserving the power of one imperial centre at the expense of another. But Rose and Koji themselves, although they come from opposite sides of the planet, are in many ways kin in a non-oppositional fashion. Their non-identical likeness, their partial similarities, work to place them side by side in a chain of atomic kinships that reverberate through time and space. Rose and the Dene Ore carrier's widow attempt to articulate the uncommon commonalities they share with Koji, in a conversation that coincides with the illness of another character, the miner, in the chain of radioactive kinship:

THE WIDOW: Where's your baby's father?
ROSE: He's down the river fishing.

> THE WIDOW: Indian? He looks sorta like an Indian but there's
> something different going on.
>
> ROSE: He's Indian enough from the other side.
>
> THE WIDOW: I can't argue with that.
>
> ROSE: Finally.
>
> THE WIDOW: Not because I can't but because I say you are like my
> daughter.
>
> THE DENE SEE-ER (v.o.): My voice grew hoarse with the sight of knowing that
> they would harm my people from the inside.
>
> *THE MINER's hat goes on. He coughs and coughs. Yellow spray comes from him
> as he coughs.* (105)

Koji is "Indian ... from the other side" in that there are similarities in appearance between some Asian people and some Indigenous people, but also because he is on the receiving end of the same logic that has caused such devastation among the Sathu Dene—a logic that has exposed them to death by cancer by employing them in the mines at Great Bear Lake without telling them about the dangers of radiation. He is also "from the other side" in the sense that, from Rose's point of view, he comes from the other side of the Pacific Ocean. Also implicit here is that Rose thinks Koji is "Indian" on the inside in that he shares with her a feeling of alterity, paradoxically "outsiderness." He is like a son to the widow because Clements has cleverly and thoughtfully double-cast the Dene ore carrier's Widow with Koji's grandmother—yet another instance of what Glissant means by *echos-monde*.

But the *echos-monde* is utterly shot through with violence. It is not utopic. For Koji to be Indian on the inside, the next character in the line of radioactive kinship, the miner, who is white, must be Asian on the inside. The miner is also double-cast as one of the LaBine Brothers—the original "discoverers" of radium. As the Miner coughs, yellow spray comes out of him. Thus Clements's kinship circle is an inclusive one. All of the characters suffer—not regardless of race but, rather, each in her or his own specifically racialized way.

In the most causal sense, the miner's radiation sickness has been caused by the American need for uranium to kill the Japanese. To take material from the depths of the earth from one location and drop it on the surface of the earth in another, in order to reveal that other place's depths, rearranges the depths and surfaces, or interiors and exteriors, of the people involved. The radioactive temporality that brings traumatized people in touch with their history is fully in play here. This radioactive *echos-monde* is also a world that is inside out and upside down. The poetics of relation enacted here are unquestionably violent and change who we are in ways that are sometimes fatal but sometimes loving and hopeful. What appear to be large geopolitical acts are, significantly, profoundly intimate. Across vast differences, across time, and across the boundary between life and death, Rose and Koji find love and make a child. It's an oddly heterosexual romance in a play that is otherwise determined to complicate all normative forms of relation.

It seems to me that Clements's gesture of respect here is the laying out of all these fraught connections so as to acknowledge violence and injustice while also trying to establish balance in the aftermath. To achieve that balance requires a reconfiguration of space and time, which is exactly what the Dene seer in the play's third movement, "Waterways," invokes. As he says: "Can you read the air? The face of the water? Can you look through time and see the future? Can you hear through the walls of the world? Maybe we are all talking at the same time because we are answering each other over time and space. Like a wave that washes over everything and doesn't care how long it takes to get there because it always ends up on the same shore" (75).

As the bomb draws closer and the end of the play begins to dawn on us, the clear separation between sight and sound, radio and television, past and present, associative and linear, becomes blurred. The Dene seer says: "My voice grew hoarse with the sight of knowing they would harm my people from the inside." (105). And then, a little later: "I sang this strange vision of people going into a big hole in the ground" (106). As sight and sound collapse, the events leading up to the atomic explosion come at us more and more quickly, but not in a linear fashion. Rather, the temporal gaps between them become greater, and the relationships among them become more random. The events are given to us in shorter snippets fired at us in rapid succession. So we see and hear the LaBine Brothers on their way to the discovery of uranium, uranium miners mining, Fat Man complaining about the darkness after the atomic blast, Round Rose after the war working in her father's souvenir shop, Koji and Rose's daughter being born, the Widow worrying about Dene men getting cancer, and Koji dying beside his cherry tree in the atomic explosion. These are the reverberations of the atomic blast, which reorganizes time, rearranges surfaces and depths, and reverses insides and outsides, but does not exactly offer the romantic return I allowed myself to dream of for a moment at the beginning of this essay.

The return, then, that I evoked at the start of this essay may be possible in Clements's terms, but it is never complete, and it never occurs without the consequences of settlement, disenfranchisement, violence, and genocide riding fully present beside the possibilities of love and hope. Clements seems to engage a poetics of relation, as Glissant describes it, a poetics that is never innocent and never pure, but rather is always stepping forward to claim responsibility and produce connection, even if, at individual and causal levels, responsibilities are not being taken and connections are not being made.

I would like to argue that in the time and space of the echoing world, kinship and responsibility are not premised on direct cause, individual agency, and incontrovertible proof of malicious behaviour, but rather through a poetics, a metaphysics, or an epistemology that emphasizes the imperative to make balance and respect wherever one sees the possibility to do so. In an epistemology of respect, as far as I understand it, we have a deep responsibility to find the new balance of the world and move towards it, instead of petulantly standing in the corner taking advantage and refusing blame while bombs fall or land and water are appropriated from our kin "from the other side."

ACTS OF NATURE
Literature, Excess, and Environmental Politics
Catriona Sandilands

In his landmark 2005 study *The Future of Environmental Criticism*, Lawrence Buell documents quite extensively that ecocriticism—a field Cheryll Glotfelty has described broadly as "the study of the relationship between literature and the environment" (xviii)—has understood itself as having political as well as critical tendencies.[1] Greg Garrard is even more direct on this point, insisting in his 2004 introductory text that "ecocriticism is an avowedly political mode of analysis" (3). Although environmental criticism is better understood, now perhaps more than ever, as what Buell calls a "concourse of discrepant practices" rather than as a critical movement per se with a clearly articulated program, in general it "gathers itself around a commitment to *environmentality* from whatever critical vantage point" (11, emphasis added). Early ecocritics—what Buell calls the "first wave"—focused on and advocated thickly descriptive, realistic nature writing as a sort of environmentalist rejoinder to "the distantiations of reader from text and text from world" (22) of which they accused much late twentieth-century literature and theory. This focus was intended as a critical politics, to be enacted through a reconnection of environmental writing and criticism with environmental *experience*, to bring criticism "back" to nature for the purposes of education and advocacy: a "modeling of ecocentric values" (22). In what he calls the "second wave," literary proponents of environmental justice rejected both the idea of nature and the insistences on nature writing and realism that had led so many ecocritics to focus on the likes of Henry David Thoreau rather than Rachel Carson.[2] As Buell notes, environmental justice literature and criticism tend to revolve around "urban and degraded landscapes" (22) rather than organically inspirational ones; the critical politics of environmental justice literature is not so much about modelling ecocentrism as it is about demonstrating, specifying, and probing ever more deeply the disturbing co-implications of racism, sexism, colonialism, and environmental degradation.

Although these divergent emphases are important, I am not as interested in the differences between Buell's first and second waves as I am in one of their similarities: in both versions, ecocriticism not only tends toward politics but also suggests particular roles for itself *in* politics. For ecocritics, literature and criticism *do* things for environmental politics that are part of its commitment to environmentality. Thus, here, the "tending toward politics" of ecocritical activity is not a reduction of literature and criticism to an "environmentalist agenda" that is incapable of valuing texts in themselves as works of art because of prior commitments to environmental ideology or strategy. Exactly the opposite: the "concourse of discrepant practices" that is ecocriticism offers a variety of perspectives on the unique ways in which literary texts in themselves, as points of environmental activity, contribute through critical practice to an environmental public culture.

To understand this contribution, we need to question ecocriticism further: What does this "avowed commitment" to politics actually look like? To continue with Buell: "criticism worthy of the name arises from commitments deeper than professionalism. Environmental criticism, even when constrained by academic protocols, is usually energized by environmental concern" (97). How is it that the act of doing literary criticism can be an expression of this environmental concern? First and foremost is the idea that there is intrinsic value in the act of taking environmental interest to the practice of reading: carefully analyzing a novel or a poem "for" nature offers a way of understanding the relations between literary depictions and embodiments of the more-than-human world and the physical environment itself. Whether a given work ecocentrically places the human figure at the margins and attempts to defamiliarize language in a bid to dislodge anthropocentrism, or whether it collects and connects instances of the relations between systemic social injustice and environmental degradation, reading a literary work for nature is important because we can then place that text in the historical and ongoing stream of works that speak to and about the natural world. Criticism energized with environmental concern, here, means showing the diverse ways in which literature has made nature its subject in order to enhance understanding of environmental relations or issues, both historically and in the present.

My primary question here, though, is not about understanding: it is about politics. I am thus compelled to ask: What *else* does ecocriticism do for the environment? In what ways does the specific constellation of activities concerning reading, writing, and criticism contribute specifically to environmental *politics*? This question is less a matter of the prior environmental commitments of ecocritical practitioners, and more one of what it is these practitioners actually do that might further their concern: this "doing," then, is my focus. This essay will reflect on ecocritical doing in three ways. First, beginning with the work of Martha Nussbaum and eventually settling on that of Hannah Arendt, it will explore some elements of the role of literary activity in public life. Here, I will consider literature and criticism as related moments in a constellation of literary activities that holds unique promise for environmental political life. Although Arendt is not an obvious choice for ecocritical attention, her understanding of the relationship between the worldliness of the work of art and the defining political activity of judgment is helpful in allowing us to think about the relations between and among the biophysical world, environmental literature, and political action in the public realm. Second, the essay will take a brief detour into the writings of Shoshana Felman, whose critical work on reading and discourse suggests a further consideration of the specificity of literature in environmental politics, here, as an interruption of the totality of environmental discourse constituted outside the literary domain. Finally, the essay will take this understanding of an eco-literary public practice to a specific act of reading environmentally in order to flesh out why this way of thinking about ecocriticism might make a difference. In specific opposition to thinkers who argue in favour of a stronger correspondence between ecocriticism and pursuit of overarching ecological "truth," I hold that ecocriticism offers the potential to *constitute*, rather than merely represent, a world among us. If literature creates a world that is open to environmentally concerned judgment and that interrupts discursive totality, then ecocriticism has a unique role in—indeed, a unique responsibility for—environmental politics.

Environmental Literature and Public Life

To say that literature has a unique role to play in politics is hardly an original statement. One of the better-known formulations of the argument comes from liberal philosopher Martha Nussbaum, who argues in *Poetic Justice* that literary experience is a necessary corrective to rational deduction in the process of making good political decisions. Briefly, for Nussbaum, the act of reading involves an experience of what she calls "judicious spectatorship," in which we feel strongly the circumstances, motivations, and actions of another—a character in a novel, for example—but still maintain our detachment from that other. We are, then, in reading, engaged spectators: we learn compassion in the empathetic but still detached act of witnessing the experience of another and imagining what we would do in the same situation. For Nussbaum, this kind of compassion is an important complement to rational, rule-based judgment of the rights and responsibilities of others. Readers of fiction, acting in the political realm, can thus simultaneously judge a course of action rationally by weighing and evaluating the evidence according to abstract moral or other criteria, and understand it compassionately by having witnessed the experience of a fictional other, whose world is revealed to us as a subjective universe that is comprehensible, if definitely not identical, to ours. "An ethics of impartial respect for human dignity," she writes, "will fail to engage real human beings unless they are made capable of entering imaginatively into the lives of distant others and to have emotions related to that participation" (xvi).

Although we might not reject entirely her insistence that reading may cultivate a kind of imaginative respect for others, there are serious problems with Nussbaum's argument. One of the largest is that she bases her case for politically relevant literary imagination on a very particular kind of literature: precisely the kind of realistic novel in which one is introduced, in a relatively intelligible way, to the feelings, experiences, inner lives, and outer actions of a character toward whom one can then feel compassion (in fact, her exemplary novel is *Hard Times*, which not only enacts but also itself explicitly argues for the importance of compassionate engagement against the dangers of excessive rationality). What, in Nussbaum's universe, is one to make of the readerly experience of, say, alienation? Or disgust? Or complete incomprehension, for that matter? As Simon Stow argues in his excellent essay critiquing Nussbaum, for a liberal philosopher supposedly interested in the individual, there is not much space for the individual reader's actual experience in Nussbaum's literary imagination. Indeed, he argues that there is in her work a decidedly "illiberal tendency to treat reader-citizens as *means* and not as *ends*" (410): the correct experience of the text for her liberal democratic purpose is, no matter what the reader might have to say about it, an enlarged ability to imagine the experience of the other, the necessity of which is given in liberal democratic reasoning, not in literary experience.

I dwell on Nussbaum for two reasons. First, she shares with some ecocritics a commitment to a literary realism that ends up getting in the way of a strong ecocritical conception of literature's contribution to environmental politics. In much the same way as Nussbaum's novels are supposed to open the reader to an empathetic relation to the other's realistically portrayed experience, nature writing is, for some "first wave" ecocritics, supposed to open the reader to some kind of authentic, theoretically unmediated experience of the natural world. Here, the literary text stands in for the world itself, and good literature mimetically reflects the complexities of the world as accurately as possible— indeed, for critics like Glen Love, as closely to the insights of ecological science as possible. In this understanding, environmental literature is a subservient form of knowledge, and Greg Garrard goes so far as to write that ecocritics "are in the unusual position as cultural critics of having to defer, in the last analysis, to a scientific understanding of the world" (10); literature's role is, here, to get nature somehow "right." As Dana Phillips, perhaps the most outspoken critic of this view, notes, this claim

> taps the vein of not just realism but outright positivism which runs thoughout ecocriticism. Its realism-cum-positivism explains why ecocriticism often seems to be a sort of rescue mission: both nonfictional and fictional references to nature—to the habits of animals, the round of the seasons, the folkways of farmers, the sense of place, and the like—are characterized by ecocritics as sweeping away the obfuscation of theory in a (counter) revolutionary (re)establishment of realistic literary priorities. (585)

In other words: reading nature literature is supposed to be a way of accessing a natural other in order to develop exactly the kind of literary imagination of the other that Nussbaum insists is necessary for good political judgment. Leaving aside the problems of ecocriticism's mimetic insistences and scientific desires, which have been well rehearsed by Phillips and others, including the impossibility of writing nature outside theory (including the theory involved in the generation of scientific knowledge), I would argue that the idea of literature as a stand-in for either the biophysical or the social world impoverishes our view of the specificity of both the world and the text, as if "representing" were the most interesting thing that literature does, and as if the world could be represented in the first place. Even if ecocritics, with Nussbaum, acknowledge that reading is a specifically imaginative act, there remains a sense in both positions that what is most important to imagine is "realistic" and that the goal of literature is as much "rightness" as anything else.

Second, as Stow also notes, Nussbaum's ultimate commitment to a liberal democracy governed by abstract moral reasoning causes her to treat literature as an "add-and-stir": an ingredient that adds a little flavour but does not really alter the recipe. As he writes, "Nussbaum believes that literature is merely a valuable addition to philosophical Reason traditionally conceived" (411); compassion enriches abstraction but does not in any way call into question the primacy of abstract reasoning as the guiding principle of public deliberation. Thus, it is not surprising that we find in Nussbaum such a narrow view of literary experience: it can only ever be supplementary data in a larger evaluative project already constructed according to the rules of rational abstraction. Here, too, I note a parallel with ecocriticism. If the "truth of ecology" actually lies in ecological science—and even in the lesser but still positivist claim that good environmental literature reflects a certain kind of empirical environmental experience—then literature can only ever clarify, contextualize, or specify ecological data that are external to literature and not specific to literary works themselves. Although I am clearly overgeneralizing what is, in fact, a more complex constellation of ecocritical relationships to realism, I find among them this disconcerting similarity: environmental literature can only ultimately give an aesthetic or empathetic edge to the hard data that have already defined the reality of environmental crisis. As Buell writes, then, "the majority of ecocritics ... look upon their texts of reference as refractions of physical environments and human interactions with those environments, *notwithstanding* the artifactual properties of textual representation and their mediation by ideological and other sociohistorical factors" (30, emphasis added).

It is the "notwithstanding" that troubles me: Surely the "refractionality" of literature is not something to be bracketed in our understanding of its political contribution? Surely there is something about the *fact* of the "artifactuality of textual representation" that might cause us to think in a more nuanced way about the specific contribution of literature, and thus also the specific contribution of the ecocritic, to environmental politics? To address these matters, I would like now to turn our attention to Arendt, for whom the work of literature is, precisely, an artifact with specific political capacities *because* of its artifactuality.

Nature, Worldliness, and Action

Let me begin this consideration with a passage from Arendt's essay "Truth and Politics":

> The transformation of the given raw material of sheer happening which the historian, like the fiction writer ... must effect is closely akin to the poet's transfiguration of moods or movements of the heart—the transfiguration of grief into lamentations or of jubilation into praise.... The political function of the storyteller—historian or novelist—is to teach acceptance of things as they are. Out of this acceptance, which can also be called truthfulness, arises the faculty of judgment—that ... in Isak Dinesen's words, "at the end we shall be privileged to view, and review, it—and that is what is named the day of judgment." (*Between Past and Future* 262)

For Arendt, the work of literature, as a work of art, is a worldly thing: it is, as David Halliburton writes, a "tangible entit[y] in an artifice of human making fashioned so as to become relatively immutable" (111). Although Arendt clearly links literature to factuality—"a good novel," she writes, "is by no means a simple concoction or a figment of pure fantasy" (*Between Past and Future* 262)—she also understands that the novelist or poet engages in transfiguration by reifying the "raw material of sheer happening" into an artificial composition that is no longer of the same register as the happenings themselves. As Halliburton notes, she uses the word "transfiguration" in an almost mystical sense: the work of literature transforms "mundane facts and events into something memorable. As in distilling, what results from the process is something that did not exist before; something that needed the already existing ingredients and yet possessed the superior capacity of changing the terms, so to say, of *how* they exist" (112–13).

If, for some ecocritics, literature is of the same organic whole as the biophysical reality it supposedly represents—in which, Phillips writes, "the complexity of ... poetic language in particular ... is seen as expressive of or even determined by the complexity of nature" (579)—for Arendt, the exact opposite is true. To her, the stuff of nature is ephemeral, fragile, and mutable; it grows and decays, flourishes, dies, and regenerates. It is obviously necessary and valuable, not least because it is the biophysical condition of human life, the basis of what she calls our capacity to labour, to reproduce our material being, but it is not all there is. Indeed, Arendt draws an important distinction between "nature" and "the world": the world is comprised precisely of those objects that human beings create in order to give us permanence in the face of natural transience. Through work, by which she means the fabrication of things out of nature into a form that provides durability, we create for ourselves a relatively stable "home," as it were, in the midst of the ebb and flow of living and dying. And literature, like all works of art, is of the *world*, not nature. Indeed, writes Arendt,

> Because of their outstanding permanence, works of art are the most intensely worldly of all tangible things. Their durability is almost untouched by the corroding effect of natural processes, since they are not subject to the use of living creatures, a use which, indeed, far from actualizing their own inherent purpose—as the purpose of a chair is actualized when it is sat upon— can only destroy them. Thus their durability is of a higher order than that which all things need in order to exist at all.... Nowhere else does the sheer durability of the world of things appear in such purity and clarity. (*Human Condition* 167–68)

The work of literature, then, precisely because it is a "thought-thing" plucked and crafted from the ephemeral flow of "sheer happening," allows that happening to endure, albeit in a completely new way: "it is the 'dead letter' in which the 'living spirit' must survive" (169). To put it differently, if reality itself is unascertainable in its ever-changing cascade of processes and events, literature is an exemplary world-making process in which a meaningful story about life is brought into being, given rest, and allowed to appear as something common among us. It is a "saying what is," and as Arendt writes, "who says what is ... always tells a story, and in this story the particular facts lose their contingency and acquire some humanly comprehensible meaning" (*Between Past and Future* 261–62). This, indeed, is what Arendt means when she says that the novelist teaches us "acceptance of things as they are": not quietism, but an agreed-upon common world that can appear to all of us despite our diverse perspectives on it.

Although it may seem odd of me to champion the relevance of so obviously un-ecocentric a political theorist to environmental literature and politics, let me go one step further. For Arendt, it is the world—not nature itself—that is the object of political action. This statement does not mean that we should not be concerned about environmental crisis, about the destruction of those life activities without which there would be no human condition of any kind. It does mean that action is only possible when there is a common world to which our action responds, and that common world is a fabrication, a "saying what is" to which literature has already contributed.[3]

Here, Arendt's conception of action requires some brief elaboration. Where labour is that portion of the human condition "which corresponds to the bio-logical processes of the human body," and work "provides an 'artificial' world of things ... meant to outlast and transcend them all" (*Human Condition* 7), action "is the only activity that goes on directly between men [*sic*] without the intermediary of things or matter"; it "corresponds to the human condition of plurality, the fact that men, not Man, live on the earth and inhabit the world" (7). Action is, for Arendt, the human capacity for distinctive speech and deed, our individual ability to bring into the world new beginnings in concert with others. It is the enactment of the human condition of *natality*, the distinctive-ness that is the unique potential of every human being, rather than mortality, the species-destiny of all of us. Action is, in other words, the activity through which the world can indeed change; by developing our unique relationships to the common world, each of us comes to hold the potential, in the political activity of speaking and acting together on matters of the common world, to bring unpredictable possibility into the world that exceeds both biological reproduction and instrumental production.

For our eco-literary purposes, there are two major elements to consider concerning action and politics. First, Arendt understood *judgment* to be the defining faculty of the political realm: developing an *opinion* on a matter of the common world as it rests, like a table, among us. Opinion is a knowledge of the world "as it opens itself to me ... not subjective fantasy and arbitrariness, but also not something absolute and valid for all" ("Philosophy and Politics" 80). Opinion is a question of taste, of appreciation, of judgment formed in relation to the world itself as it appears to us in common. It is not a question of timeless or axiomatic truth; it is not something that can be ascertained by applying scientific or philosophical principles, and it is not an application of prior moral precepts or statements of value. Political judgment is, instead, a mode of thought that is based on cultivating, from the individual's unique perception of the world, what Arendt calls an "enlarged mentality."

Second, this enlarged mentality is something that can happen only in the company of others, in other words, in a public realm that gathers together diverse individuals for speech and deed. For Arendt, when we think philosophically or scientifically, we do so by ourselves; when we develop opinions, we necessarily do so in a public realm that surrounds us with the opinions of others, against which we refine our own through conversation and persuasion. We develop, through this activity alone, the capacity for representative thought: for thinking in the place of the other. Let me offer a final passage from Arendt to elaborate on this important quality:

> Political thought is representative. I form an opinion by considering a given issue from different viewpoints, by making present to my mind the standpoints of those who are absent; that is, I represent them. This process of representation does not blindly adopt the actual views of those who stand somewhere else, and hence look upon the world from a different perspective; this is a question neither of empathy, as though I tried to be or to feel like somebody else, nor of counting noses and joining a majority but of being and thinking in my own identity where actually I am not. The more people's standpoints I have present in my mind while I am pondering a given issue, the better I can imagine how I would feel and think if I were in their place, the stronger will be my capacity for representative thinking and the more valid my final conclusions, my opinion. (*Between Past and Future* 241)

Thus now we see a crucial difference between Nussbaum and Arendt and can specify an important move for ecocriticism to make in order to think differently about its political possibility. Where, for Nussbaum, reading inspires an empathy that fleshes out rationality in the creation of good judgment, for Arendt, judgment happens in precisely a space that is informed by neither empathy nor rationality. Judgment is not something that can be derived from private feeling or from the application of overarching principle, theory, or method. It is a capacity of thought that is unique to public life and that requires the presence of others for its exercise. The role of literature in public life, then, is not as an emotional augmentation to reason. Literature is, rather, a halting of the constant movement of life so that we can apprehend it as the world, as a non-utilitarian object of public reflection around which we can then begin to cultivate the judgment that lies at the heart of the public sphere.[4]

Literature, Environmentality, and Excess

The argument for an Arendtian view of ecocritical politics is thus that litera-ture's contribution to environmentality lies neither in its ability to reflect the natural world as if it were an organ of nature nor in its expression of the "truth" of the environmental crisis in some kind of artful reflection of prevailing wis-dom in ecological science or economics. Literary works, as worldly creations, pluck out the facts of material reality; they then create from these facts a realm of enduring meaning that can then appear to us as a common world. This common world is not a collection of theoretical principles or scientific obser-vations: it is a realm of appearances in which we act politically, in which we exercise judgment and develop opinion, in which we debate our perceptions of the common world in the company of multiple and diverse others, and in which we engage in our potential for action to bring new things into the world, which is not at all the same thing as offering up literature to the public realm as a way of convincing the world of the necessity of more sustainable public policy written in accordance with good ecological science. Literature, then, is important to the ecopolitical realm because its worldly endurance allows it to appear to each of us individually as a matter of judgment; exercising judg-ment together expresses ecocriticism's capacity to cultivate a *public* practice of environmental reading "for" nature, and is thus a vital part of its real "ten-dency toward politics." What I am suggesting, then, is that literature creates a world from nature as, literally, an "act" of nature, and that ecocriticism, as a practice of judgment in concert, holds a unique potential for the development of an environmental public sphere in which we cultivate not an emotionally augmented appreciation of ecological truth—as if literature were necessarily subordinate to science and criticism a poor cousin of moral philosophy—but rather a capacity to think representatively about the natural world from the cultivated experience of "thinking in my own identity where actually I am not" (*Between Past and Future* 241).

But what difference does this view actually make to environmental liter-ature, to ecocriticism, and to the relationship between them? First and most obviously, for ecocriticism to approach politics, it needs to be practised in public. Rather than think of the environmentality of our reading practices as some kind of prior commitment we take to private, individual acts of textual encounter, and rather than think about the environmentality of a literary work as residing mostly in the text itself, I think it would make a great deal of differ-ence to insist that we cannot actually understand the environmental concern of the text without debating it with others and without forming, from that process, a judgment of it that is "hermeneutically responsible as well as rhe-torically persuasive" (Halliburton 113). This proposition is not, in fact, a very radical one: in the seventeenth and eighteenth centuries, public discussion of literature was a crucial part of the development of the bourgeois public sphere, and literary salons were—to quote Jürgen Habermas—"a training ground for critical public reflection ... a process of self-clarification of private people" (qtd. in Stow 417), a process in which the capacity for public reflection and "enlarged mentality" was actually created. But to stop with a text, to discuss it in the company of others, to remove it from the sphere of mere entertainment and allow it to appear as a part of a common world, holds a possibility for political action—simultaneously, self-cultivation and responsible imagination—that, I think, is particularly lacking in an ecopolitical universe currently dominated by green consumerist debates about the relative merits of what are, in essence, merely different kinds of technological application rather than fundamental questions about the future of the world.

This stance does not mean there should not be a critical interaction between ecological science and environmental literature; indeed, a robust practice of environmental literacy can and should insist on basic knowledge of the principles of ecology as a key part of ecological citizenship. What this stance rejects, however, is the idea that ecocritics have "to *defer*, in the last analysis, to a scientific understanding of the world" (Garrard 10, emphasis added). Therefore, I am compelled to add that environmental literary criticism might *not* actually supplement established modes of environmental investigation; indeed, it might actually *challenge* them in ways that are very important to environmental understanding and politics. Thus here, I would like us to consider very briefly a thought from Shoshana Felman: that a crucial role of literature is to mark a place of *incompleteness* in a system of thought, in this case ecology, thus preventing it from "closing in on itself, for example, by providing a complete representation of something" (Sun et al. 2).

In her book *Writing and Madness*, Felman notes that the disciplines that have attempted to understand madness—especially philosophy and psychiatry—are founded precisely on the exclusion of madness itself from their accounts; this exclusion is a foundational silence for discourses of madness that claim, rationally, to know it. "For the historian and philosopher of madness"—by which she means Foucault and Derrida in this context—"the problem then is how, while analyzing History's essential structure of muffling madness, to give it voice, restore to madness both its language and its right to speak; how to say madness itself" (42). This "saying" is actually impossible, and not only but perhaps especially within the disciplines,[5] as madness is (to quote Foucault) "a language which stifles itself, which sticks in the throat [and] collapses before having attained formulation" (qtd. in Felman, *Writing and Madness* 41). Yet madness can be rendered present, indirectly and sideways to speech, in literature, as fiction and poetry include *pathos* as well as *logos*, metaphoricity as well as factuality, both of which open up a space, for example, for delirium to emerge obliquely in among the words.

By invoking *pathos* I am not suggesting, qua Nussbaum, that a work of literature such as *The Turn of the Screw* (which Felman reads) is thus a good supplement to psychiatry because it might allow an impartially respectful subject to feel some compassion in the midst of her systematic understanding of an unspeaking Other. On the contrary, what reading James's story does is, in Felman's view, *disorient* discursive thought about madness because, as literature (not necessarily fiction), it evokes a sort of resonant experience that cannot be reduced to disciplinary knowledge about madness or, indeed, to any language about a madness that is, fundamentally, "a language … that returns, without incident, to the silence from which it had never been freed" (Foucault qtd. in Felman 41). Literature is, here, "in a position of excess, since it includes that which philosophy excludes by definition: madness. Madness thus becomes an overflow, what remains of literature after philosophy has been subtracted from it" (51).

Perhaps especially in relation to literature that reminds us of its literariness, then, reading and writing offer reminders of worlds and experiences that are excessive to the texts and discourses that attempt to totalize them. These encounters remind us that philosophy and science are not "in control," that the production of axiomatic knowledges about the world is not the only way of going about encountering it in its truthfulness, and that its essence may indeed defy speech altogether. One can certainly draw an analogy between madness in Felman's account and nature in the writing of authors such as Don McKay,[6] who most certainly considers it one of his literary tasks to call into question, in the *poetry* of his poetry, the ability of language to represent a nature that is always excessive to human speech even as it may lurk within it. But the more conservative point, here, is that literature offers us a point of textual encounter that, far from confirming ecological science—or, indeed, any environmentality—reminds us that the discursive incorporation of the more-than-human world into any kind of systematicity is interrupted by the constitutive exclusions on which that systematicity is, by definition, founded. To some extent at least, we must recognize—to change Felman's terms of reference from "literature" to "nature"—that "if we are unable to locate [nature], read it, except where it has already escaped … it is not because the question relative to [nature] does not question, but because it questions *somewhere else*" (55).

The "act" of nature that is literature, then, is important to environmental politics partly because it *reveals* its activity or, in our earlier terms, its artifactuality. Environmental literature may indeed be a creative act of enduring worldliness for public discussion and action, but its very qualities of literariness remind us that, in developing practices of representative thinking around it to form and evaluate opinions, this world is still not nature itself. Partiality, incompletion, and uncertainty are thus part of the process of judgment.

Reading for the World

In the final section of this essay, I try to offer a glimpse of the kind of ecocritical reading I have thus far sketched. Although I cannot single-handedly—according to my own definition—draw out the full ecopolitical implications of any text, I can offer a suggestion of how a work of literature might be a generative "act of nature," contributing to an enduring world of ecological concern, one in which nature is *held imperfectly* in literature in such a way that it can then offer up nature to a kind of judgment that is not always already subordinate to knowledges and interests that pre-exist their appearance as a world "that opens itself to me." I choose for this reading Dionne Brand's 1997 book of poetry *Land to Light On* partly because its nature is both vivid and unexpected, welling up in the text in encounters that are profoundly, even shockingly resonant and excessive, in Felman's terms, and partly because it insists, in both content and form, on a political reading, demanding that we develop an opinion about it.

Land to Light On begins "out here," in Ontario's "near north," in winter drives on long highways heading toward Haliburton, to a frozen place where Brand "can hear wood / breathe and stars crackle on the galvanized / steel" (11). Interwoven with this north of Brand's "out here" (1) are other places: the Caribbean, "slow purple quietness of cocoa pods" (66), of her memories and family and departure; the painful Toronto streets, "subways tender as eggshells" (24), of immigrant familiarity and unfamiliarity; and the sites of violent events of global imperialism that appear not only in the "terrifying poetry of newspapers" (13) bought with hot coffee at northern gas stations, but also in the everyday lives of her friends and family. And in her own life: the second poem of the book recounts a white man jumping out of a truck to scream his sexism and racism, his "exact hatred" at her on a country road, "something about your cunt" (4). If the book begins with a powerful sense of Brand's uncomfortable being in the particular place of this northern landscape—"is not peace / is getting used to harm" (3)—then it ends with an equally uncomfortable understanding of "her own singular life," with an imperative to locate her discomfort in the world, in "the life of a child running with her to a refugee / camp on the Burundi border, caught / in the bulb of a television camera" (99).

Many Canadian poets and novelists have written about their complex relationships to the "awesome" natural landscapes of the northern wilderness.

Brand is responding to these relationships, and to the landscape, by insisting on a different kind of awe: looking around her to the snow on the pine trees, and up into the black and frigid air, she attempts to locate the words to name and understand the inexplicable racism that has just assaulted her on this winter road, and cannot "find a language" (5). The quiet does not offer her solace or simplicity; they are not enough to allow her to be in this white place that does not welcome her, does not recognize her possibility of belonging. To understand, to confront the racist and sexist relations by which this landscape is denied her, she has "to think again what it means that I am here" (9); this thinking traces the complex geography of Brand's discomfort and links urban Toronto with northern wilderness with a gecko climbing a dirt wall in Trinidad with global imperialism and massive human displacement. Against a dominant narrative of Canadian nationality in which immigrants find freedom and belonging in the act of building a home in the wilderness, Brand offers a story in which that very wilderness is part of multiple stories of home, dislocation, violence, disappointment, and loss. The particularity of the place, the pines, the snow, and the "Quiet, quiet, earfuls, brittle, brittle ribs of ice" (8) cannot be separated from the story of her coming to it and is fully inserted into relations of global capital, like "bananas floating in the creamy eyes of business / men" (100).

The responsibility of the poet, for Brand, is to find the language that can allow her to understand and challenge the relations of landscape in which she finds herself: "I still need the revolution / bright as the blaze of the wood stove in the window / when I shut the light and mount the stairs to bed" (7). Thus the text invites not only a complex reading of nature and place, but also a deeply political one. What happens if we look at the north as a landscape of ongoing violence, as a place that is not a refuge from but rather profoundly a part of a global web of ongoing violences that connect to one another through capital flows and individual stories of coming and going? Looking closely, we find a dense network of particularities, specific body/landscape relations that Brand evokes in their sensual present: she describes the time of a Caribbean Sunday as "the violent / slowness of flour, the regular ruin of storms, seas, winds" (67); she offers an Ontario summer as "corn dangling bronze, flat / farm land growing flatter, eaten up in highways" (73). Yet the places are connected, and in complex ways; in the midst of overt references to imperialism in lists of nations and snapshots of atrocity, we find repeated mentions of sewing, "mouthsful of needles / and thread bristling and black cake packed for sisters / abroad" (59), of loss, "rooms across this city full / of my weeping," and even of common rhythms of landscape, "this new / landfall when snows come and go and come again, / this landfall happened at your exact flooding" (69). For Brand, the particularity of place—tropical, urban, northern, remote—is always already penetrated by the particularity of other places; every chapter of the world (to borrow the title of her final section) shows how particular relations to landscape form a plurality that speaks to, and of, a common world.

So, first, Brand herself represents nature as a realm that can only be understood in its socio-historical complexity when it has been given a more or less meaningful language in the world through specific acts of poetry, when the experience of nature in its particularity is crystallized into something else: at the end of the day, the experience is gone save the poem. The necessary language, however, perpetually eludes her, which is why she must continue to attempt to craft the world from words. Indeed, she explicitly writes of this artfulness as a craft:

> It
> always takes long to come to what you have to say, you have to
> sweep this stretch of land up around your feet and point to the
> signs, pleat whole histories with pins in your mouth and guess
> at the fall of words. (43)

But, second, the failure of language to fully represent nature and experience does not mean that the world cannot be made common enough to be discussed and acted upon. The perpetual incompletion of the task of the poet to craft the world from the land does not in any way blunt the clear imperative Brand gives us to listen to her attempts at its capture. We are clearly supposed to attend: she speaks to the reader directly, sometimes writing in the second person, sometimes implying that her words are a response to questions posed elsewhere; her descriptions are sometimes angry, piercing accusations. The collection is a violent rendering of violence, as it were, in which the reader is called—sometimes ordered—to respond to the specific experiences from which she, in her poetry, fabricates a world.

Consider one last fragment from *Land to Light On*:

> In this country where islands vanish, bodies submerge,
> the heart of darkness is these white roads, snow
> at our throats, and at the windshield a thick white cop. (73)

Here, we begin in a country that claims to know no particularity, no racialized embodiment in the expanse of whiteness that is Ontario in the winter—islands vanish, bodies submerge—but the invocation of Conrad[7] turns the universality of that northern white nature on its head: in this landscape it is, as she describes down the page, "three Blacks in a car on a road blowing eighty miles an hour" who are faced with the unbearable otherness of an alien nature. But she does not leave it at that principled, pointed reversal: at the windshield, there is a "thick white cop / in a blue steel windbreaker peering into our car, suspicious." She thus interrupts even her own reflection on race and landscape with a terrifying particularity, a specific experience of racism to bring to this not-so-universal-after-all northern winter understanding of nature. She interrupts the north not only with the south, but also with a staccato-rhythmed thick white cop, an immediate experience brought into carefully troubling words.

What Brand offers in *Land to Light On*, then, is a performative interruption of an idea of universal, encompassing nature, a poetry that insists, in its emphatic and deeply particular insertions of global violence—like the thick white cop—into the silent white northern landscape, on being remembered. As Arendt writes, in poetry "remembrance ... is directly transformed into memory [and] its memorability will inevitably determine its durability" (*Human Condition* 169). Brand's remembrance of the imbrications of landscape and racialized violence can become, through poetic crystallization into memory, the stuff of the world in a way that even the most detailed statistical rendering of environmental racism cannot approach: it is memorable, enduring, an object in the world that demands we figure out a relationship to its stunning if elusive crystallizations of race, nature, and violence. How we then act on that racialized and degraded world is, at that point, up for discussion.

ECOCRITICISM IN THE UNREGULATED ZONE

Cheryl Lousley

[E]cological thinking is not simply thinking *about* ecology or *about* "the environment."... It is a revisioned mode of engagement with knowledge, subjectivity, politics, ethics, science, citizenship, and agency.
—Lorraine Code, *Ecological Thinking* (2006)

The relations of democracy and knowledge are up for materialized refiguring at every level of the onion of doing technoscience, not just after all the serious epistemological action is over.
—Donna Haraway, *Modest_Witness@Second_Millennium.Female-Man©_Meets_Oncomouse™* (1997)

In striving to call public attention to ecology, to "protect the environment," to value nature, and to insist that there are laws of nature that even capitalism must respect, environmentalism politicizes nature, ecology, and environment. Just as feminism makes it a little more difficult to take women for granted, environmentalism makes it more difficult to take nature for granted, to view nature as an endless sink for the waste products of capitalist production, as a free resource ready for appropriation, or as a predictable, steady-state backdrop to social and cultural life. The parallel is not coincidental: as numerous environmental feminist thinkers have shown, both women and nature have been figured as supplements to modernity—superfluous additions or secondary matters—that turn out to be essential to its thought and productivity.[1] However, just as feminism finds that its politicization of women's lives ends up showing that the very category of woman cannot be taken for granted, but rather is constituted through political discourses and practices, so, too, does environmentalism find that nature, even in the most material sense of the term, is a power-effect, not an objective or transcendental ground for politics. The politicization of nature thus brings about a political and epistemological free fall, where nothing is certain, including the evidence on which we base our environmental criticism.

To take my cue from Larissa Lai's 2002 novel *Salt Fish Girl*, we find ourselves in an "Unregulated Zone." In the speculative fantasies of *Salt Fish Girl*, the Unregulated Zone lies outside the secured boundaries of the corporate strongholds that have replaced nation-states in the mid-twenty-first-century Pacific Northwest. Populated by sweatshops, unidentified viruses, barter networks of the unemployed, human clones, and genetically modified organisms mutating in a changing climate, the Unregulated Zone riffs on the popular tradition of environmental dystopia and the neoliberal erosion of welfare state protections. *Salt Fish Girl* is also a novel of hope, however. Structurally, the Unregulated Zone is a place without recourse to a transcendent authority— not to the laws of a state, not to a corporate contract, not even to predictable laws of nature—and this is what makes it a contested space of both nightmares and political possibility. It is a space where "the relations of democracy and knowledge" are indeed "up for *materialized* refiguring" at every single level, from DNA to climate, as much as from the family to the nation-state (Haraway, *Modest_Witness* 68).

Although many environmental critics pull back in horror from such premises, I turn to science studies, particularly the work of Donna Haraway and Bruno Latour, to find a more robust mode of environmental criticism and politics that can take them into account. Beyond the "nature-endorsing" or realist and "nature-skeptic" or social constructionist positions within social theory lies a more nuanced path that grapples with dynamic assemblages of human and non-human actors (Soper 23). I use Lai's novel as a companion for thinking through ecocriticism and environmental politics because, like the science studies approach that partly inspires it, the novel takes the Unregulated Zone as a political opening—a place from which we might reconfigure ecological relations and, in the process, also recast, as Lorraine Code argues, "modes of engagement with knowledge, subjectivity, politics, ethics, science, citizenship, and agency" (5).

Mediating Materials

In *What Is Nature?* Kate Soper outlines a stalemate between two positions in social thought, loosely termed realist versus critical or postmodern. Critical theorists from Marx onwards have argued that the appearance of something as if it were merely there, natural or given, accessible to immediate contact, occludes its socio-material underpinnings, such as, in Raymond Williams's *The Country and the City*, the capitalist relations of property and exchange that underlie rural landscapes. By showing how the "natural" is historical, cultural, and fabricated, Williams made the underlying property and labour relations publicly visible and politically contestable. Although important for tracing the operations of power, the social construction of nature critique is nevertheless limited. By bringing nature into view as always already social and cultural, it provides no grounds on which to make empirical judgments. It can thus be dangerously enabling of non-naturalistic moralisms, whether Christian creationist opposition to biology (Haraway, *Modest_Witness* 117) or industry-funded climate change skepticism (Latour, "Why Has Critique"). Moreover, the emphasis on social and cultural agency tends to reinforce how ecological matters and non-humans are rendered absent, passive, and without value in modern social affairs. Soper contrasts social constructionism with what she terms "nature-endorsing" perspectives to emphasize the latter's normative combination of realism and ethics (23). Nature endorsers aim to place moral value on nature in itself, turning to myth and literature as mechanisms for the re-enchantment of the world.

In *Ecology without Nature*, Timothy Morton attempts to develop a theory of ecological criticism that abandons nature as starting point for either remythologization or demystification, and attends instead to practices of mediation. Morton outlines a Derridean deconstruction of the quest for re-enchantment through immersion in nature. Striving for immersion and immediacy, Morton points out, actually underscores the practices of mediation, especially the boundary work involved in constituting inside and outside. Nature, especially when conceived as "the environment," is that which is "out there," just beyond the boundaries of the text, or the self, or the city, or modernity, and so on. Morton argues that continually reaching towards something "out there" makes ever more visible its *displacement* (its location elsewhere) and its *supplementarity* (its incompleteness in itself, such that nature needs so much writing to be appreciated, to be really present). Nature writing, in making the world "out there" feel real, present, and alive, is "a sprawl of sheer *text*" that achieves its rejuvenating effect in part through the quantity of its language (Morton 70). Textual mediation is not the barrier that separates us from nature, Morton argues, but the very thing that enables a sense of immersion—a sensibility that may inhibit our attending to the nuanced particularities of textual practices, ecological relations, power relations, and social responsibilities.

Latour makes a similar point in his examination of environmental politics in *Politics of Nature*. He argues that while environmental advocates usually declare that they are concerned about the loss, end, or destruction of nature, political contestation in the name of nature continually ends up pointing to its mediation, "speak[ing] of countless imbroglios that always presuppose human participation" (20). Climate change, for example, is by no means a problem concerning the atmosphere "in itself"; rather it is about emergent, frightening climate feedback loops that include a range of anthropogenic activities. More, not less, human activity is required if we want to re-establish some boundary between social life and climate systems (so that climate can be a semi-predictable background once again). The supposed objectivity of nature and science—their realism—is also underpinned by extensive human action. Each reference to scientific practices to resolve an environmental debate, whether about climate change or the health risks of toxic chemicals, may well contribute to better understandings of carbon cycles and chemical pathways, but only through more mediation:

> this nature becomes knowable through the intermediary of sciences; it has been formed through networks of instruments; it is defined through the interventions of professions, disciplines, and protocols; it is distributed via databases; it is provided with arguments through the intermediary of learned societies. Ecology, as its name indicates, has no direct access to nature as such; it is a "-logy" like all the scientific disciplines. (Politics 4)

Why, Latour asks, should we separate the toil of all these scientists and instruments from the end product called "truth," any more than we think the immersive effect of nature writing can be achieved without the writing? The practices of technoscience are "material-semiotic," in Haraway's words (Modest_Witness 11). As she explains, "their constructedness, their always unfinished articulations, are not in opposition to their reality; that is the condition of their reality" (120).

Haraway and Latour claim for empirical objects and scientific knowledge the same density, inscriptions, and heteroglossia that characterize novels. Science and technology are not simple instruments of human intention and agency (tools to answer a preconceived hypothesis or fulfill a preconceived purpose), but rather "networks," "detours," or "tropes," because of the laborious association of quite heterogeneous actors both malleable and stubborn.[2] The development of the anthrax vaccine, Latour shows in The Pasteurization of France, involved the displacement of a disease from a pasture to a laboratory where it could for the first time become visible as a microbe. Contrary to the conventional understanding of the scientist as a master figure, marshalling nature under his command, Latour characterizes the scientist as listener, translator, and stabilizer, assembling sensitive apparatuses to learn what microbes like and dislike: "If we stop the culture, if we sterilize the pipettes badly, if the incubator varies in temperature, the phenomena disappear; that is, they change their definitions" (*Pasteurization* 93). The destination is reached only by this circuitous route; like the epiphany of a novel, the phenomenon of *Bacillus anthracis* has no meaning—no definition, no stability, no visibility to human subjects—without the meticulous practices that bind together relevant participants, give them names, and sketch their characters. Over time, "the modest appearance assumed by technology comes from *habit*, which prompts forgetfulness about all these interlinked mediations" (Latour, "Morality" 251). Once stabilized and concretized, the "accumulation of folds and detours, layers and reversals, compilations and re-orderings" that make up scientific discoveries and technological inventions is hard to see ("Morality" 251). Like the reified commodity that appears free of the labour that produces it, we can refer to a vaccine as if it were an object, forgetting that creating immunity in our bodies is the action of microbes supported by a network of techniques and apparatuses.

That is, we *could* do this. During the global H1N1 (swine flu) pandemic of the late 2000s, the life, death, and agency of microbes, vaccines, agribusiness, and pharmaceutical corporations were all matters of public concern and discussion while the virus was being named and identified. Political debate was not restricted to the socio-political dimensions of the crisis; indeed, it consistently contested any clear line between the scientific and social. What role did overcrowding at hog farms play in creating the conditions for rapid mutation of the virus? This was not a question that could be answered without a detour into a laboratory, but the Mexican operations of United States agricultural subsidiaries under the North American Free Trade Agreement were surely not a matter for scientists alone. The H1N1 pandemic was a reminder of how environmental politics are about politics, not nature: the virus was undoubtedly material but it was hardly "natural." Moreover, the political debate surrounding the virus did not hinge on whether it was natural or not—the very distinction had become irrelevant—but on whether it existed, what it would do, whom it would change (harm), and who was responsible for it.

Matters of Concern

The H1N1 virus was an example of what Latour in *Politics of Nature* calls a "matter of concern." Latour recounts how in the good old days of modernity ("modernism," in his terminology), the epistemological divide fell along the lines of facts versus values: one was empirical, the other philosophical; one dealt with things, the other with ideas; one with nature, the other with humans. Sometimes one was contingent (limited by reality), the other transcendent (ideas are free); sometimes it was the other way around (ideologically bound discourse, universal laws of nature). Their forms of truth were incompatible. Now, a new kind of boundary can be articulated—the one between matters of fact and matters of concern, or between the things we habitually take as given and those we find troublesome, risky, and uncertain. Matters of concern are no more or less material than matters of fact, and matters of fact are no less historical than matters of concern. The difference lies in their public appearance.

A matter of fact has clear boundaries and defined properties; it appears in public as belonging "to the world of things, a world made up of persistent, stubborn, non-mental entities," because it is without "the researchers, engineers, entrepreneurs, and technicians" who testify to its properties and make it visible (Latour, *Politics* 22). The actors and networks that produce a matter of fact sit outside political contestation, because they are either calcified by habit, hidden from public view, or accepted as commonsense. At any moment, a matter of fact can be politicized, as *Silent Spring* author Rachel Carson accomplished in the 1960s when she launched a new social movement by gathering anecdotal and laboratory evidence in order to attach poisoned birds and people to the pesticide DDT. It is also reasonable to let the properties associated with a matter of fact stabilize (such as when feminist activists brought abortion into the regulated practices of doctors' offices). It can be good to make something *matter of fact*.

Matters of concern, by contrast, are "surprising actors" (Latour, *Politics* 103), "recalcitrant" (81) and stubborn "events" (79), and "beings of uncertain status that demand to be taken into account" (103). Because they are not yet "solid" matters of fact, the material-semiotic work of listening, translating, and arguing that might identify and stabilize them is in full swing. Matters of concern arrive accompanied by their producers and spokespeople, who "appear in broad daylight, embarrassed, controversial ... with all their instruments, laboratories, workshops, and factories" (24). Their entanglements and attachments are publicly visible, their boundaries uncertain. Matters of concern are "associations of beings that take complicated forms—rules, apparatuses, consumers, institutions, mores, calves, cows, pigs, broods—and [that are] completely superfluous to include in an inhuman and ahistorical nature" (21). We cannot call them "nature" but neither are they "human." They may be our "work," Latour notes, but they are not our "doing" (*We Have Never* 50). The active parties are forests, chlorofluorocarbons, and viruses, as well as scientists, ethicists, and journalists. "We talk about a *crisis* every time they emerge," Latour writes, because matters of concern do not fit our pre-existing categories and arrangements (*Politics* 24).

Environmental politics, in other words, have made the discursivity of science publicly visible. As a result, the aura of what Latour calls capital-s Science collapses, thereby sometimes weakening its authority in particular environ-mental battles (DDT, climate change). Latour's response is to say, in effect, "Good riddance!" Not relativism but democracy might follow. Although our sense of crisis erupts in relation to matters of concern, Latour argues that envi-ronmental (and, I would add, feminist and anti-racist) politics have politicized nature so that the authoritative rule of objectivity may no longer reign over anyone. Stabilizing the boundaries of matters of concern evidently cannot be left to scientists alone (to settle "the facts"); and showing that those matters are socially produced and culturally mediated does not make them go away. Each such matter requires complicated analysis, discussion, and experimentation. While it might be nice to imagine some technical or theoretical mechanism for dealing with matters of concern once and for all—bringing the crisis to an end—such calm can only be achieved by closing down hard-won political space.

The Politics of Contingency

If nature or ecology is not an essence underlying the series of late-twenti-eth-century imbroglios or matters of concern (forests, chlorofluorocarbons, viruses), then what is? What makes something an environmental concern? Latour insists that there is no a priori empirical element that holds together all of these imbroglios as a single crisis:

> Political ecology claims to speak of the Whole, but it succeeds in upsetting opinion and modifying power relations only by focusing on places, biotopes, situations, or particular events—two whales imprisoned on the ice, a hun-dred elephants in Amboseli, thirty plane trees on the Place du Tertre in Montmartre. (*Politics* 21)

Each of these issues is singular. Their scales, properties, and networks are in the first instance incommensurable: "[political ecology] can never array little humans and great ozone layers, or little elephants and medium-sized ostriches, in a single hierarchy" (*Politics* 22). Matters of concern surprise. Environmentalism, Latour notes, takes as a truism that everything is con-nected—that, for example, the water that comes out of the tap comes from groundwater filtered through the moraine slated for development. The Whole, in other words, is empirically constituted a priori—that's what ecology means. In practice, however, ecology shows just the opposite, that "it *does not know* what does or does not constitute a system. It does not know what is connected to what" (*Politics* 21).

This lack of certainty about matters of concern drives environmental anal-ysis to sort out who the actors are and what kinds of relations they have: to look for connections, to follow flows, and to read in context (subject-in-envi-ronment, animal-in-habitat, worker-in-workplace). Code describes Carson's empirical method as ecological precisely because of its openness to varied types of claims and evidence in trying to make visible connections across disparate domains: in the field *and* the laboratory, scientist *and* citizen testi-monies, bird *and* human health. Carson demonstrates how "the very complex-ity of each separate subject matter requires a knower to be multilingual and multiply literate ... sometimes, all for the sake of understanding something so very small as a beetle" (Code 44). Taking uncertainty as the starting point reminds us that environmental analysis is not about bringing all the actors in, as if we could reconvene all the elements under a new transcendental sign of "natureculture." Such comprehensiveness is nigh impossible, as climate sci-ence sadly shows. Rather, scientists, social scientists, activists, capitalists, and ecocritics alike are engaged in boundary-work: acts of definition and experi-mentation that reconstitute identities, beings, and worlds in the process. Har-away describes this as "'troping,' in the sense of worlds swerving and mutating through material cultural practice" (*Modest_Witness* 136).

The common world, in other words, is not already given by the empirical universality of nature, nor by the universality of humanity; rather, it is in "*the process of composition*" (Latour, *Politics* 195). As Haraway insists, "Boundary lines and rosters of actors—human and nonhuman—remain permanently contingent, full of history, open to change" (*Modest_Witness* 68). Boundaries are contingent both materially and semiotically. The boundary of the atom seemed fixed and impermeable for a long time, but the bombing of Hiroshima was a material-semiotic demonstration that that boundary had changed. Drawing on Ernesto Laclau and Chantal Mouffe, one could say that matters of concern are not inherently about "the environment"—the very ambiguity of the term "environment" (referring not to a substance but to a boundary) points to its hegemonic function. Rather, through material-semiotic politi-cal action these matters are articulated into a common struggle organized in the name of ecology as utopian possibility. The contemporary environmental movement emerged when a chain of equivalences was articulated—that air and water pollution were like DDT spraying, which was like nuclear radiation, and so on—with all of its links sharing as common antagonist a military-in-dustrial complex that disregarded life.[3] Non-humans are discursively part of that articulation. Haraway writes that

> something of an unreconstructed and dogged Marxist, I remain very inter-
> ested in how social relationships get congealed into and taken for decontex-
> tualized things. But unlike Marx ... I insist that social relationships include
> nonhumans as well as humans as *socially* (or, what is the same thing for this

odd congeries, sociotechnically) active partners. All that is unhuman is not un-kind, outside kinship, outside the orders of signification, excluded from trading in signs and wonders. (*Modest* 8)

That the "we" of any political struggle or collective identity—for example, the nation—actually includes a lot of unnoticed non-humans (such as calendars, clocks, statistics, newspapers, maps, and books) without which there is no "we" (as Benedict Anderson has shown) has already been recognized by social theory. Such things not only are instrumental but also can serve as objects of affective attachment, and this, Rey Chow suggests, somewhat resembles the attachments and affective investments that constitute a nation. What Haraway, Latour, and others in science studies add to the radical democratic project is a refusal to take for granted that non-humans (whether chemical or animal or text or myth) are socially passive and do not resist or encourage, in their different ways, their mobilization and reconfiguration.

Feminist science studies scholars point to the parallel danger of assuming that human properties are non-contingent (see Hayles on the assumption made by information technologists that human thought is disembodied). Giorgio Agamben's analysis of how the deprivations of Nazi concentration camps pushed some people outside personhood to a state of bare life (past sensibility but not yet dead) is also relevant here (54). Destabilizing and reconfiguring some material-semiotic arrangements may indeed result in a nightmare that many of us would politically resist. Although Haraway is best known for casting the boundary-blurring cyborg as a possible figure of political resistance to military technoscience, both Haraway and Latour emphasize the political role of stabilization as well as reconfiguration. As Haraway writes, "I am at least as invested in the continuing need for stabilizing contingent matters of fact to ground serious claims on each other as any child of the Scientific Revolution could be.... The important practice of credible witnessing is still at stake" (*Simians* 33).

Once stabilization is understood as a material-semiotic political act, the political work of realizing (making real) a more just and livable world will make an effort to involve the skills, techniques, and spaces of microscopic as well as macroscopic assembly (laboratories as well as factories; gene work as well as media work; the computer enabling of both chat rooms and climate [re]modelling). To date, most technoscientific knowledge/world production remains hidden from public view and contestation until after initial stabilization by accredited experts, who often distrust politicization in the hands of "ignorant masses." Most social theory, in tandem, retains a distrust of non-humans, figuring them as fetishes and screens that obscure the political rather than as allies and partners in politics.

Novel Experiments

If we consider the production of knowledge and artifacts to be a means of composing new worlds, then speculative fiction is an ideal site for experimenting with the contours of this radically contingent politics. In Lai's *Salt Fish Girl*, the twenty-first-century protagonists are themselves matters of concern. Miranda Ching's body, odorous, racialized, and diseased, is matter-out-of-place in her all-white classroom and in the gated corporate community of Serendipity. Evie is an escaped and self-named clone, genetically identical to a whole series called the Sonias, who are manufactured to work in the factories of the Unregulated Zone, producing commodities such as Pallas shoes. Another primary agent in the novel's plot is a durian, a genetically modified tropical fruit that is evolving in the Pacific Northwest in a period of climate change and nation-state decline. No less than Miranda and Evie, the durian exemplifies the absurdity of trying to settle the properties of a matter of concern by distinguishing between made and given, human and natural, local and global.

To echo Latour, is the fruit natural because it grows on a tree? Is it wild, because that tree grows from a wayward seed, or is it a cultivar, because it is nurtured by the Sonias? Is it manufactured because its genes are partly the work of scientists? Or is it manufactured because that environment is a product of greenhouse gas emissions, archaic national and urban planning, and guerilla gardening? Is it natural, because it has adapted over generations to a new environment according to the evolutionary "law" of natural selection? Is it local, because the fruit is specific to the Fraser River watershed in 2044? Or is it global, because it is a cross-Pacific hybrid? To echo Haraway, is it material, because it is tangible and edible? Or is it semiotic, because it has been brought into production by the cultural inscriptions of corporate regulations, Chinese memories, and women's desires? Is its agency merely due to a fictional text's ability to cross into the supernatural (the mythical Nu Wa)? Or does its agency lie in the quite mundane action of a ripe fruit attracting an animal through smell to propagate its seed?

Anthropologist Anna Tsing presents the durian as an exemplary case of how forests are social spaces where human/natural distinctions are not useful. In the Meratus Mountains of Borneo, where durian is thought to have evolved, durians, like many wild fruit, propagate through consumption by mammals— seedlings sprout from trash heaps and casual droppings. Durian seeds are also saved and deliberately planted. Whether planted or self-seeded, each durian tree is claimed and tended. Thus, durian trees are rarely killed; instead, when patches of forest are cleared for agriculture, the durians remain, proportionately increasing the durian population over time (Tsing 179). The forest is both wild and cultivated; the durian, too, is both wild and cultivated, an active part of a dynamic social field.

Lai's novel, with its sweeping reach across centuries, continents, and mythologies, brings together the incommensurable to propose that justice be sought through political alliances rather than naturalized identities, that power be located in public rather than private hands, and that matters of fact be produced and authorized in ways open and accountable to a more inclusive collective. By invoking matters of concern, or unruly agents that disrespect the stabilized lines between natural and unnatural, the novel exposes the active boundary work that produces the worlds of Evie and Miranda.

Boundary Work

In her classic text *Purity and Danger*, anthropologist Mary Douglas argues that dirt is a symbolic-spatial category: "Dirt is the by-product of a systematic ordering and classification of matter, in so far as ordering involves rejecting inappropriate elements" (35). "Dirt," in other words, is not soil per se, but "matter out of place" (35). The term "pollution" is even more obviously a symbolic category because it refers not to a particular substance, but rather to a defilement of a naturalized order. Monica Chiu applies the concept of dirt as "matter out of place" to Asian American women's fiction in her book *Filthy Fictions*. Chiu argues that, beginning with the historical concept of "Yellow Peril," Asian Americans have been racialized as "dirt," "filth," and "disease," often by association with animals (1). This discursive regime can be summed up in Robert Lee's assertion that in the United States "analysis of the Oriental as a racial category must begin with the concept of the alien as a polluting body" (qtd. in Chiu 18n2). Chiu and Lee focus their analysis on the specific geohistorical context of the United States; I find their concepts useful for reading Lai's Canadian text, which responds both to Canadian histories of racism, such as the Chinese Head Tax, and to the fluid border crossing and border constituting of racist discourses.

Although Chiu addresses pollution as primarily a social concept rather than an ecological one, Lai combines the two in her novel. Miranda is marked from birth by a smell "like the reek of cat pee tinged with the smell of hot peppers" (13), which is the odour of the durian smuggled in from the Unregulated Zone, the forbidden fruit that stimulates her parents' belated romance. The smell materializes the anti-Asian racism that Miranda experiences at school, but it also may be a symptom of "a new breed of auto-immune diseases, related to genetic and other industrial modifications to [the] food supply" (69). Both racism and disease are shown to be material-semiotic boundary constructions: when "medical experts" (71) identify Miranda's symptoms as part of the dreaming disease, her family is all too ready to hand her over to participate in drug trials that might cure her of this evident dis-order. The proposal makes Miranda feel "dirty" (72); she internalizes a shameful view of her own body as diseased. The condition itself brings her no pain, although her pathologized subjection to for-profit science does: "I imagined a bright searchlight and my own body splayed open like a gutted trout" (73).

Her skin is quite materially the contested terrain in the boundary work of scientific experimentation in the name of health and social experimentation in the name of comfort and security. These operations work on different bodily scales, but no single one is more or less semiotic or material than the others; nor are they merely analogous. That the violence/violation of scientific ordering is enabled by power relations of gender, racialization, and sexuality is made clear in the parallel "drowning" stories from the nineteenth and twenty-first centuries: in the former, Nu Wa dives into the river when fleeing the villagers who accuse her of sexual deviance; in the latter, the experimenting scientist Dr. Flowers places the diseased Miranda in an underwater human-sized "glass cage" (201), symbolic of both aquarium and test tube.

Several critics have noted that the odours that cling to the characters' bodies can be read in terms of Julia Kristeva's concept of abjection—the casting out or repulsion that enables the boundaries of the subject to be constituted. Joanna Mansbridge describes how the odours represent an uncanny reminder of the nation's abjection of racialized, feminized, and labouring bodies (131), while Rita Wong highlights their materialization of "silenced histories" ("Troubling" 114). Perhaps even more striking is how these odours produce an uncanny ecological re-membering (or reattaching in spectral form): their "bodies reeked of oranges, or tobacco, or rotten eggs, or cabbage. Or else of silk, of cotton, of coffee, of blood and carnage, of coal, of freshly baked bread, of machine oil, of dust and rain and mud" (Lai 70). Evie's fishy smell represents her as a queer woman, but her odour is also a spectral reappearance of the salt fish trade of the father of nineteenth-century Salt Fish Girl, and of the salty congee on which she was nourished: "She stank of that putrid, but nonetheless enticing smell that all good South Chinese children are weaned on, its flavour being the first to replace that of mother's milk" (48). Lai literalizes, or makes publicly visible, the assemblages that bodies are.

Plumwood suggests that Kristeva's description of subject-formation through the abjection of the mother's body is repeated in the ecological abjection that underwrites modernity, which, in declaring freedom from nature, exhibits a neurotic denial of the metabolic systems through which humans live. As Plumwood explains, to be defined as "nature" ... is to be defined as passive, as non-agent and non-subject, as the "environment" or invisible background conditions against which the "foreground" achievements of reason or culture ... take place. It is to be defined as a *terra nullius*, a resource empty of its own purposes or meanings, and hence available to be annexed. (4)

This is a description of the mother reduced to a material body that nourishes the child. The manual labour of women, servants, and slaves in a household, the administrative labour of secretaries, and the labour that fuels a resource economy in a colony also function as "background" or "environment" to the public life and activities of professional men and women, as well as those of the imperial metropole. Resources and women's work are taken to reproduce the conditions of life (what's given); male professionals are taken to enter history by producing the new (what's made). Since being modern means having been freed from the given, modern subjectivity is premised on a systemic "denial of dependence on biospheric processes" (Plumwood 21); this can be understood as a gendered and racialized disavowal of "dependency on the whole sphere of reproduction and subsistence" (21).

In Lai's novel, ecological and racial abjection is exposed because the "polluting bodies" that are cast out of the gated corporate city haunt its borders. Serendipity retains its veneer of order, safety, and cleanliness by displacing the metabolic work of maintenance underground, outside, and into virtual space. Beneath Miranda's school, as she discovers one day, labour the illegal Janitors, whose backs are transparent silicone sheets, displaying organs that have been gruesomely rearranged so that they do not appear human. The violence of her father's work as a tax collector, which involves taking money from the poor to maximize the corporation's profits, is displaced into a game-like virtual reality. Outside the gates lies an urban landscape in decay: "As we entered it the air grew thick with the smell of old petrol, sulphur, urine and rotten food" (37). The Unregulated Zone constitutes the supplemental space necessary to, but materially-semiotically located outside, the safe, secure, patented, and genetically controlled environments of the corporations. It is a version of the "Free Trade" or "Export Processing Zones" in Jamaica, the Philippines, China, and Mexico, where multinational corporations operate factories outside normal tariff regimes, and a version of the anarchist urban street life that generates the styles appropriated as raw material for commodity capitalism.

Those who live in the Unregulated Zone inhabit what Ulrich Beck calls a "risk position" that amplifies their socio-economic and political insecurity (23): genetic and industrial pollution has made food risky to eat, the soil risky to walk on, water risky to touch, air risky to breathe. Even when exiled to the Unregulated Zone, however, Miranda remains oblivious to and relatively untouched by the insidious conditions around her because her middle-class privilege largely saves her from riding the bus or walking the streets, where she would encounter the more vulnerable and violated others and be herself subject to greater ecological risk (Lai 157). The material construction of a body as polluted or queer or at risk is demonstrated as being due to spatialized regimes of power. The materialization of power relations in spatialized bodily acts can be read down "all the layers of the onion" to the bodily acts of leachates, groundwater, and antigens (Haraway, *Modest* 68). Environmentalism does indeed make everything potentially matter: some lowly molecules gain appearance as additional actors. As the uncanny return of the dead (waste products), they have moved from the outside to the very core of the social world.

Dark Ecology

Literary aesthetics, no less than technoscientific artifacts, are an "accumulation of folds and detours, layers and reversals, compilations and re-orderings," to repeat Latour ("Morality" 251). Literary texts are detours, looping away from the seeming task at hand (the living world "out there," the urgent issues) not just into other possible worlds but also, as Lai shows, into abject underworlds we may not want to see or acknowledge. Detouring into the dark underworlds of ecological thought reminds us that affective attachments (and detachments)—the concerns that matter—are no more self-evident and transparently readable than molecular ones. Environmental thinkers routinely search for the organizing principle or motivation that could launch an ecological politics. As Alexa Weik von Mossner points out, Beck proposes that fear could bring together the political collective in the global risk society: "the movement set in motion by the risk society ... is expressed in the statement: *I am afraid!*" (qtd. in Weik von Mossner 2). Latour, in contrast, imagines a well-managed republic constituted around a new balance of power—a house of assembly, or taking into account, and a house of putting in order. A shortcoming of such visions is their presumption of a straight, instrumental path from concern to action, for this forgets the substitutions, repressions, and displacements that enable assemblages like modernity—and the modern subject—to function.

Just as technoscience and ecological degradation are supported by fetishisms (of things-in-themselves) and disavowals (of boundaries permeable to metabolic flows), environmental counter-politics, too, will involve affective troping. To seek to avoid such detours—or the affective mediating of boundaries and attachments—is precisely the fantasy of nature immersion, which Lai reveals as a horrific disavowal of difference when Miranda and Evie encounter

Flowers's receptionist, "a lovely young woman with dark skin and smooth black hair ... [who] blended into the lush atmosphere" (254) of the tropical reception room. Part of a naturalized office landscape, which also features "a hallway that resembled a forest path, beside which a little artificial brook bubbled, effervescent and poetic," the receptionist is an uncanny reappearance of Raymond Williams's peasants rendered invisible and, as the novel points out, "a Gauguin nude" (254). Lai's gothic invocations of uncanny spectres, doubling, and haunting function to resist the pull of the immersion fantasy, which Morton especially cautions against:

> Ecological writing keeps beating itself against the glass of the other, like a fly. The constant dinging of the impact—in which the strange other, as soon as it enters into proximity, becomes an inert or threatening *thing*—indicates a loss of irony.... If irony and movement are not part of environmentalism, strangers are in danger of disappearing, exclusion, ostracism, or worse. (100)

It is the frightening openness of the Unregulated Zone that enables strangers to continually appear and surprise—often through their uncanny repetition or animation of what is presumed singular, lost, hidden, or dead.

Environmental politics are not driven only by some rationality of self-interest, to be countered with, as Beck writes, "self-limitation" (49), nor should they be. As Haraway observes, "decentering the godlike, individualist, voluntarist, human subject should not require a radical temperance project mandating abstinence from the strong drugs of networked desire, hope, and—in bell hooks' ... provocative term for an affective and political sensibility—'yearning'" (*Modest* 128). Evie's salt fish odour awakens in Miranda a memory and a yearning she did not know she had. Others with the "dreaming disease" experience such a yearning for the ocean from which life emerged that they walk into the water, never to resurface. Here is a veritable "ecological melancholy," in Morton's words: the subject cut off from, and thus through longing connected to, the life source (186). Morton calls this "dark ecology": "The ecological thought, the thinking of interconnectedness, has a dark side ... a 'goth' assertion of the contingent and necessarily queer idea that we want to stay with a dying world" (184–85). Morton suggests that an ethical impulse arises from this ecological longing—a desire for otherness qua otherness, in its unattainability. *Salt Fish Girl* places ecological melancholy within a politics of yearning.

Against the tragic figures drowning themselves in the ocean stands Evie, the quintessential political subject: the one able to make connections, judge allies, and name her own desires. For Miranda, Evie is the outlaw and the messianic figure; the other and the lover; the friend who continually surprises and thus opens up the possibility of another future. Evie is at once the figure of disruption and destabilization *and* the novel's epistemological linchpin—the one able to decode and explain what is going on and thus make it into a single comprehensible system. While Miranda thinks the newspapers are "independent," Evie is able to trace their hidden connections:

> "... They belong to Aries William, who is a major shareholder in the Central Bank." ...
> "You ever hear of a firm called Johnny Angel?"
> "Sure. They're seed designers."
> She sighed and leaned back on her elbows. "Designers. Okay. You ever hear of a shoe company called Pallas?"
> "Of course, everyone that can afford them owns a pair of Pallas shoes."
> "And they both belong to Aries William of Nextcorp fame. They've been making people for years."
> "Making people?"
> "Why do you think their labour costs are so low?" (157)

Evie embodies the mode of critique developed by Haraway and Latour: she makes connections, politically and epistemologically, allying with others to identify and respond to the acts and agents at work in assembling and stabilizing seeds, clones, humans, newspapers, shoes, diseases, and profits.

Politically, Evie is the "multilingual and multiply literate" subject that Code associates with Carson's ecological science: knowing it all, while remaining always epistemically located. Never figured in some godlike stance above the fray, Evie is everywhere the political action is: the street demonstrations, the factory revolt, the reclaiming of reproductive technologies, the subversive defetishizing messages in the shoes. Indeed, Miranda sees Evie doubled everywhere she goes—on the stage at Kubla Khan, in her brother's bed, in the aged face of Sonia 14. Evie's almost infinitely multiple situations enable her to articulate a categorically impossible comprehensive "situated knowledge" (Haraway, *Modest* 3). The epistemic closure or mastery this accumulation might suggest, however, is undone and democraticized by Evie's spectral appearance. Evie as a clone—as a horrifying disruption of the individualized social order—is visible as such only when doubled, in the uncanny moments when one is two. Evie can thus be read as the spectral form of the democratic subject, acting in Jacques Rancière's terms as if she is the democratic anyone, the one in two positions at once, ruling and ruled.

Evie is no one (not a legal person, civically dead) and everyone (doubled, tripled, a cloned repetition without end; the first woman, Eve herself; and a fish, the oceanic evolutionary ancestor). Evie embodies Rancière's notion of the "political excess" or the "democratic supplement" ("Should Democracy" 276, 277); she "acts as if [she] were the demos, that is, the whole made by those who are not countable" (278). Rancière describes this as "the 'aesthetical dimension' of politics: the staging of a dissensus—of a conflict of sensory worlds—by subjects who act as if they were the people" (278). The novel ends on just this fantastical—or, in Rancière's terms, *aesthetic*—"mode of the *as if*" (278): a mystical ascent into the coastal rainforest, the pursuing police forces vanishing in the mist. The novel stubbornly, self-referentially, insists on acting "as if" a new world could be founded, continuing on "as though the world behind had vanished. As though the minute we turned, it utterly ceased to exist" (Lai 264). The novel refuses to give way on its desire for a living world, despite all the troubling signs: "No matter how destroyed the land, the mist clings, hovers like a worried mother or lover too far gone to know her love has long since died, that what clings to the body is no longer life exactly, but something much more hungry and desperate and strange" (264). The melancholic mist, resolutely staying with the dying land, is what enables their decidedly contingent freedom—freedom to act, to dream, and to give birth to future possibilities.

Ecocritical Futures

Salt Fish Girl presents a forceful reminder that it is not only nature but also democracy that should no longer be taken for granted. It is the commitment to democratic politics and future possibilities that I find most encouraging in a mode of critique concerned with making just and public the acts of assembling and stabilizing. With its skepticism towards narratives of pollution (and alien threats), Lai's novel shows how useful it is to follow Morton's Derridean detour from an ecocritical analysis based on the natural/unnatural distinction to attend more carefully to inside/outside boundary work, when extended via science studies through all the layers of knowledge/world/subject constitution. Rather than reading for nature or for culture, ecocriticism might read for matters of concern—marks of uncertainty, anxiety, injury, grief, pleasure, or hope in the destabilization or transgression of boundaries. We might read for narratives of new or re-assembly—Lai's resistant Sonias, for example, ally with the unregulated durian tree to generate children born outside slavery. Asking about interconnection, we might read for attachments—the disjunct entanglements of markets, of chemistry, of food chains, of love. Alternatively, we might read against a text (or any other artifact) to politicize boundaries that have been unjustly stabilized. In many ways, these are reading strategies in which ecocriticism is already engaged. We are contributing to public discussion about the appearance of "unregulated zones" where the fabled modernist order is not secure—with all the possibilities and nightmares that any disso-lution of an order brings. The point is not a priori celebration of either trans-gression or stabilization but responsible and *responsive* readings.

DISTURBANCE-LOVING SPECIES
Habitat Studies, Ecocritical Pedagogy, and Canadian Literature
Laurie Ricou

Each time we enter a new place, we become one of the ingredients of an existing hybridity ... reciprocal identity is inevitably altered by the place ... by the people who are already there.
—Lucy Lippard, *The Lure of the Local* (1997)

I seek to answer the cherished and well-worn Canadian question "Where is here?" by teaching habitat.[1] Study of habitat begins with soil conditions and microclimates, air quality and aquifer status, companion species and competing species, with what eats what and what is eaten by what. Habitat Studies, the title of an English Department seminar I designed and taught for a dozen years at the University of British Columbia, begins with chiton and rock dove, with pika and kinnikinnick. What does this have to do with Canadian literature? It disrupts, even disturbs, more familiar approaches to Canadian literature,[2] and it is just the disturbance necessary to thinking bioregionally. My strategy is to talk obliquely about Canadian literature by teaching habitat. In my Habitat Studies seminar, students look for poetry through which we might "under[stand] the talk of animals" (Harjo 65), indeed, through which we might even understand the language of plants. In what follows, I comment in some detail on Don McKay's intricate poem "Pond," but in so doing I hope to argue the value of shifting ecocriticism's dominating emphasis from place towards a system of animals and plants, water and soil. To do so will necessarily disturb the long-standing primacy of landscape-place in Canadian literary criticism. Because Habitat Studies tracks the movement of plants and animals it is always already transnational and diasporic. Its other is a shrub (talking), a bird (speaking). Where the earth is disturbed, the other moves in; it transforms. Canadian literature, as I see it here, is the speaking and messaging of the species with which we share the soil and air and water. This is disturbing. It is intended to disturb.

◆ ◆ ◆

In one of my Habitat Studies seminars (2009), I sent one student searching for the yellow sand verbena (*Abronia latifolia*), and hence for some literary piece that developed a response to that gracefully clustered blossoming. I thought it would not be possible. She found two verbena poems, one of which, Richard Arnold's "A Wolf in the Choir," celebrates the pedagogy of one of the speaker's favourite teachers:

> "When it comes to truth, I'm lazy," he used to say.
> "I find it in close-by, ordinary things."
>
> The Literature he showed us was thunder clouds
> . . . .
> In music, he'd talk about the genius of Bach—
> But weep for joy when he heard the evening grosbeak.
>
> Our Sociology was dropping to hands and knees
> On beaches to watch the yellow sand-verbena
> Fling its fragrance of sex to pollinators. (n.p.)

For centuries the settler society thought it could dominate the non-human world. Industrial and post-industrial societies thought it possible to destroy others' habitats and still go on living. Now we must admit that it is not possible. Western dominion cannot continue to hold dominion. In Habitat Studies, we learn that we need to become communicators and to be in community with grosbeak and sand verbena. Birdsong and human song, Robert Bringhurst muses, are both "cultural traditions," and the arts serve to establish their community: "music, dancing, story telling, poetry are means by which we can and do embrace and participate in being, not tricks by which we prove our independence from or superiority to it" (38).

Habitat Studies

The description of my 2009 Habitat Studies seminar reads as follows:[3]

Sue Wheeler's poem "Understory" begins in the infiniteness of the infinitive: "To walk out of the field guide / and listen. To wait / for the world to approach with its dapple and hands." Don McKay, in Vis à Vis, *writes about the state of mind he calls poetic attention: "Even after linguistic composition has begun, and the air is thick with the problematics of reference, this kind of knowing remains in touch with perception … will keep coming back to the trail." Wheeler and McKay might be trying to articulate the prompts for this course. It hopes to approach, in the way of the infinitive, some verbal notion not yet subject-ed, not yet time-ed. And although we and it are made of language, it wants to listen to what the world outside of (human) language systems might be saying.*

So, although "Habitat Studies" has had several iterations since 1999, this course is still very much an experiment in ecocriticism. Because I remain convinced that the best way to encounter this relatively new field of English studies is by leaving English studies behind, each of you begins with and sustains a study of a single species of flora or fauna, one that surprises for having been randomly selected, not chosen on the basis of whatever preconception. Each participant will from day one examine a particular species and its habitat—in the fullest sense—in a project intended to push literary research into anthropology and ethnography, folk music, theatre, economic, geographical and political history, film and visual arts. But surely, and most essentially, into the sciences: into botany and zoology, lichenology and entomology, especially into ecology. Yet necessarily this course also belongs to those who have been transformed and transfixed by literature and by great teachers of literature. The idea is not to abandon your love of poetry. Indeed you must be ready to walk out and listen—somewhere the other is speaking. I want you to break away from what you thought literary study was, lose yourself, and then find your way back by becoming poet.

In tone and information, I want this description to emphasize a disturbance of the conventional English literature course, that is to say a course that presents a list of texts to be interpreted and interrogated within a set of thematic, generic, historic, etc., frameworks. Instead, we set out first to trace an animal's or plant's interdependencies.

At the TransCanada Three conference whose presentations and discussions this volume in part records, I did not read this essay, but attempted to convey the disturbance of assumptions by performing the opening class as if the assembled audience were a group of fourth-year undergraduates wondering what they had got themselves into. Such a venture requires a different medium than print to convey; hence this substitute. Quoting the full course description sets the stage for the three-part structure of this admittedly loosely structured essay. That is, the introductory pages of the course description provide a brief overview of a program I have developed and advocate for ecocritical pedagogy in English departments—and hence in Canadian literary studies. The course description ends with poetry, partly to reassure prospective students, and partly to acknowledge that I have no wish to abandon the sorts of courses

I have taught since the late 1960s. In order to do ecocriticism effectively and responsibly in Canada, or anywhere, we need to understand boundaries in a different way. Hence my use of the term Habitat Studies: the boundaries are the limits of where this or that species can live and reproduce, boundaries for example of watershed, or climate, or elevation, or soil type.

Later in this essay I focus on an environmentally sensitive and ecologically informed poem by Don McKay and read it within my limited knowledge of pond ecology. Much of this part of the essay takes the form of annotations. That is, it does not attempt a sustained, singular reading of McKay's poem, but compiles some teaching notes that might contribute to reading some of the interdependencies alive in the systems of pond, and humans living in connection to ponds. This approach is admittedly closer to "doing" Nature Writing than it is to Habitat Studies as I urge it on my students. A student might, for example, bring the poem into a project report if her assigned species were *alder*, in which case, she would have different questions about the poem.

The following includes a brief consideration of the term disturbance found in my title—a reminder of the various resonances intended to infuse the whole. Disturbance—say a volcano, or fire—for an ecologist allows or necessitates a new succession of species. So disturbance enables renewal. But the human animal is the ultimate and most aggressive of disturbers, and often its disturbances allow for invasion, in which a monoculture replaces a rich biodiversity. Hence we have the "problem" of invasive species. In this essay the concept is complicated by the attention to disturbance within a pond—its effects both chemical and aesthetic. And McKay embodies the technique and process as well: that is, disturbance is a method of poeming, even given the seemingly placid focus on a placid pond. Perhaps most interesting—and the source of my title—is the other side of destructive disturbance in human caring.

◆ ◆ ◆

Ben Quinn has seen almost nothing of his sister Kate since they left high school. Ten years later, he travels to West Africa to identify her body; she has died of complications after mistaken surgery. The short story "Disturbance-Loving Species," from the collection of the same name, is author Peter Chilson's imagining of Ben's need to tell in "chunks" what his sister has left him.

He tells of bouncing across the hills in Kate's Land Cruiser and colliding violently with a vulture, and of racing blind in the same vehicle through sand and dust storms. He tells movingly of Kate's work in the Peace Corps, seeking out those desperately ill of cholera and wading into excrement and vomit to help. Kate is the positive exemplar: she seeks out disturbance and recognizes that disturbance demands her empathy, her caring, and her comfort.

Ben is a botanist. He is uneasy "in the language of science" where subjects are "stripped of character." One of his favourite plants, an ideal representative of "'a disturbance-loving species'" (Chilson 149), is the alpine lupine, *Lupinus latifolius*:

> The lupine is a plant that defies the neighbourhood, which makes it a sort of kindred creature to me, the kind of personality I admire but do not possess. Once, on a collecting trip when I was an undergraduate, I found a lupine where it shouldn't have been—where no plant should have been—growing in a desert of blasted rubble on a slope inside the burnt-out core of Mount St. Helens.... After the volcano blew, lupines were among the first plants to sprout on those plains, splashing purple and blue across soil the consistency of ground glass.... Lupines live where other plants cannot, breathing nutrients into torn-up soil so others might grow. But I was the first to find any plant where this particular lupine had taken root, this botanical commando showing off its brilliant purples near the lava cone steaming and growing inside the crater. A sort of "Fuck You!" from the plant world to the earth's most awesome power. (Chilson 150)

Finding disturbance congenial, Kate heals. Ultimately, the "'war'" she is fighting is the "'struggle to protect the land itself'" (158). The land needs protecting from the ultimate disturbance-loving species. American West and West Africa. *Lupinus latifolius* and *Vibrio cholera*. Early in the story, Ben summarizes difference: "I liked plants, Kate liked people" (148). The disturbance he almost discovers through Kate is that the two passions cannot be separated or differentiated.

POND

Eventually water,

having been possessed by every verb —

been rush been drip been

geyser eddy fountain rapid drunk

evaporated frozen pissed

transpired — will fall

into itself and sit.

      Pond. Things touch

or splash down and it

takes them in — pollen, heron, leaves, larvae, greater

and lesser scaup — nothing declined,

nothing carried briskly off to form

alluvium somewhere else. Pond gazes
into sky religiously but also
gathers in its edge, reflecting cattails, alders,
reed beds and behind them, ranged
like taller children in the grade four photo,
conifers and birch. All of them inverted, carried
deeper into sepia, we might as well say
pondered. For pond is not pool,
whose clarity is edgeless and whose emptiness,
beloved by poets and the moon, permits us
to imagine life without the accident-
prone plumbing of its ecosystems. No,
the pause of pond is gravid and its wealth
a naturally occurring soup. It thickens up
with spawn and algae, while,
on its surface, stirred by every
whim of wind, it translates air as texture —
mottled, moiré, pleated, shirred or
seersuckered in that momentary ecstasy from which
impressionism, like a bridesmaid, steps. When it rains
it winks, then puckers up all over, then,
moving two more inches into metamorphosis,
shudders into pelt.
                    Suppose Narcissus
were to find a nice brown pond
to gaze in: would the course of self-love
run so smooth with that exquisite face
rendered in bruin undertone,
shaken, and floated in the murk
between the deep sky and the ooze?

◆ ◆ ◆

I turn now to a reading of Don McKay's poem "Pond," both because of the
pleasure the poet takes in disturbing as a way of caring, and because the poem
is local but unlocated. A pond can be found, and made ready contact with, in
most places across Canada, the country that McKay has called home.[4]

"Pond" is a poem rich in particulars of flora and fauna, morphology, and the vocabulary of light. Answering my interest in the intersections of literary study, habitat, and ecology, this resonant particularity makes the poem an appropriate study. McKay seems to have been taught by pond ecology: the poem's persona is a scrupulously attentive observer but also a bookish student who eventually turns to classical myth to invert his imagining. But "Pond" also hums the vibrato of a poet's poem, luxuriating in the texture of words, words whose intricate expressiveness teaches an ecology of the pond's habitat beyond what attentive observation or months of measurements might provide.

As with good poems everywhere, McKay's "Pond" sustains multiple readings and multiple definitions of its structure. In my configuration of its form, "Pond" is in four movements. The first is a remarkable exercise in slowing verbs, especially water verbs, into stillness. The second, beginning with the single-word, single-syllable sentence, "Pond," details the "natural" features of pond. The third begins by contrasting pond and pool and ends in a *tour de force* of visual rendering. Finally the Narcissus myth is invoked, to discover surprising animality in the observer and an artistic function shared by ponderer and pond. The poem invites and allows an exhilarating close reading and hence declares my method and training and continuing conviction (and reactionary nostalgia). It serves to demonstrate an ecocritical approach to Canadian writing by using scientific study of pond ecology as one means of reading the movement of the poem. As much as the poem draws us into the learning of being lost, it registers that its author comes to its writing with a strong commitment to "plumbing ... ecosystems" (12–13).

Almost every McKay poem will suddenly turn sharply sideways into some topic—often both banal and pop cult—that opens up a whole set of playful ironies and cautions us not to take the poet, or the subject—or our aspirations to groundbreaking scholarship—too seriously. As such, "Pond" lends itself to classroom anecdotes. I once began a different course—"Nature Writing"—by reading this poem. On the first day of class, we all went out into the central campus garden to look at a "real" pond. Within twenty seconds, one student jumped in, breaking through the skim of ice that translated its surface and, in the process, illustrating the disturbance-loving species.

◆ ◆ ◆

"Man's world begins among stones, rocks, frogs, and cicadas ... this is quite another world from Plato's realm of forms or from Descartes' clear and distinct ideas," as Edward Said writes in *Beginnings* (348).

◆ ◆ ◆

The verb "pond" gathers things in by virtue of the stilling power of its sound, which is at once transpiration and inspiration, a breathing in and a breathing out, sounding ä. Hence, pond will necessarily gather scaup [skŏp], pollen [pä/ an], alder [ölder], conifer [känafa(r)] and spawn [span], not to mention, of course, pause [pöz].[5] Any listener aware of McKay's salute to apostrophe (*Vis à Vis* 66–67), will recognize here the "ah!" of surprised discovery and the "awe" of hushed reverence.

"Pond"'s introduction of awestruck grade four children serves as a simile to describe the appearance of successive stands of plants at a pond's edges. The allusion to grade four is startling, even incongruous, and in its slightly odd juxtaposition, it challenges the reader to uncover fresh understandings—in this case, both of "conifers and birch" and of nine- and ten-year-old children. For an ecocritic, what we might call pond pedagogy (that is, using an accessible, manageably sized system to teach science) provides the surprising—paradoxically because most obvious—connection. It is in ponds, whether near the school or in jars and aquariums in the classroom, that many schoolchildren, around grade four, encounter their first learning of biology and, at least indirectly, their first instruction in ecology.

It is much easier to show a schoolchild a pond, and some of the creatures in it, than to begin with, for example, grasslands ecology, or rainforest ecology, or even estuarine ecology. One primer on pond ecology reminds us that "many professional zoologists have started their careers as [child] collectors of pond animals" (Burton 7), going on to celebrate accessibility: "By definition a pond is a small, shallow body of water, so it can be explored with a long-handled net.... A small pond, only a few yards across, may contain an incredible wealth of animal life. Within this volume of water there will be representatives of almost every class of living thing" (8).

◆ ◆ ◆

How we inhabit the planet is intimately connected to how we imagine the land and its creatures.
—Scott Russell Sanders, "Speaking a Word for Nature" (194)

◆ ◆ ◆

So massive and daunting are the environmental crises facing us—facing the earth—that nothing short of a massive reimagining, a shift in the imaginary, will work. Our role as writers, teachers, readers, is in part to contribute to that foundational reimagining. Kathleen Dean Moore, speaking at the Association for Literature and the Environment Conference in Victoria, BC, in June 2009, urged the importance of moving away from the old ways of thinking about how we can dominate the non-human world. The feedback loop is not work-ing, so we must learn to be communicators, to find community with spider and bird. Moore reminds us that wonder closes the distance between what is and what ought to be. At the same time, she insists that witness is not enough: reverence must be engaged and active.

In its focus on habitat, is Habitat Studies ignoring race, class, and gender? Habitat Studies demands cross-cultural sensitivity. It attends to culture in the root sense of *growing*. As seasonal patterns change, and as species go extinct at an unprecedentedly accelerated space, cultural definitions as foundational as our sense of time or our concept of beauty alter. The TransCanada proj-ect points to a crucial dimension of opening up categories of engagement, and Habitat Studies promotes the contact of university students with workers (oyster farm and pet store owners) and challenges the sentimentalization of Aboriginals and Métis (trappers) as *not* working.

◆ ◆ ◆

Stay together / learn the flowers / go light. (Snyder 84)

◆ ◆ ◆

Habitat Studies takes place within an English Department, with an ENGL designation in the timetable and on transcripts. It depends on the methods of language and literary analysis to develop an imaginary, to test that impossible ecocentrism that McKay proposes. It translates science and seeks disciplinary interdependence. Learn the flowers. Habitat Studies encourages writing that can and will be published outside the academy and specialized readership. If we are going to change things, then we need to go public. We need our *students* to go public. These days I am writing for my granddaughters. Wonder closes the gap. Witness with engagement.

◆ ◆ ◆

The ultimate verb in McKay's exuberant opening series of verbs is "sit." And following that quiet monosyllable, McKay leaves two-thirds of the next line blank—a long pause—and then the single-word sentence: "Pond." As a noun, "pond" seems to function here as an apostrophe, without the overtly identifying "Oh" or "Ah." McKay's definition of apostrophe is "the gawk of unknowing ... an opening into awe" (66). It initiates a second series of possessings of nouns, the names for items of flora and fauna whose less overt verbness is implicit in the action of their continual growing. "Pond" in this section is a generous accepting and comprehensive wholeness: it takes everything in. "[N]othing declined" (12). What disturbs it does not disturb it. Pond is home: we might as well say *eco-* ... from the Greek for home.

"Gathers" is the crucial verb in this second sequence. "Pond," we realize, draws everything in and comprehends it—in its literal accepting of whatever falls in or near it, swims on or in it, grows on or in it, but also in its mirror function as a reflection of what surrounds it. I choose the term "comprehends" both for its sense of togetherness and for its reminder that "gather" is also a *ponder* word: as in "infer" or "understand."

At the point of comprehensive gathering, McKay dares that abrupt change in tenor mentioned earlier. He disturbs our perceptions as readers, and we love it—at least this reader does. The reflected "conifers and birch" are "ranged" surprisingly, "like taller children in the grade four photo." This simile, I suggest, challenges us to read everything that precedes in a different way. As we wonder "Where did *that* come from?" we relax into the exuberant playfulness of the entire poem.

◆ ◆ ◆

"Pond" realizes the buoyant playground inventiveness of a gaggle of ten-year-olds at the same time that it suggests classroom and teaching. "Pond," with its lists of associated species, its calling attention to the forming of alluvium, its mention of spawn and algae, is a *teaching* poem, and McKay, in his pondering, is also instructing.

A teacherly voice initiates the third movement of the poem. "[P]ond is not pool," the speaker intones, drawing now on principles of logic to define by difference. The vital difference is not intellectual, however. The verb "gathers," here, referring to material drawn together in folds, anticipates the aesthetic appreciation of pond in the third movement, where it is carried by a third—and the most audacious—accumulating verbal series, words to describe the textures of fabric and particularly the characteristics of light in or on surfaces:

> mottled, moiré, pleated, shirred or
>
> seersuckered in that momentary ecstasy from which
>
> impressionism, like a bridesmaid, steps. (*Strike/Slip* 13)

The vocabulary here reads beauty in the dappled: spotted and smeared and wavy and unstable—we might as well say disturbed. Pond becomes a work of art, a painting, a moment in which we comprehend not only an intricate interdependency of scaup and pollen and a nurturing, global, watery circulation system, but also a place and way to *see the air*: it enables the viewer to understand the language of breathing and gases we cannot see or feel.

◆ ◆ ◆

Annotations, "teaching notes," and, following McKay's punning, a catalogue of some questions I have pondered about some of the ways in which pond ecology connects to the poem and can shape a reading of it:

Stirred by every / whim of wind   Although its effects are "more influential in large ... lakes than in small ... ponds" (Brönmark and Hansson 9), wind is crucial to pond ecology, creating turbulence and hence an environment "far more homogenous than terrestrial habitats" (9). McKay's fabric-making verbs enrich our sense of surface texture, but they must also be read as the "visible result" of "subsurface turbulence" (9). McKay's invocation of "metamorphosis" at the end of this movement is a reminder of the dynamic processes of succession taking place under water.

The course of self-love   Among bodies of water on the globe, ponds, more so than most except perhaps canals and irrigation ditches, are likely to have been *made* by human beings. That is, the apparently placid, undisturbed pond most often exists because of the human animal's dedication—that is, it is not incidental—to disturbing the environment in which it finds itself. Altering the wisdom of Lysander's pronouncement, McKay touches the paradox that what seems undisturbed is a product of disturbance.

Gathering   In its "gathering it *all* in" (emphasis added), McKay's pond remembers the global. That is, the entire planet's water is continuously falling to earth, flowing, evaporating, and again falling. Linda Hogan's observation makes an apt gloss on this aspect of the pond: "Between earth and earth's atmosphere, the amount of water remains constant; there is never a drop more, never a drop less. This is a story of circular infinity, of a planet birthing itself" (106). The amount of water in and around the earth is stable and unchanging. Pond gathers totality; pond gathers all.

Pleated   "Manifold" seems best to describe—if *one* modifier can—McKay's pond. It enfolds the word "fold" and evokes for me the catalogue of pleatings and fabric-phenomena that texture McKay's description. In opening his poem with the adverb "eventually," which embeds the verb "come," he sets up, lingeringly and longingly, the conviction of the overlapping and concealing accumulation that is a manifold pleating.

◆ ◆ ◆

To a hydrologist or an ecologist, pond *reflects* in a not immediately visible but crucial sense. As a reflection of its whole surrounding watershed, an ecologist would "read" pond for an understanding of its contributing water sources (ground water aquifer, stream flow, surface runoff), the characteristics of its watershed (geology, soils, topography), and culture (forestry, agriculture, silviculture, residential, commercial, industrial uses) ("Primer"). When McKay salutes the pond's capacious receptivity—"nothing declined"—he is remarking on all the ways in which this apparently unremarkable body of water registers the entire water cycle that is so vital to sustaining any and all life.

Narcissus, when imagined encountering pond—not pool, over which he once hovered fixated—might have recognized in self-love a threat, "shaken," to the very ecosystem of which he was a part, as a handsome human youth and as the flower he became.

◆ ◆ ◆

The song-poem, Bringhurst proposes, is a "means by which we can and do embrace and participate in being" (38). Attuned, in the opening movement of "Pond," McKay wonders at the continuous movement of water as the continuous movement of language. He is participating in the apparent stasis. He introduces water with the verb "possess" but in the passive voice. The possessor is language, particularly that part of speech—the verb—that denotes movement. Indeed, consistent with a motif of enclosed completeness, McKay invokes every verb and then follows in the opening movement with thirteen verbs—not quite "every" verb, even in English, but enough to convey amplitude. Consistent with the poem's title, and the word water, many of the verbs are also nouns: rush, drip, drink, piss, fall. Conversely, many of the nouns are also verbs: geysers, eddy, and perhaps fountain. The verbs run up against one another without the pause of punctuation, but within a pause set off by em-dashes, both stilled into thingness as nouns and mobile as verb cascading.

◆ ◆ ◆

Further pondering:

wealth   The wealth of ponds might first be recognized in their numbers: "they … typically outnumber[] larger lakes by a ratio of about 100 to 1 and occur in virtually all terrestrial environments" (Céréghino et al. 2). The pond's "wealth," McKay continues in the next line, consists in "a naturally occurring soup," the modifier "occurring" sustaining a sense of the unexpected (and hence of muted wonder) that runs through the poem, as well as the vocabulary of casual thinking: of gaze and gather and ponder. The metaphor of soup will evoke not only liquid nourishment but also mixing and jumbling constituents. But it is the modifier "naturally" that signals—with a touch of irony—that the poet's sense of wealth is also ecological. The aquatic ecologist ponders ponds specifically because "they support considerably more species, and specifically more scarce species, than other freshwater waterbody types" (Céréghino et al. 1). Pond is a wealth of "biodiversity," of "greater biotic and environmental amplitudes than rivers and lakes" (2).

with spawn and algae   As the poem's accumulation accumulates, the life forms identified get smaller. In an (imaginary) pond without any organisms, simple algae would be an early biological influence, raising the oxygen level through photosynthesis and creating conditions hospitable to other organisms. Spawn, from fish and amphibians, for example, or even as producers of fungi, would likely come late in a cycle of succession. In the case of algae, most "have a higher density than water and will eventually (cf. McKay's opening line) sink to the sediment surface"; accordingly, "most algae have adaptations to reduce sinking rate" (Brönmark and Hansson 8). "The most common morphological adaptation to reduce sinking in, for example, diatoms and blue-green algae, is to form *colonies*" (9). So we see how McKay attends to the "accident- / prone plumbing" of the pond's ecosystem. Evolutionary adaptation both slows to a "thickening" and densifies to maintain soupiness.

when it rains   "The catchment (or drainage) area ... is ... the region ... that drains the rain to the lake" (Brönmark and Hansson 1). The size of the catchment dictates the time it takes for the rain to reach the pond, and thus the amount of nutrients it gathers. An ecological dimension inheres in the loving response of pond to rain that McKay figures: wink, then pucker, and eventually shudder—an erotics of nutrient accumulation, perhaps gravid.

in bruin undertone   "The colour of the water in a ... pond is mainly derived from organic material ... lakes, and ponds in catchment areas dominated by coniferous forests are generally brown in colour because of the slow degradation of pine tree litter" (Brönmark and Hansson 2).

accident- / prone plumbing   "In oxygenated sediments where animals can live, sediment layers are disturbed by mechanical mixing. This *bioturbation* is caused by foraging fish, worms, insect larvae, and mussels moving around and mixing sediment layers" (Brönmark and Hansson 36).

◆ ◆ ◆

McKay ends his poem by returning, as it were, albeit interrogatively, to the catalogued verbs that "possess" water. The last word in the poem is the noun/ verb "ooze," situated as one of the two defining limits of pond ("deep sky" is the other). Ooze designates the muddy deposits at the bottom of the pond and implies some motion of slow exuding. Perhaps more slyly and playfully, McKay exploits the less familiar meaning of "ooze" as "an infusion of oak bark or other vegetable matter, used in tanning" ("Ooze"). The word picks up the odd introduction of "pelt" at the end of the poem's third movement. "Ooze," then, is the fourth explicit colour word in a poem with surprisingly little variety of palette colours. "Sepia," interestingly secreted by cuttlefish, moves changes from "brown" to "bruin": all is monochromatic shades of brown.

Although pond is essentially local—it is by definition small and still—the poem's opening sequence is global: geyser (heated water from deep within the earth) becomes eddy (in the backwater of a salmon stream) becomes frozen (in ice cap and glacier). Furthermore, the sequence moves to include and conclude with the circulation of water within bodies, pissed out by animals, transpired through skin, or lungs, or leaves.

TRANSLOCAL REPRESENTATION
Chief Buffalo Child Long Lance, Nello "Tex" Vernon-Wood, and CanLit
Julie Rak

> Like most Indians I have always been a great user of canvas rubber-soled shoes. When my old schoolmate, Chief Long Lance, and I were running with and against one another on the track team of the Carlisle Indian school, I remember how we used to kick out the rubber-soled shoes we had to wear in our athletics ... little did I think then that Long Lance himself would some day design this shoe.
> —Attributed to Jim Thorpe, advertisement for the Chief Long Lance Shoe (1930)[1]

> Does beat hell how complicated life's getting up here in the hills. Take this pilgrim [tourist] wrangling, fr'instance. Used to be, a man could bust out for a month on the trail, with a few plugs of spitting tobacco, and his other socks. As long as you had plenty sow belly, beans, flour, tea and sugar, with the odd fish hook, that's all anybody looked for. Try and get away with that now. We got to have grapefruit for breakfast, and a table to eat it off.
> —Nello "Tex" Vernon-Wood, "Us Winter Sports," *Sportsman* (1931; rpt. in *Mountain Masculinity*, Vernon-Wood 71)

Jim Thorpe, Chief Buffalo Child Long Lance, Tex Wood: these are not names associated with any literary canon, and certainly not with CanLit, "the informal shorthand which establishes it [Canadian Literature] as an established formation" (Brydon 2). However, the content of these quotations illustrates

problems of identity and representation that are, or could be, central to considering what CanLit is and what scholars might make of it now. Although the
subject of the first quotation is authenticity, little is authentic about the ad copy
supposedly by Jim Thorpe, a mixed-race athlete and celebrity raised on the
Sac and Fox Nation in the United States, including its endorsement of Chief
Buffalo Child Long Lance as an American Indian man and a designer of shoes:
technically, he was neither. The second quotation is about the transition of wilderness travel in the Canadian Rocky Mountains from a simpler (and manlier)
style that relied on hunting and fishing as methods of provision, to a fancier
mode of travel that is not "of" its place because it evokes capitalism's cease-
less movement of goods and services to where they do not belong. Like the
rich, urbanized travellers who consume it, grapefruit should never be found
in the Rocky Mountains. Ironically, the writer of these observations is Nello
Vernon-Wood, who represented himself as a former member of the English
aristocracy and invented a persona as a working-class wilderness guide "Tex
Wood," a clever, well-read social commentator who understood what "real" life
in the mountains was. In fact, Nello Vernon-Wood was Nello Wood, an illegitimate son of a working-class dressmaker from Birmingham, England. Just as
Sylvester Long, a mixed-race North Carolina man with Native ancestry classed
as "coloured," successfully passed for a time as a full-blooded Blackfoot chief
from a Blood reserve in Canada, so Vernon-Wood, a working-class man with
a difficult past, was able to pass as another kind of working-class man: a tough
mountain guide who was as authentic as the Canadian West he wrote about.

When we look at the lives and writings of Long Lance and Vernon-Wood
within the national frame of Canadian literature, neither fits. Both of these
men depended on a certain idea of Canada to construct their identities, but
Long Lance—a journalist who worked for Canadian newspapers—was born
in and ended his life in the United States, and Wood—who lived the latter
half of his life in Banff, Alberta—wrote about Canada for American magazines. When we look at either of them as writers, their status as journalists
means that their writing does not qualify as literary, either. When we look at
them as impostors—as many have at Grey Owl—somehow this invalidates
them both as people and as writers (Braz 53–55). The position of imposture,
however, relies on the very acceptance of secure identities that cannot travel.
During the 1930s in Canada, Britain, and the United States, much of the
reading public needed to believe that Canada was a frontier where Native
people could exist as alternatives to industrialization and where it might be
possible to rediscover some kind of primitive connections to that world; this
helped create what today look like creaky fictions of identity in the writings of
so-called imposters. The audience *wanted* to believe—so much so that in order ·
to succeed as writers, people like Long Lance, Tex Wood, E. Pauline Johnson

(who was technically half Mohawk, but who often performed her poetry as a generic Indian Princess), and even Grey Owl himself created fictions of the ideal Indian, or ideal frontiersman, for that audience. This version of identity imposture sees the act of being someone else *for others, demanded by those others*, as potentially challenging the idea of a secure identity, and of a secure literature based on identity:

> Imposture cannot be constituted outside a relationship: that is, imposture exists not as a pose undertaken in isolation but as a pose *imposed* on others. Second, it implies that imposture must be conceived of both as an act of misrepresentation and as a process of ascription, as a label. As an ascribed identity, imposture exists in the eyes of an audience. But because imposture exists as an ascription of a specifically fraudulent identity, it presupposes the possibility of a plenitudinous, fully self-cognizant subject capable of a "truthful" and totalizing self representation. (Dawson 224)

The self-reinventions of Long Lance and Tex Wood in the "New World" challenge our understanding of the rubrics of nation and literature, and even of what cultural production can be about. Because they were not strictly speaking imposters—rather, they were less glamorous members of the groups to which they pretended to belong—Long Lance and Wood serve as interesting examples of the construction of authenticity in the Canadian West; they also exemplify part of the problem of authenticity in Canadian literature. In this, they are both like and unlike Grey Owl.[2]

How can we examine these figures today? *Why* should we? A more traditional approach to thinking about Vernon-Wood and Chief Buffalo Child Long Lance would involve making them authentically Canadian and literary, "fitting them" into a CanLit discourse that continues to be remarkably slow to accept certain kinds of identities and certain types of writing. However, when we argue that Long Lance and Vernon-Wood are part of Canadian literature, we run the risk of critiquing ideas about national belonging without thinking about why these writers might be part of a discourse of national literature in the first place. Problematizing the nation without problematizing the literary means that half of our work is left undone. The literary as a category of knowledge deserves the same scrutiny that nation and state have received. As Smaro Kamboureli has observed, "literature has irrefutably emerged as a major player in the transformation the Canadian state has been undergoing in this era of global market economies" ("The Culture of Celebrity" 39). Why has the literary been so well suited to promoting the national project abroad, instead of Canadian visual art, dance, or performance?[3] What exactly *is* the literary, and what is it about the literary that seems to make it travel so well between states, regions, institutions, and economies? Examining national and literary imperatives together will help us answer this question.

Literary and cultural studies scholars are already fully engaged in critiquing ideas of nation in the English Canadian and Quebec cultural fields. The "TransCanada project" itself evokes the category "transnational"—at least metaphorically—as a way to talk about literature, institutions, and citizenship. If the transnational can be loosely understood as recognizing that social movements and cultural capital do not remain safely within national borders, then as Diana Brydon suggests, the concept of CanLit as a national and institutional formation must be rethought along with the idea of "the literary" as a prized category of knowledge:

> Like literature, "Canada" is an institutionally produced entity. With globalization, as institutional contexts change and come under scrutiny, literature, Canada and the notion of a national literature have all become problematized concepts. With the rise of new technologies, reading and entertainment are changing their functions, and literature no longer seems as important as it once did. With transnational mobilities of capital and people, nation-state functions are changing and the legitimacy of this institution is also being questioned. (5)

Brydon goes on to advocate that we investigate Canadian literature as an institution supported by other institutions. One way to do this is to look at limit cases of literariness, racial affiliation, class, and nationality such as those of Vernon-Wood and Long Lance. At the limit, we can think about how the mobilities of the transnational work to highlight "national literature" as a concept that—when it is critiqued—in fact *does not travel*. We now know that CanLit is a global product and an institutional imperative, but only when it appears to offer solid identities and cultural products to the market so that consumers "know" what kind of Canada they are getting. Inevitably, this version of Canada is limited to that of its most mainstream literary producers. How are we to study texts and identities that refuse to obey the dictates of either literariness or Canadianness—texts and identities that move around and evade capture, that are of the market more than literature itself but, because they are not literary, are somehow unharnessed from the reproduction of nationality? How then can we understand the movements of texts and people between regions, states, and racial and class identifications? In this essay, I suggest that the figures of Vernon-Wood and Long Lance have the potential to help CanLit scholars rethink the meaning of national literatures—including the "lit" of CanLit itself—as examples of the translocal. I suggest the translocal as a way to identify these kinds of movements and track their rather bumpy course across spaces and identities in order to interpret what cannot be fully "placed" within a state, a body of writing, or an identity.

Transnational to Translocal

I am suggesting the translocal as a term rather than the transnational, even though the latter is better known. I will take some space here to discuss what the transnational is and why it does not suit the transitory and even occasional kinds of movements I want to examine. The transnational has emerged in several fields—most notably in anthropology, sociology, and cultural studies—as a way of understanding how mobile populations create "the social, economic, cultural, and political linkages that migrants in host societies establish with their home countries—usually with an emphasis on the emergence of networks that cut across the borders of two or more nations" (Veronis 7). The transnational in this context serves as an acknowledgment that immigration does not occur unilaterally and that national borders do not cut off the flow of information or people between immigrant communities and their countries of origin. Other uses of the transnational relate to its status as a critique that helps scholars understand networks and flows in the wake of globalization— or, in some cases, before globalization occurs. For example, Riva Kastoryano has described as transnationalist groups that appear to act nationally but that operate beyond national borders in a series of networks. Transnationalism, then, is "deterritorialized," but instead of developing new national paradigms, it relies on the continuance of nation-states and on the interdependence of territory and state:

> The emergence of transnational communities is also a post-national phenomenon. That is, emigration took place after the age of nationalism, and the immigrants involved in constructing transnational communities do not refer to a "mythical" territorial state, but come from and refer to a territorialized nation-state.... The cultural and political specificities of national societies (host and home) are combined with emerging multilevel and multinational activities in a new space beyond territorially delimited nation-states, inevitably questioning the link between territory and nation-state. ("Settlement" 307)

Transnational communities challenge the assumed link between nation and people, but they do not do so consistently. There is a "balance" between territory and nation-state, since in transnational communities the flow of people, goods, and information occurs both ways and continues over time. A new nation is not formed from this relationship. Rather, as Kastoryano writes, transnationalism is "an institutional expression of multiple belonging, where the country of origin becomes the source of identity, the country of residence a source of rights, and the emerging transnational space, a space of political action combining the two or more countries" (311). As Paul Hopper points out in *Understanding Cultural Globalization,* this way of seeing migrant identities within globalization as flexible and multi-faceted explains why transnationalism is both a description and a critique of migrants' relationship to nation-states:

> To an extent this popularity [of transnationalism in academic discussions of globalization] may be due to the perceived inadequacies of internationalism, which continues to conceptualize the world in terms of nation-states and the extension or otherwise of national power, and thereby pays insufficient attention to the range of cultural forms, forces and tendencies that both extend beyond their borders and at the same time move within them.... Transnationalism is effectively an acknowledgement that many contemporary flows are not truly global, and are simply anchored in more than one nation-state. (52)

There is currently a debate about what transnationalism looks like in migrant communities (Hopper 53–55) and whether it is a better way to describe migrant connections than diasporic nationalism (Kastoryano, "The Reach of Transnationalism"; Cho 98–99); clearly, though, transnationalism is a way to describe how people are moving—literally and imaginatively—between nation-states and challenging the primacy of thinking about nation-state formations as they do. For instance, if CanLit were reconceived as transnational, it might be possible to understand at least some of its literatures (and the migrants who write them) as participating in the flows within and beyond nation-states in conditions of globalization, rather than as existing (and being studied) in splendid isolation.

But the emphasis on the "national" in transnational creates problems for my own study; the usefulness of that term for describing migrant connections is also problematic. For transnationalism to accurately describe a networked community, the nation-state must still be operating, even if its functions of providing an identity and providing rights and privileges of citizenship are spread across one or more states, as Kastoryano suggests they are ("Settlement"). It was not always the case that groups of people migrated to Canada from another nation. Some moved to (and within) Canada when Canada itself was not yet a nation-state but rather part of an empire. Also, some parts of Canada, such as Quebec and Nunavut, have complex relationships with the nation-state that affect the movement of people and how their identities are formed. Furthermore, as we shall see in the case of Long Lance, many people have come to Canada without citizenship rights in their "home" countries; it is difficult to discuss these migrants as transnational, since they were not able to "belong" fully to their home nations. In the case of Aboriginal people in Canada, national belonging is neither desirable nor even possible, because of the ongoing effects of colonization and dispossession. In fact, the need to belong fully and imaginatively to a place is what makes Tex Wood and Long Lance limit cases in a discussion of literature and citizenship: both of them shed their old identities in an attempt to make lives (and writing lives) for themselves that would never have been available to them in the spaces they once occupied and in the identities they once had. The process, as we shall see, is not easy. It involves passing as another kind of person, lying about origins, and inventing new ones. Those new identities are prey to what market forces demand in terms of identity politics, and those who invent new identities move places and shift identities in response to the ways that people with power demand and define "authentic" identity for their own purposes and enjoyment.

In this sense, the translocal participates in the politics of mobility that Mark Simpson has described in an American context as "the contestatory processes that produce different forms of movement, and that invest these forms with social value, cultural purchase, and discriminatory power" (xiii–xiv). As a term coined by Arjun Appadurai to explain how—because of globalization— communities reconstitute the borders of their groups in ways that unhook the identities and practices of their members from fixed territories, the translocal has become a way to talk about how identities are created on the move without reference to consistent national borders (Appadurai 8). Also, the term "translocal" fits a "post-national" understanding of collaborative art curation and production.[4] In human geography, "translocal" has been used instead of "network" as a means to understand how place-based social movements communicate with other places and indeed extend beyond their original place as they become mobile (McFarlane 562).

Thus, translocality does not need to focus on nations. As a concept, the translocal performs the function for place that "transgender" performs for gender identity: instead of tracking the permeability of communicative networks, it represents the capacity of identities, affiliations, and even texts to exist between and across places that do not have to be nation-states. It can track the movement and permeability of subjects. It can trouble the boundaries of what we understand epistemically in an emphasis on networked spaces and flows. In this sense, I am suggesting that "translocal" is not just a way to talk about how identities based on place can move and exceed their places of origin; translocality can also be connected to the development of identity itself. The translocal can sometimes challenge what we know about national belonging and citizenship. At other points, translocal subjects return this kind of knowledge to the status quo and support conventional ways to think of identity and nation. The translocal, then, can be a description of movement as well as a critique of mobility within a nation-state. In this sense, it can remind us of the importance of local places within Canada, at the same time resisting the impulse to subordinate the regional to the national in the Canadian imaginary, since translocal subjects move between regions, which sometimes include national borders. This is how, for instance, we can use the translocal to look at how movement happens between the American and the Canadian wests, which are shared geographic and social locations, and between the idea of the "West" and its manifestations as part of the national imaginaries of both nations.

To examine how the translocal can be a critique of nation, identity, and the idea of the literary, I next consider the two authors I began this essay with, both of whom helped create the idea of the Canadian West as the last "wild" place on earth. During the 1920s and 1930s, journalist and silent film star Sylvester Long pretended to be Chief Buffalo Child Long Lance, a member of a Blackfoot tribe near Calgary, Alberta. Nello Wood reinvented himself as Vernon Wood in the early twentieth century, then as Nello Vernon-Wood, and finally, during the 1920s and 1930s, as Tex Wood, a homespun Canadian Rocky Mountains guide. The identities and writings of Long Lance and Wood challenge what it means to be authentically "of a place." At the time, they also helped create fantasy locations and the idea of the Canadian West as a tourist destination. Reading them today poses the challenge of the translocal to both the Can and the Lit in CanLit.

Tex Wood

Who was Tex Wood and where did he come from? This question is more complicated than it might seem, particularly in light of the investigations into Wood's identity that Andrew Gow (Wood's great-grandson) and I did for the book *Mountain Masculinity: The Life and Writing of Nello "Tex" Vernon-Wood in the Canadian Rockies, 1906–1938*. That book is a collection of writings by Nello Vernon-Wood and his alter ego Tex Wood as well as photographs and reminiscences about Tex from members of his family. It includes a critical introduction by Andrew Gow and me in which we discuss Nello as "a gentleman born and bred" (Gow and Rak 9) who was able to "pass" (with winks at his readers) as a cowpoke and mountain guide by writing pieces in homespun vernacular, albeit heavily larded with allusions to the classics. We thought that Tex's wry comments about the ineptitude of English and American elite clients in the Canadian wilderness were part of his "real" identity as an insider who had given up being an aristocrat. That identity was not meant to be hidden, however (18–20)—he did, after all, sign each of his "Tex" pieces, as well as two pieces where he did not write as Tex, as "N. Vernon-Wood." We assumed that he did this because, as Nello, Vernon-Wood was a lifelong socialist (he subscribed to the *Manchester Guardian*). He was also the husband of a working-class Irish woman and an avid reader, so we concluded that his socialist beliefs had led him to abandon his class position in England, although he never really left some of his old habits behind (25–28). We concluded that the "Tex" persona was meant to be read as an identity performance by the readers of his articles in magazines for the sporting elite, who knew that in the end, he was "the right sort" of Englishman who could be relied on to be both authentic and genteel. His gentle critiques of those who belonged to the elite reflected his socialist desire to be a working man himself, while his performance of "book learning" was a reflection of his own identity as an elite person (34–35).

Gow and I were wrong on many of these counts. Nello Vernon-Wood, the aristocratic son of an army physician who was killed in Egypt and a woman named Ruth Hunter, a native of Stratford-upon-Avon, who had a single picture of his family home (Gow and Rak 11), never existed. He was actually Nello Wood, a working-class man of humble origins, and was probably the illegitimate son of Ruth Wood, a dressmaker who lived with her sister in a suburb of Birmingham, England, for more than twenty years. According to British census records from 1891 and 1901, Nello lived with Mary Ann, his aunt and the family head, and Ruth in at least two different row houses on Homer Street in Balsall Heath, a working-class neighbourhood of Birmingham. Ruth and Mary Ann had a half-sister living nearby named Ellen, whose nickname could have been Nell. Perhaps, then, she was Nello's namesake, as at least one family story suggests (1901 UK Census 24; Gow and Rak 11). Nello could have been Ellen's child, taken to the city to be raised away from prying eyes, or he could have been Ruth's son, born far from any possibility of gossip in Darlaston, the village where she had grown up and where she had worked "out" as a maid when a young woman. Did Ruth have a liaison with a young aristocrat in the place where she worked and, when she became pregnant, was she forced to leave and live with her sister Mary Ann? Was she working in the house that appears in Wood's only photograph of what he said was his family home? No one knows. When he was six, the 1891 census listed Nello Wood as a student. Ten years later, he had received enough education to become a legal clerk. He is also listed in that census as "Nello V.," which is probably a reference to his middle name, Vernon (1891 UK Census 44; 1901 UK Census 105). Nello must have been successful enough at school to get a job as a clerk later on. He could have become an avid reader there and learned about socialism and the plight of the British working class from the excellent public library, which was around the corner from his house (Dargue n.p.). It is possible to imagine that, as a young man, he read in that library about the possibilities of the Canadian West as he learned about socialism, or perhaps he saw one of the many posters that advertised resettlement there for young English men. He may have dreamed of escaping from a life with few prospects for social advancement, especially if his illegitimacy were discovered. Thus, as one of the family accounts about him says, he went to Canada in 1903, when he was about eighteen (Gow 215–16).

Nothing appears about Nello Wood after that, but Nello, perhaps because of his dislike for his given name, probably became "Vernon." The 1906 Census of the Northwest Provinces lists a V. Wood living in Medicine Hat and working as a ranch hand, as he told his relatives he did do. His year of migration from England is listed as 1906 (although this could be an error), and he is twenty years old (1906 NW Census 12). The 1911 Canadian census lists a "Vernon Wood" as a resident of Alberta who was born two years before Nello, in 1882 (1911 Canada Census 4). This is probably Nello.

At some point, Vernon acquired the name Tex—possibly, from a set of big "Texas" chaps he bought to help him in his work as a rancher in Medicine Hat (Gow 219). Whatever the case, he became known only as Tex even to his own family, and he somehow became Vernon-Wood, a hyphenated name that an English aristocrat would have. His family believed this was his real name. His fabricated origins probably helped him get guiding jobs, since English guides were thought to be "gentlemen" who could guide women and men without difficulty.

In 1930, presumably to supplement his guiding income, Wood began writing articles for American sporting magazines about his experiences in the persona and voice of Tex Wood, unflappable wilderness guide. Early on, the editor of the *Forum* specifically asked Vernon-Wood to write in vernacular because his readers would find this enjoyable. The request from editor E.W. Smith is worth quoting in its entirety:

> How would you [Nello Vernon-Wood] like to try an 1800-word travelogue for *The Forum* on "Big Game Hunting in the Rockies." You can work in some of your most exciting experiences. And if you will use your own most pictu[r]esque language, and do not stumble into academic English, thinking it is for *The Forum*, you might produce something very original and refreshing for our readers. We will be willing to gamble $35.00 on the experiment, anyhow. (qtd. in Gow and Rak, 18–19n24)

Vernon-Wood must have agreed, since most of the articles he wrote for magazines like the *Forum*, the *National Sportsman*, and the *Sportsman* used this type of language. It is interesting to note how careful the editor is to direct

Vernon-Wood to write as Tex: he asks Vernon-Wood to use his "own" language, which assumes that he has a language of his own, but he also takes care to tell him not to "stumble" or lapse into academic English, for he knows that Vernon-Wood is capable of speaking and writing this way and might even *want* to write this way. Smith says his readers will find picturesque language "original and exciting"—an indication that he is asking Vernon-Wood to write inauthentically (since the editor's detailed instructions show it is not easy to do) in order to create an authenticity for an audience that wants it. Finally, he offers a considerable sum if Vernon-Wood is actually able to do this: it is an "experiment," both in writing persona and in identity performance.

Vernon-Wood was able to rise to this challenge: as Gow and I point out, he succeeded in performing as a gentleman (Vernon-Wood) who was pretending to be a working-class man, although at the time we thought it was the upper-class performance that was real. In the story "Sawback and the Sporting Proposition," Tex Wood's sidekick, Sawback, makes the following speech: "Well, there's also a fardel of fish down where Skookumchuk Crik empties into the lake. I dunno about you, but I'm fed up on lean venison, so I rid over to see you'd consider postponin' your various inutile pursuits, an' concentrate on decoyin' the odd Christivomer outer his native element" (Vernon-Wood 193–94). The words "fardel," "inutile," and "Christivomer" (a Latin word for lake trout)—words that an educated person would use—are deliberately placed beside slang words and deliberate malapropisms like "Crik," "rid over" and "outer." In the same story, Tex uses the word "aerated" in one breath and "billygoat" in another (196). At other times, Tex combines two unlikely words in one phrase, such as "bobtail hellion" for lynx (93), or he refers to a dictionary as "Webster's masterpiece" (92). The audience for these stories was educated; readers were meant to "get" the joke that a guide had the intelligence and education to use language in this way. Just as an Indian was meant to be seen as a "Noble Savage" and not as an actual Native person, so Tex Wood was meant to be homespun but also familiar to his readers in a comic manner. Many of Vernon-Wood's Tex stories lampoon tourists who do not understand what wilderness life. Often, in sporting magazine articles from the period, guides are lampooned by clients. In Vernon-Wood's articles, the guide literally talks back to his masters. In "Fifth Avenue Pilgrims amid the Goats," for example, Tex's slight build is mocked by his rich client, but in the end it is the guide who proves to be stronger (Vernon-Wood 40–41). "William, Prepare My Barth" mocks big-game hunters who treat their guides like servants and affirms that Tex's identity is "colonial" and therefore authentic (64–66); "Pipestone Letters No. 1" (part of a series of "letters" Vernon-Wood wrote for the magazine *Hunting and Fishing* in 1932) features a New Yorker who has to be taught by his guide how to hunt and live properly in the back country (104–5).

At other times, Tex Wood shows himself to be an authentic outdoorsman who does not care about social rules. In "Tex Reads His Permit," Vernon-Wood mocks park wardens who are university-educated but who lack proper outdoor skills and, more importantly, any understanding of wilderness conduct. Tex is educated—he calls the economic downturn of the 1930s "financial flaccidity," for instance (127)—but park wardens take useless subjects like "Sikology, Practical Prospectin', an' Needlepoint Embroidery" (128). Tex is hunting for "ovid canandesis" as a specimen for the Smithsonian Institution (he describes this job in a story—not written in vernacular—called "Rams") and is accused of poaching by a warden who asks for his permit. Tex demands the warden's credentials and then is made to go back to his camp for his documentation. The scene ends with Tex beating the warden up when the warden decides not to read the permit (128–29). Here, Tex's wilderness ethic (outdoorsmen should trust one another) triumphs over the park warden's lack of experience. In other stories, Tex says that contrary to popular wisdom, women are often just as good or better than men in the back country: "any woman I have had to do with fitted in like a cartridge in a rifle. I figure that if a woman don't like the outdoors she never gets far enough to get here" (51). Here, "fitting in" refers to the ability of men or women to adhere to back country values and to demonstrate hunting and camping skills. Since women are not expected to be good at a traditionally masculine pursuit such as hunting, Tex Wood's beliefs are comic because they turn the tables on gender norms. In "It's a Woman's World," for instance, the female client proves to be a much better hunter and dresser of game even than the guides (210–14). In "This Guiding Game," the women in the hunting party prove to be tougher than the man with them, and happily leave him behind when the trip becomes difficult (52).

In 1931, Tex's suspicion of non-wilderness ideas is also used to lampoon the new sport of skiing in "Us Winter Sports," where Tex and his friends try out skis in an effort to educate themselves as ski guides. This story is a reference to the founding of Skoki Lodge by the Ski Club of the Canadian Rockies (Gow and Rak in Vernon-Wood 69), but in this story much is made of the fact that Tex cannot ski: "I try stem turns, jump turns, telemarks and a lot that aint in our book, and finish in a nose dive" (Vernon-Wood 74). Yet only one year later, Vernon-Wood published a "straight" piece for *Canadian Alpine Journal* about the building of Skoki Lodge in 1930, which included a first ski ascent of Mount Ptarmigan. Here, Vernon-Wood presents himself as a highly educated traveller:

> In Skoki Valley, immediately north of Lake Louise they [the Canadian Ski Club] found their desideratum. Here, conditions, approximated the best of European ski centres, slopes on which the novice may try his 'prentice hand,

open alplands, spruce filled valleys.... The northern slopes [of Mt. Ptar-
migan] are glacier hung, with a stupendous ice-fall terminating in a small
unnamed lake of surprising beauty. (97–98)

Vernon-Wood's language here is clearly more elevated, although he still uses
the slang word "'prentice," and there are no references to any inability to ski.
Tex is suspicious of tourism and tends not to describe the mountains; by contrast, Vernon-Wood in this persona talks about the benefits of the Skoki Valley for tourists and later describes the wilderness summit in romantic terms:
"the world seemed snow-covered and silent. A brooding calm, accentuated
occasionally by the roar of a distant avalanche" (99). It might be tempting to
think of this literary voice as the "real" Vernon-Wood; however, his position
as someone who has "double-passed" as both a hard-bitten wilderness guide
and a highly educated former member of the English gentry means that in fact
this persona is no more authentic than that of Tex. Like the persona in the
Tex Wood stories, it is aimed at a specific market that might be interested in
this version of the Canadian West as an unspoiled wilderness. In his writing
and even as a performance for his family, Wood created the Vernon-Wood
persona as a way to show how authentic he had become. Vernon-Wood is what
allows Tex to pass as a working-class man. Ironically, it is "Tex Wood," the
clever, self-educated man of the people, who represents more accurately who
Nello, and then Vernon-Wood, was: the largely self-educated working-class
Englishman and socialist who may well have dreamed of a place where he
would not face class restrictions, a place where one could live by one's wits and
intelligence. It seems that N. Vernon-Wood was the way for Tex Wood to be
that man of the New World, a man who had left the old one behind and who
no longer had to account for his love of books, especially the Latin classics
and Shakespeare, by talking about the difficult parts of his origins. He could
disavow them by creating a new set of origins to disavow (Gow and Rak 12).

Wood did not entirely disavow anything, however, and this is what makes
him translocal, a person between identities and places. Tex Wood, or Tex
Vernon-Wood, or Nello Vernon-Wood, or Nello Wood never really gave up
any of his identities; instead, he acquired more of them, slipping between
each just as his language slipped from vernacular to malapropisms to Lati-
nate references as he performed Canada for American markets. Wood's use
of slippage between places as a marker of authenticity, for the West and for
himself, was a response to the demand for regions and those who are regional
to be "authentic" for their audiences and other consumers of that authenticity.
Alison Calder has identified this tendency in the demand for regional writing
to be authentic, especially in the case of the Canadian West, due to a rigid
connection between environment and identity:

> The demand for authenticity, for the authorial experience requiring an insider's view thus also conserves a reliance on the genus loci: it is exposure to the "natural environment" that confers both authenticity and authority.
>
> The authority of the insider, or native speaker, is derived from the reader's faith in the insider's capacity to function as a regional representative, to speak for the region and in some way embody what are perceived to be distinct regional characteristics. This capacity is closely linked to the text's truth-value: readers trust the author to provide them with a true, insider's view of regional life. (59–60)

This idea about region, Calder says, is based on Northrop Frye's original premise in *The Bush Garden* that an artist may move from one region to another and be accepted by others while nevertheless remaining foreign when she or he tries to represent the region (59). This kind of absolute demand for authenticity, which asked Nello Vernon-Wood to become Tex Wood and then to write in his own "picturesque language" for American magazine markets, is what creates the authentic region of the Canadian West as a fantasy location for others. Wood's response to this is translocal. He creates a "straight" persona, which becomes the alternative to the supposedly false, homespun character Tex Wood, and then he allows the layers of identity, customs, language, and class to overlap one another. Ultimately, Tex Wood does "wink" at his readers—indeed, at the idea of authenticity itself—even while he appears to support what authenticity stands for. In this "wink," this refusal to let go of any forms of belonging, we can see the challenge of translocality and its refusal to connect region to identity.

Chief Buffalo Child Long Lance

The story of how Sylvester Long became Chief Buffalo Child Long Lance is a fascinating example of the problems of race and belonging in the United States and Canada. The facts of Long Lance's life have been well documented by Donald Smith: Sylvester Long was born in 1890 in Winston-Salem, North Carolina, to two former slaves, Sallie and Joe Long. Sallie and Joe lived as "coloured" (that is, black) people in Winston-Salem, although both maintained that they were white and Indian. This is probably true, but because they had been slaves, they were unable to prove this, so they had to live as black people in a segregated society. The community of Winston-Salem accepted that the Longs had some Indian ancestry, which if they could have documented it, would have led them to be classified either as Indian—as was possible in some southern counties—or as white (Smith, *Chief Buffalo* 32–33, 281–82). Thus the Long children—Walter, Abe, and Sylvester—had to attend a school for blacks even though they lived next to the white school.

Sylvester wanted to escape this stifling life. In 1904 he ran off with a circus that had a Wild West show. With his straight, dark hair and sharp features, he was able to pass as an Indian. He returned home, but after a failed attempt to pick up his grade seven education, he joined another circus, passed easily as an Indian, and learned to ride a horse so well that some thought he had been born on a ranch. He befriended a Cherokee man and learned rudimentary Cherokee and some Cherokee lore before he went home in 1909 (Smith, *Chief Buffalo* 38–39).

With help from his father, who wrote on the forms that his son was "half Indian of the Cherokee tribe," Sylvester Long was admitted to the Carlisle Indian School in Pennsylvania, an institution founded to help Native children succeed in the white world. At Carlisle, the students were suspicious of Long's claims, complaining (at first) that he was not purely Native and calling him a "Cherokee nigger" (Smith, *Chief Buffalo* 50). Long worked hard to earn their approval and learn their traditions and history. By the time he graduated in 1912, he was calling himself Sylvester Chahuska Long Lance. He tried to get into West Point but failed the entrance exams.

With West Point no longer a possibility, Long Lance went to Canada in 1916, where he enlisted in the Canadian Army. He fought at Vimy Ridge, and was wounded a month later and sent to England for the rest of the war. After he was discharged, he did not return to the United States. At the time, the United States was beset with racial strife: seventy African Americans were lynched in 1919, the year Long Lance was discharged, and there were race riots in twenty-five American cities that same year (Smith, *Chief Buffalo* 80). The segregated United States could not have appealed to Long Lance, who had already lived a life of adventure and possibility by pretending to be someone else. After he was discharged in Canada, he went west to Alberta. His decision to go to Alberta involved more than a desire to distance himself from his origins. As Nancy Cook points out, many Americans during this period, including Long Lance himself, saw the Canadian West as the "unspoiled" part of the West, a place where Indians seemed to be less assimilated than those in the United States. This view of the Canadian West persisted among Americans well into the 1920s (Cook 152). For Long Lance, the Canadian West would have represented a place where it was possible to live in a land of opportunity without barrriers or the threat of violence. In Long Lance's 1927 article for *McClure's* called "Princes Go West, but What of the Young Man without Money?", however, opportunity comes only for those who are British royalty or full-blooded Indians (Cook 142–43). Long Lance's subsequent desire to *become* a full-blooded Plains Indian was linked to the idea of the Canadian West as more authentic than the American West, and as a place where some groups , unlike the Cherokee, had not been conquered, humiliated, and forced to assimilate. In other words, Canada was the place where Long Lance could work out a pure Native identity for himself, far from people who might question his origins. He would not have to face becoming a black person again.

Long Lance worked as a journalist for the *Calgary Herald* from 1919 until the late 1920s. During those years, he began to publish stories about the Blackfoot and Blood in the area. He was formally adopted by the Blood nation in 1922, at which time he was given the name Buffalo Child. Long Lance's reinvention of himself as a Plains Indian truly began shortly afterwards, once he started working as a journalist in Vancouver. He began using the byline "Chief Buffalo Child Long Lance." He also began writing articles about the conditions on reserves and about the need for Canada's Native people to resist oppression; all the while, he wrote about the nobility of Native people's traditions, making sure to represent their views as accurately as he could. He also began referring to himself as a Blood Indian. Why would he do this?

As a child and as a young man, Long Lance had experienced racial inequality, and in particular, the failure of American law and social custom to acknowledge who mixed-race people were. Until very recently, American law and social practice held that Americans could only be one race. Only since the 1980s has this belief been challenged. It was not until 2000 that the US census even allowed respondents to declare that they were of more than one race (Garroutte 7–9). This was partly due to the commonly held idea in the United States that "colour" and "blood," rather than ethnic background or culture, were what determined racial identity. The "one-drop rule" in the American South after the Reconstruction, for instance, created a set of social and legal practices that determined that even "one drop" of African American blood made a person black, regardless of how many generations back this might have occurred (Wald 11). The US government and some Native American groups also used blood quantum to determine who was a member of a tribal roll and who was not (Garroutte 16). As a consequence, racial belonging was conceptualized as a single affiliation, and white as a pure norm that could be corrupted by any other racial affiliation. Mixed-race people in the United States have been viewed as a threat to the social order, or they have been categorized—as the current President Barack Obama often is—as not-white. In the nineteenth century, the result of this, as Gayle Wald has pointed out, was that passing became a strategy for negotiating the absolute assessments of the one-drop rule and Jim Crow laws. Indeed, Wald suggests, the idea survives to this day. In essence, passing has been constructed as a transgression of racial purity—a transgression that the law is supposed to protect Americans from (Wald 11–12). What is more, at the time of the Jim Crow laws, passing was the only way that Southern blacks could actually become American, because being black meant it was impossible to be a citizen or even a full human being.

The Jim Crow laws and the one-drop rule, then, created an embodied sense of citizenship. To be American was to have a white body (Wald 13).

In this social situation, many black people tried to pass as white; but for Long Lance, there was another way to leave behind the world of segregation and racial prejudice. Long Lance's parents had always insisted that they were mixed race but not black. If Long Lance could pass as a Native person, he could acquire a pure identity and, it followed, the rights and privileges of full citizenship that had been denied him and his family. I believe this is why he went to Canada to join the army; it was so that, as an Indian, he could participate fully as a citizen. And this is why he chose to live and build his identity in the Canadian West before moving to New York as a full-fledged celebrity. The one-drop rule did not seem to apply in Canada, particularly in the West; in Canada, Native people could even, if they were chiefs, be treated as equals. At a time when the Ku Klux Klan was on the rise in the United States, Long Lance must have found it appealing to pursue a pure identity in Canada.

More and more often, Long Lance represented himself in public as a member of the Blood nation. He even appeared at a Blackfoot Sundance in 1923 as an investigative reporter; he made many mistakes at the encampment, however, and the Blackfoot barred him from the sacred ceremonies, refusing to recognize him as one of them. In the aftermath, he turned away from activism and started "playing" Indian for non-Native people. He began leading the Indian contingent, in full regalia, at the Calgary Stampede each year; he also began working for the Banff Springs Hotel each summer as a publicist and an entertainer of VIPs. At the hotel, he became the "resident Indian" for the rich tourists, who enjoyed his sophistication and were enthralled by his stories of Indian life and lore.

A cartoon from this period shows how Long Lance was able to appear as an authentic Native person by *not* appearing in costume (D. Smith, *Chief Buffalo* 180). In the cartoon, Cicero Sapp, a white man, dresses up in cowboy costume to meet "a real Indian chief at the hotel" because, as he says to his wife, "this is a he-man's country out here. You don't think I'm going to meet an Indian dressed like a cake-eater, do you?" To his horror, he is introduced to a suave man in a tuxedo, who turns out to be Long Lance (180–81). The scene's comedy arises from the inauthenticity of Sapp, who can dress up as a cowboy and act manly, but whose expectations of Native people mean that he finds Long Lance's lack of machismo (he has sensuous lips in the cartoon) and his upper-class manners mark him as a *real* chief and Sapp as the counterfeit cowboy. The hidden real exposes the displayed fake. In an article for *McClure's* in 1927, Long Lance wrote that "all of the genuine cowboys on the plains are as pedigreed as a Boston Terrier" and that "the real cowboy dresses less like he is pictured as dressing than those who masquerade as cowboys"; he added that he recognized a "real" cowboy in street clothes during the Calgary Stampede (qtd. in Cook 143). The authentic Western person, then, did not need to be in costume for other authentic people of the West to recognize him. However, Long Lance neglected to say that he would have been leading the Indian contingent in full regalia at the time, in costume. What does this say about authenticity? According to Cook, if authenticity requires an inauthentic other in order to be authentic, then an authentic Native person or cowboy needs to be able to play two roles: one symbolizing the link to the past (costume), and one representing the link to modernity (tails or street clothes). Long Lance's ability to shift roles made it possible for him to *see* the authentic where others could not; this was how he could *appear* authentic precisely by not acting the part (145–46). The same economy of Western authenticity held true for Tex Wood, who required Nello Vernon-Wood, the educated and aristocratic Englishman, to exist as the guarantee of his authentic self, who could then evaluate whether others, such as tourists or park wardens, were authentic or not.

By 1927, Long Lance's stories about Plains Indian life for American magazines had become stories about himself and his origins. His self-inventions had become more pronounced: he was now claiming, for instance, that he had graduated from West Point, and he even wrote a short "autobiographical" piece in which he said he wanted to be like a white man but was also proud of his Indian heritage (D. Smith, *Chief Buffalo* 186). The American public eagerly consumed these fictions.

Sylvester Long would never have experienced the fame and adulation that his creation Long Lance was now receiving, and he would have faced a life of segregation, poverty, and violence. The lure of pretending to be an Indian on an even bigger stage was too much for him to resist. When Ray Long asked Long Lance to write a boy's adventure book to be called *The Story of an Indian Boy* about the Blackfoot communities for *Cosmopolitan*'s book publishing company, he agreed. In 1927, however, just before the contract was finalized, Long made an important suggestion: he should write a memoir instead, beginning the story in the 1890s, when he was a child (194–95). The reasons why are clear: a boys' book would undoubtedly have an attracted an audience that had been primed on dime westerns and the stories of James Fenimore Cooper; a memoir by Long Lance would find an audience interested in "authentic" accounts of the West by someone who had experienced it. Long Lance, who had never been asked to account for any of the fictions he had created about himself, agreed to write the book as his life story. Using stories told to him by his friend Mike Eagle Speaker, a member of the Blood nation near Calgary, and some of his pieces for newspapers and magazines, he constructed a tale of life as a Blackfoot (Cook 148).

The resulting book, *Long Lance*, was an instant bestseller in 1928. It was well reviewed by the international press, and even prominent experts on Native people praised it. By 1929, its author was a full-fledged celebrity, endorsing a line of athletic shoes by B.F. Goodrich (for which Jim Thorpe willingly put his name on the advertising copy), giving lectures on Native people, and, in 1929, starring in the film *The Silent Enemy*, a fictional documentary that aimed to represent the problems of Native people in a non-exploitive way. However, legal counsel for *The Silent Enemy* investigated a claim by one of the Aboriginal actors that Long Lance could not be Native, and found out that he was Sylvester Long of North Carolina. Long Lance fled to Los Angeles, where he was hired to be the bodyguard of the heiress Anita Baldwin. He killed himself in Anita Baldwin's library in 1932.

On publication, *Long Lance*[5] had been generally lauded as a true account of the Blackfoot because, unlike the more lurid boys' tales of the period, it did contain some accurate information about pre-contact Blackfoot ways. Most of the information in the book was based on what Mike Eagle Speaker had told him about the earlier times of the Blackfoot and on Long Lance's own interviews with elders, so this material was accurate (D. Smith, *Chief Buffalo* 201–4), although he had to set the story in the 1890s in northern Montana and on the Canadian prairies to make it believable as his memoir. This meant he had to claim that bison still roamed the plains and were being hunted by nomadic groups in the 1890s, when in fact they were almost extinct by then and the Blackfoot were living on reserves. Significantly, Long Lance did not present the American West as a wilderness at that time; instead, he described Canada before 1905 as a wild and untamed wilderness:

> Until 1905 Alberta and Saskatchewan were known as the Northwest Territories, a wild untamed region of North America, which had seen its first white settlers only twenty years before. The Indians of this vast stretch of high rolling plains still remember the first white man they ever saw. (Long Lance 11)

This was an idealized—and of course, inaccurate—picture of Canada for American readers. Long Lance was describing a wilderness where Indians could still live without the influence of white contact. Most American readers of *Long Lance* would have known about the Indian Wars in the United States (including Custer's Last Stand and the massacre at Wounded Knee) but little or nothing about the Canadian West; thus, Long Lance's book made it possible for them to imagine a place where non-Native people had not yet dominated or destroyed Native people and their way of life. As Cook points out, however, this "stateless" wilderness where the Blackfoot were free to roam can be read today not just as an idealization of the frontier, but as a representation of Long Lance's own desire for mobility:

> As a child in North Carolina, Long Lance had been trapped by geography,
> whereas in Blackfeet country Indians cross state, provincial, territorial and
> national boundaries routinely. His catalogue of the Indians' extensive terri-
> tory reinforces the idea that freedom of movement is the paramount marker
> of political freedom.... In fact the movement across borders was stopped by
> treaty in 1877 and most Blackfeet were settled on reservations or reserves
> by the early 1880s. (150)

The same holds true for the picture in *Long Lance* of the Blackfoot as fearless
warriors whose male children took baths in snow and icy water "to harden
our bodies" (Long Lance 20) but whose mothers (as Long Lance's own mother
did) took sole charge of their moral instruction (22).

Long Lance is not really a memoir, yet it is still possible to read it, as Cook
does, as an expression of Long Lance's own yearning for mobility, for a close
family (he had not seen most of his family in years), and for a pure identity.
Karina Vernon points out (63–66) that in a passage near the beginning of
Long Lance, the author raises and then disavows the possibility of his own
blackness: "They [story tellers of other tribes] even told us of 'black white men'
who lived under the sun, where it rested when it went under the horizon, and
who were 'scorched' until they were black" (Long Lance 17). This detail is not
necessary to the rest of the passage, which is actually about enemy groups
and then the coming of white people during Long Lance's youth, with their
"big houses" on water and a "long house" that spat fire and smoke (17). Why
include it, with its racist assumptions about the origins of blackness? One
answer is that it ends the introductory section of the book, where Long Lance
talks about his early memories as "a dull, deep bluish grey. That was the color
of my early world. Everything I saw was tinted with this mystic greyness. It
represented danger, mystery and distance" (16–17). Given the account of an
exciting and action-packed life as a Blackfoot child that follows, this melancholic beginning seems to make little sense. It may be that Long Lance
is talking about his own childhood in North Carolina and that "the mystic
greyness" refers to the hopelessness of his life there, or perhaps to his own
identity as "coloured," to a time when everything seemed uncertain and he
was powerless to change anything.

After the first sections about his Blackfoot boyhood, the middle section
of *Long Lance* describes a war between his community and the Crow people.
When peace is finally achieved with the Crow, the story shifts to an account
of the rebellion of Almighty Voice. Here, *Long Lance* critiques the land take-
over by wondering why the young people do not rise up and rebel when their
elders will not:

And sometimes, as the sun was setting and it started to get cold on the butte, we would all huddle close together in the gathering darkness—and just sit and think. Though powerless little children, we, like all youngsters, felt a great responsibility in the things that were going on about us. We felt that if our old people would let us fight we could soon clear up the situation. I supposed all boys are like that. (212)

This passage reflects Long Lance's belief, expressed in his later magazine articles, that younger Native people might be able to help their groups withstand assimilation. However, its evocation of "all youngsters" and "all boys" also indicates that he could be referring to other instances of childhood helplessness, including that of his own childhood, when his mother constantly told him and his brothers not to fight discrimination but to bear it because it was God's will (D. Smith, *Chief Buffalo* 28).

This need to resist, and to present a *pure* Indian resistance to white tyranny, might be why *Long Lance* does not end with an account of Louis Riel, who as leader of the Métis of the Red River Colony, with Cree allies, created the largest full-scale resistance to white dominance in Canada. Riel, as Long Lance would know, was a mixed-race person because he was Métis, and therefore he could not represent the romantic image of the pure Indian that Long Lance needed a figure like him to be. This could be why the rest of the narrative focuses on a romantic interpretation of the resistance of Almighty Voice, a Cree who in 1895 was arrested in Duck Lake, Saskatchewan, for slaughtering a government cow. Almighty Voice escaped from prison when an officer joked that he could be hanged. He evaded capture until 1897, when he and two of his relatives were killed after a dramatic shootout (Nestor n.p.). Long Lance had already researched the story of Almighty Voice and had interviewed his parents and photographed them. He had previously sold a romanticized version of the story to magazines, containing invented dialogue and an expanded role for Spotted Calf, Almighty Voice's mother (D. Smith, *Chief Buffalo* 164–65).

In *Long Lance,* however, the story of Almighty Voice exists to create an imagined family connection where Long Lance himself can imagine fighting a good fight with the support of his parents. In Long Lance's version, Almighty Voice appears at his mother's door after escaping, making a raft to ford a river, . and running fourteen miles (Long Lance 215–16). Long Lance uses this detail to claim an adopted parent for himself:

His [Almighty Voice's] mother Spotted Calf is also my adopted mother, and that is why I am able to record the inside story of this famous manhunt, which today is so amply deal with in history and in all books on the

> Northwest Mounted Police. Spotted Calf and her husband Sounding Sky are
> still living on the One Arrow Indian Reserve, at Duck Lake, Saskatchewan—
> mother and father of Almighty Voice. (216)

Long Lance has gone far beyond being a Blood Indian here and is claiming
membership in a Cree family. Why would he do this? Partly, it is to establish that he truly knows Native people, because he interviewed the parents of
Almighty Voice. It is also, I suggest, to construct a family for himself within his
identity as an Indian because he is distraught about the family he left behind.
Two years later, Long Lance would meet his brother Walter, who had come
to New York to ask him for money to help with his parents' medical bills, and
he would write to Walter that "I have not yet fully untangled these emotions:
my own darling brother whom I used to romp and play with, coming to me
after twenty-two years, wondering if I were going to be ashamed of him" (qtd.
in D. Smith, *Chief Buffalo* 291–92). Clearly, Long Lance suffered from guilt
about his neglect of his family, and he missed them. Therefore, in *Long Lance*
he attempts to "borrow" a Native family to replace the family he lost: the
story of adoption also authorizes Long Lance as the only person who can tell
the story of what happened to Almighty Voice while he was in hiding (Long
Lance 218). According to Long Lance, the police somehow know there is a
special bond between father and son: "they sensed that there was a strong
tie between Almighty Voice and his father Sounding Sky," so they use his
father to trap Almighty Voice at the One Arrow reserve (219). During the final
standoff, Spotted Calf sings encouragement to her son, who tells her how he
is doing. She refuses to leave the battlefield (226) and then changes her song
to a death song just before Almighty Voice dies. At the end of the story, it is
Long Lance himself who brings Spotted Calf to the site where Almighty Voice
died. She is described as a "wonderful woman" who in mourning is a "pathetic
figure" crying by the hole where her son was shot (23–33). Long Lance ends
the episode by declaring that he is proud to be her son and that "my highest
hope in the new life that I have adopted from the white man is that I shall
never do anything to bring shame upon that name—Spotted Calf" (234). The
book ends only two pages later by saying that all tribes agreed that Almighty
Voice's resistance was the final one and that Native people would accept the
coming of reservations and residential schools, where young warriors would
"have to work like women," hoeing and learning their letters as they fit into
the new way of life (236). The end of *Long Lance* is an evocation of helplessness and loss, much like the greyness of the beginning, with children working
like farmhands (or, perhaps, like slaves); but it is also an affirmation of family
connections.

Although Karina Vernon has suggested that it is possible to read *Long Lance* as a novel and that this makes Long Lance a literary ancestor for other African Canadian writers (96), I would suggest that this tactic serves to incorporate him into a CanLit paradigm where he does not fit well. It is more fruitful to read *Long Lance* as something other than a novel, since it was read as an autobiography when it was published and was until the 1950s still marketed that way. It makes more sense to think of *Long Lance* as a translocal document between sets of genres because it is a *roman à clef*, an ethnographic account of some real memories of Long Lance's friend—Mike Eagle Speaker—and, as I have argued, a hidden expression of Long Lance's own history and desires. It is more meaningful to think of Long Lance himself as something other than African Canadian, because technically, he was neither black nor Canadian. He himself moved between identities in ways that failed to stabilize any of them. But the request made to Long Lance to write his own memoir did create in him what I would call a translocal response much like Vernon-Wood's, where Long Lance mixes details about Blackfoot life into his own chronology in an invented West, letting his own desires for freedom, heroism, and family become part of this narrative. *Long Lance* moves its characters freely across national boundaries, imagining a time when no one had to hide or compromise who they were, when an identity could be pure, and when family ties could be created that remained unbroken even in hardship. The fact that neither *Long Lance* nor Long Lance could ever really be pure, and that neither the text nor the identity could stand up to any kind of scrutiny, shows how identities and life stories might be able to cross boundaries, disrupting the narratives of identity that are prescribed for us, but how, ultimately, the movement between localities is not always a joyous one. Movement does not always lead to empowerment and belonging. This kind of transgression, when it is discovered, can be difficult and even painful for the person who tries it. So it was for Long Lance, who ended his life after he broke a wedding engagement because he could not tell the woman he loved who he really was.

Conclusion

What does it mean to claim that Vernon-Wood and Long Lance constitute a translocal critique of CanLit at the limit? Neither of these figures had a fixed identity (no matter how much they may have desired one), and both were able to write from the place of instability, despite the privileges afforded them by their gender. Canada was the stage and the condition for their masquerades, even though Long Lance was not a citizen of Canada and Nello Vernon-Wood wrote for American readers. Their translocal movement across places and names and other marks of identity in fact enabled them to write about authenticity inauthentically and to construct Canada as an authentic place. As Karina Vernon says, Long Lance "could not have been both black and the writer that he became" (75), while Vernon-Wood could not have been a professional writer without becoming, and performing, Tex Wood. They both are—and are not—Canadian writers. Are they literary figures? Neither wrote what is usually considered to be literature, although both enjoyed popularity in their own day. What is important about them is that they are a part of the writing about Canada that has helped form ideas about mobility, race, class, and region that remain with us to this day. For that reason, they, and other writers like them, can help us let go of the need for writing to be literary in an institutionally recognized sense, the desire that national identity be easy, and the idea that writers should be from backgrounds that are recognizably Canadian and middle class. Long Lance and Vernon-Wood are not CanLit. They unmake it.

JAZZ, DIASPORA, AND THE HISTORY AND WRITING OF BLACK ANGLOPHONE MONTREAL

Winfried Siemerling

I

On 30 June 2009, Montreal jazz pianist Oliver Jones and singer Ranee Lee opened the thirtieth Montreal Jazz Festival in its new venue, L'Astral.[1] After a hiatus, Jones was returning to a festival that his presence had graced since its second year, 1981. Two years earlier, in April 2007, he had headlined a benefit concert attended by Daisy Peterson, his former piano teacher. Her brother Oscar, that other Montreal jazz legend, was represented by a large photograph on stage. That concert had been a fundraiser to help reopen the former Negro Community Centre (NCC), founded in 1927, whose mission had been to "alleviate social and economic conditions among Blacks in Montreal." Oliver Jones had spent much of his time there as a child. Now he was back for a benefit that served as a vivid reminder of the strong, ongoing presence of one of Montreal's oldest black communities. The beginnings of this black anglophone community date back to the late nineteenth century. It is preceded by the "oldtimers" of the Underground Railroad and, even before them, the black slaves of Montreal.[2]

The evening's celebration of black musical traditions, institutions, and community history evoked cultural geographies that are rarely present in a wider public imaginary. In her 1984 memoir *Growing Up Black in Canada*, Carol Talbot uses the term "folk geography" when writing about "the 'felt' geography of a particular group [that] can indicate significant factors which will not be revealed by an orthodox scientific approach" (19). Cultural geographers such as Joyce Davidson and Christine Milligan have explored such "emotional geographies" (523–32) in their field, and Canadian postcolonial scholar Katherine McKittrick has used the same approach to discuss Angélique, the Montreal slave accused of having started a fire that burned down most of Montreal in 1734. There are now many black communities in Montreal; the city's Haitian diaspora in particular has found literary expression and in some cases significant francophone reception, with English translations of Dany Laferrière perhaps being the most notable exception. Yet the pre-1960s black geographies of Quebec have rarely been imagined so as to narrate their emotional contours. Canadian classics set in this space and time either elide black emotional geographies or treat them problematically. Pierre Nepveu's comment in *Lecture des lieux* (2004) remains pertinent: "Lire Montréal, ce pourrait être, par exemple, raconter son histoire et réinventer en particulier son commencement" (49; "To read Montreal could mean, for instance, to tell its history and reinvent in particular its beginning"). Or perhaps one could say that it is time to "wake up," not so much from the dream of the nineteenth century (as in Walter Benjamin's *Arcades Project*), but from the images of Montreal that were part of the dream to finally put Canada and Quebec on the map against European and US culture. This dream was partly realized by some of the most important novels of the mid-twentieth century, but the priorities and perhaps necessities of that dream and "the hoary battles of the national epic" (Simon, *Translating Montreal* 7) have eclipsed more complex realities that come to the fore retrospectively in more recent texts that afford other perspectives.

While I will briefly examine earlier moments, this essay focuses on the period from the 1920s to the 1950s that includes Montreal's jazz age. This era in the city's history was heavily marked by black cultural contributions that appear non-existent or problematic at best in geographies offered by literary texts about the period. Consider, for example, three of the canonical novels about 1940s and 1950s Montreal: Hugh MacLennan's *Two Solitudes* (1945), Gabrielle Roy's *Bonheur d'occasion* (1945; translated as *The Tin Flute* [1947]), and Morley Callaghan's *The Loved and the Lost* (1951). MacLennan's *Two Solitudes* is a sweeping portrait of interwar Quebec that also claims to reimagine Canadian national space. Montreal, which was Canada's most important city at the time, serves MacLennan in the first pages as a metonymic microcosm of modern industrial Canada, with its social and ideological practices governed by linguistic difference. In that city, MacLennan writes, "two old races" meet, using an older nomenclature still evident in later documents (such as the Royal Commission on Bilingualism and Biculturalism in the 1960s),[3] in which the term refers to the anglophone and francophone white settlers of Canada respectively: "Two old races and religions meet here and live their separate legends, side by side. If this sprawling half-continent has a heart, here it is. Its pulse throbs out along the rivers and railroads; slow, reluctant and rarely simple, a double beat, a self-moved reciprocation" (2). The Quebec countryside of *Two Solitudes* is home to francophone agricultural labourers working the fields for the inheritors of the seigneurial regime under the ultra-montane Catholic clergy; Montreal is the site of the francophone working poor and an anglophone capital that reaches deep and aggressively into the surrounding countryside for ever more resources of capital accumulation. But while the "two races" in Quebec, and specifically in Montreal, are charted in the Canadian national space that MacLennan weaves out of personal and "emotional geographies" (Davidson and Milligan 523), non-white characters remain invisible.

This is also the case in another "classic" portrait of Montreal that appeared in 1945, the same year as MacLennan's novel: Roy's *Bonheur d'occasion*. The absence here is particularly striking given that Roy's setting is working-class Saint-Henri in southwest Montreal, which had been the home of a small but growing black community since the end of the nineteenth century. After arriving in Montreal from Manitoba (via Europe) in 1939, Roy had taken a deep interest in Montreal as a meeting place of diasporas. For *Le Bulletin des agriculteurs*, she wrote a series of reportages titled "Tout Montréal," which took note of the city's cosmopolitan population. Yet when she wrote her fictional account of francophone working-class life in Saint-Henri, she expunged almost all indications of a multiracial Montreal.[4] True, when her protagonist Florentine is invited to a party in a house on Place-George-Étienne-Cartier, in one of the quarter's "better" neighbourhoods, a turn of the radio knob fills the room with "un air de jazz, furieux, à grands éclats de saxophone" (136; "A savage blast of music, with saxophones blaring", 88).[5] The younger generation opts to dance, embracing the swing music that so many white bands also played at the time. The originators of this music, however, are identified here only when Létourneau, a member of the parents' generation and a "marchand d'objets de piété, d'ornements et de vin eucharistique" (133; "a dealer in religious objects, ornaments and church wines," 86), inquires pejoratively: "Qu'est-ce que c'est que cette danse de nègres?" (137; "'Is that some new Negro dance?'" 89).

Roy focuses her novel on the francophone Montreal working class, especially its women; even so, it is striking how she renders invisible another universe that existed at the same time in the same Montreal neighbourhood. Oscar Peterson grew up a very short distance from Place-George-Étienne-Cartier and had begun attrracting attention from 1942 onward as a black musician in one of Montreal's popular white swing bands. Place Saint-Henri, at the very centre of the universe described by Roy, served as inspiration for the eponymous composition that became part of his *Canadiana Suite* (1964). The trains continually crossing Saint-Henri loom large in Roy's novel. But she is more preoccupied with their noise and with the coaldust they shower on the neighbourhood than with their travellers and destinations—or the black porters and redcaps whose lives were interwoven with the railway's North American networks as much as they were a part of Saint-Henri. In 1955, in *Rue Deschambault* (*Street of Riches* 1957), her book of vaguely autobiographical stories about her childhood in Saint-Boniface, Manitoba, Roy would write about the black porters who boarded at her parents' and neighbours' houses. In "Les deux nègres," she emphasizes their love of music, and one of them is assigned to the Montreal–Halifax run, thus fleetingly evoking the city and the neighbourhood she had portrayed a few years earlier in so much detail but without black residents.

Black Montreal features prominently in Callaghan's *The Loved and the Lost* (1951). The novel contrasts the rich Westmount district with the rest of Montreal, describing the former as "a rock of riches with poverty sprawling around the rock" (166). Within this particular geography, the black jazz milieu of the St-Antoine district appears as the other, dark side—and ultimately the downfall—of the white hero's quest for wealth and social standing.[6] Black jazz, although an important theme here, ultimately serves as the background for a white character's unsuccessful search for meaning. Black Montreal and its music hold an ambivalent place in this novel: they are threats to the social order, yet they also hint at a utopian chronotope of interracial possibility. In any case, the perceptions of Callaghan's protagonist remain caught in primitivist stereotypes:

> Music came from the ground-floor open window, the music of a cello and a piano, and he could see three figures, one a Negro at a piano, another, who looked like a French Canadian, at the cello, and the third figure, the face hidden, was bending over the piano. The piano and the cello achieved an hypnotic effect in primitive counterpoint, repeating a simple theme over and over with curious discords; but it was the posture, the attitudes of the musicians as they played their solitary theme that held him spellbound: the cello twanged, the piano repeated the minor chords with a little variation, the musicians were held in their strange rapture, and there was nothing in the world for them but the lonely little theme and that one room in the cold night and their own intensity. (57)

Perhaps the third figure with the hidden face is the placeholder for a position that Callaghan's protagonist considers for himself. The image conveys social intimacy even while withholding the readability of the face. The protagonist remains an observer. Jim McAlpine's assertion of himself as an Emersonian "independent man," and his quest for innocence—which in the novel is connoted repeatedly with the colour white—use black St-Antoine as background. Callaghan is "playing in the dark"; the neighbourhood, with its blackness, becomes here a space for what Toni Morrison calls the "projection of the not-me" and a "playground for the imagination" containing "a fabricated brew of darkness, otherness, alarm, and desire" that *pace* Morrison is *not* "uniquely American" (38). In *The Loved and the Lost*, blackness is construed along stereotypical significations, portrayed as exotic and ultimately potentially murderous and destructive otherness.[7] The novel can therefore hardly convey a sense of Montreal and the St-Antoine district as the home of everyday black lives that have long been part and parcel of the city and its history. One must look elsewhere for perspectives that bring black geographies and lives to the fore, and heed Nepveu's injunction that "to read Montreal could mean ... to tell its history and reinvent in particular its beginning."

II

Although its numbers were very small in the beginning, the black diaspora has always been integral to the history and settlement of what is now Quebec. Canada's first documented slave, Olivier Le Jeune, lived in the first half of the seventeenth century in Quebec City. In the *Jesuit Relations*, Father Le Jeune even gave him a voice: "You say that by baptism I shall be like you: I am black and you are white, I must have my skin taken off then in order to be like you" (qtd. in Winks 1). While Le Jeune presented this remark as a child's naïveté and historian Marcel Trudel (14) reproduces the passage without further comment, Robin Winks gives a certain ontological weight to the utterance (1). Most remarkable, however, was the very fact that a black voice was transcribed at all in the first person—a rare exception. About a century later, in 1734, when there were perhaps between forty and fifty black slaves in Quebec (Gay 29; Trudel 86),[8] the Montreal slave Angélique was tried and hanged for allegedly burning down the better part of Montreal. Her responses to interrogation—as rendered in the third person in court documents—were her only words transmitted.[9] In recent decades, however, a heterotopic Montreal of the eighteenth century has emerged in neo-slave dramas and narratives around the case of Angélique, in plays by Lorris Elliott (1985) and Lorena Gale (2000) and in novels by Paul Fehmiu Brown (1998) and Micheline Bail (1999). As George Elliott Clarke points out, Angélique is also the subject of a song and a movie ("Raising"), while in 2006 Afua Cooper dedicates a monograph and Katherine McKittrick devotes an important book chapter to the topic.

In 1760, a few decades after Angélique was hanged, England and France signed a peace treaty that confirmed the continuation of slavery in Quebec under the English (Trudel 66). The number of slaves rose in 1783, when United

Empire Loyalists arrived with them (86); however, slavery ended in Quebec early in the nineteenth century, well before it was abolished throughout the British Empire in 1834 (13, 85).[10] Trudel found 1,443 documented black slaves overall in Quebec, in addition to 2,683 Native slaves or *panis* (69–99).

Black slavery in Quebec is generally perceived by historians to have been less brutal than elsewhere. In part, this is because most black slaves here were house slaves (rather than field slaves) and considerably more valuable than Native slaves (Winks 10–11, 15; Rhodes 29). This difference hardly prevented them from seeking freedom, however, or from attempting to flee in considerable numbers. In the *Quebec Gazette* between 1769 and 1794, "advertisements for runaway slaves were more frequent ... than were those for the sale of slaves" (Winks 15).[11] While black slaves were less significant in number than elsewhere, they certainly contributed to the building of Quebec. Slave labour was employed by the clergy and the military as well as by notaries, doctors, and printers (Trudel 123–42). Consider, for instance, William Brown, who with Thomas Gilmore founded the first newspaper in Quebec in 1764, the bilingual *Quebec Gazette—Gazette de Québec* (see Audet). Brown remained sole owner of the paper and its slaves after 1773. His slave, Joe, fled at least six times between 1777 and 1789, once by escaping from prison (Trudel 161). "Wanted" ads for Joe must have been printed in the very paper he normally helped produce. Having been trained as a printer, he was obviously valuable enough, despite all his resistance, for his master to have incurred considerable expenses to maintain his services (205–7). François-Xavier Garneau, the most important nineteenth-century historian of French Canada, omitted the fact that slavery existed in Quebec in his *Histoire du Canada* in 1846 (however, the fourth edition, issued by his son in 1882, ended this denial [Winks 19]). Documentary evidence and the work of other historians shed at least some light on this chapter of black French Canadian history.

On 1 August 1834, black Montrealers congregated in a hall at St. Ann's Market to celebrate the abolition of slavery in the British Empire (Mackey 92–96). French Canada (and Montreal in particular) was an Underground Railroad destination, although the numbers who arrived were much smaller than in Upper Canada. The slave narrative of Lavina Wormeny was reported in the Montreal *Gazette*. A child of free parents in Washington, Wormeny was abducted and enslaved; after multiple attempts, she escaped to Montreal in January 1861.[12] An earlier case has been minutely reconstructed by Gary Collison in *Shadrach Minkins: From Fugitive Slave to Citizen* (1997). For that study, Collison used census records, city directories, newspaper accounts, and other sources to document a slave's escape from Norfolk, Virginia, to Montreal in February 1851. Despite spotty documentary evidence, Collison offers interesting conjectures about the size of Montreal's black community at the time:

> But just how many African-Americans joined Shadrach Minkins in Montreal, or where they came from, is unclear. Although the *Gazette* argued that there were more than four hundred, the published census of 1861 indicated only 46 Black residents. Manuscript census slips, however, show 228, and since this figure almost certainly represents an undercounting, the actual numbers may have been fairly close to the *Gazette* estimate. (206)

Interestingly, by 1860 Shadrach Minkins had moved from the old city to what was then—and remained in Callaghan's novel—the St-Antoine district in southwest Montreal. At the end of the nineteenth century, a larger black community began to develop there. From the 1920s on, the area became a crucial site for the development of Montreal jazz.

Just to the south, by the second half of the nineteenth century the Lachine Canal had emerged as Canada's industrial heartland: "iron works, flour mills, the Chemical and India Rubber Works, the Oil and Colour Works, the Candle Works, and the Canada Marine Work, among others" (Collison 205).[13] This canal, opened in 1825 (the same year as its competitor, the Erie Canal in New York), was the realization of a dream of opening up the Great Lakes hinterland to trade. It had been dug to circumvent the Lachine Rapids, which since Jacques Cartier and the search for Cathay[14] had prevented ships from entering the Great Lakes. In many ways, the rapids and the efforts to circumvent them "explain[ed] Montreal" (Desloges and Gelly 9). Part of a century-long international "canal craze" (9), the Lachine allowed the more rapid transportation of goods.After 1846, it provided hydraulic power for flour and saw mills, grain elevators, foundries, nail factories, and other industries; after 1893, it also provided electricity (129). The canal attracted numerous industries that together would turn Montreal into the industrial and commercial heart of Canada.

Yet soon after they were built, canals had to compete with railways as the most effective conveyors of goods and people. A few years after the Champlain and St. Lawrence (Canada's first railway) was completed in 1836, the Montreal and Lachine Railroad was inaugurated in 1847 to bypass the Lachine Rapids, although it could not compete with the lower freight rates on the Lachine Canal (Tulchinsky 172). The 12 kilometre track was soon incorporated into a network of lines connecting Montreal to the western hinterland and the Atlantic seaboard (127–200). A generation later, after the railways began hiring blacks as redcaps and porters—one of the few reliable livelihoods for black Montrealers—a larger black community began to develop in the St-Antoine district. By the late 1850s, the Grand Trunk Railway connected Montreal with Toronto and Chicago (D. Williams 32); by the 1880s, the American Pullman Palace Car Company, the Grand Trunk Railway, and the Canadian Pacific Railway were employing black sleeping car porters, with the latter company doing so directly out of Montreal (Calliste, "Sleeping Car Porters" 2; D. Williams 32–33). At first, many of these porters used Montreal as only a temporary home because of immigration restrictions (D. Williams 33). After this, the "period between 1897 and 1930" "marked the beginning of a genuine black community in Montreal. Major institutions such as the Union United Church (Union) in 1907, the Universal Negro Improvement Association (UNIA) in 1919, and the Negro Community Centre (N.C.C.) in 1927 were established" (38). These landmark institutions, which were so crucial for the development of Montreal's black community, are often overlooked in the city's history.

The black community contributed in various ways to another important chapter of Montreal history, the development of jazz—although the acceptance of that musical genre by the community was hardly smooth. Many parents preferred that their children learn classical music. Some aspects of jazz were met with suspicion and rejection by respectable members of the community, in large part because the genre was associated with alcohol. The Prohibition Era in the United States lasted from 1920 to 1933. Nancy Marrelli notes that "Quebec was the last Canadian province to get prohibition in 1918 and it was the first to repeal it, 1919" (14). As Dorothy Williams remarks, this made Montreal attractive for many: "as a result of Prohibition, Montreal was *the* place to be" (44). Prohibition favoured the development of jazz in Montreal: "From the 1920s until the early 1950s Montreal had an international reputation as a glamorous wide open city with a lively nightlife" (Marrelli 9). In his history of Montreal jazz, John Gilmore notes that "work for musicians was plentiful" (43). Many of the bands and venues were exclusively white. Marrelli offers the following racial geography of Montreal jazz from the 1920s to the early 1950s:

> The Montreal club scene was one of complex race, class, and language relations, as well as territorial boundaries. The "downtown" clubs were on St-Antoine Street, where many blacks lived because it was close to the railways where many of the men worked as porters.... There was an active music scene in the black community, although there was a long history of discrimination in the unions until the early 1940s, and mixed black and white bands were not common. At various times it was trendy to have black musicians and black shows, particularly in east-end clubs, but all-white policies were the rule in hotels and were common for uptown clubs in the early years. The downtown clubs usually had black musicians and entertainers and their patron policies were wide open. That's where you could almost always find great music, and it was where other musicians went to "jam" after their shows in theaters or clubs in other parts of town. (10–11)

Gilmore also chronicles, after some earlier black entertainers, a "second wave of black musicians who had heard tales about the exciting city and ventured north…. By the end of the decade [the 1920s], it had drenched Montreal with talent and with the sounds of the latest black music" (43). Together with these musicians from elsewhere, home-grown talents like the pianists Steep Wade, Oscar Peterson, Oliver Jones, Joe Sealy,[15] and Milt Sealey (Miller, *Companion* 178–79)—all sons of railway employees—became part of Montreal jazz history.

III

Particularly fascinating and influential—if historically elusive—was Steep Wade, although there are no recordings of his saxophone playing and very few of him on piano.[16] But his influence on pianists like Peterson, Sealey, and Jones is a matter of record. Born in Montreal in 1918, Wade began as an alto saxophonist and played with the Canadian Ambassadors, the "most successful of Canada's few black jazz bands active during the 1930s" (Miller, *Companion* 37). While his lifestyle caused notoriety, he gained musical fame as the pianist for the mixed-race International Band from 1947 to 1949 (Gilmore 141–54; Miller, *Companion* 207). This formation was led by Louis Metcalf, a trumpeter who had played with Duke Ellington, Jelly Roll Morton, and King Oliver in New York. They became the first band to try bebop on Montreal audiences. This incursion took place during their 1947–50 residency at the Café St-Michel (Gilmore 115–40; Miller, *Companion* 136). This club and Rockhead's Paradise across the street became "The Corner," the internationally known headquarters of black Montreal jazz.[17]

This is where Oscar Peterson fell under the spell of Steep Wade. From 1942 onwards, Peterson played with the orchestra of Johnny Holmes, a white trumpeter whose swing band regularly packed eight hundred dancers into Montreal's Victoria Hall (Gilmore 99)—an episode to which I will return below. While still a teenager, Peterson also listened at Rockhead's to Wade, among other musicians, and was occasionally asked by him to fill in: "'They used to sneak me in because I was under age at the time. Steep used to call me 'kid.' On different nights when he used to go for a walk or listen to someone else's music, he'd say 'Okay, kid, go on and play the show for me. I'll be back.' That's where I really served my jazz apprenticeship—in that environment'" (Lees 42). At the Café St-Michel as well, late at night after performing with his own trio at the Alberta Lounge between 1948 and 1950, Peterson listened to Wade and sat in with the Metcalf International Band to familiarize himself with bebop; later he would identify Wade as "my favourite pianist" (Miller, *Jazz in Canada* 127). According to legend, Peterson's engagement at the Alberta Lounge near the CPR Windsor station led to his appearance at Carnegie Hall and his subsequent international career (Gilmore 109–10).

Peterson's career is part of jazz history. But his life, like Steep Wade's and Oliver Jones's, was also closely linked to the black anglophone community in southwest Montreal, including institutions like the Union United Congregational Church, the Negro Community Centre, and the UNIA with its (often moved) Liberty Hall. Peterson was born in 1925 next to Union United Church on Delisle Street and later would be married there (Lees 22). Oliver Jones played his first public boogie-woogie at one of the church's events when he is five years old (Sansregret 30). One day, across Atwater Avenue in Little Burgundy, Jones heard beautiful music through an open window and knocked at a door, which happened to be Peterson's. That is how, at the Negro Community Centre, Jones became a student of Daisy Peterson, who also taught her brother as well as Joe Sealy. In 1954, that centre would move to Coursol Street, where Jones had been born before growing up on intersecting Fulford (now called George Vanier), where the Universal Negro Improvement Association's Liberty Hall was located. While these locations are in what is now called Little Burgundy, for Jones they were all part of Saint-Henri. "I grew up in Saint-Henri," he confirmed during the intermission of a concert by Keith Jarrett at the 2007 Montreal Jazz Festival (a few days later, Jones would play the festival's closing concert). Jones's personal geography thus united under the name of Saint-Henri the experiences of his childhood and a network of connections and lives that were part of Montreal's oldest black community. The area roughly coincided with what had earlier been called the St-Antoine district; as the historian Dorothy Williams writes, it was "synonymous with the growth of the black community in the southwest core of the city of Montreal" (36–37).

We are fortunate to have Dorothy Williams's history and other accounts of wider segments of that community (e.g., Bertely, Hostesses). Jazz historians like John Gilmore, Mark Miller, and Nancy Marrelli, and a number of documentaries, have delineated aspects of the more public, visible, and audible side of black Montreal represented by jazz. Examples include *In the Key of Oscar, Oliver Jones in Africa, Crossroads—Three Jazz Pianists,* and *Show Girls.* Oliver Jones and the singer Ranee Lee still perform in Montreal. Recordings of Oscar Peterson, bassist Charlie Biddle, guitarist Nelson Symonds, and others form part of the unique musical and cultural contributions of that community. But strangely enough, as noted above, its presence has remained all but unheralded in literary portraits of Montreal.

IV

One text that does focus on the black community of southwest Montreal of that era is Mairuth Sarsfield's historical novel *No Crystal Stair* (1997).[18] It opens in the spring of 1942, and like Roy's *Bonheur d'occasion* and parts of MacLennan's *Two Solitudes*, it has the Second World War as a background. Like Callaghan's *The Loved and the Lost*, it utilizes not just the city but often the very streets where black Montreal jazz was born. But Callaghan treats black Montreal as a backdrop against which white trajectories play out; Sarsfield, by contrast, places that culture at the novel's centre, shows its inner workings and contradictions, and explores how it relates to other cultural groups. Musical and (to some extent) literary traditions are key to Sarsfield's project.

In Sarsfield's Montreal, multiple diasporas and cultures meet,[19] and black Montreal is shown to be itself international and heterogeneous. The novel's cast includes black characters from the Caribbean and the United States and features fictive and historical participants in the Harlem Renaissance and famous black exiles in Europe between the wars. Earlier black history in Quebec is evoked with slavery in Quebec City and the events surrounding Angélique in Montreal (86), while Nova Scotian history surfaces briefly with the Jamaican Maroons shipped to Nova Scotia and the exodus of black settlers from there to Sierra Leone (87). A number of diasporic connections appear through the protagonist's work environment as part of the Westmount YMCA staff, yet at the centre is the black community of the St. Antoine district and its institutions, including the Union United Congregational Church, a focal point of the community since its founding in 1907 by railway porters, and the Marcus Garvey Debating Society and Garvey's Universal Negro Improvement Association (UNIA). In Dorothy Williams's words, in "the heyday of the UNIA in Montreal (1919–1928), people attended Union Church in the morning and UNIA social activities at Liberty Hall in the afternoon" that often featured a "focus[ed] on Pan-Africanism" (61).[20] Sarsfield also refers variously to the Coloured Ladies Club (5 and passim),[21] Asa Philip Randolph's Brotherhood of Sleeping Car Porters, the importance of the railways as purveyor of employers, and Montreal Jazz.

Directly or indirectly, the railway influences most of Sarsfield's black characters, connected as they are with work- and community-related aspects of black Montreal such as unions and (in particular) Garveyism. Marion Willow, the novel's protagonist, is the widow of a railway redcap who is a McGill dentistry student. At "a Back to Africa rally in the old UNIA hall on Fulford Street" (24), she meets Edmond Thompson, a Guyanese chemist turned railway porter. Like him, she participates in the Marcus Garvey Debating Society. Thompson's attitudes reflect a dual strategy that was the choice of many

Montreal porters at the time. In Marion Willow's thinking, "above all, he was a true Garveyite. He believed, like she did, in the need for self-sufficiency for Black folks" (146). At the same time, however, this very Garveyite porter urges "his cricket-playing teammates … to join the American J. [*sic*] Phillip [*sic*] Randolph Movement to form a Pullman porters' union" (22). Randolph's racial integrationism stood in stark contrast to the self-segregation advocated by Garvey.[22] As Dorothy Williams points out, Garvey's anti-union message—strengthened by union racism and the very slow acceptance of blacks by many unions[23]—did not convince blacks in Montreal: "By the mid-thirties, Randolph was embraced and honoured by all but the staunchest Garveyites in Montreal" (59). Sarsfield thus evokes accurately the contradictions but also the productive transfigurations of Garveyism in Montreal.

A comparable double strategy of black self-reliance and integration is adumbrated in Sarsfield's portrayal of jazz and the role of Oscar Peterson within it. The novel features the legendary Rockhead's Paradise and Café St-Michel at "The Corner," a location that is glossed here as the centre of "the nightlife around Montreal's Mountain Street, with its Jazz entertainers and brown-skinned chorus girls imported from New York's Harlem. Both clubs were owned by former railway porters who—gossip contended—had made their initial nest eggs rum-running in the decade when Prohibition in the United States made smuggling liquor across the border profitable" (Sarsfield 58). Besides writers and entertainers from the United States (Langston Hughes, Sammy Davis, Jr), a number of Montreal musicians are mentioned, including Steep Wade (73, 142), Lou Hooper (137), Maynard Ferguson (135), Paul de Marky (137), and Johnny Holmes. What these musicians have in common is their connection with the Peterson family, and Daisy Peterson Sweeney and Oscar Peterson both appear briefly in the novel. Given Sarsfield's dual strategy of emphasizing both black strength and lively interaction across racial boundaries, it is not coincidental that a longer passage staging a discussion of tradition and influence in terms of black cultural specificity turns around Oscar Peterson.

Peterson was trained in both classical and jazz piano. One of his important early solo concerts, at age twenty at the Majesty's Theatre in Montreal in 1946, featured both classical and jazz pieces (Gilmore 107). From 1942 onward, as we have noted, Peterson played with the Johnny Holmes Orchestra, usually as its only black musician, and this led to a few racist incidents.[24] Peterson continued to play in mixed bands throughout his career. At the same time, Peterson was an icon of black Montreal's culture and community, which he credited with his success; at one point in his autobiography, *A Jazz Odyssey* (2002), he even emphasizes the formative role of the UNIA and of Marcus Garvey's visit to Montreal.[25] This endorsement of a black cultural leader who was mostly associated with black nationalism might be surprising, but it hardly minimizes Peterson's integrationist stance, illuminated strikingly by the dedication of one of his best-known compositions, "Hymn to Freedom," to Martin Luther King, Jr.

In *No Crystal Stair*, an early Oscar Peterson concert with the Johnny Holmes Orchestra—probably in the fall of 1942—gives rise to a heated post-concert discussion among a racially mixed group (135–39, 141–42). The debate mostly concerns influences on Peterson's style, and pitches his right-hand arpeggios against his left-hand bass. Affinities with Liszt and Rubinstein strike a white commentator as significant; a black observer, however, sees Peterson as more "influenced by Duke Ellington's mastery of harmonic chords" and insists: "It's a soul thing" (141). This insistence rejects recognition on the basis of whiteness as a norm. Emphasizing aspects of Peterson's technique that appear comparable to those of famous white musicians prevents a re-cognition of artistic possibility and excellence, eclipsing the specificity that makes Peterson's style different.[26] Whiteness here "constitutes itself as a universal set of norms by which to make sense of the world" (Fiske 42, qtd. in G. Lewis 140).[27] In the words of Sarsfield's character, "Here we go again: Ole Whitey's discovered him, so he must be for real" (142).

In this musicological debate staged by Sarsfield, the denial of difference is thus met by an insistence on Peterson's music as expressive of "race spirituality," which in turn is countered by a two-step protest: "You can't deny the European influence. Music doesn't have boundaries." The first statement is accurate in Peterson's case. The second seems a simple reiteration, yet in fact it denies difference and any kind of social aesthetics. Another character objects: "Yes, it does, and until Europe acknowledges the influence of jazz on its culture, there's no dialogue" (142).[28]

Significantly, this protest is voiced not by a black participant in the debate, but by a white Jewish woman. The discussion here switches to the issue of "passing," another important issue in the novel (Wegmann-Sánchez 147–54). Of the two women present, one is of mixed Russian and black Caribbean descent and passes as white, while the other is Jewish Canadian. Both women feel constrained to pass by dissimulating their "ethnic" names at work to fit in socially and professionally—Marushka and Sarita becoming Maria and Sara (142–43). The novel thus connects prejudicial pressures on racial and ethnic identities that lead to passing with the "whitening" of black jazz through forms of re/cognition that reaffirm Eurocentric vantage points. The insistence on black jazz as a constitutive element in North American culture and on a "dialogue," by contrast, implies multiple vantage points and traditions.

Yet the novel indeed goes out of its way to emphasize *as well* the influence of European music on Peterson's style, and it certainly does not deny cross-cultural influence. Similar issues are raised by some of the novel's inter-textualities as well as its theme of reading. Beginning with the title, which cites Langston Hughes's poem "Mother to Son" and its call for perseverance against harsh odds, the novel references a "Who's Who" of black culture; in addition to those already named, it includes not only musicians and entertainers like the Fisk Jubilee Singers, Bessie Smith, Cab Calloway, Duke Ellington, Sammy Davis Jr., Josephine Baker, and Paul Robeson, but also writers like Frederick Douglass, W.E.B. Du Bois, Claude McKay, and Frantz Fanon. Some of the writers appear in an impassioned discussion about education, during which Marion Willow realizes that her bookish daughter's voracious reading of British literature should be balanced by readings from the black tradition. *Anne of Green Gables*, however, also holds a special place in the novel; the daughter blasts an unfortunate playmate with "'There's no poetry in your soul'" (16), worries about the absence of "'a kindred soul'" (17), emphasizes her plight as a demi-orphan (21), and reads *Rilla of Ingleside* (30). Sarsfield's text emphasizes the wealth of black geographies and traditions in Montreal, while relying at the same time on intertextualities that are at least "double-voiced" (Gates xxiii), as demonstrated by repeated references to the black tradition and the Harlem Renaissance but also Lucy Maud Montgomery. A related strategy pertains, as we have seen, to the novel's discussion of jazz.

V

In Sarsfield's portrait of black Montreal culture of the 1940s, jazz is only one element, albeit a highly visible one. It constitutes a specific and remarkable contribution (among many) to Montreal history and culture. The debate about different cultural specificities and their dialogues takes on a wider meaning in that context. Evoking black jazz as a community-specific and culturally rooted yet cross-culturally receptive and influential matrix, Sarsfield's novel is relevant for its reimagining of the multiple emotional and imaginary geographies that constitute Montreal's history. This is underscored by the historical depth of the community it portrays. Jazz is a visible and audible sign of that community, whose rooted history is intertwined with the founding of modern Montreal in the nineteenth century and its earlier black history, which the novel cites back to Angélique and slavery in Montreal (86).

The role of black performers—and here, particularly, of Oscar Peterson—in Montreal jazz serves Sarsfield in her portrayal of black diasporic geographies as integral to Montreal and to Canadian culture. The novel stages an inter-culturally active version of multiculturalism, although black self-reliance and Garveyism play at least equally important roles. *No Crystal Stair* thus outlines a dual strategy. Instead of playing opposite options against each other by insisting on *either* black nationalism *or* integration, it pursues multiple possibilities by emphasizing both black culture and its intercultural or transcultural options. The novel thus stages a "rooted cosmopolitanism" (Appiah 213–72) that rests on a culturally specific, grounded openness.

No Crystal Stair is part of a wider group of texts that make anglophone black Montreal come alive in literature. Also set in Little Burgundy is Ernest Tucker's 2006 crime novel *Lost Boundaries*, in which a black lawyer crosses racial boundaries in the name of justice, while his mother, an anglophone much worried about the announcement of a referendum, seeks to solve the same murder case in her own ways. Nigel Thomas's *Behind the Face of Winter* (2001), a Caribbean immigrant's coming-of-age story, is set in 1980s Montreal outside of Little Burgundy, but references its division through highway construction (115) and as the place of his mother's congregation, which had "come to Canada looking for green pastures beside still waters; the Lachine Canal bordering their warehouse church was still enough" (124). Cecil Foster, who has dedicated a chapter of his *A Place in Heaven: The Meaning of Being Black in Canada* to black suburban Parc Agrignon Montreal, is at work on a novel involving Montreal, the railways, and jazz.[29] And George Elliott Clarke, whose jazz opera *Québécité* (2003) is provocatively set in Quebec City as one of the whitest cities in Canada and whose Trudeau in the eponymous 2007 jazz opera is a regular at bassist Charlie Biddle's nightclub in Montreal, features plenty of jazz in *George and Rue* (2005). Montreal appears here as both the "fabulous Montreal" (18) that is Cynthy's black Nova Scotian dream getaway (18–23 and passim) and the site of George's wartime enlistment and eventual jailing (75–82), and is thus remembered as "a burgh of cops and jail" (84). These often jazz-inflected black anglophone Montreals are joined, of course, by a much larger corpus in French, produced by writers mostly from Haiti, who include Dany Laferrière, Emile Olivier, Gérard Étienne, Anthony Phelps, Max Dorsinville, Jean Jonassaint, Joël Des Rosiers, Edgar Gousse, and Marie-Célie Agnant (see Siemerling, "Ethics"). Their heterogeneous black diasporic Montreals make for multiple rereadings of the city, a project that texts such as Pierre Nepveu and Gilles Marcotte's *Montréal imaginaire*, Nepveu's *Lecture des lieux*, and Sherry Simon's *Translating Montreal* have advanced so much in other ways. Together with Sarsfield's *No Crystal Stair*, which reminds us of black Montreal historical continuities that are also evoked in Oliver Jones's present-day musical interventions and his championing of community renewal, they invite us to see black diasporas and their cultures as integral to a social and cultural architecture that, like the Arcades for Benjamin's Paris, make up and help explain Montreal.

TRADITION AND PLURALISM IN CONTEMPORARY ACADIA

François Paré

Like hundreds of present-day minority cultures, at once the most fragile and the most resilient of all societies, contemporary Acadia continues to evolve on the outskirts of geographical representation, as an "identity-based nation" marked to the core by past and present constructs of displacement and itinerancy. How can one describe a culture's stylized absence from any national space? In contrast to the earlier topography of New France, current maps of Canada and of New Brunswick—and of Nova Scotia—do not show a well-circumscribed place named Acadia. For a long time, writes Herménégilde Chiasson in *En marge*, "Acadia wrestled with the terms of its representation" (n.p.), and it is this unusual tension between rising Acadian nationalism and the invisibility of the Acadian nation that the present essay seeks to explore. This is a culture without a centre, a fundamental periphery, defined by the vast regions of outlying precariousness on the American continent, where Acadia stages itself as a festive, resilient, and nostalgic space. Here, invisibility is a signature on a well-known landscape. Acadians are not alone in this predicament. How many linguistic and cultural groups do not appear on national maps? Tyrolean, Navajo, Cree, Kurdish, Catalan, and Acadian cultures all partake in a topography of oblivion that is, after all, an essential component of the postmodern world.

This essay focuses on the concept of pluralism and the search for new areas of social cohesion within traditional cultural minorities. Oscillating between literature and cultural anthropology, it attempts to respond to two of the questions raised by Moncton sociologists Greg Allain and Isabelle McKee-Allain in the final pages of their 2003 study of Acadian postmodernity: "La société acadienne en l'an 2000: identité, pluralité et réseaux." First, can the concept of pluralism be used to describe effectively contemporary Acadia in its national and diasporic manifestations? And second, what roles do systems of tradition play in a minority society such as Acadia? By bringing these two questions together under one conceptual roof, I will begin to investigate the theoretical relations between diversity and minority sites at the margins of contemporary North American society.

In his study of French Canada, Roger Bernard suggests that cultural communities are based on two fairly complex systems of tradition. First, the existence of the group rests on a set of "objective traditions," measured by recognizable identity factors such as language, territory, census counts, and other observable elements. Objective traditions, however, cannot entirely account for the "implicit construction" of identities within the minority culture. To gain an understanding of what goes on inside the minority community, one needs, according to Bernard, a set of "subjective traditions" from which "un sentiment d'appartenance" (a sense of belonging) can emerge, making cultural "communalisation" possible (38–39). In this model, it is assumed that a reference to common narratives constitutes the link between objective and subjective systems of tradition, an assumption that Anne Gilbert and Marie Lefebvre, in their study of the vitality of francophone communities in Canada, put into question, given the "difficult articulation" between the individuals and their fragile communities (376). Like Gilbert and Lefebvre, Joseph Yvon Thériault questions the validity of the concept of tradition in dealing with minority communities, especially Acadia (177–79). Yet he finds the reference to systems of tradition a requisite not only in ensuring the survival of minority cultures themselves, but also in considering their past evolution and their future in the interstices of our globalized economies. Cultural minorities may well be like canaries in the coal mine, warning of an impending disaster; their slow demise could be the sign of a widespread disintegration of the world's cultural and linguistic ecology.

For many Acadian intellectuals such as Thériault, there can be no understanding of Acadian cultural identity and political institutions without referring to the powerful founding narrative of the eighteenth-century Deportation. While still alive in public discourse throughout Acadia, the teleological meaning of the "Grand Dérangement" has recently been submitted, like so many other national narratives in the Western world, to the displacements imposed by a more pluralistic world view. National narratives are not readily transferable to newcomers and rarely resonate outside the minority community. Should recent francophone immigrants moving to Moncton, New Brunswick, or Meteghan, Nova Scotia, be encouraged to visit the Grand Pré or

Memramcook Acadian memory sites? Surely, immigrants cannot be expected to honour the same memory protocols as native Acadians. Moreover, newcomers to Acadia would not be alone in questioning the validity of the Deportation narrative. Paul Émile d'Entremont's short film *Seuls, ensemble*, produced for the National Film Board in 2000, shows the extraordinary complexity of modern Acadian identity, even for Acadians themselves. As he stands on the shores of the Baie Sainte-Marie, symbolically burning masks in a campfire on the beach, not far from Meteghan, Nova Scotia, one of d'Entremont's characters, Simon, wonders about finding a place for himself, as a homosexual and an Acadian, and for everyone else in such an exiguous place. Isn't everyone an adopted child in this world, he asks? Yet the depth and meaningfulness of his Acadian identity never leave him.

In *The Quest for Autonomy in Acadia*, André Magord also suggests that the Acadian nation, with its lack of access to political statehood, needs to build its finality on a strongly articulated commonality of traditions (29–30). Acadia would belong, then, to what Thériault terms "des mouvements nationalitaires, c'est-à-dire des communautés culturelles sans État, mais dotées d'attributs qui les rapprochent des configurations nationales" (179) (nationalistic movements, i.e. stateless cultural communities with attributes similar to those of a nation). By renouncing the past and by fully embracing models of pluralism, Acadians, it seems, would saw off the branch on which they have been sitting for centuries. Acadia, Thériault contends, continues to see itself as an autochthonous nation, one that has emerged from a highly significant past and that congeals around a shared language, a lost homeland, and a common memory (179).

Virtually all minorities in the world are confronted by cross-border mobility and the globalization of cultural politics. Finding an appropriate course of action in defending minority rights is not an easy task in the current context, especially in Western-style democracies. Should scholars mobilize on behalf of threatened languages and cultures and promote the "advocacy of democratic cultural autonomy," as Joshua A. Fishman recommends in the introduction to his collection of essays on threatened languages? Or does the responsibility ultimately lie with the minority communities themselves (7)? Speaking in New Brunswick in 2009, Graham Fraser, Canada's Commissioner of Official Languages, recognized the challenges posed by pluralism to modern-day Acadians: "Identity issues," he stated, "are complex and difficult. How can you stick together and be welcoming of others at the same time? How can you share a culture that has been shaped by historic struggles and often marked by rejection and discrimination by the majority? How can you expand the meaning of 'we' without losing the sense of who you are?" To his credit, the commissioner couched the problem in an appropriate and relevant manner.

However, he tended to reduce the Acadian minority to its use of the French
language as sole factor in the community's identity:

> In Acadia, as in other official language minority communities, language is
> a unifying factor, especially considering the new face of Canada and the
> Francophonie. These communities now bring together diverse faces, dialects,
> cultures and traditions. But they all have a common thread: language. Here
> in Acadia, sharing the French language enables native Acadians and new-
> comers to come together and find common ground within a larger society.
> And we must recognize that the Finns, Kenneys and Smiths are also native
> Acadians. (Fraser n.p.)

Such a perspective on francophone minorities in Canada has become com-
monplace since the introduction of bilingualism policies in 1969, and it lies at
the core of Canada's immigration practices and multicultural ideals. A common language, however, does not make a nation. The commissioner's stance
tends to dismiss as obtrusive references to issues beyond a shared linguistic
code, such as collective memory, homeland, and national aspirations. Only
Indigenous communities seem exempted from this multicultural analysis,
since none is expected to welcome into its midst newly arrived immigrants.
Later in his speech, Fraser expressed his admiration for Ottawa councillor
Clive Doucet, who, in a book published in 2000, considers himself an exiled
Acadian. Ironically, if language alone were the defining factor in developing
cultural membership, would Doucet not be happy to become a Franco-Ontar-
ian? What part of Acadian identity cannot be reduced to the French language?
What is Doucet in exile from?

There is no doubt that Acadians form a national community within Canada, in sociological as well as political terms. This status, of course, is not
recognized officially by the federal and provincial governments. Present-day
discourse reveals a great deal of unease when dealing with cultural and linguistic minorities that do not have access to the structures and the legitimacy
provided by a national state. Indeed, is the concept of nation—as bestowed on
Quebec by the Canadian government—truly thinkable outside the enabling
organic forces contained within the concept of statehood? What is so troubling
about an Acadian national identity? It seems too easy, too convenient, at least
in the context of the dominant discourses on nationalism and multiculturalism, to dismiss those "identités nationalitaires" as if they were relics of past
centuries, or as if they only and rightfully belong to Indigenous peoples. Is it
not a self-serving stance and an admission of intellectual paralysis to attempt
again and again to draw a flimsy line between a historical "before" and an
unlikely "after" for all emerging national movements? How does one deal

with land claims and homeland symbolism in the absence of the structuring conventions of a state? Where is governance located in stateless minorities? In 1972, Raymond Guy LeBlanc, one of Acadia's most revered twentieth-century poets, called for the awakening of "les petits peuples":

> Neither threats nor tear gas
>
> Neither lies nor insults
>
> Neither laws nor prisons
>
> Will prevent small nations
>
> To take their fair share of food
>
> And dignity (145; my translation)

LeBlanc's concern for the status of the Acadian people in 1972, less than a decade before Quebec's first referendum on sovereignty-association, reflects the ambient uncertainty about the future of French Canada. But his call for resistance goes well beyond the political preoccupations of the period. More research is needed on the symbolic nature and the structural potential of national identities at the margins of nation-states. Minorities are fascinating thresholds, translucent partitions separating larger cultural or national spaces. Acadians, for one, are experts at looking both ways before moving ahead.

Acadian nationalism is rooted not only in an organic vision of a tragic past, but also in diasporic North American modes strongly represented in literature and popular culture. In the past thirty years, a number of important Moncton poets, such as Gérald Leblanc, Fredric Gary Comeau, Serge Patrice Thibodeau, Dyane Léger, and Sarah-Marylou Brideau, have sought to define Acadian identity as a blend of traditions and urban uprootedness that is reminiscent of the interesting concept of "ethni-cité" coined by Jacques Beauchemin and Joseph Yvon Thériault to talk about hybrid rural-urban communities (Beauchemin and Bock-Côté 279–90). In his 1999 collection of poetry, *Je n'en connais pas la fin*, Gérald Leblanc evokes the ambiguity associated with his much-loved Moncton streetscapes:

> we live in the same city
>
> it is our foremost script, our only one
>
> between our home geography
>
> stretches out like a landscape of illusions (38; my translation)

Leblanc's references in earlier books to what he calls his "navigable ambiguity" in the middle of his "culture métisse" (Métis culture) demonstrates that his native Acadia increasingly strikes him as "une communauté lousse" (a loosely shaped community), one that calls nonetheless for the most entrenched membership and commitment. Serge Patrice Thibodeau's *Nous, l'étranger* (1995) also exposes the euphoric tensions between the togetherness of the Acadian landscape (yet cut off from its very history) and the strong invocation of foreign lands at the core of the poet's language of hope:

> where do you want us to go in this foggy land
>
> we, foreigners, pilgrims in search of those misty shorelines
>
> where the event took place
>
> the need to inscribe the white stone seal a printed letter
>
> high above the fire of our written memory
>
> . . . .
>
> we are such timeless relics (59; my translation)

Both Leblanc and Thibodeau bear witness to the strategic displacement of collective representations in Acadia. Theirs is a vision of a continent-wide Acadia, determined by the forces of dislocation and relocation that are shaping linguistic and cultural groups across North America, from Puerto Rico to Quebec. Yet nowhere in their works is the ontological meaning of the past, the centrality of the Deportation, ever questioned. Leblanc died in 2005, leaving an uncanny emptiness on the streets of Moncton. His involvement, through his development of a highly recognizable Acadian poetic landscape was decisive in shaping contemporary Acadia as both a homeland and a point of departure, a coastal space and a wharf extending into the sea.

Serge Patrice Thibodeau's appointment, after many years in Montreal, as director of Moncton publisher Éditions Perce-Neige confirms the importance of his engagement in Acadian cultural life. Indeed, several poets of Leblanc's generation saw Acadia's obvious lack of access to statehood as a paradoxically enabling factor, one that would lead to a powerful and truly original Acadian presence in Canada and in the francophone world. Acadia seemed to be a nation free of the constant preoccupation with state structures; cultural initiatives and educational institutions, such as publishing firms and the Université de Moncton itself, played a much larger role in terms of governance. These purely cultural aspirations were often overstated by Leblanc and many others (Roy, Arsenault, Raymond Guy Leblanc, Chiasson) in the 1980s and 1990s. But in the face of Quebec's own political agenda during the same period, literary and artistic activism appeared to be the only realistic vision for Acadia. From refugee status in the eighteenth century to cultural nationhood, a huge historical expanse could be reclaimed and transformed into collective affirmation. Much of late-twentieth-century Acadian literature focused on creating a working chronotope for an itinerant nation.

Constructing themselves as the hosts and sole guarantors of diversity, dominant societies typically vow to harbour both sameness and difference. There is no doubt that contemporary Canadian society likes to associate its most recent evolution with this high moral goal. Tamed and often trivialized, cultural and linguistic differences are only welcome as appropriate manifestations of collective affirmation when they are subsumed under the apparently harmonious environments that present-day developed societies strive to foster within their borders. In fact, the fundamental value afforded to diversity in dominant discourses in Europe and North America generally leads to the implicit denial of otherness as the site of resistance and disharmony. The soft and seamless assimilation to diversity as an illusion of difference is one of the most directly relevant ideological conditions confronting minority communities today, especially in Canada.

Far from being sheltered societies, cultural minorities tend to be inhabited by diasporic tensions, as they accommodate all differences. Indeed, from all perspectives, minority subjects are the embodiment of difference. In *Le discours antillais*, Édouard Glissant has drawn our attention to the fundamental creolization of postcolonial societies, not only in the use of language aggregates, such as Creole, but also in the acceptance of mixed, wavering identities. One is reminded of Jacques Derrida's insightful comments in *Judéités, questions pour Jacques Derrida*. In this well-known series of interviews, Derrida muses about his Jewish identity. His childhood, he writes, was determined by a double injunction based on the ambiguity of his cultural heritage. Derrida's text is difficult to translate, for it plays in French on the various meanings of the verbs "garder" (to keep, to preserve), "se garder de" (to distrust, to protect oneself from), and "prendre garde" (to watch out for). "Protect yourself from the Jew in you in order to preserve your Jewishness," writes Derrida in this important passage. "Watch out for the Jew in you":

> The phrase, the contradictory injunc-tion, that would thus have ordered my life seemed to say to me, in French,—*garde-toi du Judaisme—ou même de la judéité,* ... keep yourself from it in order to keep some of it, keep yourself from it, guard yourself from being Jewish or keep and guard the Jew in you. Guard yourself from and take care of the Jew in you. (*Judeities* 6)

In *Psyche, Inventions of the Other*, Derrida again describes identities as infinite displacements: "when a traveler turns into or sets out along an infinite way and one asks him where he is, he replies that he has come from the way; and if one asks him where he is going, he replies that he is going from the way to the way"

(*Psyche* 237). His strategy "consists in not being careful, taking care of nothing, being careful of nothing [prendre garde, garde de rien, garde à rien]" (237). Amidst the uncertainties reflected in the verbs "garder" (to preserve) and "se garder" (to guard oneself from) lies the dramatic tension that shapes minority identities in Derrida's works on judeity. Oscillating between an obsessive preoccupation for the past and a need to guard themselves from it, members of minority communities particularly enjoy acting out the dominant discourse, espousing its powerful idiosyncrasies to the point of self-effacement, while thriving on resistance. Wavering between denial and affirmation can be a dangerous game, for the endangered community may be swallowed whole by the theatrical effects. Shifting magically from one language to the other, hiding under new or mispronounced names, playing out the other as though one is the master of otherness itself, these trademarks of minority communities suggest both the fragility of their collective existence and their subtle resourcefulness in the face of extinction. The pleasure found in games of masks, in borrowed identities, and in learning different languages stems from the desire to act out who they are not. Cultural and linguistic minorities are masters at the game of *passer pour un autre*, at crafting vanishing identities. One is reminded of Emmanuel Levinas's metaphor of the face—*le visage*—which is, in the terms of the exalting encounter imagined by the philosopher, the manifestation of otherness in one's daily existence. This *visage de l'autre*, which the author of *L'humanisme de l'autre homme* contemplates with such extraordinary fondness, tends to be for minority subjects a part so deeply enmeshed in their own identity that it becomes at times totally indistinguishable from the self.

Modern-day Acadia is an unfailingly open society. It is open even to the point of fracture. Yet for all cultural or linguistic minorities, the elaborate multicultural construct on which Canadian modernity is built remains deeply problematic, for it tends to invalidate or even erase references to collective identities. Thériault wonders about the relevance of the notions of conflict and resistance in the construction of a modern Acadian society. Acadians formed a marginal but largely accommodating group as early as the late 1700s. He notes that Acadians have generally sought to live in harmony with their neighbours, especially in New Brunswick (35). Cultural and linguistic survival had to be expressed in terms of marginality instead of conflict. Yet Acadian historians, as early as Michel Roy in *L'Acadie perdue*, his important 1978 text, and Jean-Paul Hautecoeur in his *L'Acadie du discours*, have construed this non-conflictual state of apartness as a subtle form of resistance. The strategic construction of a distinct but harmonious historical subject, Thériault points out, can only be the result of "*une participation différenciée*" (52). One may conclude that marginality and resistance are two sides of the same coin and that Acadian identity is the product of both self-affirmation and self-effacement.

The work of poet and folksinger Fredric Gary Comeau illustrates this fundamental ambivalence in *Routes* and, more recently, in *Naufrages*. Comeau's persona in *Naufrages* seems indifferent to his roots. He lives a life of transience, alternating between an intense desire for homelessness and a fundamental sadness in what he sees as an exiled existence. Is identity what one leaves behind? Or, better said, is identity the distance that separates the subject from the very moment of departure? Is that moment in which a distance was created the source not only of subjective identity, but also of Acadian culture itself? Is culture that very distance in space and time? Obsessed with the fractured certainties of his past, Comeau's narrator counts on the redemptive qualities of displacement:

> I remember those eyes from the other side of the world
>
> watching out for another image to emerge
>
> between the night and my devastated language
>
> between existence with its air of certainty
>
> and doubt, my very last chance
>
> I remember those eyes from the other side of the world
>
> and blindly I move forward (*Naufrages* 20; my translation)

In *Routes*, the Acadian landscape is defined by its endlessness. Beyond the silent confines of the villages, the poet hears "feverish voices" and urban beats from those like him who "refuse to negotiate, their eyes scarred by exile" (*Routes* 56; my translation). In Comeau's work, sadness and longing characterize the lost sense of belonging. His Acadian identity is precisely that loss as it projects itself onto the future like a barred horizon. Not all contemporary Acadian poets are as deeply motivated by a melancholic sense of futility. In Rose Després's *La vie prodigieuse*, for instance, the female voice at first appears to be cut off from her native language, a foreign tongue in an all too familiar guise:

> A disconnected language
>
> As foreign as other languages may be
>
> Rings through me unidentified
>
> It stays apart, on its own
>
> Anchored nonetheless
>
> Vibrating to other beats (30; my translation)

Throughout Després's work, the linguistic fracture within the self paradoxically leads to self-affirmation. "Chez nous ça rage," she declares in a poem entitled "Al dente":

> Ideas like blood-sucking bats wait for the night
> They climb along the walls and colonize the ceilings
> Like frantic cats (40; my translation)

In *Mourir à Scoudouc* and other early poetic works, Herménégilde Chiasson offers momentous depictions of Acadia as a fleeting homeland. In the "Red" section of his Acadian flag trilogy, for instance, he evokes the fragmentation of the Acadian space:

> Acadia, my beautiful love, violated, on stand-by on all five continents, on stand-by amidst all galaxies, scattered among narrow church steeples filled up to the sky with saints, my far away love. Take off your blue dress, red stars printed on your breast, and move forward deep into the sea, the red sea will open its arms for us, there in front of us our own escape from Egypt. (43; my translation)

Chiasson's entire work reflects the poet's ambivalence towards his own culture, as he is torn between "garder" and "se garder de" (to preserve the past and to abstain from it), between the fragility of the national space, yet also the inescapable quest for identity.

Poets such as these are at the core of contemporary Acadian culture. They do not speak for everyone, of course. But it is hard to imagine that cultural transfers would occur without them. Their strong presence in the media in Moncton and Caraquet, and, via the Université de Moncton, in the wider social discourse, is a reflection of the fragile structures underpinning cultural minorities as they seek to make sense of a fast-erasing historical narrative. Although they often reject the systems of tradition on which the Acadian national identity continues to build itself, asserting values of individuality and freedom, their work contributes nonetheless to the construction of powerful areas of meaning.

The shift from a historical paradigm of dispersion, loss, and *retrouvailles* to the composite and interlocking spaces of roots/routes described by James Clifford in his seminal study of diasporas in North America, *Routes: Travel and Translation in the Late Twentieth Century*, continues to resonate throughout Acadia, from the Internet portal Acadie.net, which developed new pages on the diaspora circa 2000, to the Université Sainte-Anne's summer seminar on the continental Acadian landscape, also in 2000. In their superb 2007 book on plural *Acadies*, Martin Pâquet and Stéphane Savard offer, with the help of a dozen academics, the best multidisciplinary essays on the new territorialities shaping Acadian/Cajun identity(s) and culture(s) from New Brunswick to Louisiana.

In many ways, with the organization in 1994 of the first Acadian World Congress and with the subsequent development of strategic and symbolic links with Louisiana's Cadian and Cajun communities, the last fifteen to twenty years have arguably been a resounding response to statelessness as a mode of entrenching Acadianness. If the "Grand Dérangement" broke the unity of the Acadian chronotope, the reconciliation with the diversity of the concept of "américanité" as applied to Acadian culture was bound to mend the historical fracture. Many Acadian poets and essayists—Leblanc and Thériault first and foremost—worked on that assumption. Ties quickly developed with the Acadian historical diaspora in Louisiana and with countercultural movements in the Northeastern United States. A new connectedness with a particular brand of continental identity is bound to move Acadian identity well beyond its linguistic and historical confines.

◆ ◆ ◆

No one could have predicted that the tiny village of Memramcook, New Brunswick, would become the diasporic homeland of post-Deportation Acadia. This is a stunning part of New Brunswick, broken into two inseparable, yet rival, shorelines along the Petitcodiac River. There is a powerful sense of resistance in this slow-moving, absorbing maritime landscape. With its church parish, founded in 1700, and its college, a huge building for such a small community, Memramcook is a testimony to the educational goals and ambitions of nineteenth-century Acadians. Acadian families first regrouped in the valley of the Memramcook River after 1755, and from there many migrated north to settle in villages and towns on the eastern shore of New Brunswick. This forced migration is only a small part of a very well-known story: the Acadian refugees reached virtually all corners of the continent, from the town of L'Acadie, Quebec, to the parishes around Lafayette, Louisiana. Along the Petitcodiac, scattered Acadian villages, always so surprisingly centreless, lie on both shores from the city of Dieppe, near Moncton, to Grandes Buttes, Boudreau Village, and minute settlements all the way to the Bay of Fundy. Perhaps this complex and extraordinary movement, back and forth, between crystallization and dissolution, is nowhere better symbolized than in the gigantic volume of the Petitcodiac River moving in both directions, towards the land and towards the sea, as if this made sense in some basic, fundamental way. Here the river is a metaphor for a culture. How would one know that something significant continues to happen here beyond that which the cartographer's eye can see?

CRITICAL ALLEGIANCES

Christl Verduyn

What is "new," then, is disciplinary consciousness. (32)
A field's political unconscious can re-script its primal scene only via
epistemic and methodological shifts. (36)
—Smaro Kamboureli, "Shifting the Ground of a Discipline: Emergence and Canadian Literary Studies in English"

"Something has happened to English Canadian literary studies."
With this declaration, Smaro Kamboureli opens her introductory essay,
"Shifting the Ground of a Discipline: Emergence and Canadian Literary Studies in English" (1), in the second of the three volumes that have emerged from
the TransCanada conferences project.[1] This essay is at the heart of the transformative exercise that the TransCanada project has been.

As Kamboureli explains, the field of English Canadian literary studies has
shifted "toward a foregrounding of the situational and material conditions"
(1) that influence literary production in the country and that "broaden our
understanding of what the literary entails and invite a reassessment of the
disciplinary contexts within which we customarily read literature" (2). Something has indeed happened to English Canadian literary studies, and in this
essay I argue that the TransCanada project is a vital part of what has happened.

The TransCanada project refers primarily to three linked conferences that
began in Vancouver in 2005, that continued in Guelph in 2007, and that concluded at Mount Allison University in Sackville, New Brunswick, in 2009. In
addition to the conferences, the project included workshops, research seminars, and academic events sponsored by the TransCanada Institute under the

directorship of Smaro Kamboureli at the University of Guelph (2005–2013). Drawing widely and creatively on new disciplinary discourses and approaches, the TransCanada conferences gathered together a remarkable array of participants in a national discussion about the possible new directions that Canadian literary studies might take. These conferences have generated three extensive essay collections—including this volume—that trace the disciplinary transformation—or transdisciplinary discussion—that has unfolded in Canadian literary studies over the past decade.

In this concluding essay, I offer some reflections on the paths charted during this journey—from the first collection, *Trans.Can.Lit: Resituating the Study of Canadian Literature* (2007), through the second, *Shifting the Ground of Canadian Literary Studies* (2012), to this third and final collection, *Critical Collaborations: Indigeneity, Diaspora, Ecology, and Canadian Literary Studies* (2014). As I have suggested, Kamboureli's expansive essay is at the heart of this triptych. Nominally, it serves as an introduction to the second volume; substantively and strategically, however, it speaks to the TransCanada project as a whole. As such, it offers a useful, productive, and consequential lens or focus for some closing comments, reflections, and suggestions about the collective and collaborative venture of the conferences, about the publications they have produced, and about future directions for transdisciplinary literary studies.

The present essay has four sections. The first two focus directly on Kamboureli's strategic concerns about methodology and epistemology, in particular the two key concepts of "emergent events" and transdisciplinarity. The third and fourth direct my focus concretely to the broad areas of Canadian Studies and Canadian literature and, finally, to Indigenous Studies as a necessary foreshadowing of the future shape and character of transdisciplinary literary studies.

Emergent Events

Methodological concerns are for Kamboureli a "guiding principle." As she explains: "I attempt to examine how the field of Canadian literary studies has been reconfigured as a discipline through what I call 'emergent' events or discourses" (3). The concept of emergent events expresses Kamboureli's view of the changes in Canadian literary studies in recent years. These changes have not been based on sudden, radical paradigm shifts. Rather, they are part of an ongoing or incremental process, stemming from events or circumstances that "emerge" only episodically. In this emergence, they "disturb" their surroundings (8)—in this case, the field of Canadian literary studies—by introducing new ways of seeing and doing. These new perspectives and practices then lead to further developments. Kamboureli cites as examples of this process the 1983

Women and Words conference in Vancouver; the 1988 Third International Women's Book Fair in Montreal; and the 1994 Writing Thru Race conference in Vancouver. To this list of emergent events, I would add the TransCanada project itself.

Through its conferences and publications, the TransCanada project has promoted and performed different ways of knowing and as well as the "nodal function" that Kamboureli ascribes to emergent events. By this she means that these events "operate within and across different communities as (sometimes loose, sometimes organized) network formations that gradually pick up momentum ... [establishing] *allegiances* through interrelationships that mobilize *across different constituencies*" (11, emphasis added). The episodic character of emergent events resists any chronological and progressivist interpretation of the changes they effect. They raise questions about what and how we know—that is, the concerns of epistemology, methodology, and transdisciplinarity that are central to Kamboureli's essay and, by extension, to the TransCanada conference publication project as a whole.

Kamboureli explains that emergent events come in different forms, from conferences such as those mentioned above, to individual and collective writings and publications, such as Joy Kogawa's novel *Obasan* (1981), Lee Maracle's *Oratory: Coming to Theory* (1990), the journal *Tessera*, and the magazine *f(l)ip* (Kamboureli, "Shifting" 11). These and other examples constitute emergent event "nodes," which have the capacity to network within and across different constituencies and boundaries, intervening or disrupting them, exposing the vested interests of a field and its foundations (11–12). For example, the impact of Kogawa's novels extended well beyond literary studies into the field of Canadian history, studies of Canadian multiculturalism, and the Japanese Canadian Redress movement of the 1980s. Maracle's *Oratory: Coming to Theory* troubled traditional academic practices of theory. Publications like *Tessera* and *f(l)ip* intervened in multiple disciplinary fields by reimagining them from feminist, lesbian, queer, and other non-dominant perspectives.

In short, emergent events have the effect of triggering change in a "field-imaginary." This is a term that Kamboureli borrows from Donald E. Pease, who uses it to denote what might be understood as the basic inside elements of a field—Pease's phrase is "fundamental syntax" (8).[2] Emergent events disrupt a field with material conditions, or contingencies from "outside," which can seem strange because they are extraneous to the field; and, being strange, they can cause a sense of uneasiness, nervousness, or even anxiety. Informed by Foucault and Nietzsche, Kamboureli develops the concept of "emergence" to express the process and effect of "making strange" (8) and to convey her perception of the process whereby, recalling Pease, "the Canadian field-imaginary begins gradually and steadily to change its syntax" (9).

In the first instance, the key to this process of change has been the end of its "romanc[e]" with "the nation and . . . CanLit as a statist institution" (9). The examination of literature, then, in the second instance, began its relationship with "notably, but not exclusively, indigeneity, racialization, gender, and queerness" (9).

The essays in the three TransCanada volumes have carried out this twofold examination. Many of them exhibit the "strangeness" of their material relative to "familiar" Canadian literary studies—that is, to the "traditional" themes and imagery, forms, and genres of the field. They illustrate how that field is shifting away from "the great themes of the nation-building narrative" as Diana Brydon describes these in her essay for the first volume, *Trans.Can.Lit: Resituating the Study of Canadian Literature:* "transportation and communication; a movement from east to west, from sea to sea, from civilization to wilderness; a march of progress; a resistance to north-south pulls and to the ethos of the United States" (13). In the "strangeness" of their "different" foci, the essayists are aware of the uneasiness or resistance that their explorations might elicit. As Brydon notes, asking the question "Is Canadian literature an institution?" "goes to the heart of the uneasiness some participants [in the TransCanada project] felt in worrying that what were once sociological questions were now overwhelmingly more properly literary ones" (3).

In the same volume, Lily Cho reports on the "perplexity about the situation of Asian Canadian literature within Canadian literature, the situating of Native literatures within and against majoritized Canadian literature ... [and] the uneasiness of simply containing minor literatures under the umbrella of CanLit" (100). Just as Brydon brings government departments, the market sector, and civil society into the literary arena (5), Cho injects complexities of citizenship and diaspora, while other contributors to the three volumes explore Canadian literary studies in relation to debates in globalization, neoliberalism, multiculturalism, colonialism, social justice, the law, ecology, Environmental Studies, Indigenous Studies, Political Studies, Translation Studies, Throne Speeches, the Cold War, jazz, even taxidermy and café menus, among other fields and foci of study.

In short, the shift of literary studies from its familiar foundations into what may at first seem to be strange new fields is the effect of emergent events, such as those mentioned and numerous others.[3] As I am arguing here, the TransCanada project joins that list of emergent events. Cumulatively, the TransCanada conferences and publications have served, in Kamboureli's words, "as conduits through which turning points occur, shifts that ... undiscipline the discipline" ("Shifting" 12–13).

Undisciplining Canadian literary Studies: Inter/trans/disciplinarity

For Kamboureli, a discussion of interdisciplinarity and transdisciplinarity is critical to and instrumental in opening the field of English Canadian literary studies to new ways (methods) of knowing (epistemology). Interdisciplinarity has a long-standing place in my other scholarly home, Canadian Studies. Kamboureli is cautious, and rightly so, about too closely aligning Canadian literary studies with Canadian Studies. Yet both fields have endured identification with the nation, even as they have transcended this by contesting and critiquing the nation. In its transdisciplinary development, Canadian literary studies can draw insights from Canadian Studies' interdisciplinary experience. Reflecting on the changes within Canadian literary studies in recent years, then, it serves to recall Canadian Studies' early engagement with knowledges and methodologies across disciplinary boundaries.

Kamboureli acknowledges that the notion of shifting disciplines—or even "undisciplining" disciplines (8)—is not particularly new today. What is new, she proposes, is the increased awareness or "disciplinary consciousness" in (Canadian) literary studies (14). What has caused this heightened academic consciousness? Kamboureli suggests that it has been its "outward mobility" (14). Canadian literary studies, she suggests, has developed and benefited from "the shuttling of the critical gaze from the 'inside' to the 'outside' of the discipline—along with the characteristic interdisciplinarity it involves" (17).

The shift towards interdisciplinarity is one of the most striking features of the TransCanada conference publications, as the examples mentioned above have illustrated. But Kamboureli maintains that interdisciplinarity—with its "shuttling" back and forth between the "inside" and the "outside" of disciplines (3)—is not sufficient to generate real change in a field-imaginary and its "political unconscious" (10). She is concerned that interdisciplinarity is simply a kind of "value-added" to humanities scholarship. In *Retooling the Humanities: The Culture of Research in Canadian Universities* (2011), Daniel Coleman and Kamboureli track the shift to interdisciplinarity and its "ancillary development"—collaboration in humanities research (57)—to a "privileging of knowledge-as-commodity" (57) in academic culture. This ultimately serves as an instrument in the management of knowledge production.

Kamboureli suggests that this interdisciplinarity is functioning "vertically," in contrast to a form of interdisciplinarity that operates horizontally as a "dialogue across different fields of knowledge" (Schagerl 106, qtd. in Kamboureli, "Shifting" 32–33). She further explores the duality of how interdisciplinarity may work in literary scholarship through Alan Liu's model of "thin" and "thick" interdisciplinarity ("Shifting" 33). "Thin" interdisciplinarity is the "shuttling back and forth" variety mentioned above. It may well generate dialogue across disciplines, but it does so primarily in a superficial or "thin" manner that does not alter a field and its political unconscious. To achieve the latter requires more than simply crossing disciplinary boundaries or bringing the "outside in." It requires reconceptualizing the outside and inside of disciplinary formations (16). As Kamboureli argues,[4]

> mere incorporation within a discipline's domain of those other subjects or of different ways of knowing does not necessarily disrupt its political unconscious; inclusion can become an instance of policing and fetishization, a means of containment, a strategy designed to pre-empt any radical restructuring of the discipline. (15)

"Thick" interdisciplinarity does not merely borrow across disciplinary boundaries; it also broadens them, challenging and "recalibrat[ing]" a field-imaginary (35). "Thin" interdisciplinarity may use another discipline's methods, concepts, or theories incorrectly or problematically. In contrast, "thick" interdisciplinarity accepts "the limits of knowledge and methods" (35). Indeed, interdisciplinarity's potential lies precisely in that it recognizes the limits of knowing. Liu discusses the "feeling of wordlessness" (184), also expressed or experienced as the "*sublime*" or its "other"—*dejection/abjection* (184)—"in the face of an unknown world" (185). He suggests that we "ask more usefully whether there might not be other minds a bit more open than [one's] home knowledge" (177).

I believe this is an extremely useful, productive, and consequential framing of the issue. In guest lectures I gave during the late 1990s to the graduate M.A. classes in the core course of the Frost Centre for Canadian and Indigenous Studies at Trent University, I used the expression "epistemological humility." By that I was referring to the limits to knowledge derived from interdisciplinary practice. "Limits" here does not have a negative connotation but rather a positive one of respectful awareness that there may be understandings that are quite simply beyond one's own, that belong to someone other. The notion of epistemological humility also accorded with the awareness of cultural appropriation that arose in the 1990s. Interestingly, in light of Kamboureli's discussion of disciplinary awareness, I titled these lectures "Beware—Be Aware—Interdisciplinary Vigilance."[5]

Liu's "thick" and "thin" interdisciplinarity recalls J.S Kelley's earlier notion of "wide" and "narrow" interdisciplinarity,[6] as well as Jill Vickers's reflection on "strict" interdisciplinarity, and other terms and analyses of interdisciplinarity by such scholars as Julie Thompson Klein, and Liora Salter and Alison Hearn. In all, interdisciplinarity is "a hard notion to define, as well as a complex and diverse practice to perform," Kamboureli concludes (33), a statement that echoes Salter and Hearn:

It is evident that interdisciplinarity is a *complex* phenomenon and that it involves much more than the combination of two or more disciplines in research. This complexity is compounded by the fact that the discussion of interdisciplinarity is permeated with *essentially contested* concepts. (*Report* 24, emphasis added)

These explorations and discussions of interdisciplinarity took place earlier within various Canadian Studies forums.[7] Canadian Studies has had a long and close relationship with interdisciplinarity, from the 1975 Symons Report, *To Know Ourselves*, through a regular series of self-conscious reflections on Canadian Studies and interdisciplinarity, among them the 1992 conference "Theoretical Discourse in the Canadian Intellectual Community," the 1994 Cameron Report, *Taking Stock*, and special publications of interdisciplinary journals such as *Arachne: An Interdisciplinary Journal of the Humanities* and the *Journal of Canadian Studies*. For example, the 1997 issue of *Arachne* was devoted to the topic of interdisciplinarity and Canadian Studies. In it, Jill Vickers's essay "'[U]nframed in Open, Unmapped Fields': Teaching the Practice of Interdisciplinarity" was an early articulation of how new knowledge fields— she mentioned Women's Studies and Native/Aboriginal Studies in particular—have "powerfully disrupted our ways of understanding knowledges both in disciplinary and I-D [interdisciplinary] ventures" (13). Vickers tackled the potentially problematic use of another discipline's methods, concepts, or theories with suggestions for collaborative research and "self-consciousness about epistemological questions" (20). She critiqued Julie Klein's notion of interdisciplinarity as "*essentially* a process for achieving an integrative synthesis" and thus "an attempt to impose (or retain) a totalizing account of difference, since integration usually involves the absorption of the weaker by the stronger" (21). Finally, she saw a particular role for Canadian Studies precisely because it "does not have a shared paradigm, canon or common epistemological base" and is instead an "open, cross-roads field" (34) with "an important contribution to make, for example, in developing an understanding of the ethics involved in cross-cultural borrowing/harvesting of knowledge" (36).

Interdisciplinarity, Canadian Studies, and Canadian Literature

One of the TransCanada project's objectives has been to resituate the study of Canadian literature, to shift its epistemological and methodological grounds, and to reconfigure Canadian literary studies. This recent effort finds an antecedent in earlier efforts within Canadian Studies to "un-discipline" Canadian literature and its study. Vickers's article in *Arachne* offered an excellent articulation of the discussion of new understandings and approaches to knowledge that animated Canadian Studies throughout the 1990s. In the same issue of *Arachne* on interdisciplinarity and Canadian Studies noted above, I argued for the benefits and value of interdisciplinarity to the study of Canadian literature, citing the work on ethnicity, race, and Canadian literature by Enoch Padolsky, Francesco Loriggio, and Arun Mukherjee, as well as the then relatively new genre of life writing. For example, in his 1987 article "The Question of the Corpus: Ethnicity and Canadian Literature," Loriggio called for more attention to be paid to the "circumstances" of the work of literature (54), meaning the social, historical, and political contexts, conditions, or circumstances of its production. Referencing Loriggio's article a decade later, I noted: "Circumstances—or what cultural anthropologist Victor Turner called liminalities[8]—the specifics of time and place make the difference. They challenge the assumption that literature is produced in a uniform and unitary context—or in a vacuum" (Verduyn 79). Various 1990s Canadian literary and critical texts further illustrate the point:

> Thus, for example, Lee Maracle's *Sundogs* is significantly enhanced by reader awareness of the 1990s Oka Crisis. Afua Cooper's poem "The Power of Racism" is a critique of the 1990 Royal Ontario Museum exhibit "Into the Heart of Africa," protested by members of Canada's black communities for its (mis) representation of elements of their history and culture. Arun Mukherjee's critical "aesthetics of opposition" uncovers the political dimension of a-historicity or claims to the universal. Her stance is confrontational, Mukherjee acknowledges, "not out of choice but out of necessity": "I have tried to point out how the dominant discourses in North America dehistoricizes and depoliticizes everything so that non-white, non-male, working-class ways of apprehending reality seldom get a hearing." (Verduyn 79–80)

Arun Mukherjee asked why so much critical work was ignoring aspects of literary texts that were the most important considerations for her, such as "poverty, exploitation, social inequality, social and political conflicts, imperialism, racism" (Mukherjee, *Oppositional Aesthetics* viii, qtd. in Verduyn 81). Approaching Canadian literature from an interdisciplinary perspective did not simply add "value-added," sociological, political, or other disciplinary analyses into the mix. Interdisciplinarity asked new questions, focusing less on the "what" and more on the "how" and "why." Thus, Lee Maracle's *Sundogs* addressed much more than the question, "What was Oka?" Interdisciplinary literary analysis asks "the how and why of the crisis and its literary representation, specifically in reference to its literary expression" (Verduyn 82).

One of emergent events' nodal functions is to present allegiances with earlier literary approaches. Indeed, the TransCanada project's powerful interrogation of traditional disciplinary boundaries in Canadian literary studies presents a continuum or an allegiance with earlier interdisciplinary approaches to Canadian literature from within Canadian Studies. That said, Kamboureli suggests not unreasonably that "interdisciplinarity as manifested in the Canadian field-imaginary is not always strictly speaking interdisciplinary" ("Shifting" 33). The same may be said of Canadian Studies, in that some of its work might more aptly be described as multidisciplinary.[9] For Kamboureli, the term transdisciplinary is more appropriate. This term better expresses the new awareness or "disciplinary consciousness" ("Shifting" 14) that she discerns in the study of Canadian literature, along with the new intention to transgress disciplinary boundaries as "an act of practicing criticism responsibly" (36). This understanding of the term aligns well with Vickers's view of transdisciplinarity as an approach "integrating materials from fields with quite different epistemological bases. This is highly productive in terms of the emergence of new theoretical insights, which are then borrowed back into the disciplines" (Vickers 39).

As with emergent events, so too with transdisciplinarity: it does not take the form of precipitous paradigm shifts. Kamboureli is guarded about the idea that Canadian literary studies are undergoing sudden major changes. This is because of the underlying assumption that "there was a single, or easily identifiable, dominant paradigm in the first place" (19). Kamboureli challenges this aspect of or assumption in Canadian literary studies in a compelling "case study" of Canadian thematic criticism.

Long viewed as paradigmatic of Canadian literary studies, thematic criticism has been widely associated with such 1970s publications as Margaret Atwood's *Survival: A Thematic Guide to Canadian Literature* (1972), D.G. Jones's *Butterfly on Rock: A Study of Themes and Images in Canadian Literature* (1970), and John Moss's *Patterns of Isolation in English Canadian Fiction* (1974). Thematic criticism has played a dominant but not an exclusive role in Canadian literary studies. It has by no means encompassed all critical discourse in the field, as Kamboureli shows in a convincing analysis of work by Warren Tallman (his 1960 essay "Wolf in the Snow"), Eli Mandel (his 1971 *Contexts of Canadian Criticism*), and E.D. Blodgett (*Configurations: Essays on Canadian Literatures*, 1982) as three examples of "non-thematic discourses that disturbed the idea of a singular critical model, that did not obsess with the nation, and that did not posit the national character of Canadian literature as the determining feature" (20).

Such a clear-eyed look at Canadian literary studies' past has had the same corrective effect in Canadian Studies. A careful rereading of key documents in the field reveals that strikingly similar questions have been raised about assumptions made of Canadian Studies. This point can be illustrated by the following excerpts from the Symons Report:

The most valid rationale for Canadian Studies is not any relationship that such studies may have to the preservation or the promotion of national identity, or national unity, or national sovereignty, or anything of the kind. The most valid and compelling argument for Canadian studies is the importance of self-knowledge, the need to know and to understand ourselves: who we are; where we are in time and space; where we have been; where we are going; what we possess; what our responsibilities are to ourselves and to others. (Symons, *To Know Ourselves* 12)

If Canadian studies are designed to advance self-knowledge rather than performed in a narrow type of nationalism, some important implications follow. For one thing, the concept of self-knowledge ... opens windows on the street of the world instead of shutting them.... It makes knowledge of other lands and other times essential to our understanding ... knowledge of ourselves cannot fully succeed if accompanied by an unthinking indifference or hostility to non-Canadian studies. Studies that do not relate to Canada in an immediate and obvious way may none the less be a prerequisite to self-knowledge. (14)

These excerpts describe Canadian Studies as a field that is open to the "outside," to the world beyond Canada, and that is neither closed to other disciplines nor obsessed with national character or the nation. Symons stated in no uncertain terms that "patriotic appeals to preserve and develop Canadian identity do not constitute, in practice or in principle, an adequate rationale for Canadian studies at any level" (12). Perceptions of Canadian Studies as nationalistic may and do exist, but they do not comprise its definition any more than thematic criticism is the paradigm of Canadian literary studies. In this manner, Canadian Studies' commitment to interdisciplinarity has enabled interrelationships with other, "different" disciplines and constituencies, other ways of knowing (epistemology), and different ways of doing (methodology).[10]

Kamboureli sees that transdisciplinarity has served in similar fashion in contemporary Canadian literary studies. It has expanded the epistemological and methodological breadth and depth of Canadian literature and critical practice. Indeed, the three volumes of essays generated by the TransCanada project provide ample evidence of this, as Kamboureli sums up:

As "a critical evaluation of terms, concepts, and methods that transgresses disciplinary boundaries" (Dolling and Hark 1195), transdisciplinarity performs ... both thematically and methodologically. If transdisciplinarity reflects at once an awareness of the territoriality of disciplines and an intention to transgress their boundaries as an act of practicing criticism responsibly, then the disciplinary territorialism troubled here is consonant with territoriality as it concerns aboriginality and land claims; white settler society, sovereignty, and the nation-state; cultural and publishing spaces claimed for by racialized and diasporic subjectivities; the travel of literature across languages and their cultural domains through translation; and market places where CanLit as a national or globalized formation circulates. The articulation and treatment of these themes demand that they be addressed contextually across and through the different discursive sites where we encounter them. (35–36)

Sui Generis (and a Nod to Sa'ke'j Henderson)

The TransCanada conferences and publications have explored many new transdisciplinary relationships in relation to Canadian literary studies. One area that recurs with particular presence, and that calls for a few further comments, is Indigenous Studies. This is by no means to diminish the role and impact within Canadian literary studies of such vital areas as globalization, citizenship, politics, environment, and other areas investigated across the three collections of essays. But another striking feature of the volumes' essays is the value that the TransCanada contributors have discerned in Indigenous knowledges and practices, particularly Indigenous legal studies. This area presents an especially compelling and potentially consequential transdisciplinary approach to Canadian literary studies.

In his essay "The Long March to 'Recognition': Sa'ke'j Henderson, First Nations Jurisprudence, and *Sui Generis* Solidarity," for the second volume (*Shifting the Ground*), Len Findlay argues that:

> literary scholars and cultural workers need to know as much about this legal-jurisprudential *turn* as they do about linguistic and cultural and ethical turns. From such ongoing self-education and receptivity to difference, *sui generis* solidarity may arise, and with it new distributions of authority and responsibility, indeed new knowledge systems, within and beyond the Canadian academy. (247)

Henderson explains his use of the Latin *sui generis* in his essay for the present volume, "Trans-Systemic Constitutionalism in Indigenous Law and Knowledge" as follows: "*sui* (of its own) connected with *generis*, genitive of *genus* (kind)—[it] means self-generating; of a kind of one's own; without equal; absolutely unique. In other words, this is a knowledge system distinct from Eurocentrism." He explores the innovative methods and principles that are being developed through "the trans-systemic synthesis of the Supreme Court of Canada's … constitutional framework of Canada." These are being developed in the legal system to protect Indigenous rights and treaties as useful models for other areas and disciplines of study. Thus, Indigenous legal studies offer an example *par excellence* not just of collaborative research but also of work with real social justice effects, work that challenges "dominant understandings of what knowledge is" (Findlay, *Shifting the Ground* 239).

Distinguishing Indigenous traditions of knowledge and practice from those of European provenance can make a crucial difference in literary studies. This is a key theme in the essays presented by many TransCanada contributors, such as Marie Battiste and Lee Maracle, Julia Emberley and Larissa Lai. For Battiste, "there is no greater promise and hope than ... the increased awareness and work of Indigenous people that has been emerging.... The theme of trans-systemic knowledge, which operates between two or more distinct knowledge systems, displacing Eurocentrism suggests sites of emerging change and innovation that come from Indigenous peoples animating IK [Indigenous Knowledge]" (84). In "Oratory on Oratory" (*Trans.Can.Lit*), Lee Maracle point outs that

> [i]n the study of literature, Western instructors often pose the question, "What was the author thinking, doing, intending?" Salish thinkers and philosophers (orators) regard such questions as invasive, and do not grant themselves the right to ask them, much less answer, in the absence of the author. Such questions are meaningless in terms of the function of story in our society. The point of hearing (and now reading) story is to study it in and of itself, *to examine the context* in which it is told, *to understand the obstacles* to being that it presents, and then to see ourselves through the story, that is, *transform* ourselves. (55, emphasis added)

Extending the "turn" in understanding that Maracle's "oratory on oratory" illustrates, Julia Emberley and Larissa Lai draw with respect and acknowledgment on Indigenous knowledge and historical experience in their literary critical work. Emberley presents a reading of Eden Robinson's *Monkey Beach* "in the context of Indigenous spiritual epistemologies" (71). Based on the Haisla Spirit Canoe journey, Emberley examines the novel's structural organization as a history of residential school violence and its consequences for Indigenous communities. Lai examines Lee Maracle's short story "Yin Chin," SKY Lee's novel *Disappearing Moon Cafe*, and theatre productions by The Movement Project (a Toronto-based group of First Nations women and women of colour) by David Khang, and by Marie Clement for their depictions of Indigenous and Asian Canadian relations and the historical and political realities and inequities that characterize them.

This is not to suggest that exclusive focus on the future should be placed on Indigenous legal studies narrowly or technically defined. Rather, participants across the TransCanada project can turn to Indigenous studies with new awareness or consciousness of what Canadian literary studies can learn from Indigenous knowledge and practice.

In/conclusion

The TransCanada project has been conceived from multiple needs: the concern for "the state of CanLit" (Kamboureli, Preface x); a "summons for developing new terms of engagement" with it (x); and a response to "pondering not only on the methods but also on the institutional and material conditions that have shaped CanLit and its study as an institution since the early 1990s" (Kamboureli, "Shifting" 30). In their execution, the TransCanada conferences and publications have "opened up" the field of Canadian literary studies and shifted its critical gaze "from the 'inside' to the 'outside' of the discipline" (3).

At its outset, three elements of the TransCanada project were seen as crucial. First, the focus would be on "CanLit" in the broader contexts of study—"globalizing processes and critical methodologies, but also ... institutional structures such as the Humanities, the cultural industries, curricula, and anthologies" (Kamboureli, Preface xii–xiii). Methodologies and method would provide "constitutive rather than supplementary" objects (xiii) and would be key to this focus, with the task at hand "a major rethinking of the assumptions that had governed the field of CanLit studies" (xiii). Second, the project would be future-oriented in that it would aim to generate momentum for ongoing work beyond the TransCanada project itself. Third, it would be a sustained collaborative effort, with transdisciplinarity playing a significant and productive role.

The TransCanada project has substantially and successfully combined and addressed these elements. In the process, I suggest that it has performed the "nodal function of emergent events"—operating within and across different communities while establishing allegiances through interrelationships across different constituencies (Kamboureli, "Shifting" 11). I further suggest that Indigenous Studies and Canadian Studies are front and centre among these allegiances and interrelationships. The questions these fields raise about what and how we know—about epistemology and methodology—are the questions of Canadian literary studies today, as well as those going forward. The pursuit of these questions will undoubtedly lead to other "happenings" like the TransCanada project.

NOTES

Introduction

1   On this point, see also Robert Ian Vere Hodge and Vijay Mishra, *Dark Side of the Side: Australian Literature and the Postcolonial Mind* (Sydney: Allen And Unwin, 1990), esp. 196.

2   In their influential *The Empire Writes Back: Theory and Practice in Post-Colonial Literatures*, Bill Ashcroft, Gareth Griffiths, and Helen Tiffin also refer to settler cultures as "white diaspora" (see 19–20), but their use of "diaspora" neutralizes its impact—an impact that Maracle problematizes.

3   I echo here Stoler, who sees epistemic habits as being "steeped in history and historical practices, ways of knowing that are available and 'easy to think,' called upon, temporarily settled dispositions that can be challenged and that change" (39).

4   On this question, see *Is Canada Postcolonial? Unsettling Canadian Literature*, ed. Laura Moss (Waterloo: Wilfrid Laurier UP, 2003).

5   The TransCanada project encompasses the serial conference TransCanada: Literatures, Institutions, Citizenship that I co-organized in collaboration with Roy Miki (Vancouver 2005 and Guelph 2007) and Christl Verduyn (Sackville 2009); the workshops and other activities initiated by the TransCanada Institute that I founded and directed at the University of Guelph (2005–12); and the various publications that resulted from these activities. See http://www.transcanadas.ca.

6   Carol Boyce Davies employs the same term, in *Black Women, Writing, and Identity: Migrations of the Subject* (New York: Routledge, 1994), but she applies "elsewhereness" to the Black diaspora (26). I employ the term in a broader sense to suggest that some of the most significant changes the study of Canadian literature has undergone of late have occurred under the signs of diaspora, postcoloniality, and Indigeneity, but also to draw attention to the "outward movement" such studies are marked by. See my "Introduction" in *Shifting the Ground* (1–36).

7   I have in mind here, for example, the changes in the cultural marketplace, specifically the Random House–Penguin merger and its expected negative impact on Canadian literature. See Steve Ladurantaye and Marsha Lederman, "Random House–Penguin Merger to Squeeze Canadian Publishers," *The Globe and Mail*, 20 October 2012. Web. http://www.theglobeand mail.com/report-on-business/random-house-penguin-merger-to-squeeze-canadian-pub lishers/article4784552. See also a compilation of comments in response to the merger by publishers, editors, literary agents, and authors: "How Will the Random House–Penguin Merger Affect Canadian Publishing?", compiled by Robert Everett-Green and Marsha Lederman, *The Globe and Mail*, 29 October 2012. Web. http://www.theglobeandmail.com/arts/books -and-media/how-will-the-random-house-penguin-merger-affect-canadian-publishing/ article4744576.

8   I elaborate on this concept in my introduction to *Shifting the Ground* (32–36).

9   I engage with this issue more directly in my introduction to *Shifting the Ground*.
10 In *Adorno*, Martin Jay hyphenates force-field, while in his later work, *Force Fields*, he drops the hyphen. See also Richard Leppert's "Introduction" to Adorno's *Essays on Music: Selected, with Introduction, Commentary, and Notes* by Richard Lippert, trans. Susan H. Gillespie (Berkeley: U of California P, 2002): 1–84.
11 See Mary Louise Pratt, *Imperial Eyes: Travel Writing and Transculturation*, 2nd ed. (New York: Routledge, 1992); and Katie Pickles and Myra Rutherdale, eds., *Contact Zones: Aboriginal and Settler Women in Canada's Colonial Past* (Vancouver: U of British Columbia P, 2005).
12 See also Perry Anderson's *A Zone of Engagement* (London: Verso, 1992).
13 Rancière's *litteralité* is now translated as literality, now as literariness; along the same lines, some of his readers use the concepts interchangeably, while others distinguish between the two. See also my engagement with literariness in my Introduction to *Shifting the Ground* (6–8).
14 See, for example, *Disagreement: Politics and Philosophy* (55).
15 See Findlay's essay, "Redress Rehearsals: Legal Warrior, COSMOSQUAW, and the National Aboriginal Achievement Awards."
16 The two have collaborated extensively. See, for example, *Protecting Indigenous Knowledge and Heritage: A Global Challenge* (Saskatoon: Purich Publishing, 2000).
17 In 1847, Dumas established the Théâtre Historique in Paris, which he inaugurated with the production of his play *La Reine Margot*. This theatre "exorcises the 'old' that appropriates the place of the present.... It tears it to pieces, fragmenting it in individual plays; it acts it out" (de Certeau 151).
18 For recent examples of work that engages with this issue, see Justin Edwards, Cynthia Sugars and Gerry Turcotte, and Marlene Goldman and Joanne Saul.
19 See Margaret Atwood, *The Animals in That Country* (Toronto: Oxford UP, 1968), 36–39.
20 I have in mind here Homi Bhabha's essay "Of Mimicry and Man: The Ambivalence of Colonial Discourse," *The Location of Culture* (London and New York: Routledge, 1994), 85–92.
21 Young develops his point by analyzing, and tracking the pervasive influence of, Joseph Arthur comte de Gobineau's *The Inequality of Human Races*, vol. I, trans. Adrian Collins (London: Heinemann, 1915).
22 Though Kertzer contends that "the *genius loci* always retains something of its unruly, demonic character" (61), the overall tenor of his study reflects a desire to contain this unruliness.
23 Indigenizing here doesn't operate in the ways in which Len Findlay exhorts us to "Always Indigenize"; nevertheless, I employ the term deliberately so that it signifies in its literal sense but also echoes the silencing of Indigenous voices.
24 I hear *apostrophe* in its original Greek sense of averting one's gaze, looking away because of shame, anger, or embarrassment.
25 Sneja Gunew, in *Haunted Nations: The Colonial Dimensions of Multiculturalism* (London and New York: Routledge, 2004), also touches on hauntology and Canada; see especially the conclusion to her book.
26 I have in mind here Fanon's critique of the Oedipal complex. As he says: "The Oedipal complex is far from being a black complex" (130). Still, Fanon doesn't entirely reject psychoanalysis; early in the same book he writes that "only a psychoanalytic interpretation of the black problem can reveal the affective disorders responsible for this network of complexes" (xiv). See *Black Skin, White Masks*, trans. Richard Philcox, with a Foreword by Kwame Anthony Appiah (New York: Grove, 2008).
27 See, for example, Daniel Francis, *The Imaginary Indian: The Image of the Indian in Canadian Culture* (Vancouver: Arsenal Pulp, 1992).
28 For an analysis and critique of this issue, see Monika Kin Gagnon and Yasmin Jiwani, "Amplifying Threat: Reasonable Accommodations and Quebec's Bouchard–Taylor Commission Hearings (2007)," in *Shifting the Ground* (129–49).

29 Beyond anticipating Daniel Coleman's study *White Civility: The Literary Project of English Canada* (Toronto: University of Toronto Press, 2006), the implications of Kertzer's civil project are also evident in his calling minoritized groups and their literatures "disaffected subcultures within well-established nations" (173), a formulation that leaves undisturbed the very system that produces their minoritized conditions.

30 As Deleuze and Guattari write, "the colonized resists oedipalization, and oedipalization tends to close around him" (169).

31 As Findlay goes on to say, cultural portage is an "activity with an important history which no one today can monopolize." Moreover, as "a term strongly associated with the innumerable waterways of the northern plains," we can see it "as a distinctive, locally inflected version of the notion of movement intrinsic to creativity itself" (24). Equally important about the relevance of this critical trope is its direct association with natural habitats, the fact that it is generated by and is responsive to them.

32 I quote here Spivak's translation of these lines as it appears in her essay "Responsibility" (20). The original translation, "to let ourselves be approached by the resistance which 'once' may offer thought," does not make full sense without the rest of the paragraph, where Derrida proceeds to meditate on "once."

33 See David M. Schneider, *American Kinship: A Cultural Account* (Chicago: U of Chicago P, 1980); Thomas R. Trautmann, *Lewis Henry Morgan and the Invention of Kinship* (Berkeley: U of California P, 1987); Kath Weston, *Families We Choose: Lesbians, Gays, Kinship* (New York: Columbia UP, 1991); and Judith Bulter, *Antigone's Claim: Kinship between Life and Death* (New York: Columbia UP, 2000).

34 In keeping with employing typography as a semantic and political tool in his other works, here, too, Kiyooka capitalizes a large number of nouns.

35 For details about Kiyooka's experience, see the other posthumous publications by him: *Mothertalk: Life Stories of Mary Kiyoshi Kiyooka*, edited by Daphne Marlatt (Edmonton: NeWest, 1997); Roy Miki's Afterword to *Pacific Windows: Collected Poems of Roy K. Kiyooka*, which he edited (Vancouver: Talonbooks, 1997); and my own Afterword to *Pacific Rim Letters*.

36 See, for example, William Little, *The Tom Thomson Mystery* (Toronto: McGraw-Hill, 1970); Joan Murray, *Tom Thomson: The Last Spring* (Toronto: Dundurn, 1994); Sherrill Grace, *Inventing Tom Thomson: From Biographical Fictions to Fictional Autobiographies and Reproductions* (Montreal and Kingston: McGill–Queen's UP, 2004); and Roy MacGregor, *Northern Light: The Enduring Mystery of Tom Thomson and the Woman Who Loved Him* (Toronto: Random House, 2010).

37 Kiyooka refers to many of these sources, albeit in ways that are both faithful to the originals and playful. And as is typical in this text, he also plays with the names of historical figures so that, for example, Judge Little who wrote one such book is referred to as Judge Small. See Miki's Afterword for a detailed treatment of this aspect of the text.

Belief as/in Methodology as/in Form: Doing Justice to CanLit Studies

1 See, for instance, Robert Lecker's "'A Quest for the Peaceable Kingdom': The Narrative in Northrop Frye's Conclusion to the *Literary History of Canada*," and the essays collected in *Where Is Here Now?* (ed. Lecker and Flynn), a special millennium issue of *Essays on Canadian Writing*.

2 It is difficult not to wonder whether Szeman would have reached the same conclusion had he chosen to focus on poetry, and especially the Canadian long poem, where questions of place, localism, regionalism, and centralism have been heavily debated in what can be read as nation-bounded frameworks. I am thinking of the long-poem poets such as Margaret Atwood, Dennis Lee, Eli Mandel, Robert Kroetsch, bpNichol, George Bowering, Daphne Marlatt, and Fred Wah (and there are others).

The Accidental Witness: Indigenous Epistemologies and Spirituality as Resistance in Eden Robinson's *Monkey Beach*

1   Further to the use of pronouns in the middle voice, Barthes argues that the pronoun, for example, "which is without doubt the most staggering of the 'shifters,' belongs structurally to speech (*parole*). That is its scandal, if you like, and it is on this scandal that we must work today, in linguistics and in literature. We are all trying, with different methods, styles, perhaps even prejudices, to get to the core of this linguistic pact (*pacte de parole*), which unites the writer and the other, so that—and this is a contradiction which will never be sufficiently pondered—each moment of discourse is both absolutely new and absolutely understood" (144).

It is the incomprehensibility of residential school abuse and the incomprehensibility of an Indigenous genocide in Canada that shifts this "linguistic pact" between "the writer and the other" to a textual kinship between writer and reader, a shape shifting that is necessary and essential to the reconciliation process. But this mode of reconciliation is about the importance of writing and culture to democracy and the need for real democratic change in which difference and alterity are embraced rather than crushed. This might also mean that the way the stories or testimonies of the Indian Residential Schools are told will also be different, with a new set of kinship affiliations, obligations, and responsibilities emerging on the horizon.

2   The rhetoric of healing must also be situated in an Indigenous epistemic framework. Jo-Ann Episkenew writes that an Indigenous approach to healing

> does not imply that Indigenous people are sick, however.... Colonial is sick; under its auspices and supported by its mythology, the colonizers have inflicted heinous *wounds* on the Indigenous population that they set out to civilize. Although Indigenous people understand their need to heal from colonial trauma, most settlers deny that their society is built on a sick foundation and, therefore, deny that it requires a cure. (11)

Marlene Brant Castellano conceptualizes the approach to healing taken by the Aboriginal Health Foundation (AHF) in its publication *From Truth to Reconciliation: Transforming the Legacy of Residential Schools* in the following terms: "the AHF framed the components of residential school resolution in the quartered circle of a medicine wheel, a figure widely used in First Nations teaching circles" (385). Those four components consist of acknowledgment, redress, healing, and reconciliation, where "healing restore[s] physical, mental, emotional, and spiritual balance in individuals, families, communities, and nations" (385).

Ambidextrous Epistemologies: Indigenous Knowledge within the Indigenous Renaissance

1   Centralization is explained fully in Daniel Paul's book *We Were Not the Savages: Collision of European and Native American civilizations*, 3rd ed. (Nimbus, 1993; Fernwood, 2000, 2006) and on his website http://www.danielpaul.com/CentralizationAbandoned-1950.html.

Epistemologies of Respect: A Poetics of Asian/Indigenous Relation

I would like to acknowledge Larry Grant, Rita Wong, Lorraine Weir, David Khang, and Richard Cavell for their generous feedback on this essay. Thanks also to SSHRC for its generous financial support.

1   Sid Chow Tan, president of the Head Tax Families Society of Canada and a tireless activist on the Head Tax issue, argues that the Harper government offered redress as cheaply as it could for the sake of optics, by offering a settlement only to living Head Tax payers, whose numbers at this late date are very small, and their living spouses, but not to Head Tax payers' now adult children, who also have directly suffered the consequences of that wrong. In so doing, Tan argues, the Harper government has cheated many Head Tax families of real justice. In a speech to the Head Tax Families Society of Canada at their First Annual General Meeting in December 2007, Tan described the political wiliness of the Harper government

as follows: "The Stephen Harper government has shown itself to be shrewd. They have taken a two step agreement, which was an inclusive agreement. They did the first step. They took the photo ops, they pandered for votes, and then they shut the door on those affected sons and daughters of elderly head tax payers" (Tan n.p.). The Residential School apology has been criticized as insufficiently broad to recognize the full extent of ongoing genocidal policies and practices against Indigenous peoples. James Sa'ke'j Henderson, for instance, calls for a reconciling of Canadian law with the Aboriginal and treaty rights entrenched within it (115). Paulette Reagan argues that the testimonies given by Residential School survivors as part of the Truth and Reconciliation process are a gift to settlers and that settlers have an obligation to respond in a meaningful way (18). The apology is not a gift but only the start of a conversation.

2 I take Nancy up here with the awareness that his concept of the "singular plural" is arrived at by carefully thinking through the problem of the individual and the collective as they have been conceived in the European philosophical tradition. I have a strong sense that there are other cultural ways of perceiving and articulating such a concept. This is certainly something I intend to research.

3 In this regard, in their essay "Behind Enemy Lines: Toxic Titties Infiltrate Vanessa Beecroft," Julia Steinmetz, Heather Cassils, and Clover Leary offer a scathing critique of the work of the American artist Vanessa Beecroft.

4 Khang's collaboration with Hopkins at the diegetic and extra-diegetic levels extends the boundaries of the performance even further, so that it exceeds both the temporal specificity of the performances and the doors of Centre A. Thus, it becomes yet another gesture of becoming, one that now includes us, as writer and as readers, in the singular plural engaged and produced by *How to Feed a Piano*.

5 Given that the cherry was used as a symbol of Japanese military nationalism during the Second World War—in particular, as a symbol of beautiful dying youth meant to encourage young Japanese men to become kamikaze pilots—Clements's use of the cherry tree here is somewhat troubling, although I don't think she intends to use it in a military/nationalist sense. Certainly, though, its association with tragic youthful beauty continues to work in relation to this character.

6 There is arguably a logical flaw in the play here, in the sense that Fat Man's hi-fi set is figured as a technology that propagandizes, that cannot offer any deep or ethical truth. Clements's "active radio," by contrast, although it cannot exist without a conception of technology, is figured as an instrument of genuine insight. I reconcile these two conceptions of technology by thinking of Clements's active radio in Donna Haraway's sense, as a sort of cyborg radio. But it seems to me that further thinking is required in this regard.

7 The play also offers an excellent critique of the politics of apology, but I do not have the space to address it here.

Acts of Nature: Literature, Excess, and Enviromental Politics

My thanks to Smaro Kamboureli and Christl Verduyn for inviting me to be part of this conversation about literature, institutions, and citizenship. Earlier versions of this essay were presented at Queen's University and Trent University in the winter of 2009; thanks to Molly Wallace and Douglas Torgerson for their invitations to conversation as well. A small portion of the final section was included in "'I Still Need the Revolution': Cultivating Ecofeminist Readers," in Laird Christensen, Mark C. Long, and Fred Waage, eds., *Teaching North American Environmental Literature* (New York: Modern Languages Association of America, 2008), 58–71.

1 While many scholars have pronounced preferences for different terms—environmental criticism, environmental literary criticism, ecocriticism—I am interested in their common political orientation and so use the terms interchangeably in this essay.

2 Thoreau is often considered a seminal figure in nature writing in the United States; in particular, some ecocritics read his later work, with its emphasis on describing "the solid earth! the actual world! the common sense! Contact! Contact!" (*The Maine Woods* 79),

as a defence of the sensuous, natural present against the onslaughts of obfuscating and alienating social relations (and, by extension, social theory). By contrast, many advocates of a more environmental-justice-oriented ecocriticism view Carson's *Silent Spring* as the originary text of a more politicized view of nature, one in which conditions of toxicity and environmental degradation generate a "nature writing" that foregrounds the destructive social and economic relations in which experiences of nature cannot help but take place, thus giving rise to advocacy rather than appreciation.

3   For Arendt, that common world is as much under threat as the biosphere. In a society fixated on the pursuit and ingestion of increasingly ephemeral consumer goods oriented to the satisfaction of individual desires, there is a diminishment of the world in the sense of a realm of permanent creations upon which to reflect and from which to derive the "acceptance of what is" that is the enduring story undergirding the possibility of the common world. It is not so much that there is no "real" literature any more to do that work; it is that we treat works of art as mere objects to consume in the space "which is ... left over after labor and sleep have received their due" (*Between Past and Future* 205). Kerry Whiteside has rightly pointed to the relationship between this loss of a common world and the devastation of the biosphere.

4   Whiteside also makes the important argument that the "cultivation" of nature—its worldly reconstitution as culture—removes it from the mode of utility. Judgment of the worldly object (the object having been created in the mode of utility) occurs after the object has already been created. Thus, "culture becomes a matter of nurturing things because one sees intriguing, non-instrumental qualities in them" (34).

5   Felman is relating Derrida's critique, in *Writing and Difference*, of Foucault's *Madness and Civilization*. Derrida's argument is that the "normality" of the sentence precludes the emergence of madness into *any* speech: "Any philosopher ... who is trying to evoke madness *inside* of thought ... can only do so in the dimension of *possibility* and in the language of fiction or the fiction of language" (Derrida qtd. in Felman, *Writing and Madness* 47). If madness is silence, then it cannot be said.

6   McKay, one of Canada's best-known contemporary "nature poets" (I don't think he would object to that description), makes a strong case in *Vis à Vis* for an ecopoetic practice that builds into the nature poem the failure of language to represent the natural world, but also the responsibility of the poet to attempt to do so despite and in the midst of that failure, thus including in the poetic form the ethical/experiential recognition of the linguistic failure of all poetry to make the world knowable in writing.

7   Conrad's *Heart of Darkness* (1902) explores the ways in which the tropical "wilderness" of the Congo invokes and creates an experience of utter environmental and social strangeness for the novel's protagonist; in so doing, he highlights the negative effects of colonialism.

Ecocriticism in the Unregulated Zone

I would like to thank Cate Sandilands for her incisive comments following the first presentation of this paper at the TransCanada Three conference. Our discussion provided the groundwork for the further development and clarification of my ideas.

1   See, for example, Susan Griffin, Carolyn Merchant, Val Plumwood, and Joni Seager.

2   "Network" is a concept Latour develops in *Science in Action* and *We Have Never Been Modern;* "detour" appears in his essay "Morality and Technology." "Tropes" is Haraway's term (*Modest_Witness* 135).

3   Carson uses the analogy of nuclear radiation extensively in *Silent Spring* to introduce the new set of risks, as did other environmental writers and thinkers of the time.

Disturbance-Loving Species: Habitat Studies, Ecocritical Pedagogy, and Canadian Literature

1   Northrop Frye's resonant question is playfully unpacked in Roy Miki's essay in this collection.

2   Land and its analogues have been an obsession in Canadian letters, from Francis Brooke's *The History of Emily Montague* to Timothy Taylor's *Stanley Park*, from the *roman du terroir* to *le pays d'en haut*. Critics of Canadian Literature have been roughing it in the bush from E.K. Brown through Northrop Frye and Margaret Atwood to Alison Calder. As Calder's name reminds us, much recent study has sought to rewrite mythologies of place and region to recognize cultural, gendered, and racial dimensions within and beyond them. Yet somewhat surprisingly, Canadian literary scholarship has been slow to embrace ecocriticism. (One anecdote has it that at the TransCanada project's first conference, an intervenor in one discussion provoked approving laughter by dismissing the emerging subfield with the epithet "earth critters.") From another angle, we might say (consider the convention that the animal story is a "Canadian" genre) that Canadian literary criticism is always already ecocritical. A useful, compact introduction to the range of approaches in the field of environmental criticism may be found in Sabine Wilke's "'The Sound of a Robin after a Rain Shower': The Role of Aesthetic Experience in Dialectical Conceptions of Nature."

3   See http://www.english.ubc.ca, "English Courses Offered: Archive." For a more detailed description of the pedagogy of Habitat Studies, see my article "Out of the Field Guide: Teaching Habitat Studies" in *The Bioregional Imagination: Literature, Ecology, and Place*, ed. Tom Lynch, Cheryll Glotfelty, and Karla Armbruster (Athens: U Georgia P, 2012), 347–64.

4   I also chose the poem as homage to and reading of the Sackville Waterfowl Park—once saltwater marsh, now freshwater refuge—which sits so compellingly on the edge of the Mount Allison University campus, where TransCanada Three took place. My memory of the Waterfowl Park shaped my early conception of this essay. I had not remembered—and was delighted to rediscover during the TransCanada conference at Mount Allison—that the campus geography centres on a pond, known as the Swan Pond. The campus buildings form rippling semicircles around the pond, overlooking it and its modest fountain. At the "Speak to the Wild Conference," September 2013, Trevor Goward told us the poem was inspired by the pond—and the several teaching sites surrounding it—that is a central feature of his home, Edgewater Blue, in Wells Gray Provincial Park.

5   "For any who may require in their transcribing a symbol for the unrounded vowel that occurs in *cot* and a symbol for the rounded vowel that occurs in the same word and is distinct from the vowel of *caught* (kȯt), we suggest \0\ for the rounded" (36a). *Webster's Third New International Dictionary* (Springfield: Merriam-Webster, 1993).

Translocal Representation: Chief Buffalo Child Long Lance, Nello "Tex" Vernon-Wood, and CanLit

I would particularly like to thank Danielle Fuller for her work in revising the received interpretation of who Nello Vernon-Wood was. Thanks to Andrew Gow. Thanks to the participants and audience at my plenary panel in TransCanada 3 who helped me think about what the translocal could signify.

1   The text and image of the advertisement for the Chief Long Lance shoe appear in Donald Smith, *Chief Buffalo Child Long Lance: The Glorious Imposter* (253–54).

2   Like Long Lance, Archie Belaney learned about the traditional ways of a First Nations group in Canada. Eventually he assumed the identity of Grey Owl, a half Apache, half Scottish man, initially as an attempt to escape his origins (D. Smith, *From the Land of the Shadows* 35–46; Chapin, "Gender and Indian Masquerade in the Life of Grey Owl" 91–110) and then as a way to publicize his writing about ecological issues. Like Wood, Grey Owl was actually a working-class Englishman from an impoverished family who had lost at least one parent and come to Canada to make a new life. His writing career almost exactly paralleled Wood's own. But unlike either Wood or Long Lance, Belaney wrote about and publicized his identity at first, and primarily, for the Canadian and then the British public. In this sense, Grey Owl can be claimed more easily as a Canadian writer (and film star for the National Film Board), and then as a Commonwealth writer of non-fictional books. This could be why he has been written about extensively. Also unlike Wood and Long Lance, Belaney was

a cultural and racial imposter who could move from one place and identity to another in a specifically British context. Although Wood moved in this way, he did not assume another racial and cultural identity, and he did not write for a Canadian market. Long Lance's own performance, as we shall see, was more complex than Belaney's because he actually was a person of Native heritage forced to perform as a "coloured" man.

3   It was not always the case. The art of the Group of Seven and Emily Carr, for example, also performs this nationalist function in the public sphere, albeit as a sign of Canada's artistic *past*, not its present.

4   This is particularly true in the case of European visual art networks. See the website trans-local.org for an example of this approach: http://www.translocal.org. The site http://www .translocal-practices.net is also attempting to make critical use of "translocal" to describe networking in art production.

5   All quotations are from the Corgi Books edition of *Long Lance*, published in 1956 in the United Kingdom. Interestingly, the cover of this book says it is "an authentic story of tribal life and rites by a chieftain of the northern Blackfeet," and the other paratextual elements present it as a memoir even at this late date. Corgi Books was an imprint of Faber and Faber, which originally published *Long Lance* in Britain. It published "Wild West" stories for boys.

Jazz, Diaspora, and the History and Writing of Black Anglophone Montreal

1   I would like to acknowledge support in the preparation of this article from a Standard Research Grant of the Social Sciences and Humanities Research Council of Canada. I would also like to thank my research assistant Jay Rawding for editorial assistance.

2   As Marcel Trudel's *Deux siècles d'esclavage au Canada* and other sources on the subject make clear, only about one third of the slaves in New France were black; the majority were Natives or *panis*.

3   Volume IV of the Commission on Bilingualism and Biculturalism's *Final Report* reiterates its mandate to "recommend what steps should be taken to develop the Canadian confederation on the basis of an equal partnership between the two founding races, taking into account the contribution made by the other ethnic groups" (3). But it also states: "We repeat that we accept the words 'race' and 'people' only in their traditional sense—meaning a national group, with no biological significance—and we prefer to emphasize the facts of language and culture rather than the concepts of 'race,' 'people,' or even 'ethnic group'" (7).

4   See especially "Tout Montréal 1: Les deux Saint-Laurent." Mary Jean Green observes: "In *Bonheur d'occasion* … the multiethnic city she described in 1941 has disappeared, replaced by a bipolar city divided between rich and poor anglophone and francophone, where the only 'immigrants' are Roy's impoverished French-Canadian characters, who have migrated into the city from nearby farms.… Although *Bonheur d'occasion* broke new literary ground by placing its French-Canadian characters in an urban setting, it did not go so far as to integrate Roy's early vision of the city as a place of hybridity" (Green 13).

5   Like all further translations from *Bonheur d'occasion*, this is taken from Hannah Josephson's translation of the novel, *The Tin Flute*.

6   Sherry Simon points out that *The Loved and the Lost* and Roy's *Bonheur d'Occasion* are among the few novels that "have used the vertical drop between mountain and river as dramatic material to be exploited"; many other works have concentrated instead on the east–west linguistic split (Simon, "The Post-Industrial South-West" 4).

7   David Leahy has argued that, "given the semiotic field of blacks in the novel it is difficult to imagine that predominantly white readerships in the early 1950s would not have presumed Peggy's murderer was black" (37).

8   Negro slavery in New France was authorized by Louis XIV in 1689—four years after the *Code Noir* regulated slavery in the West Indies—but the decision had no direct impact because of intervening wars and perhaps for reasons of insufficient capital (Trudel 34–48; Winks 5–23).

9   George Elliott Clarke has suggested that such transmissions should also be read as slave narratives ("This Is No Hearsay" 17–18).

10 Blacks had standing in courts, which often ruled in their favour (Winks 11) and this ren-dered slavery impracticable; see the chapter "Charlotte, She Got the Ball Rolling" in Mackey (25–32).

11 In 1799 and again in 1800, slaveowners petitioned for legislative support to quell the increas-ing numbers of absconding slaves, after several of them secured their freedom through the courts (Mackey 4; Trudel 304–12).

12 The account appeared in the *Gazette* (Montreal) on 31 January 1861; it is reprinted in Mackey (162–66).

13 As Collison remarks: "By moving to Mountain Street Shadrach Minkins put himself in the center of the most dynamic area of the city" (204). Tulchinsky and Day both illustrate this claim. For a history of Saint-Henri, see Société Historique de Saint-Henri.

14 Hence the name of the Lachine Canal: "Upon arriving in New France, Cavalier de La Salle ... dreamed of discovering this very route [to China]. Later, his seigneury [*sic*] located near the rapids was mockingly dubbed La Chine—the name in French for China" (Desloges and Gelly 9).

15 Sealy won a Juno award in 2000 for *Africville Suite*, partially inspired by his Africville-born father. Sealy still performs actively and is a co-owner of the jazz record label Triplet Records, established in 1989.

16 Mark Miller notes: "His only recorded solo of any consequence, an 84-bar improvisation on *Now's The Time*, was made at Parker's side and issued 40 years later on the CD *Charlie Parker, Montreal, 1953* (Uptown)" (*The Miller Companion* 207).

17 Marrelli points out that "'The Corner' was "close to where the black community lived, and to the trains where many blacks worked as porters. At 'The Corner' black entertainment was the drawing card, but both black and white audiences were welcome" (100).

18 Sarsfield's text was a finalist in the 2005 edition of "Canada Reads."

19 The novel brings up, for instance, the predicaments of French Canadian women during that period, and features characters from Italian, Russian, and other backgrounds, as well as a fully multicultural wedding that combines a Russian Orthodox ceremony with the temptations of Creole cooking.

20 On the UNIA in Montreal and in Canada, see Bertley and Marano.

21 "The Coloured Ladies Club" (5) in the novel corresponds to the Coloured Women's Club of Montreal, which was founded in 1902. Initially, it was "an exclusive club of only fifteen women—all wives of American porters," that assisted the black community and its newly arrived immigrants (D. Williams 50–51); on the important role of women in the UNIA, see D. Williams (60–61).

22 Randolph "advocated a grand alliance between blacks and the trade union movement.... Many blacks regarded organized labor as an enemy of racial integration, because blacks were barred from most of labor's craft unions. Randolph relentlessly attacked unions that excluded black workers" (George Meany Memorial Archives).

23 For Canada, see Calliste, "Sleeping Car Porters in Canada" and "Blacks on Canadian Railways."

24 On at least one known occasion, Holmes had to fend off racist exclusionary tactics by a ballroom when Peterson became one of the first black musicians to play with the Holmes Orchestra at the Montreal Ritz-Carlton (see Marrelli 86; Gilmore 103–5; Lees 51–52, 59).

25 As a child, Peterson was expected to perform on the piano during Marcus Garvey's visit to Montreal; he describes his impressions of Garvey and the UNIA:

> He drove home that it would only be with the courage and determination to create and sustain our very own black industries, grocery stores, taxis, airlines, and even shipping lines that we would at last be truly free from the economic bondage that we endured. Intriguingly, if we thrust that form of thinking forward to today's world, Marcus Garvey was dead on the mark.... When I think back to those countless Sunday afternoons, I realize that I got more from those [UNIA] meetings than I was aware of at the time. Not only did the repeated public performances in the hall increase my musical confi-dence, but—more importantly—I learned from Marcus Garvey and others the need for

dedication and devotion to any cause that one sincerely believes in. Many of the young Montreal blacks of today may not even have heard of the UNIA; nevertheless, it served their forebears as a place of spiritual sustenance and personal reconstruction. (Peterson 28–29)

26   I have used the notational form of "re/cognition" elsewhere to emphasize the ambivalent and often contradictory duality by which cognitive change ("re-cognition") draws on available categories in a process of pattern matching ("recognition") that often produces identification as acceptance under dominant standards. In this sense, "recognition" limits "re-cognition" because the former assimilates potential difference to what is already known or accepted. I have developed this problem of re/cognition in the context of "New" World paradigms and of W.E.B. Du Bois's elaboration of "double consciousness," as a framework to study North American cultures comparatively and as the ongoing results of conflicted complex processes and articulations of cultural emergence (see Siemerling, *The New North American Studies*).

27   For Fiske, whiteness exercises power through "exnomination" as "the means by which white-ness avoids being named and thus keeps itself out of the field of interrogation and therefore off the agenda for change" (42 qtd. in G. Lewis 140).

28   In an influential discussion of "Afrological" and "Eurological" perspectives, the trombonist and music scholar George Lewis draws on Fiske and other commentators on whiteness to highlight, for example, the paradoxical status of boundaries in John Cage's statements about experimental music, which turn on notions of "indeterminacy" and "chance operations" (136–37) but entirely dismiss jazz (138). This is all the more surprising given the influence of bebop on the New York school of which Cage was a member (139). With respect to Cage's elision of black traditions, Lewis writes that "despite such declarations as 'the world is one world now' … it is clear that Cage has drawn very specific boundaries, not only as to which musics are relevant to his own musicality but as to which musics suit his own taste" (138).

29   Personal communication, 30 January 2010.

Critical Allegiances

1   This essay appears in *Shifting the Ground of Canadian Literary Studies* (2012), the volume resulting from the second TransCanada conference.

2   Kamboureli, quoting Donald E. Pease's introduction to his guest-edited special issue of *boundary 2*: "New Americanists: Revisionist Interventions into the Canon" (11). She notes that this introduction appears as the opening chapter to his 1994 book *Revisionary Interventions into the Americanist Canon* (Durham: Duke UP, 1994), as well.

3   Kamboureli cites works by these Aboriginal writers: Lee Maracle—*Bobby Lee: Indian Rebel* (1975; rev. 1990), *I Am Woman* (1988), and the earlier-mentioned *Oratory: Coming to Theory* (1990); Beatrice Culleton—*In Search of April Raintree* (1983); Jeannette Armstrong—*Slash* (1985); her own co-edited (with Shirley Neman) collection of feminist criticism—*A Mazing Space: Writing Canadian Women Writing* (1986); and Barbara Godard—*Gynocritics/ Gynocritiques: Feminist Approaches to Canadian and Quebec Women Writers* (1987).

4   Here, Kamboureli recalls Foucault's critique of disciplinary discourse, "The Order of Discourse," trans. Ian McLeod, in *Untying the Text: A Post-Structuralist Reader*, ed. Robert Young (Boston and London: Routledge and Kegan Paul, 1981), 15.

5   More recently, in 2008, the idea of epistemological humility remained relevant in an invited paper, titled "What Means? Interdisciplinarity in 2008," that I presented to the "Breaking Boundaries, Forging Connections: Feminist Interdisciplinary Theory and Practice" conference at Mount Saint Vincent University (13 April 2008).

6   Vickers explains Kelley's "narrow" interdisciplinarity as "involving efforts to resolve problems 'so that we may gain manipulatory control over our environment and the material conditions of our existence' (Kelley 6)" and "wide" interdisciplinarity as that which "draws together 'input from disciplines that share different epistemological positions' (Kelley 6)" (Vickers 29).

7   Thus, for example, the special issue of *Arachne* discussed below was the publication outcome
     of a conference on the topic of interdisciplinarity and Canadian Studies at Laurentian Uni-
     versity, Sudbury, Ontario, 13–15 October 1995. This conference was itself a continuation of
     discussions about interdisciplinarity and Canadian Studies at the earlier Canadian Studies
     conference "Theoretical Discourse in the Canadian Intellectual Community," St-Jovite,
     Quebec, 23–27 September 1992. It resulted in the publication *Canada: Theoretical Discourse/*
     Discours théoriques, ed. Terry Goldie, Carmen Lambert, and Rowland Lorimer (Montreal:
     Association for Canadian Studies, 1994). The Association for Canadian Studies' newsletter
     (*ACS Newsletter/Bulletin*) was the venue for regular reflections on interdisciplinarity during
     the 1990s. See, for example, the Spring 1994 issue (16.1): *Another Look at Interdisciplinarity /*
     Réflexions sur l'interdisciplinarité.
8   See Kathleen M. Ashley, ed., *Victor Turner and the Construction of Cultural Criticism:*
     Between Literature and Anthropology (Bloomington: Indiana UP, 1990).
9   In "Interdisciplinarity and Canadian Literature," I distinguish interdisciplinary literary
     analysis from "such sociological or historical approaches to literature as may have been
     practised earlier in this century. These might be said to illustrate multidisciplinary analysis
     more than interdisciplinarity. They operated under different questions—what, instead of
     how or why. One body of knowledge ('what' was known by, say, sociology) was set up
     against a given literary corpus (another 'what'), with insights into the latter deriving from
     perspectives provided by the former. This juxtaposition of two 'whats,' productive as it may
     be, is a different undertaking from that which sets out to identify or articulate why or how"
     (Verduyn 81–82).
10   Indeed, Canadian Studies' commitment to interdisciplinarity greatly facilitated the inte-
     gration into academia of such other fields as Women's Studies, Indigenous Studies, Envi-
     ronmental Studies, and Global Studies. Thus, for example, in the mid-1980s, Canadian
     Studies at Trent University fostered the initiative to create a Women's Studies program at
     the university.

WORKS CITED

Agamben, Giorgio. *Remnants of Auschwitz: The Witness and the Archive.* New York: Zone, 1999.

Allain, Greg, and Isabelle McKee-Allain. "La Société Acadienne en l'An 2000: Identité, Pluralité et Réseaux." Ed. André Magord. *L'Acadie plurielle: Dynamiques Identitaires Collectives et Développement au Sein des Réalités Acadiennes.* Moncton: Centre d'Études Acadiennes, 2003. 535–65.

Alonso, Ana Maria. *Thread of Blood: Colonialism, Revolution, and Gender on Mexico's Northern Frontier.* Tucson: U of Arizona P, 1995.

Anderson, Benedict. *Imagined Communities: Reflections on the Origin and Spread of Nationalism.* Rev. ed. London: Verso, 2006.

"A. Philip Randolph, 1889–1979, Trade Union Leader." *National Labour College.* 9 Mar. 2001. Web. 25 Oct. 2007.

Appadurai, Arjun. *Modernity at Large.* Minneapolis: U of Minnesota P, 1996.

Appiah, Kwame Anthony. *The Ethics of Identity.* Princeton: Princeton UP, 2005.

Arnold, Richard. "A Wolf in the Choir." *Trumpeter* 18.1 (2002): n.p. Web. 16 June 2012.

Arendt, Hannah. *Between Past and Future.* New York: Penguin, 1954.

———. *The Human Condition.* Chicago: U of Chicago P, 1958.

——— . "Philosophy and Politics." *Social Research* 57.1 (1990): 73–103.

Aschcroft, Bill, Gareth Griffiths, and Helen Tiffin. *The Empire Writes Back: Theory and Practice in Post-Colonial Literatures.* London and New York: Routledge, 1989.

Attridge, Derek. "'This Strange Institution Called Literature: An Interview with Jacques Derrida." Trans. Joshua Wilner. *Acts of Literature: Jacques Derrida.* Ed. Derek Attridge. New York and London: Routledge, 1992. 33–75.

Audet, F.J. "William Brown (1737–1789), premier imprimeur, journaliste et libraire de Québec; sa vie et ses œuvres." RSC Trans., 3rd ser. 26 (1932): i.97–112.

Austin, John. *Lectures on Jurisprudence.* 3 vols. London: John Murray, 1861–63.

———. *The Province of Jurisprudence Determined.* 2nd ed. London: John Murray, 1861–63.

Barsh, Russel Lawrence, and James Youngblood Henderson. "Aboriginal Rights, Treaty Rights, and Human Rights: Indian Tribes and Constitutional Renewal." *Journal of Canadian Studies* 17.2 (1982): 55–81.

Barthes, Roland. "To Write: An Intransitive Verb? Discussion: Barthes—Todorov." *The Structuralist Controversy: The Languages of Criticism and the Sciences of Man.* Ed. Richard Macksey and Eugenio Donato. Baltimore: Johns Hopkins UP, 1970. 134–56.

Battiste, Marie. "Mi'kmaq Literacy and Cognitive Assimilation." *Indian Education in Canada: The Legacy.* Vol. 1. Ed. Jean Barman, Yvonne Hébert, and Don McCaskill. Vancouver: U of British Columbia P, 1986. 23–44.

———. "Nikanikinútmaqn." *The Mi'kmaw Concordat.* Black Point: Fernwood, 1997. 13–20.

———, ed. *Reclaiming Indigenous Voice and Vision.* Vancouver: U of British Columbia P, 2000.

———. "The Struggle and Renaissance of Indigenous Knowledge in Eurocentric Education." *Indigenous Knowledge and Education: Sites of Struggle, Strength, and Survivance.* Ed. Malia Villegas, Sabina Rak Neugebauer, and Kerry R. Venegas. Cambridge: Harvard Educational Review, 2008. 85–91.

———. *Decolonizing Education: Nourishing the Learning Spirit.* Saskatoon: Purich Press, 2013.

Battiste, M., L. Bell, I.M. Findlay, L. Findlay, and J.Y. Henderson. "Thinking Place: Animating the Indigenous Humanities in Education." *Thinking Place: Animating the Indigenous Humanities in Education.* Spec. issue of *Australian Journal of Indigenous Education* 34 (2005): 7–19.

Battiste, Marie, and James Youngblood Henderson. *Protecting Indigenous Knowledge and Heritage: A Global Challenge.* Saskatoon: Purich, 2000.

Beauchemin, Jacques, and Mathieu Bock-Côté. *La Cité Identitaire.* Montreal: Athéna, 2007.

Beck, Ulrich. *The Risk Society.* Trans. Mark Ritter. London: Sage, 1992.

Bell, Vikki. *Culture and Performance: The Challenge of Ethics, Politics, and Feminist Theory.* Oxford: Berg, 2007.

Berlant, Lauren Gail. *The Queen of America Goes to Washington: Essays on Sex and Citizenship.* Durham: Duke UP, 2002.

Bernard, Roger. *Le Canada Français: Entre Mythe et Utopie.* Ottawa: Le Nordir, 1998.

Bertley, L. *Montreal's Oldest Black Congregation: Union Church.* Pierrefonds: Bilongo, 1976.

———. "UNIA of Montreal, 1917–97." Diss., Concordia U, 1980.

Beverly, John. *Testimonio: On the Politics of Truth.* Minneapolis: U of Minnesota P, 2004.

Birney, Earle. "Can. Lit." *Canadian Literature in English: Texts and Contexts.* Vol. II. Ed. Laura Moss and Cynthia Sugars. Toronto: Pearson Longman, 2009. 117

Blaut, James M. *The Colonizer's Model of the World: Geographical Diffusionism and Eurocentric History.* New York: Guilford, 1993.

Blow, Peter, dir. *Village of Widows.* Lindum Films, 1999. Film.

Borrows, John. "Sovereignty's Alchemy: An Analysis of *Delgamuukw v. British Columbia.*" *Osgoode Hall Law Journal* 37.3 (1999): 537–96.

Brand, Dionne. *Land to Light On.* Toronto: McClelland and Stewart, 1997.

Braz, Albert. "The Modern Hiawatha: Grey Owl's Construction of His Aboriginal Self." *Auto/biography in Canada: Critical Directions.* Ed. Julie Rak. Waterloo: Wilfrid Laurier UP, 2005. 53–68.

Bringhurst, Robert. "Singing with the Frogs: The Theory and Practice of Literary Polyphony." *Everywhere Being Is Dancing: Twenty Pieces of Thinking.* Kentville: Gaspereau, 2007. 33–62.

Brönmark, Christer, and Lars-Anders Hansson. *The Biology of Lakes and Ponds.* Oxford: Oxford UP, 1998.

Brydon, Diana. "Metamorphoses of a Discipline: Rethinking Canadian Literature within Institutional Contexts." Kamboureli and Miki 1–16.

Brydon, Diana, and Marta Dvořák, eds. Introduction. *Crosstalk: Canadian and Global Imaginaries in Dialogue.* Waterloo: Wilfrid Laurier UP, 2012.

Buell, Lawrence. *The Future of Environmental Criticism.* Malden: Blackwell, 2005.

Burton, Robert. *Ponds: Their Wildlife and Upkeep.* Newton Abbot: David and Charles, 1977.

Butler, Judith. *Gender Trouble: Feminism and the Subversion of Identity.* London: Routledge, 1990.

———. *Excitable Speech: A Politics of the Performative.* New York and London: Routledge, 1997.

Calder, Alison. "Getting the Real Story: Implications of the Demand for Authenticity in Writings from the Canadian West." *True West: Authenticity and the American West.* Ed. William R. Handley and Nathaniel Lewis. Nebraska: U of Nebraska P, 2004. 56–71.

Callaghan, Morley. *The Loved and the Lost.* Toronto: Macmillan, 1983.

Calliste, Agnes. "Sleeping Car Porters in Canada: An Ethnically Submerged Labour Market." *Canadian Ethnic Studies* 19.1 (1987): 1–20.

———. "Blacks on Canadian Railways." *Canadian Ethnic Studies* 20.2 (1988): 36–52.

Canada. Constitution Act 1867 (U.K.), 30 & 31 Victoria, c. 3. 1867. Web. 18 Aug. 2011. http://laws.justice.gc.ca/eng/Const/page-1.html.

———. 1916 Census of Manitoba, Saskatchewan, and Alberta. Web. 9 May 2011. http://www.ancestry.ca.

———. Royal Commission on Bilingualism and Biculturalism. *Final Report.* Vol. IV. Ottawa: Queen's Printer, 1969.

———. The Canada Act 1982 (U.K.). 1982, c. 11.

———. Canadian Charter of Rights and Freedoms. 1982. Web. 18 Aug. 2011. http://laws .justice.gc.ca/eng/Charter/page-2.html#anchorbo-ga:l_I-gb:s_34.

———. Royal Commission on Aboriginal Peoples. *Report.* 5 vols. Ottawa: Minister of Supply and Services Canada, 1996.

———. Auditor General. *Chapter 4—Indian and Northern Affairs Canada. Elementary and Secondary Education.* Ottawa: 2004. Web. 6 May 2011. http://www.parl .gc.ca/HousePublications/Publication.aspx?DocId=1031727&Language=E&Mode =1&Parl=36&Ses=2.

Canadian Council on Learning. *Aboriginal Holistic Learning Models.* 2007. Web. 6 May 2011. www.ccl-cca.ca.

Cardinal, Harold. *The Unjust Society.* Edmonton: Hurtig, 1969.

———. *The Rebirth of Canada's Indians.* Edmonton: Hurtig, 1977.

Castellano, Marlene Brant. "A Holistic Approach to Reconciliation: Insights from Research of the Aboriginal Health Foundation." Castellano, Archibald, and DeGagné 385–400.

Castellano, Marlene Brant, Linda Archibald, and Mike DeGagné. *From Truth to Reconciliation: Transforming the Legacy of Residential Schools.* Aboriginal Healing Foundation. 2008. Web. 6 May 2011.

Castoriadis, Cornelius. *World in Fragments: Writings on Politics, Society, Psychoanalysis, and the Imagination.* Ed. and trans. David Ames Curtis. Stanford: Stanford UP, 1997.

CDS Indigenous Peoples' Caucus. "Dialogue Paper by Indigenous Peoples." *Indigenous Affairs* 4.1 (2001): 12–25.

"Centre A / about." *Centre A.* Vancouver International Centre for Contemporary Asian Art, n.d. Web. 14 June 2012.

Céréghino, R., J. Biggs, B. Oertli, and S. Declerck. "The Ecology of European Ponds: Defining the Characteristics of a Neglected Freshwater Habitat." *Hydrobiologia* 597 (2008): 1–6.

Chapin, David. "Gender and Indian Masquerade in the Life of Grey Owl." *American Indian Quarterly* 24.1 (Winter 2000): 91–110.

Chiasson, Herménégilde. *Mourir à Scoudouc.* Moncton: Éditions d'Acadie, 1974.

———."Les Lieux Nomads." Bureau des regroupements des artistes visuels de l'Ontario (BRAVO). *En marge.* Trois-Rivières: Éditions d'art Le Sabord, 1999.

Chilson, Peter. *Disturbance-Loving Species: A Novella and Stories.* Boston: Houghton Mifflin, 2007.

Chiu, Monica. *Filthy Fictions: Asian American Literature by Women.* Walnut Creek: AltaMira, 2004.

Cho, Lily. "Diasporic Citizenship: Contradictions and Possibilities for Canadian Literature." Kamboureli and Miki 93–110.

Chow, Rey. "Fateful Attachments: On Collecting, Fidelity, and Lao She." *Critical Inquiry* 28 (2001): 286–304.

Clarke, George Elliott. "Raising Raced and Erased Executions in African-Canadian Literature: Or, Unearthing Angélique." *Essays on Canadian Writing* 75 (2002): 30–61.

———. *Québécité: A Jazz Fantasia in Three Cantos.* Kentville: Gaspereau, 2003.

———. "'This Is No Hearsay': Reading the Canadian Slave Narrative." *Papers of the Bibliographical Society of Canada* 43.1 (2005): 7–32.

———. *Trudeau: Long March, Shining Path.* Kentville: Gaspereau, 2007.

Clements, Marie. *Burning Vision.* Vancouver: Talonbooks, 2003.

Clifford, James. *Routes: Travel and Translation in the Late Twentieth Century.* Cambridge: Harvard UP, 1997.

Code, Lorraine. *Ecological Thinking: The Politics of Epistemic Location.* Toronto: Oxford UP, 2006.

Coleman, Daniel. *In Bed with the Word: Reading, Spirituality, and Cultural Politics.* Edmonton: U of Alberta P, 2009.

Coleman, Daniel, and Smaro Kamboureli, eds. *Retooling the Humanities: The Culture of Research in Canadian Universities.* Edmonton: U of Alberta P, 2011.

———. "Canadian Research Capitalism: A Genealogy of Critical Moments." Introduction. Coleman and Kamboureli 1–39.

Collison, Gary. *Shadrach Minkins: From Fugitive Slave to Citizen.* Cambridge: Harvard UP, 1997.

Comeau, Frédric Gary. *Routes.* Trois-Rivières: Écrits des Forges, 1997.

———. *Naufrages.* Moncton: Éditions Perce-Neige, 2005.

Conaglen, Matthew D.J. "Judicial Supremacy: An Alternative Constitutional Theory." *Auckland University Law Review* 7 (1994): 665–90.

Cook, Nancy. "The Only Real Indians Are Western Ones: Authenticity, Regionalism, and Chief Buffalo Child Long Lance, or Sylvester Long." *True West: Authenticity and the American West.* Ed. William R. Handley and Nathaniel Lewis. Nebraska: U of Nebraska P, 2004. 140–54.

Cooper, Afua. *The Hanging of Angélique: The Untold Story of Canadian Slavery and the Burning of Old Montreal.* Toronto: Harper, 2006.

Cover, Robert M. "Foreword: *Nomos* and Narrative." *Harvard Law Review* 97.4 (1983): 4–68.

Critchley, Simon. *The Ethics of Deconstruction: Derrida and Levinas.* Oxford: Blackwell, 1992.

Cruikshank, E.A., ed. *The Correspondence of Lieutenant Governor John Graves Simcoe, with Allied Documents relating to his Administration of the Government of Upper Canada.* Vol. 3 Toronto: Ontario Historical Society, 1925.

Dargue, William. "Balsall Heath." *A History of Birmingham Places and Names: A to Y.* Web. June 2009. http://billdargue.jimdo.com/placenames-gazetteer-a-to-y/places-b/balsall-heath.

Davidson, Joyce, and Christine Milligan. "Editorial: Embodying Emotion Sensing Space: Introducing Emotional Geographies." *Social and Cultural Geography* 3.4 (2004): 523–32.

Dawson, Carrie. "Never Cry Fraud: Remembering Grey Owl, Rethinking Imposture." *Essays on Canadian Writing* 65 (Fall 1998): 120–40.

Day, Samuel Phillips. *English America, or, Pictures of Canadian Places and People.* London: T. Cauthley Newby, 1864.

de Certeau, Michel. "The Theatre of the *Quiproquo*: Alexandre Dumas." *Heterologies: Discourse on the Other.* Trans. Brian Massumi. Foreword by Wlad Godzich. Minneapolis: U of Minnesota P, 1986. 150–55.

Deleuze, Gilles, and Félix Guattari. *Anti-Oedipus: Capitalism and Schizophrenia.* Trans. Robert Hurley, Mark Seem, and Helen R. Lane. Preface by Michel Foucault. Minneapolis: U of Minnesota P, 1983.

d'Entremont, Paul, dir. *Seuls, ensemble.* National Film Board, 2000. Film.

Derrida, Jacques. "The Principle of Reason: The University in the Eyes of Its Pupils." *Diacritics* 13.3 (1983): 3–20.

———. "*From* Shibboleth: For Paul Celan." Trans. Joshua Wilner. *Acts of Literature. Jacques Derrida..* Ed. Derek Attridge. London and New York: Routledge, 1992. 370–413.

———. *Specters of Marx: The State of the Debt, the Work of Mourning, and the New International.* Trans. Peggy Kamuf. New York: Routledge, 1994.

———. *Psyché: Inventions de l'autre.* 1987. Paris: Galilée, 1998.

Desloges, Yves, and Alain Gelly. *The Lachine Canal: Riding the Waves of Industrial and Urban Development, 1860–1950.* Trans. Donald Kellough. Sillery: Septentrion, 2002.

Després, Rose. *La vie prodigieuse.* Moncton: Éditions Perce-Neige, 2000.

Dicey, Albert Venn. "Introduction: The True Nature of Constitutional Law." *Introduction to the Study of the Law of the Constitution.* 1885. 3rd ed. London: Macmillan, 1889. 1–34.

Douglas, Mary. *Purity and Danger: An Analysis of Concepts of Pollution and Taboo.* London: Routledge, 1970.

Dumbrill, Gary C., and Jacquie Green. "Indigenous Knowledge in the Social Work Academy." *Social Work Education* 27.5 (2008): 489–503.

Duran, Eduardo, and Bonnie Duran. *Native American Postcolonial Psychology.* Albany: SUNY P, 1995.

Edwards, Justin D. *Gothic Canada: Reading the Spectre of National Literature.* Edmonton: U of Alberta P, 2005.

Emberley, Julia. "Epistemic Encounters: Indigenous Cosmopolitan Hospitality, Marxist-Anthropology, Deconstruction, and Doris Pilkington's *Rabbit-Proof Fence*." *English Studies in Canada* 34.4 (2010): 147–70.

Episkenew, Jo-Ann. *Taking Back Our Spirits: Indigenous Literature, Public Policy, and Healing*. Winnipeg: U of Manitoba P, 2009.

Erasmus, George. Introduction. *Cultivating Canada: Reconciliation through the Lens of Cultural Diversity*. Ed. Ashok Mathur, Jonathan Dewar, and Mike DeGagné. Ottawa: Aboriginal Healing Foundation, 2011. vii–x.

Erikson, Kai. "Notes on Trauma and Community." *Trauma: Explorations in Memory*. Ed. Cathy Caruth. Baltimore: Johns Hopkins UP, 1995. 183–99.

Felman, Shoshana. *Writing and Madness (Literature/Philosophy/Psychoanalysis)*. Trans. Martha Noel Evans and the author, with the assistance of Brian Massumi. Ithaca: Cornell UP, 1985.

———. "Education and Crisis, or the Vicissitudes of Teaching." *Testimony: Crises of Witnessing in Literature, Psychoanalysis, and History*. Ed. Felman and Dori Laub. New York: Routledge, 1992. 1–56.

Findlay, Len. "TransCanada Collectives: Social Imagination, the Cunning of Production, and the Multilateral Sublime." Kamboureli and Miki 173–86.

———. "The Long March to 'Recognition': Sa'ke'j Henderson, First Nations Jurisprudence, and *Sui Generis* Solidarity." Kamboureli and Zacharias 235–47.

———. "Redress Rehearsals: Legal Warrior, COSMOSQUAW, and the National Aboriginal Achievement Awards." *Reconciling Canada: Critical Perspectives on the Culture of Redress*. Ed. Jennifer Henderson and Pauline Wakeham. Toronto: U of Toronto P, 2013. 217–35.

———. "Lori Blondeau: Cultural Portage and the (Re)Markable Body." *Lori Blondeau: Who Do You Think You Are?: Performance, Installation, Documentation, 1996–2007*. Ed. Dan Ring. Saskatoon: Mendel Art Gallery, 2009. 17–27.

Fishman, Joshua A., ed. *Can Threatened Languages Be Saved? Reversing Language Shift, Revisited: A 21st Century Perspective*. Clevedon: Multilingual Matters, 2001.

Fiske, John. *Media Matters: Everyday Culture and Political Change*. Minneapolis: U of Minnesota P, 1994.

Foucault, Michel. *The History of Sexuality*. Trans. Robert Hurley. Vol. 1. New York: Vintage, 1978.

———. *Ethics: Subjectivity and Truth*. Ed. Paul Rabinow. New York: New Press, 1994.

Fraser, Graham. "Cultural Diversity and Its Role in the Changing Canadian Identity." Caraquet Conference on Culture and Identity. Caraquet, New Brunswick. 27 Mar. 2009. Web. 6 May 2011. http://www.ocol-clo.gc.ca.

Freud, Sigmund. *Civilization and Its Discontents*. Ed. and trans. James Strachey. New York: W.W. Norton, 1961.

Frye, Northrop. "Conclusion to a *Literary History of Canada*." 1965. *Bush Garden: Essays on the Canadian Imagination*. Toronto: Anansi, 1971. 213–51.

Gandhi, Leela. *Postcolonial Theory: A Critical Introduction*. New York: Columbia UP, 1998.

Garneau, David. "Imaginary Spaces of Conciliation and Reconciliation." *Reconcile This!* Spec. issue of *West Coast Line* 74.46 (2012): 28–38.

Garrard, Greg. *Ecocriticism*. Oxford: Routledge, 2004.

Garroutte, Eva Marie. *Real Indians: Identity and the Survival of Native America*. Berkeley: U of California P, 2003.

Gates, Henry Louis, Jr. *The Signifying Monkey: A Theory of Afro-American Literary Criticism*. New York: Oxford UP, 1988.

Gay, Daniel. *Les Noirs du Québec, 1629–1900*. Sillery: Septentrion, 2004.

George Meany Memorial Archives. "A. Philip Randolph, 1889–1979, Trade Union Leader." *National Labour College*. 9 Mar. 2001. Web. 25 Oct. 2007.

Gilbert, Anne, and Marie Lefebvre. "Un Espace Francophone sous Tension." *Territoires francophones: Études Géographiques sur la Vitalité des Communautés Francophones au Canada*. Ed. Anne Gilbert. Québec: Septentrion, 2010. 339–82.

Gilmore, John. *Swinging in Paradise: The Story of Jazz in Montreal*. Montreal: Véhicule, 1988.

Glissant, Édouard. *Le discours antillais*. Paris: Gallimard, 1997.

———. *The Poetics of Relation*. Ann Arbor: U of Michigan P, 1997.

Glenn, H. Patrick. "Doin' the Transsystemic: Legal System and Legal Traditions." *McGill Law Journal* 50 (2005): 863–98.

Glotfelty, Cheryll. "Introduction: Literary Studies in an Age of Environmental Crisis." *The Ecocriticism Reader: Landmarks in Literary Ecology*. Ed. Glotfelty and Harold Fromm. Athens: U of Georgia P, 1996. xv–xxxvii.

Godard, Barbara. *Canadian Literature at the Crossroads of Language and Culture: Selected Essays by Barbara Godard, 1987–2005*. Ed. Smaro Kamboureli. Edmonton: NeWest Press, 2008.

Goldman, Marlene, and Joanne Saul. "Talking with Ghosts: Haunting in Canadian Cultural Production." *University of Toronto Quarterly* 75.2 (2006): 645–55.

Goldsworthy, J. *The Sovereignty of Parliament: History and Philosophy*. Oxford: Clarendon, 1999.

Gow, Andrew, and Julie Rak. Introduction. Vernon-Wood 9–35.

Gow, John R. "Tex Vernon-Wood: Recollections by His Grandson, John R. Gow." Vernon-Wood 215–20.

Green, Mary Jean. "Transcultural Identities: Many Ways of Being Québécois." *Textualizing the Immigrant Experience in Contemporary Quebec*. Ed. Susan Ireland and Patrice J. Proulx. Westport: Praeger, 2004. 11–22.

Griffin, Susan. *Woman and Nature: The Roaring Inside Her*. New York: Harper and Row, 1978.

Halliburton, David. "Hannah Arendt: Literary Criticism and the Political." *Extreme Beauty: Aesthetics, Politics, Death*. Ed. James E. Swearingen and Joanne Cutting-Gray. New York: Continuum, 2002. 110–23.

Haraway, Donna J. *Simians, Cyborgs, and Women: The Reinvention of Nature*. New York: Routledge, 1991.

———. *Modest_Witness@Second_Millennium.FemaleMan©_Meets_Oncomouse™: Feminism and Technoscience*. New York: Routledge, 1997.

Harjo, Joy. *How We Became Human: New and Selected Poems*. New York: W.W. Norton, 2002.

Hart, H.L.A. *The Concept of the Law*. Oxford: Clarendon, 1961.

Hautecoeur, Jean-Paul. *L'Acadie du discours: Pour une sociologie de la culture acadienne*. Québec: Presses de l'Université Laval, 1975.

Hawken, Paul. *Blessed Unrest: How the Largest Social Movement in History Is Restoring Grace, Justice, and Beauty to the World*. New York: Penguin, 2007.

Hayles, N. Katherine. *How We Became Posthuman: Virtual Bodies in Cybernetics, Literature, and Informatics*. Chicago: U of Chicago P, 1999.

Henderson, James [Sa'ke'j] Youngblood. *First Nations Jurisprudence and Aboriginal Rights: Defining the Just Society*. Saskatoon: Native Law Centre, 2006.
———. *Indigenous Diplomacy and the Rights of Peoples: Achieving UN Recognition*. Saskatoon: Purich, 2008.
———. "Incomprehensible Canada." *Reconciling Canada: Critical Perspectives on the Culture of Redress*. Ed. Jennifer Henderson and Pauline Wakeham. Toronto: U of Toronto P, 2013. 115–26.
Henderson, James [Sa'ke'j] Youngblood and Jaime Battiste. *Philosophy and Aboriginal Rights: Critical Dialogues*. "How Aboriginal Philosophy Informs Aboriginal Rights." Ed. Sandra Tomsons and Lorraine Mayer. Don Mills: Oxford UP, 2013. 66–101.
Hibbits, Bernard J. "Coming to Our Senses: Communication and Legal Expression in Performance Cultures." *Emory Law Journal* 41 (1992): 874–960.
Hill, D.L. "Holistic learning: A Model of Education Based on Aboriginal Cultural Philosophy." M.Ed., Saint Francis Xavier U, 1999.
Hogan, Linda. *Dwellings: A Spiritual History of the Living*. New York: W.W. Norton, 1995.
Hopkins, Candice. "On Gesture and Becoming Animal." *How to Feed a Piano: La Monte Young Projects 2003–2008*. Vancouver: Centre A, 2008. 65–72.
Hopper, Paul. *Understanding Cultural Globalization*. Cambridge: Polity, 2007.
Hostesses of Union United Church. *Memory Book: Union United Church, 75th Anniversary, 1907–1982*. Montreal: Hostesses of the United Church, 1982.
Huggan, Graham. *Australian Literature: Postcolonialism, Racism, Transnationalism*. Oxford: Oxford UP, 2007.
Hughes, Langston. "Mother to Son." *Selected Poems of Langston Hughes*. New York: Vintage, 1959. 187.
Immordino-Yang, Mary Helen, et al. "Neural Correlates of Admiration and Compassion." *Proceedings of the National Academy of Science* 106.19 (12 May 2009): 8021–26.
Inglis, Stephanie H. "Speaker's Experience: A Study of Mi'kmaq Modality." Diss., St. John's Memorial U of Newfoundland, 2002.
Jay, Martin. *Adorno*. Cambridge: Harvard UP, 1984.
———. *Force Fields: Between Intellectual History and Cultural Critique*. New York: Routledge, 1993.
Justice, Daniel Heath. "Go Away Water! Kinship Criticism and the Decolonization Imperative." *Reasoning Together: The Native Critics Collective*. Ed. Craig S. Womack et al. Oklahoma: U of Oklahoma P, 2008. 147–68.
Justinian Institutes. *L'Interprétation des Institutes de Justinian*. Ed. M. le duc Pasquier. Paris, 1847.
Kamboureli, Smaro. "The Culture of Celebrity and National Pedagogy." *Home-Work: Postcolonialism, Pedagogy, and Canadian Literature*. Ed. Cynthia Sugars. Ottawa: U of Ottawa P, 2004. 35–56.
———. "The Limits of the Ethical Turn: Troping Towards the Other, Yann Martel, and Self. *University of Toronto Quarterly* 76.3 (2007): 937–61.
———. Preface. Kamboureli and Miki vii–xv.
———. "Shifting the Ground of a Discipline: Emergence and Canadian Literary Studies in English." Kamboureli and Zacharias 1–45.
Kamboureli, Smaro, and Roy Miki, eds. *Trans.Can.Lit: Resituating the Study of Canadian Literature*. Waterloo: Wilfrid Laurier UP, 2007.
Kamboureli, Smaro, and Robert Zacharias, eds. *Shifting the Ground of Canadian Literary Studies*. Waterloo: Wilfrid Laurier UP, 2012.

Kastoryano, Riva. "Settlement, Transnational Communities, and Citizenship." *International Social Science Journal* 52.165 (2000): 307–12.

———. "The Reach of Transnationalism." Social Science and Humanities Research Council online papers on globalization. Web. June 2009. http://www.ssrc.org/sept11/essays/kastoryano.htm.

Kelsen, Hans. *The Pure Theory of Law*. 1934. Trans. M. Knight. Berkeley: U of California P, 1967.

Kertzer, Jonathan. *Worrying the Nation: Imagining a National Literature in English Canada*. Toronto: U of Toronto P, 1998.

Khang, David. *How to Feed a Piano: La Monte Young Projects 2003–2008*. Vancouver: Centre A, 2008.

Kirby, Michael D., "The Struggle for Simplicity: Lord Cooke and Fundamental Rights." *Commonwealth Law Bulletin* 24.1–2 (1998): 496–516.

Kiyooka, Roy K. *Pacific Rim Letters*. Ed. and afterword. Smaro Kamboureli. Edmonton: NeWest Press, 2005.

———. *Transcanada Letters*. 1975 Ed. Smaro Kamboureli. Edmonton: NeWest, 2005.

———. *The Artist and the Moose: A Fable of Forget*. Ed. Roy Miki. Vancouver: LineBooks, 2009.

Klein, Julie Thompson. *Interdisciplinarity: History, Theory, and Practice*. Detroit: Wayne State UP, 1990.

Klein, Yves. "The Chelsea Hotel Manifesto." *Long Live the Immaterial*. Ed. Yves Klein and Gilbert Perlein. New York: Delano Greenwood, 1961. 85–87.

———. "The Evolution of the Immaterial: Lecture at the Sorbonne, 3 June 1959." *Overcoming the Problematics of Art: The Writings of Yves Klein*. Trans. Klaus Ottoman. Putnam, Spring 2007. 71–98.

Kristeva, Julia. *Powers of Horror: An Essay on Abjection*. Trans. Leon S. Roudiez. New York: Columbia UP, 1982.

LaCapra, Dominick. *Writing History, Writing Trauma*. Baltimore: Johns Hopkins UP, 2001.

Laclau, Ernesto, and Chantal Mouffe. *Hegemony and Socialist Strategy: Towards a Radical Democratic Politics*. London: Verso, 1985.

Ladislav, Holy. *Anthropological Perspectives on Kinship*. London: Pluto, 1996.

Lai, Larissa. *Salt Fish Girl*. Toronto: Thomas Allen, 2002.

Lambropoulos, Vassilis. *The Rise of Eurocentrism: Anatomy of Interpretation*. Princeton: Princeton UP, 1993.

Latour, Bruno. *Science in Action: How to Follow Scientists and Engineers through Society*. Milton Keynes: Open UP, 1987.

———. *The Pasteurization of France*. Trans. Alan Sheridan and John Law. Cambridge: Cambridge UP, 1988.

———. *We Have Never Been Modern*. Trans. Catherine Porter. Cambridge: Harvard UP, 1993.

———. "Morality and Technology: The End of the Means." *Theory, Culture and Society* 19.5–6 (2002): 247–60.

———. *Politics of Nature*. Trans. Catherine Porter. Cambridge: Harvard UP, 2004.

———. "Why Has Critique Run Out of Steam? From Matters of Fact to Matters of Concern." *Critical Inquiry* 30 (2004): 225–48.

———. "From Realpolitik to Dingpolitik, or How to Make Things Public." *Making Things Public: Atmospheres of Democracy*. Ed. Latour and Peter Weibel. Cambridge: MIT P, 2005. 14–41.

Leahy, David. "Race, Gender, and Class Enigmas in *The Loved and the Lost* and *Au Milieu, La Montagne.*" *Textual Studies in Canada* 5 (1994): 32–45.

Leblanc, Gérald. *Je n'en connais pas la fin.* Moncton: Perce-Neige, 1999.

LeBlanc, Raymond Guy. *La mer en feu: poèmes 1964–1992.* Moncton: Perce-Neige, 1993.

Lecker, Robert. "'A Quest for a Peaceable Kingdom': The Narrative in Northrop Frye's Conclusion to the *Literary History of Canada.*" *Making It Real: The Canonization of English-Canadian Literature.* Toronto: Anansi, 1995. 191–204.

Lecker, Robert, and Kevin Flynn, eds. *Where Is Here Now?* Spec. issue of *Essays on Canadian Writing* 71 (2000): 6–13.

Lee, SKY. *Disappearing Moon Cafe.* Vancouver: Douglas and McIntyre, 1990.

Lees, Gene. *Oscar Peterson: The Will to Swing.* Toronto: Lester and Orpen Dennys, 1988.

Levinas, Emmanuel. *L'humanisme de l'Autre Homme.* Paris: Fata Morgana, 1996.

Lewis, George. "Improvised Music after 1950: Afrological and Eurological Perspectives." *Black Music Research Journal* 16.1 (1996): 91–122.

Lewis, Joe. "Pond Ecology." Yale–New Haven Teachers Institute. Curriculum Guide. 1992. Web. 7 Mar. 2009. http://www.yale.edu/ynhti/curriculum/units/1992/5/92.05.07.x.html.

Lippard, Lucy R. *The Lure of the Local: Senses of Place in a Multicentered Society.* New York: New Press, 1997.

Little Bear, Leroy. "Aboriginal Rights and the Canadian 'Grundnorm.'" *Arduous Journey: Canadian Indians and Decolonization.* Ed. J. Rick Ponting. Toronto: McClelland and Stewart, 1997. 243–59.

Liu, Alan. *Local Transcendence: Essays on Postmodern Historicism and the Database.* Chicago: U of Chicago P, 2008.

Lomosits, Helga. "Future Is Not a Tense." *Signs, Texts, Cultures: Conviviality for a Semiotic Point of View / Zeichen, Texte, Kulturen. Konvivialität aus semiotischer Perspektive.* Ed. Jeff Bernard. Wien: Herausgeberin, 2004. Web. 18 Aug. 2011. http://www.inst.at/trans/15Nr/01_2/lomosits15.htm.

Long Lance, Chief Buffalo Child. *Long Lance.* 1928. London: Corgi, 1956.

Loriggio, Francesco. "The Question of the Corpus: Ethnicity and Canadian Literature." *Future Indicative: Literary Theory and Canadian Literature.* Ed. John Moss. Ottawa: U of Ottawa P, 1987. 53–70.

Love, Glen. "Ecocriticism and Science: Toward Consilience?" *New Literary History* 30.3 (1999): 561–76.

Macfarlane, Scott. "The Haunt of Race: Canada's *Multiculturalims Act,* the Politics of Incorporation, and Writing Thru Race." *Fuse* 18.3 (1995): 19–31.

Mackey, Frank. *Black Then: Blacks and Montreal 1780s–1880s.* Montreal and Kingston: McGill–Queen's UP, 2004.

MacLennan, Hugh. *Two Solitudes.* Toronto: Stoddart, 1993.

Magord, André. *The Quest for Autonomy in Acadia.* New York: Peter Lang, 1998.

Mansbridge, Joanna. "Abject Origins: Uncanny Strangers and Figures of Fetishism in Larissa Lai's *Salt Fish Girl.*" *West Coast Line* 38.2 (2004): 121–33.

Maracle, Lee. *Oratory: Coming to Theory.* North Vancouver, BC: Gallerie Publications, 1990.

———. "Yin Chin." *An Anthology of Canadian Native Literature in English.* Ed. Daniel David Moses and Terrie Goldie. Don Mills: Oxford UP, 1997. 290–94.

———. "Oratory on Oratory." Kamboureli and Miki 55–70.

Marano, Carla. "'Rising Strongly and Rapidly': The Universal Negro Improvement Association in Canada, 1919–1940." *Canadian Historical Review* 91.2 (2010): 233–59.

Marrelli, Nancy. *Stepping Out: The Golden Age of Montreal Night Clubs, 1925–1955.* Montreal: Véhicule, 2004.

McConaghy, Cathryn. *Rethinking Indigenous Education: Culturalism, Colonialism, and the Politics of Knowing.* Flaxton: Post Pressed, 2002.

McFarlane, Colin. "Translocal Assemblages: Space, Power, and Social Movements." *Geoforum* 40.4 (2009): 561–67.

McKay, Don. *Vis à Vis: Field Notes on Poetry and Wilderness.* Wolfville: Gaspereau, 2001.

———. "Pond." *Strike/Slip.* Toronto: McClelland and Stewart, 2006. 12–13.

McKittrick, Katherine. *Demonic Grounds: Black Women and the Cartographies of Struggle.* Minneapolis: U of Minnesota P, 2006.

Menchu, Rigoberta. *I, Rigoberta Menchu: The Story of a Guatemalan Woman.* Ed. Elisabeth Burgos-Debray. New York: Verso, 1984.

Merchant, Carolyn. *The Death of Nature: Women, Ecology, and the Scientific Revolution.* San Francisco: HarperCollins, 1980.

Mercredi, Ovide, and Mary Ellen Turpel. *In the Rapids: Navigating the Future of First Nations.* Toronto: Penguin, 1994.

Merryman, John Henry. *The Civil Law Tradition: An Introduction to the Legal Systems of Western Europe and Latin America.* 2nd ed. Stanford: Stanford UP, 1985.

Miki, Roy. "Interface: Roy Kiyooka's Writing, A Commentary/Interview." *Broken Entries: Race Subjectivity Writing.* Toronto: Mercury, 1998. 54–76.

———. "Asiancy: Making Space for Asian Canadian Writing." *Broken Entries: Race, Subjectivity, Writing.* Toronto: Mercury, 1998. 101–25.

———. "Afterword." *The Artist and the Moose: A Fable of Forget.* By Roy K. Kiyooka. Ed. Roy Miki. Vancouver: Linebooks, 2009. 135–73.

Miller, Mark. *Jazz in Canada: Fourteen Lives.* Toronto: U of Toronto P, 1982.

———. *The Miller Companion to Jazz in Canada and Canadians in Jazz.* Toronto: Mercury, 2001.

Mills, Aaron James. "An open letter to all my relations: On Idle No More, Chief Spence and non-violence." *Rabble.* 10 Jan. 2013. Web. 3 Feb. 2013. http://rabble.ca/news/2013/01/open-letter-all-my-relations-idle-no-more-chief-spence-and-non-violence.

Minnich, Elizabeth. *Transforming Knowledge.* Philadelphia: Temple UP, 2005.

Moore, Kathleen Dean. "The Missing Premise: Bringing Ethics into the Conversation at the End of the World." Association for the Study of Literature and Environment. 8th Biennial Conference. Victoria, BC. 3 June 2009. Unpublished conference paper.

Moore, MariJo, and Vine Deloria, Jr. *Genocide of the Mind: New Native American Writing.* New York: Nation, 2003.

Morrison, Toni. *Playing in the Dark: Whiteness and the Literary Imagination.* New York: Vintage, 1990.

Morton, Timothy. *Ecology without Nature: Rethinking Environmental Aesthetics.* Cambridge: Harvard UP, 2007.

Mukherjee, Arun. *Towards an Aesthetic of Opposition: Essays on Criticism and Cultural Imperialism.* Stratford: Williams-Wallace, 1988.

———. *Oppositional Aesthetics: Readings from a Hyphenated Space.* Toronto: TSAR, 1994.

N.C.C. / Charles H. Este Community Centre. "Our History." 2007. Web. 28 Dec. 2009.

Nancy, Jean-Luc. *Being Singular Plural.* Stanford: Stanford UP, 2000.

Nandy, A. *The Intimate Enemy: Loss and Recovery of Self under Colonialism.* Delhi: Oxford UP, 1983.

Nepveu, Pierre. *Lectures des lieux: Essais.* Collection Papiers Collés. Montréal: Boréal, 2004.

Nepveu, Pierre, and Gilles Marcotte. *Montréal Imaginaire: Ville et Littérature*. Montreal: Fides, 1992.

Nestor, Rob. "Almighty Voice." *The Encyclopedia of Saskatchewan*. Web. June 2009. http://esask.uregina.ca/entry/almighty_voice_1875-97.html.

New Brunswick. *Wolastoqiyik, Portrait of a People*. Exhibition Catalogue (2000–05). Web. 6 May 2011. http://www.gnb.ca/0007/Heritage/virtual_exibition/ Portraits/schedule .htm.

Nichol, bp. "'Syntax Equals the Body Structure': bpNichol, in Conversation, with Daphne Marlatt and George Bowering." *Meanwhile: The Critical Writings of bpNichol*. Ed. Roy Miki. Vancouver: Talonbooks, 2002. 273–97.

Northwest Provinces. 1906 Census. Web. 9 May 2011. http://www.ancestry.ca.

Nussbaum, Martha. *Poetic Justice: The Literary Imagination and Public Life*. Boston: Beacon, 1995.

O'Brien, John, and Peter White. Introduction. *Beyond Wilderness: The Group of Seven, Canadian Identity, and Contemporary Art*. Ed. John O'Brien and Peter White. Montreal and Kingston: McGill-Queen's UP, 2007. 3–6.

"Ooze." *Oxford Dictionaries*. April 2010. Oxford University Press. Web. 21 June 2012.

Ouellet, François, ed. "La littérature acadienne débarque!" *Nuit Blanche* 115 (2009): 20–21.

Pâquet, Martin, and Stéphane Savard, eds. *Balises et références. Acadies. francophonies*. Québec: Presses de l'Université Laval, 2007.

Paul, Daniel. *We Were Not the Savages: Collision between European and Native American Civilizations*. 3rd ed. Halifax: Fernwood P, 2006

Pease, Donald E. "New Americanists: Revisionist Interventions in the Canon." *New Americanists: Revisionist Interventions into the Canon*. Spec. issue of *boundary 2* 17 (1990): 1–37.

Peterson, Oscar. *A Jazz Odyssey: The Life of Oscar Peterson*. London: Continuum, 2002.

Phillips, Dana. "Ecocriticism, Literary Theory, and the Truth of Ecology." *New Literary History* 30.3 (1999): 577–602.

Plumwood, Val. *Feminism and the Mastery of Nature*. London: Routledge, 1993.

"Primer on Pond & Lake Ecology & Watershed Dynamics." Aqua Link, Inc. Product Information. 2002. Web. 7 Mar. 2009. http://www.aqualinkinc.com/LakeEcology .aspx.

Rancière, Jacques. "Should Democracy Come? Ethics and Politics in Derrida." *Derrida and the Time of the Political*. Ed. Pheng Cheah and Suzanne Guerlac. Durham: Duke UP, 2009. 274–88.

Rancière, Jacques. *Disagreement: Politics and Philosophy*. Trans. Julie Rose. Minneapolis: U of Minnesota P, 1999.

———. *The Politics of Aesthetics*. Trans. and intro. Gabriel Rockhill. Afterword by Slavoj Žižek. London and New York: Continuum, 2004.

———. *Dissensus: On Politics and Aesthetics*. Ed. and trans. Stephen Corcoran. London and New York: Continuum, 2010.

———. *The Politics of Literature*. Trans. Julie Rose. Cambridge: Polity, 2011.

———. "'This Strange Institution Called Literature': An Interview with Jacques Derrida." Wilner and Attridge 33–75.

Raz, Joseph. *Concept of Legal System—an Introduction to the Theory of Legal System*. Oxford: Clarendon, 1970.

Regan, Paulette. *Unsettling the Settler Within: Indian Residential Schools, Truth Telling, and Reconciliation in Canada*. Vancouver: UBC Press, 2010.

Rhodes, Jane. *Mary Ann Shadd Cary: The Black Press and Protest in the Nineteenth Century*. Bloomington: Indiana UP, 1998.

Robinson, Eden. "Queen of the North." *Traplines*. Toronto: Vintage, 1996. 185–215.

——. *Monkey Beach*. Toronto: Vintage, 2000.

——. *Blood Sports*. Toronto: McClelland and Stewart, 2006.

Rotman, Leonard I. "'My Hovercraft Is Full of Eels:' Smoking Out the Message of *R. v. Marshall*." *Saskatchewan Law Review* 63 (2000): 617–44.

Roy, Gabrielle. "Tout Montréal 1: Les deux Saint-Laurent." *Le Bulletin des agriculteurs* 37.6 (1941): 8–9, 37, 40.

——. "Les deux nègres." *Rue Deschambault*. Montréal: Beauchemin, 1967. 8–28.

——. *The Tin Flute*. Ed. Malcolm Ross. Trans. Hannah Josephson. Toronto: McClelland and Stewart, 1969.

——. *Bonheur d'Occasion*. Montréal: Boréal, 1993.

Roy, Michel. *L'Acadie perdue*. Moncton: Éditions d'Acadie, 1978.

Ryder, Bruce. "Aboriginal Rights and *Delgamuukw v. The Queen*." *Constitutional Forum* 5.2 (1994): 43–48.

Said, Edward. *Beginnings: Intention and Method*. New York: Columbia UP, 1985.

Salter, Liora, and Alison Hearn. *Report to the Social Sciences and Humanities Research Council of Canada on Interdisciplinarity*. Ottawa: SSHRC, 1991.

——. *Outside the Lines: Issues in Interdisciplinary Research*. Montreal and Kingston: McGill-Queen's UP, 1996.

Sanders, Scott Russell. "Speaking a Word for Nature." *The Ecocriticism Reader: Landmarks in Literary Ecology*. Ed. Cheryll Glotfelty and Harold Fromm. Athens: U Georgia P, 1996. 182–95.

Sandilands, Catriona. "Opinionated Natures: Toward a Green Public Culture." *Democracy and the Claims of Nature: Critical Perspectives for a New Century*. Ed. Ben A. Minteer and Bob Pepperman Taylor. Lanham: Rowman and Littlefield, 2002. 117–32.

Sansregret, Marthe. *Oliver Jones, le musicien et l'homme*. Outremont: Stanke, 2005.

Sarsfield, Mairuth. *No Crystal Stair*. Toronto: Moulin, 1997.

Schagerl, Jessica. "Taking a Place at the Table." Coleman and Kamboureli 95–111.

Seager, Joni. *Earth Follies: Coming to Feminist Terms with the Global Environmental Crisis*. New York: Routledge, 1993.

Siemerling, Winfried. *The New North American Studies: Culture, Writing, and the Politics of Re/Cognition*. New York: Routledge, 2005.

——. "Ethics as Re/Cognition in the Novels of Marie-Célie Agnant: Oral Knowledge, Cognitive Change, and Social Justice." *University of Toronto Quarterly* 76.3 (2007): 838–60.

Simon, Sherry. *Translating Montreal: Episodes in the Life of a Divided City*. Montreal and Kingston: McGill-Queen's UP, 2006.

——. "The Post-Industrial South-West." *Used / Goods*. Ed. Gisele Amantea, Lorraine Oades, and Kim Sawchuk. Montreal: Conseil des Arts, 2009.

Simpson, A.W.B. "The Common Law and Legal Theory." *Oxford Essays in Jurisprudence*. Ed. Simpson. Oxford: Oxford UP, 1973. 119–40.

Simpson, David. *Situatedness, or, Why We Keep Saying Where We're Coming From*. Durham: Duke UP, 2002.

Simpson, Mark. *Trafficking Subjects: The Politics of Mobility in Nineteenth-Century America*. Minneapolis: U of Minnesota P, 2005.

Smith, Donald B. *From the Land of the Shadows: The Making of Grey Owl*. Saskatoon: Western, 1990.

———. *Chief Buffalo Child Long Lance: The Glorious Imposter*. Red Deer: Red Deer Press, 1999.

Smith, Graham. "Kaupapa Maori Theory and Praxis." Diss. U of Auckland. 1997.

Smith, Linda Tuhiwai. *Decolonizing Methodologies: Research and Indigenous Peoples*. London: Zed, 1999.

Snyder, Gary. *Turtle Island*. New York: New Directions, 1974.

Société Historique de Saint-Henri. "Histoire de Saint-Henri: Saint-Henri, Avant, Pendant et Après le Canal." *CLSC Saint-Henri*. 1999. Web. 27 Feb. 2010.

Soper, Kate. *What Is Nature? Culture, Politics, and the Non-Human*. Oxford: Blackwell, 1995.

Spivak, Gayatri Chakravorty. "Responsibility." *boundary 2* 21.3 (1994): 19–64.

Steinmetz, Julia, Heather Cassils, and Clover Leary. "Behind Enemy Lines: Toxic Titties Infiltrate Vanessa Beecroft." *Signs: Journal of Women in Culture and Society* 31.3 (2006): 753–83.

Stoler, Ann Laura. *Along the Archival Grain: Epistemic Anxieties and Colonial Common Sense*. Princeton and Oxford: Princeton UP, 2009.

Stow, Simon. "Reading Our Way to Democracy? Literature and Public Ethics." *Philosophy and Literature* 30 (2006): 410–23.

Strathern, Marilyn. *After Nature: English Kinship in the Late Twentieth Century*. Cambridge: Cambridge UP, 1992.

Strong, Thomas. "Kinship between Judith Butler and Anthropology? A Review Essay." *Ethnos* 67.3 (2002): 401–18.

Sugars, Cynthia, and Gerry Turcotte. "Introduction: Canadian Literature and the Postcolonial Gothic." *Unsettled Remains: Canadian Literature and the Postcolonial Gothic*. Ed. Cynthia Sugars and Gerry Turcotte. Waterloo: Wilfrid Laurier UP, 2009. viii–xxvi.

Sun, Emily, Eval Peretz, and Ulrich Baer, eds. *The Claims of Literature: A Shoshana Felman Reader*. New York: Fordham UP, 2007.

Suzuki, David. *The Sacred Balance: Rediscovering Our Place in Nature*. Vancouver: Greystone, 1997.

Symons, Thomas H.B. *To Know Ourselves: The Report of the Commission on Canadian Studies*. 2 vols. Ottawa: Association of Universities and Colleges of Canada, 1975.

———. *The Symons Report: An Abridged Version of Volumes 1 and 2 of To Know Ourselves: The Report of the Commission on Canadian Studies*. Toronto: McClelland and Stewart, 1978.

Szeman, Imre. "The Persistance of the Nation: Literature and Criticism in Canada." *Zones of Instability: Literature, Postcolonialism, and the Nation*. Baltimore: Johns Hopkins UP, 2003. 152–98.

Talbot, Carol. *Growing Up Black in Canada*. Toronto: Williams-Wallace, 1984.

Tan, Sid. "Chinese Head Tax/Exclusion Redress." *The Activist Network*. 18 Dec. 2007. Web. 2 Feb. 2011.

Terdiman, Richard. *Imagined Places*. Oxford: Blackwell, 1992.

Thériault, Joseph Yvon. *Faire société: société civile et espaces francophones*. Sudbury: Prise de parole, 2007.

Thibodeau, Serge Patrice. *Nous, l'étranger.* Trois-Rivières: Écrits des Forges; Echternach: Éditions Phi, 1995.
Thobani, Sunera. *Exalted Subjects: Studies in the Making of Race and Nation in Canada.* Toronto: U of Toronto P, 2007.
Thomas, Nigel. *Behind the Face of Winter.* Toronto: TSAR, 2001.
Thoreau, Henry David. *The Maine Woods.* 1864. New York: Cosimo, 2009.
Trudel, Marcel, with collaboration from Micheline d'Allaire. *Deux Siècles d'esclavage au Québec; suivi du Dictionnaire des esclaves et de leurs propriétaires au Canada français sur CD-ROM.* Montréal: Hurtubise HMH, 2004. CD-ROM.
Tsing, Anna Lowenhaupt. *Friction.* Princeton: Princeton UP, 2005.
Tucker, Ernest. *Lost Boundaries.* Bloomington: Authorhouse, 2006.
Tulchinsky, Gerald J.J. *The River Barons: Montreal Businessmen and the Growth of Industry and Transportation, 1837–53.* Toronto: U of Toronto P, 1977.
United Kingdom. 1891 Census. 1891. Web. 9 May 2011. http://www.ancestry.ca.
———. 1901 Census. 1901. Web. 9 May 2011. http://www.ancestry.ca.
United Nations. *Declaration of the Rights of Indigenous Peoples.* United Nations, 2008. Web. 18 Aug. 2011 http://www.un.org/esa/socdev/unpfii/documents/DRIPS_en.pdf.
Van Vleet, Krista E. *Performing Kinship: Narrative, Gender, and the Intimacies of Power in the Andes.* Austin: U of Texas P, 2008.
Verduyn, Christl. "Interdisciplinarity and the Study of Canadian Literature." *Arachne: An Interdisciplinary Journal of the Humanities* 4.2 (1997): 77–88.
Vernon, Karina J. "The Black Prairies: History, Subjectivity, Writing." Diss. U of Victoria, 2008.
Vernon-Wood, Nello. *Mountain Masculinity: The Life and Writing of Nello "Tex" Vernon-Wood in the Canadian Rockies, 1906–1938.* Ed. Andrew Gow and Julie Rak. Athabasca: Athabasca UP, 2008.
Veronis, Luisa. *Rethinking Transnationalism: Latin Americans' Experiences of Migration and Participation in Toronto.* Working Paper 51. Toronto: CERIS, 2006.
Vickers, Jill. "'[U]nframed in Open, Unmapped Fields': Teaching and the Practice of Interdisciplinarity." *Arachne: An Interdisciplinariy Journal of the Humanities* 4.2 (1997): 11–42.
Wade, H.W.R. "The Basis of Legal Sovereignty." *Cambridge L.J.* 13.2 (1955): 172–97.
———. *Constitutional Fundamentals.* London: Stevens, 1980.
Wald, Gayle. *Crossing the Line: Racial Passing in Twentieth-Century US Literature and Culture.* Durham: Duke UP, 2000.
Walker, G. deQ. *The Rule of Law—Foundations of Constitutional Democracy.* Melbourne: Melbourne UP, 1988.
Wegmann-Sánchez, Jessica. "Rewriting Race and Ethnicity across the Border: Mairuth Sarsfield's *No Crystal Stair* and Nella Larsen's *Quicksand and Passing.*" *Essays on Canadian Writing* 74 (2001): 136–66.
Weik von Mossner, Alexa. "Still Widening the Circle: The Environmental Challenge to Contemporary Theories of Cosmopolitanism." Ecocriticism, Globalization, and Cosmopolitanism Seminar, Association for the Study of Literature and Environment (ASLE). U of Victoria, BC. 2 June 2009. Unpublished conference paper.
White, Richard. "'Are You an Environmentalist or Do You Work for a Living?': Work and Nature." *Uncommon Ground: Toward Reinventing Nature.* Ed. William Cronon. New York: W.W. Norton, 1995. 171–85.

Whiteside, Kerry. "Worldliness and Respect for Nature: An Ecological Application of Hannah Arendt's Conception of Culture." *Environmental Values* 7 (1998): 25–40.

Whitman, Walt. *Leaves of Grass: The First (1855) Edition.* Ed. Malcolm Cowley. New York: Viking, 1959.

Wilke, Sabine. "'The Sound of a Robin after a Rain Shower': The Role of Aesthetic Experience in Dialectical Conceptions of Nature." *Interdisciplinary Studies in Literature and the Environment* 16.1 (2009): 91–117.

Williams, Dorothy W. *The Road to Now: A History of Blacks in Montreal.* Montreal: Véhicule, 1997.

Williams, Raymond. *The Country and the City.* New York: Oxford UP, 1973.

Winks, Robin W. *The Blacks in Canada: A History.* Montreal and Kingston: McGill–Queen's UP, 1997.

Winstead, Ray L. "Pond Ecology." August 2005. Web. 7 Mar. 2009. http://www.nsm.iup.edu/rwinstea/pond.shtm.

Winterton, George. "The British Grundnorm: Parliamentary Supremacy Re-examined." *Law Quarterly Review* 92 (1976): 591–617.

Wong, Gein, et al. *How We Forgot Here.* Unpublished manuscript, 2008.

Wong, Rita. "Troubling Domestic Limits: Reading Border Fictions Alongside Larissa Lai's *Salt Fish Girl*." *BC Studies* 140 (2003–04): 109–24.

———. "Decolonizasian: Reading Asian and First Nations Relations in Literature." *Canadian Literature* 199 (2008): 158–80.

Young, La Monte. "Piano Piece for David Tudor #1." *La Monte Young, Compositions.* New York: La Monte Young and Jackson MacLow, 1960. 2.

Young, Robert. *Colonial Desire:Hybridity in Theory, Culture and Race.* London and New York: Routledge, 1995.

Yu, Henry. "Global Migrants and the New Pacific Canada." *International Journal* 64.4 (2009): 1011-1-26.

Court Cases

Delgamuukw v. British Columbia. 3 S.C.R. 1010. Supreme Court of Canada. 1997.

Haida Nation v. British Columbia (Minister of Forests). 3 S.C.R. 511. Supreme Court of Canada. 2004.

Mitchell v. M.N.R. 1 S.C.R. 911. Supreme Court of Canada. 2001.

Paul v. British Columbia (Forest Appeals Commission). 2 S.C.R. 585. Supreme Court of Canada. 2003.

Quebec Secession Reference. Re Reference by the Governor General in Council Concerning Certain Questions Relating to the Secession of Quebec from Canada. 2 S.C.R. 217. Supreme Court Reports, Canada. 1998.

Reference re Manitoba Language Rights. 1 S.C.R. 721. Supreme Court Reports, Canada. 1985.

R. v. Burah. 3 A.C. 889. Appeal Case. 1878.

R. v. Côté. 3 S.C.R. 139. Supreme Court Reports, Canada. 1996.

R. v. Kapp. 2 S.C.R. 483. Supreme Court Reports, Canada. 2008.

R. v. Marshall (No. 1). 3 S.C.R. 456. Supreme Court Reports, Canada. 1999.

R. v. Sparrow. 1 S.C.R. 1075. Supreme Court Reports, Canada. 1990.

R. v. Van der Peet. 2 S.C.R. 507. Supreme Court Reports, Canada. 1996.

CONTRIBUTORS

MARIE BATTISTE, a Mi'kmaw educator from Potlo'tek First Nation, Nova Scotia, is a full professor in the College of Education at the University of Saskatchewan. Her research interests are in initiating institutional change in the decoloniza- tion of education, in particular humanities, language and social justice policy and power, and post-colonial educational approaches that recognize and affirm the political and cultural diversity of Canada. She is leader of a national hub at the University of Saskatchewan for the Canadian Prevention Science Cluster aimed at identifying approaches to culturally appropriate school-based violence prevention and also leader of the Animating Indigenous Humanities project, both funded by SSHRC. Newly elected Fellow to the Royal Society of Canada, and with three honorary degrees, she is the author of *Decolonizing Education: Nourishing the Learning Spirit* (2013), co-author, with J. Youngblood Henderson, of *Protecting Indigenous Knowledge and Heritage: A Global Challenge* (2000), which received a Saskatchewan Book Award in 2000. In addition to writing many articles and books, she has edited *Reclaiming Indigenous Voice and Vision* (2000) and co-edited a special edition of *Australian Journal of Indigenous Edu- cation* (May 2005), and was the senior editor, with Jean Barman, of *First Nations Education in Canada: The Circle Unfolds* (1995).

JULIA V. EMBERLEY is a Professor in the Department of English and Writing Studies at Western University. In addition to her two earlier books, *The Cultural Politics of Fur* and *Thresholds of Difference: Feminist Critique, Native Women's Writings, Post-Colonial Theory*, she has published *Defamiliarizing the Aboriginal: Cultural Practices and Decolonization in Canada* (2007). She edited a special issue of *English Studies in Canada* on *Skin* (2009) and has published numerous articles in the fields of testimony studies, post-colonial and Indigenous litera- tures, and cultural studies. Her forthcoming book, *The Testimonial Uncanny:*

Indigenous Storytelling, Knowledge, and Reparative Practices will be published by SUNY Press in their Native Traces series.

JAMES [SA'KE'J] YOUNGBLOOD HENDERSON is the Director of the Native Law Centre of Canada at the College of Law, University of Saskatchewan. He was born to the Bear Clan of the Chickasaw Nation in 1944 and is married to Marie Battiste, a Mi'kmaw educator. He received a Juris doctorate in law from Harvard Law School (1974). He served as a constitutional adviser for the Mi'kmaw Nation and the Assembly of First Nations (1978–83). He advocates uniting treaty federalism with provincial federalism to create shared rule, democracy, and government in Canada in "Empowering Treaty Federalism." He was one of the strategists who created Indigenous diplomacy, working through the Four Direction Council, an NGO, in the UN system, and was part of the team that drafted many of the existing documents. His award-winning books are *Aboriginal Tenure in the Constitution of Canada*, *Treaty Rights in the Constitution of Canada*, and *Indigenous Diplomacy and the Rights of Peoples: Achieving UN Recognition*. He has been awarded the Indigenous Peoples' Counsel Award (2005) and the National Aboriginal Achievement Award for Law and Justice (2006), and an Honourary Doctorate of Laws, Carlton University (2007). He is a Fellow of the Royal Society of Canada.

SMARO KAMBOURELI joined the Department of English at the University of Toronto as Professor and Avie Bennett Chair in Canadian Literature in 2013. Prior to this, she was Canada Research Chair, Tier 1, in Critical Studies in Canadian Literature at the University of Guelph, and Director of TransCanada Institute (2005–2013). She has edited and co-edited many volumes, most recently with Kit Dobson, *Producing Canadian Literature: Authors Speak on the Literary Marketplace* (2013); with Robert Zacharias, *Shifting the Ground of Canadian Literary Studies* (2012); with Daniel Coleman, *Retooling the Humanities: The Culture of Research in Canadian Universities* (2011); and with Roy Miki, *Trans. Can.Lit: Resituating the Study of Canadian Literature* (2007). She is also the author of *On the Edge of Genre: The Contemporary Canadian Long Poem* (1991) and *Scandalous Bodies: Diasporic Literatures in English Canada* (2000, 2009), and the editor of the two editions of the anthology *Making a Difference: Canadian Multicultural Literature* (1996, 2006). She is the General Editor of Wilfrid Laurier University Press's TransCanada Series, and the Editor of NeWest Press's The Writer as Critic Series. Most recently, she edited a special issue of the *University of Toronto Quarterly, Writing the Foreign in Canadian Literature and Humanitarian Narratives* (2013).

LARISSA LAI is a poet, novelist, critic, and Assistant Professor in the Department of English at the University of British Columbia. Her publications include *Salt*

Fish Girl (2002), *sybil unrest* (with Rita Wong, 2008), and *When Fox Is a Thousand* (1995). She has been the Writer-in-Residence at the University of Calgary, Simon Fraser University, and, most recently, the University of Guelph. Her first solo full-length poetry book, *Automaton Biographies* (2009), was a finalist for the Dorothy Livesay Poetry Prize.

CHERYL LOUSLEY is an Assistant Professor in English and Interdisciplinary Studies at Lakehead University Orillia. Her research focuses on Canadian literature and contemporary environmental literary and cultural studies. Her research has been published in *Canadian Literature, Essays on Canadian Writing, Environmental Philosophy*, and *Interdisciplinary Studies in Literature and Environment*. She is also the series editor for the Environmental Humanities book series at Wilfrid Laurier University Press.

ROY MIKI is a writer, poet, and editor who lives in Vancouver. He is the author of several books, including *Redress: Inside the Japanese Canadian Call for Justice* (2004), a work that explores the Japanese Canadian redress movement. His third book of poems, *Surrender* (2001), received the Governor General's Award for Poetry. His most recent books are *Mannequin Rising* (2011), a collection of poems and photo collages, and *In Flux: Transnational Shifts in Asian Canadian Writing* (2011), a collection of essays. He received the Order of Canada in 2006 and the Order of British Columbia in 2009.

FRANÇOIS PARÉ teaches French and Francophone Literatures at the University of Waterloo. He is the author of several books and journal articles on cultural and linguistic diversity, and on francophone minorities in Canada. He is a member of the Royal Society of Canada. His first book, *Les littératures de l'exiguïté* (1992), won the 1993 Governor General's Award for non-fiction in French. In 1997, a translation of this book was published by Wilfrid Laurier University Press under the title, *Exiguity: Reflections on the Margins of Literature*. His 2003 book, *La distance habitée*, won the Trillium Book Award offered by the Ontario government and the Prix Victor-Barbeau presented by the Académie des Arts et des Lettres du Québec. In addition to *Traversées*, an epistolary essay with François Ouellet (2000), *Shifting Boundaries / Frontières flottantes* with Jaap Lintvelt (2001), and *Le fantasme d'Escanaba* (2007), Paré also published, in collaboration with Stéphanie Nutting, a collection of articles on Franco-Ontarian playwright and novelist Jean Marc Dalpé (*Jean Marc Dalpé. Ouvrier d'un dire*, 2006). His latest book, written jointly with François Ouellet, is an epistolary essay on Quebec novelist Louis Hamelin (*Louis Hamelin et ses doubles*, Nota Bene, 2008, Prix Gabrielle-Roy, 2008). François Paré is currently working on a new book on the erasure of the Name in North American diasporic cultures and literatures.

272 Contributors

JULIE RAK is a Professor in the Department of English and Film Studies at the University of Alberta. She is the author of several books and essay collections about autobiography and culture. Her latest book is *Boom! Manufacturing Memoir for the Popular Market* (Wilfrid Laurier University Press, 2013). Her latest collection, edited with Anna Poletti, is *Identity Technologies: Constructing the Self Online* (2014). Julie is writing a SSHRC-funded book called *Social Climbing: Gender in Mountaineering Writing and Film*.

LAURIE RICOU is a specialist in Canadian literary regionalism, who has recently been questioning how borders are written in the Pacific Northwest. He taught English at the University of British Columbia from 1978 to 2010, where he developed undergraduate and graduate courses in Habitat Studies over the past fifteen years. In summer 2011, he taught a version of the course at Trier University (Germany). He is the author of two recent books on the Pacific Northwest literary bioregion: *The Arbutus/Madrone Files: Reading the Pacific Northwest* (Oregon State University Press, 2002), and *Salal: Listening for the Northwest Understory* (NeWest Press, 2007).

CATRIONA SANDILANDS is a Professor in the Faculty of Environmental Studies, York University. She is the author/co-editor of three books, most recently (with Bruce Erickson) *Queer Ecologies: Sex, Nature, Politics, Desire* (2010). "Acts of Nature" is part of a larger project on the contributions of environmental literature to environmental politics, which includes an anthology entitled *Green Words/Green Worlds: Environmental Literatures and Politics* and a monograph on the literary and activist contributions of Jane Rule to multiple public cultures.

WINFRIED SIEMERLING is a Professor of English at the University of Waterloo and an Associate of the W.E.B. Du Bois Institute for African and African American Research at Harvard. His study *The Black Atlantic Reconsidered: Black Canadian Writing, Cultural History, and the Presence of the Past* is forthcoming with McGill–Queen's University Press. Earlier books include *Canada and Its Americas: Transnational Navigations* (co-ed., 2010), *The New North American Studies* (2005, French trans. 2010), *Cultural Difference and the Literary Text* (1996–97, co-ed.), *Writing Ethnicity* (1996, ed.), and *Discoveries of the Other* (1994). He has written a chapter on Canada in *The Cambridge History of Postcolonial Literature* (2012), and is a co-researcher in the SSHRC-funded Partnership Grant, "International Institute for Critical Studies in Improvisation: A Partnered Research Institute" (2013–20).

CHRISTL VERDUYN is cross-appointed to the Department of English and the Canadian Studies Program at Mount Allison University, where she is the Davidson Chair in Canadian Studies and Director of the Centre for Canadian Studies. Her research interests include Canadian and Québécois literatures, women's writing and criticism, multiculturalism and minority writing, life writing and Canadian studies, and she has published numerous articles and several books in these areas. Recent titles include *Canadian Studies: Past, Present, Praxis* (with J. Koustas, 2012), *Archival Narratives for Canada: Re-Telling Stories in a Changing Landscape* (with K. Garay, 2011), *Marian and the Major: Engel's Elizabeth and the Golden City* (2010), and *Asian Canadian Writing Beyond Autoethnography* (with E. Ty, 2008). Before joining the faculty at Mount Allison, she taught at Wilfrid Laurier University (2000–6), where she chaired the Canadian Studies Program, and at Trent University (1980–2000), where she was Chair of Women's Studies (1987–90) and Chair of Canadian Studies (1993–99).

INDEX

abjection, 154
Aboriginal Education Research Centre, 96
Aboriginal Health Foundation (AHF), 244n2
Aboriginal Learning Knowledge Centre, 96
Aboriginal rights, 9–10, 49, 50, 52, 57, 60–61, 62. *See also* First Nations
Aboriginal Studies, 233
Acadians, 8, 11, 215–25
Acadian World Congress, 225
L'Acadie, Quebec, 225
L'Acadie du discours (Hautecoeur), 222
L'Acadie perdue (Roy), 222
Acadies (Pâquet and Savard), 225
Adorno, Theodor, 5
affiliation, 8, 17
Africville Suite (Sealy), 249n15
Agamben, Giorgio, 151
agency, 113
Agnant, Marie-Célie, 213
"Al dente" (Després), 224
Algonquin Park, 24, 45
Allain, Greg, 215–16
allegory, 21, 103
alliance: anti-colonial, 99, 100; in a balanced consciousness, 101; of blacks and trade unions, 249n22; and kinship, 22; trans-generational, 9, 50
Almighty Voice, 194, 195–96
ambivalence, 1–2, 12, 77, 224
American literature, 11, 13, 31, 153
Anderson, Benedict, 151
Angélique, 200, 203, 209, 212
Anne of Green Gables (Montgomery), 212

Anthropometry projects, 110
A Place in Heaven (Foster), 213
apology, 14, 104, 244n1
Appadurai, Arjun, 181
Arachne (journal), 233–34, 251n7
Arendt, Hannah, 129, 132–35, 142, 246n3
Arnold, Richard, 162
Arsenault, Guy, 220
The Artist and the Moose (Kiyooka), 21–27, 44–47
Asian Americans, 153
Asian Canadians: as anti-Oedipal subjects, 24; as a formation, 43–44; and Indigenous Peoples, 8, 11, 99–126, 238; literature by, 47, 230
assemblage, 144, 154, 156
assimilation: Canadian Literature and, 13; cognitive, 87; and education, 83; and multiculturalism, 221; settler states' preference for, 89; UN Declaration on the Rights of Indigenous Peoples on, 96
Association for Literature and the Environment Conference, 168–69
atomic bomb, 114
Atwood, Margaret, 12, 235, 243n2, 247n2
Australia, 57
authenticity, 187–88, 191–92, 198
authorship, 113

Bail, Micheline, 203
Baker, Josephine, 212
Baldwin, Anita, 193
Barthes, Roland, 77, 109, 244n1
Battiste, Marie, 8–9, 83–98, 101, 104, 238
Battiste, Tom, 87

"The Long March to 'Recognition'" (Find-
lay), 237
Loriggio, Francesco, 234
Lost Boundaries (Tucker), 213
Louisiana, 225
Louis XIV, King of France, 248n8
Lousley, Cheryl, 4, 7, 11, 143–60
Love, Glen, 130
The Loved and the Lost (Callaghan), 200,
202–3, 248n6

Macfarlane, Scott, 14
MacLennan, Hugh, 200
Madness and Civilization (Foucault),
246n5
Magord, André, 217
Mandel, Eli, 235, 243n2
Manitoba Language Rights (legal case), 54
Mansbridge, Joanna, 154
Maracle, Lee: and Canadian Literature,
3; on Diaspora, 2, 8; on Indigenous
approach to literature, 238; *Oratory*,
229; "Yin Chin," 8, 102, 103–4
Marcotte, Gilles, 213
Marcus Garvey Debating Society, 209
Marky, Paul de, 210
Marlatt, Daphne, 243n2
Marrelli, Nancy, 206, 208, 249n17
Marshall (legal case), 52, 54
Marshall, Albert, 88
Marshall, Murdena, 88
Martel, Yann, 41
Marx, Karl, 64
Massey Commission, 36, 43
materiality, 12, 20, 23, 39, 72
Mathur, Ashok, 47
matters of concern/matters of fact, 4, 147–
49
McClure's (journal), 189, 191
McKay, Claude, 212
McKay, Don, 138, 161, 163, 164, 165–68,
169–74, 246n6
McKee-Allain, Isabelle, 215–16
McKittrick, Katherine, 200, 203
McLachlin, Beverley (Chief Justice), 49, 58
medicine wheel, 73–74, 76, 244n2
memory, 74, 80, 97, 103, 107, 142
Memramcook, New Brunswick, 225

Menchú, Rigoberta, 70
Metcalf, Louis, 207
Metcalf International Band, 207
methodologies, 17, 19, 37–38, 39, 228–29,
239
Métis, 72, 195, 219–20
middle voice, 77, 244n1
Miki, Roy: on *The Artist and the Moose*, 22,
23, 24; on "Asiancy," 109; on Canadian
Literature, 6, 7, 29–48; on the local, 5
Mi'kmaq nation, 9, 83, 85, 101
Miller, Mark, 208, 249n16
Milligan, Christine, 200
Mills, Aaron James, 19–20
Minkins, Shadrach, 204–5, 249n13
Minnich, Elizabeth, 90
minorities: and agency, 109; and identity,
221–22; literatures, 38–39, 41; and
multiculturalism, 19; and nationalism,
46, 243n29; and pluralism, 215–18; as
translucent thresholds, 219
mobility, 5, 7, 182, 193–94, 197
modernity, 5, 11, 143, 147–48, 154, 156,
192
Mohegans, 101
Moncton, 224
Monkey Beach (Robinson), 8, 72–81, 238
Montgomery, Lucy Maud, 212
Montreal: black communities in, 8, 11,
200, 205–8, 212–13; industrialization,
205; jazz festival, 199; literary portray-
als of, 200–203, 209–13
Montréal imaginaire (Nepveu and Mar-
cotte), 213
Moore, Kathleen Dean, 168–69
Morrison, Toni, 203
Morton, Jelly Roll, 207
Morton, Timothy, 145, 157
Moss, John, 235
"Mother to Son" (Hughes), 212
Mouffe, Chantal, 150
Mountain Masculinity (Gow and Rak), 182
Mount Allison University, 227
Mourir à Scoudouc (Chiasson), 224
The Movement Project, 104, 109, 238
Mukherjee, Arun, 234
multiculturalism, 14, 43, 100, 218, 221,
222, 229

Books in the TransCanada Series
Published by Wilfrid Laurier University Press

Smaro Kamboureli and Roy Miki, editors
Trans.Can.Lit: Resituating the Study of Canadian Literature / 2007 / xviii + 234 pp. /
ISBN 978-0-88920-513-0

Smaro Kamboureli
Scandalous Bodies: Diasporic Literature in English Canada / 2009 / xviii + 270 pp. / ISBN
978-1-55458-064-4

Kit Dobson
Transnational Canadas: Anglo-Canadian Literature and Globalization / 2009 / xviii +
240 pp. / ISBN 978-1-55458-063-7

Christine Kim, Sophie McCall, and Melina Baum Singer, editors
Cultural Grammars of Nation, Diaspora, and Indigeneity in Canada / 2012 / viii + 276 pp. /
ISBN 978-1-55458-336-2

Smaro Kamboureli and Robert Zacharias, editors
Shifting the Ground of Canadian Literary Studies / 2012 / xviii + 350 pp. / ISBN
978-1-55458-365-2

Kit Dobson and Smaro Kamboureli
Producing Canadian Literature: Authors Speak on the Literary Marketplace / 2013 / xii +
208 pp. / ISBN 978-1-55458-355-3

Eva C. Karpinski, Jennifer Henderson, Ian Sowton, and Ray Ellenwood, editors
Trans/acting Culture, Writing, and Memory / 2013 / xxix + 364 pp. / ISBN
978-1-55458-839-8

Smaro Kamboureli and Christl Verduyn, editors
Critical Collaborations: Indigenity, Diaspora, and Ecology in Canadian Literary Studies /
2014 / viii + 288 pp. / ISBN 978-1-55458-911-1

Larissa Lai
Slanting I, Imagining We: Asian Canadian Literary Production in the 1980s and 1990s /
forthcoming 2014 / 270 pp. / ISBN 978-1-77112-041-8